CANNA

D1151620

CANNA
THE STORY OF A HEBRIDEAN ISLAND

BY

J. L. CAMPBELL

Nam bithinn-sa roinn an fhearainn,
Bu libh Rùm is Eige 's Canaidh.

Seann Òran Luadhaidh

If I were the land dividing,
You'd have Rum and Eigg and Canna.

Old Waulking Song

THIRD EDITION
Published
by
THE CANONGATE PRESS

First published in Great Britain in 1984 for the National Trust for Scotland by
Oxford University Press.
Reprinted with revisions 1986.

Third edition published in 1994 by
Canongate Press Ltd,
14 Frederick Street,
Edinburgh EH2 2HB

© *J.L. Campbell 1984, 1986, 1994*

All rights reserved.

The publishers gratefully acknowledge contributions from the National Trust
for Scotland towards the publication of this volume.

The National Trust for Scotland gratefully acknowledges subsidies towards
the publication of the first edition of this book in hardback from:

The Rosalind Franklin Charity Trust
The Lady and Lord Gough Charitable Settlement
Highland and Islands Development Board
The Scottish Arts Council
The Scottish Transport Group

British Library Cataloguing-in-Publication Data
A catalogue record for this book is available on request from
The British Library

ISBN 0 86241 430 X

Printed and bound in Finland by W.S.O.Y.

DO
NAOMH CALUM CILLE
ABSTOL AGUS TEARMANNAICHE
EILEAN CHANAIDH

PREFACE

After the National Trust for Scotland had become the owner of the islands of Canna and Sanday, with the aid of an endowment from the National Heritage Memorial Fund, in the summer of 1981, Sir James Stormonth Darling, then Director of the Trust, suggested to me that I might write a book on Canna. Although I had been collecting material for the information of myself and my friends for many years, I had not seen much prospect of ever publishing it. Not long ago Mr Noel Banks had collected a great deal of information about the parish of the Small Isles, the five islands of Eigg, Rum, Canna, Muck, and Heisgeir (misnamed 'Oigh-sgeir' on some OS maps) and had written a book about it for a publisher who had told him that the Small Isles were of insufficient general interest and that he must include the islands of Coll and Tiree too – which he did, to the detriment of the space devoted to the original subject of the book, the Small Isles. This was not encouraging.

I could see that Canna would have to be treated differently. I was not interested in writing a mere guide to Canna, nor would a bald account of events connected with it, or of its natural history, be of overwhelming interest. But what made it a more promising subject was the links that connected it with outside causes and institutions. A small but fertile and sheltered island with a good harbour, it was always a valuable piece of property. Far from being intellectually isolated, it had remarkable links with the outside world. The Gaelic language connected it with Ireland, St Columba, the kingdom of Dalriada, the early kings of Scotland; its many Norse place-names connected it, through the Vikings, with Norway; its political history connected it with the Lordship of the Isles and the Jacobite cause; its religion connected it with Iona, and Ireland, and Rome, and the sufferings of Scottish Catholics in the dark centuries after 1560; its population had never been divided on sectarian lines, a fact which I am certain has a lot to do with the happy atmosphere that visitors have told me they can feel here;

when I think of islands where the people are divided socially
between Catholics and Protestants, and the Protestants themselves into more than one form of Protestantism, I can easily
agree with them.

In religion, Canna has been influenced by three great orders,
the Benedictines who held the abbey on Iona from 1203 until
1560, part of whose endowment the island was; the Franciscans,
whose heroic Irish missionaries saved the Faith in the Southern
Outer Hebrides and the Small Isles and Moidart in the early
seventeenth century; and the Vincentians, who in the second
half of the seventeenth century consolidated the work begun
by the Irish Franciscans. In the last thirty years Canna's link
with the Benedictines has been renewed through Fort Augustus
Abbey.

From an agrarian point of view, the history of Canna illustrates two matters of importance; the first is the way that
Church land was engrossed by the Highland clan chiefs –
particularly by the Earls of Argyll and the MacLeans of Duart
– after the Scottish Reformation, so that starting as technically
feudal vassals of the Bishops of the Isles, they became eventually outright owners subject only to nominal feu-duties; the
second, arising directly out of the first but reinforced by the
unequal incorporating union of Scotland with England in 1707
and the failure of the Jacobite Risings of 1715 and 1745, was the
complete power the owners of such formerly Church (and
other) lands in the Highlands and Islands had in the nineteenth
century to clear their lands of tenants-at-will without any kind
of compensation, in order to improve their own financial
position. Canna had ample experience of both these aspects of
Highland history.

I therefore felt that any story of the island had to be set
against this broader background, especially as unless this was
done, a good many allusions in Canna's historical record
would probably be misunderstood or misinterpreted. I felt
also that this should be written from what I would call the
Gaelic point of view, which meant regarding official records
with a good deal of cynical scepticism. In the matter of Highland history, in the absence of the lost records of the
Benedictine Monastery of Iona, and of the Lordship of the
Isles, apart from the Irish Annals, the Book of Clanranald, and

Hugh MacDonald's history of his clan, the bulk of the written material available to historians lies in official Scottish records such as the Acts of Parliament of Scotland, the reports of the Scottish Privy Council, and so on, and these are consistently hostile to the Highlanders and Islanders and to the Gaelic language and institutions; but they occupy the great part of the available written record, and unless a historian possesses some knowledge of the Gaelic language and its written and oral literature, and has the insights that that knowledge bestows, it is very difficult not to be borne down by the accumulating weight of official assertions and propaganda, and arrive at the mental state of accepting them without question. But now we are better acquainted with ideological politics than the Victorians, questions have become inevitable.

It follows that some readers may find this book not what they are accustomed to, something that used to be a considerable obstacle to book publication in Scotland. If so, I hope it will help to acquaint them with a new point of view. Far too long have the Scottish Gaels been treated by historians as non-persons with no legitimate point of view. Barbarous things certainly happened in the Highlands and Islands of Scotland, but they equally certainly happened in other parts of Scotland as well, and in England too for that matter. The Scottish Gael is fundamentally of a very conservative nature. I see the history of the Hebrides as a sustained attempt to retain the semi-independence of the Lordship or Kingdom of the Isles and its institutions, and a determination to restore the Lordship after it had been brought down; when this failed, the clans of the western Highlands and Islands developed into a kind of splintered resistance movement to preserve what local liberties they could, against a centralizing government whose laws were imposed from outside, laws which were not always felt to have a strong moral basis. It is indeed regrettable that the Lordship of the Isles did not survive to develop into something like the local independence now enjoyed by the Channel Islands and the Isle of Man.

Modern ecologists and others concerned with the growing interest in conservation such as members of the National Trust for Scotland, should appreciate the conservation-mindedness of the old Highlanders and Hebrideans, who were so careful to apportion fairly shares in their arable land, under the run-rig system, in their common grazings, their fishing banks, and their bird-cliffs, as can be read, for instance, in Alexander Carmichael's *Grazing and Agrestic Customs of the Outer Hebrides*.* To such people the idea that one man might prosper by encroaching on the shares of his neighbours in such resources was highly offensive and improper.

But it was part of the philosophy of *laissez-faire*, which began to infiltrate the Highlands early in the eighteenth century, and to which no local resistance was possible anywhere after 1746. After that time the resources of the Highlands, their forests, fisheries, and grazings – often partly, as on Canna, consisting of former arable ground cultivated for centuries – were open to exploitation by outsiders, while their manpower, after having been of the greatest use to Great Britain in the Napoleonic Wars, was left at the mercy of the blind economic forces that dominated the nineteenth century.

In writing this book, I have preferred to quote my sources verbatim as far as possible, believing that this adds much to the vividness of the narrative. But it can lead to some difficulties over varying spellings of certain local place-names. While personally I prefer to use the correct Gaelic versions of such names as Corra-dhùn, Cill, and so on, the commonly written and used English versions, *Coraghon, Keill,* are too well established in literature to be abandoned entirely.

The material used in the writing of this book was collected over many years, and there are many persons I have to thank for aid in obtaining much of it. I acknowledge with gratitude my indebtedness to Dr Peter Anderson, Registrar of the Scottish Record Office, and members of its staff, and to Dr I. C. Cunningham, Dr Ann Matheson, and Mr Ronald Black of the National Library of Scotland, for valuable help in my researches, and express my thanks to these institutions for permission to publish material from their archives relating to the Isle of Canna.

I am grateful to the Trustees of the 10th Duke of Argyll and to the present Duke of Argyll for permission to publish extracts from the lease of Canna to the MacDonalds of Morar in the seventeenth century, and to the late Mr Eric Cregeen of

* *Report of the Crofter's Commission of 1883*, pp. 451–82.

the School of Scottish Studies for drawing my attention to the existence of this lease, which throws important light on the story of the island in the seventeenth century. I am also grateful to Mr David Scott Moncrieff, WS, for giving me copies of items relating to Canna in the Clanranald Papers, not long after I acquired the island in 1938; and to John MacLeod Esq. of MacLeod for permission to publish Mór MacLeod's defence against the matrimonial charges of her husband Donald of Clanranald in 1680.

I am indebted to my predecessor Mr R. V. G. Thom of Canna, now living in Cornwall, for much interesting information from time to time relating to the times of his family's ownership (1881–1938) and for permission to use pre-1914 photographs of Canna taken by members of the family. I must also acknowledge important information on local traditions and place-names given me by the late Angus MacDonald ('Aonghus Eachainn', 1860–1947), Angus MacLeod (1862–1951), Charles MacArthur, John MacLeod, and Duncan MacLeod of the Gaelic-speaking community of Canna; and permission received from the late Professor Delargy, and Dr A. MacLean, holder of the copyright, to publish some of the material collected on Canna for the Irish Folklore Commission by the late Dr Calum MacLean in 1947.

As regards the place-names of Canna I must express my gratitude to Mr Hugh Barron, secretary of the Gaelic Society of Inverness, for sending me a long holograph collection of Canna place-names made by his well-known predecessor, Mr Alexander Nicolson, on vacations on Canna in the 1920s. Mr Nicolson was brought up on Canna, where his father was the first state schoolmaster.

I am very grateful to Mr Noel Banks, author of *Six Inner Hebrides*, for most generously putting at my disposal information on Canna which he had discovered during his researches on the history of the Small Isles, and to Sir Archibald Ross, KCMG, who has put at my disposal very interesting material unearthed in his researches on the MacNeills who occupied Canna from 1781 to 1827, and owned it from 1827 to 1881, with whose family Lady Ross is connected.

Other persons I must thank for help and information are the Revd W. Grant Anderson and Mrs Anderson; the Revd Mark

Dilworth, OSB; Dom Augustine Grene, OSB; Mr Donald Erskine and Mr George Russell, WS, of the National Trust for Scotland; Mr David Fox, whose great grandfather came to Canna for a while as farm manager for Donald MacNeill after 1854; Mr John S. Gibson, author of *Ships of the '45*; Mr W. T. Johnston; Mrs Delia Lennie, for translations of Vatican papers relating to Canna, written in Italian; the late T. C. Lethbridge, author of *Boats and Boatmen*, and many other interesting and stimulating books, who took a great interest in the archaeology of Canna, and whose yacht used to be a frequent visitor to Canna Harbour; the Revd R. MacDonald (Dunoon); Professor Angus McIntosh, Edinburgh University; the Revd Michael Sharratt, Registrar of Ushaw College; the late Professor Alf Sommerfelt, Oslo; Messrs. George Waterston, Roger Waterston, and E. C. Pelham Clinton, for encouragement and help in the study of the natural history of the island.

I must also express my gratitude to the present (March 1983) Director of the National Trust for Scotland, and to Dr Morton Boyd, head of the Nature Conservancy in Scotland, and to many members of both bodies, including the members of the National Trust for Scotland and other friends who have most generously contributed to the cost of producing this book, for much encouragement while I was writing and researching for it. I must also thank Dr Ann E. Berthoff of the University of Massachusetts, who kindly read through the whole of this book in typescript, and made valuable suggestions from the point of view of the American reader.

I am also indebted to my wife for constant encouragement, and for valuable help in the selection of illustrations, many from her own photographs; and to Miss Penny Davies, without whose help in typing, correcting, and research this book would have taken several times longer to write.

I must also thank Mrs P. M. McDougall for preparing the Index to this book, and the Very Revd Canon John MacLean and Miss Irene Stirling for help in reading the proofs.

Isle of Canna   JOHN L. CAMPBELL
14 March 1983

CONTENTS

APPENDICES

COLOUR ILLUSTRATIONS

MONOCHROME ILLUSTRATIONS

1. 'The Witches' Home', Coroghon (*Victoria and Albert Museum*)
2. Robert Thom, Laird of Canna 1881–1911 (*Mrs J. G. Sewell*)
3. Canna House, c.1885 (*Mrs J. G. Sewell*)
4. Robert Thom and a Porbeagle Shark (*Mrs J. G. Sewell*)
5. Yachts and fishing boats in Canna Harbour, c.1890
6. Herring curing at Canna Pier
7. Canna Estate employees and crofters, 1885 (*Mrs J. G. Sewell*)
8. Filling wool bags in the old days (*Mrs J. G. Sewell*)
9. Builders of the Bute Memorial chapel on Sanday (*Mrs J. G. Sewell*)
10. Barra fishing boats in Canna Harbour (*Mrs J. G. Sewell*)
11. The Farm Steading devastated, 1926 (*R.G.V. Thom*)
12. Canna at sunset (*J.L.C.*)
13. Coroghon Bay and the Isle of Rum (*Margaret Fay Shaw*)
14. Aerial view of Canna Harbour, 1981 (*Stewart Guthrie*)
15. The Snake Stone (*Margaret Fay Shaw*)
16. The Celtic Cross, front (*Kitty Clark, Royal Commission on the Ancient Monuments of Scotland*)
17. The Celtic Cross, obverse (*Kitty Clark, RCAMS*)
18. Salving timber after storms, 1947 (*J.L.C.*)
19. Shearing at Canna fank, c.1950 (*Margaret Fay Shaw*)
20. The Haymakers, 1981 (*Stewart Guthrie*)
21. Angus MacDonald (*Margaret Fay Shaw*)
22. The late Hector MacDonald (*Margaret Fay Shaw*)
23. The author and his wife (*Tom Weir*)
24. Lester Borley and Ian MacKinnon, 1983 (*Richard Seligman*)
25. Cliff Section, Langanes, Canna, 1983 (*David Pattison*)

LIST OF MAPS

The Hebrides and the Western Highlands, from Cathaldus Giblin's
The Irish Franciscan Mission to Scotland, 1619–1646.

1 ST COLUMBA AND CANNA

Saint Columba, 'Colum Cille', originally called Criomhthann ua Cuinn, is by far the most important historical personality connected with Gaelic Scotland, let alone with the Isle of Canna, where the original chapel was dedicated to him, and which he certainly must have visited on his missionary travels during his exile in Scotland, AD 563–97. The Irish Franciscans, whose labours in the Hebrides between 1619 and 1646 recall those of Columba and his disciples more than a thousand years earlier, recorded the strength of the local tradition connecting Canna with St Columba. Fr. Cornelius Ward (Conchobhair Mac an Bháird) recorded on his visit to Canna in October 1625 that Canna was

once held by St. Columba, whom all the inhabitants . . . hold in veneration, like a second God. The place itself is most pleasing and charming. St. Columba gave it his blessing, that it should support or nourish no frog nor other poisonous animal as neither do other districts blessed by St. Columba, in however great a multitude they may be found in the neighbourhood and surrounding parts. I noticed there standing on the shore a stone having the likeness of a toad. A firm tradition relates that when St. Columba had freed by his bless-ing that district from poisonous creatures of this kind, a single toad put in there from the neighbouring island of Rum,* and was changed into this stone by the prayers and curse of the saint. . . .[1]

A story that could have come straight from the pages of Adamnan's Latin or O'Donell's Irish life of St Columba, or from Geoffrey Keating's History of Ireland (*Foras Feasa ar Éirinn*). In passing, it may be said that this tradition about the petrified toad is not remembered on Canna now; the stone of which the shape most strongly suggests the toad of the story is a very big boulder on the shore at the east end of Canna, now called *Òrd Mhic 'uirich* – 'MacVurich's Hammer' – the MacVurichs of course were the famous hereditary poet-historians of the MacDonalds of Clanranald, whose connec-tion with Canna will be discussed later.

* A source of evil in Canna eyes, see p. 125.

From the large number of anecdotes connected with St Columba or Colum Cille that have been preserved, many of them of a type of fantasy that pleases the Gaelic mind but irritates exceedingly the materialistic rationalist, one can easily form a picture of the character and personality of the man. Colum Cille was highly born, being on his father's side the son of Feidhlimidh, great-grandson of Niall Naoighiallach, 'Niall of the Nine Hostages', High King of Ireland, so called because he had taken five hostages from the provinces of Ireland, and four from Scotland; according to Geoffrey Keating, he brought Patrick then aged sixteen as a captive to Ireland on one of his raiding expeditions. He is the traditional forebear of the O'Neills in Ireland and the MacNeils or MacNeills in Scotland. His mother Eithne was the daughter of Dioma, son of Naoi, of the race of Cairbre Nia Fear, King of Leinster.

He was thus qualified for election to the High Kingship of Ireland, had he chosen a secular career. As it was, religion did not keep him out of contemporary Irish politics, which almost invariably involved violence sooner or later. He was obviously a man of very strong character, in which a failing of pride and hot temper was balanced by a great quality of asceticism and devotion to his duty inspired by his devotion to Our Lord Jesus Christ. This was typical of an age in which extreme violence on the one hand was balanced by extreme asceticism and personal saintliness on the other. It is obvious from many of the stories told about him that Colum Cille possessed the gift, which some would call the burden, of second sight. Highland second sight, which has attracted the curious interest of enquirers since the late seventeenth century, is, in the opinion of the writer, the best attested of so-called psychical phenomena, being regarded as an affliction by its unwilling exponents, to whom the faculty brought neither pleasure nor financial gain nor social advantage – indeed in the seventeenth century, the risk of prosecution for witchcraft. Readers who are inclined to find this kind of thing and other marvels in Adamnan's and O'Donell's lives of Colum Cille irritating must remember that we are dealing with a very different age and different level of human consciousness and time dimension, and one in which oral tradition, something that has nearly disappeared from the English-speaking world, played a very important part.

St Columba's nature is best shown by two important incidents told of his life, the quarrels and fighting that arose over his copying without permission of St Fintain's holy manuscript book, leading to his banishment from Ireland, and his later intervention at the Convention of Druim Ceat, to which he was brought from Scotland blindfolded to plead for the poets of Ireland who were then threatened by King Aedh mac Ainmirech with expulsion from Ireland (because they had become very numerous and their exactions, procured by threats of satirizing their unwilling hosts, very burdensome; it was not the first time their expulsion from Ireland had been proposed); for the release from imprisonment of Scannlan, and the exemption of the Scottish–Gaelic Kingdom of Dal Riada from tribute. The case of Fintain's or Finnian's holy book must be one of the earliest copyright actions on record. Colum Cille had been on a visit to Fintain of Druim Finn, and obtained a loan of this valuable manuscript, which he copied surreptitiously in church, staying there after Mass and Office were over in order to do so. On the last night when the copying was nearly complete, Fintain sent a messenger for the book, and discovered what Colum Cille had been doing. He told Colum Cille that he had acted wrongly in copying the book without permission. A dispute arose, and the matter was referred to the High King of Ireland, Diarmaid mac Cearbhuill, for adjudication. The High King gave the famous judgement 'to every cow its calf and to every book its copy' against Colum Cille, who was furious. Colum Cille was also angry with the High King for having put a young man, Curnan mac Aedha, to death following a manslaughter. Curnan was under Colum Cille's protection at the time; other stories show that Colum Cille was very touchy indeed about persons under his protection being harmed or threatened. Colum Cille told King Diarmaid he would go to his relations the clans of Conall and of Eogan (i.e. the descendants of King Niall of the Nine Hostages, who occupied the present Counties Tyrone and Donegal) and get them to wage war on him in consequence of his bad judgement about the book and his execution of Curnan.

The clans of Conall and Eogan prepared for battle at a place in Connacht called Cuil Dreimhne or Culdrevny under their Kings Ainmire mac Setna, and Ferghus and Domhnall. Colum Cille spent the night fasting and praying on their behalf. Next day the Archangel Michael appeared to Colum Cille in a vision, and told him that God would grant him his request, but that 'for having made such a worldly request God would not be pleased with him until he would exile himself beyond the seas, and never return to Ireland's shore, nor partake of her food and drink, except during his outward journey nor behold her men and women for evermore'.[2]

In the battle, Diarmaid mac Cearbhuill was defeated with the loss of 3,000 men; then Colum Cille made peace with him and gave him back the Kingdom 'for he thought it sufficient to have punished him for his evil judgment, and he could then have held the Kingdom of Ireland, had he not renounced it for the sake of God'. The copy Colum Cille had made of the book become his most important relic in the land of the race of Conall, Donegal.[3]

Colum Cille's part in the instigation of this battle (and one or two others) did not please his fellow clerics 'considering all the people that were slain in these battles as a result of his counsel'. On their advice Colum Cille went to St Molaisse of Damh-Inis to make confession of his sin. 'St Molaisse ratified the sentence the [Arch]angel [Michael] had passed on him previously, namely to abandon Ireland and never to behold her and to abstain from her food and drink, and the sight of her men and women, and never to tread her soil.'[4]

Thus Colum Cille was exiled to Scotland and Iona for the last thirty-four years of his life. Going he said

> Far I gaze across the ocean
> From a deck of oaken planks;
> Many are the tears my eye is shedding,
> As I look back on Erin.
>
> There is a grey eye
> Looking back on Ireland,
> That will never see again
> Her men or her women.
>
> Early and late my lamentation,

Alas, the journey I am making;
This will be my secret bye-name
'Back turned on Ireland'.

Colum Cille and his monks made their monastery on Iona a mission centre for much of the north and north-west of Scotland, including the Inner Hebrides. Amongst the islands specifically mentioned in Adamnan's Life of Colum Cille are Islay, Mull, Coll,* Tiree, Eigg, and Skye, and there are also allusions to his having been in Ardnamurchan on the mainland. Other islands mentioned under what must have been their pre-Norse names are not easy to identify precisely.

One of these is the mysterious 'Hinba' or 'Himba'. Adamnan refers to incidents involving Colum Cille on Hinba six times and also refers to one of his disciples, Feargna, spending the rest of his life there after Colum Cille's death. From these allusions we learn the following things about Hinba: (1) it was inhabited, (2) there was a monastic settlement there, (3) there was a considerable sea inlet there, 'Muirbolc Már' ('Great Sea-bag' – *Már* = *Mór* in Old Irish), and (4) Colum Cille had a revelation of spiritual secrets and difficult passages of Scripture in a house there, and regretted that his foster son Baithin (who was his cousin and successor as abbot of Iona) was not present and able to write these things down. 'Baithin however could not be present, being detained by winds in the Egean Island',[5] i.e. the Isle of Eigg.

These circumstances point to the strong possibility, to say the least, that Canna can be identified with Hinba. (1) Archaeological remains prove it was inhabited long before Colum Cille's mission to the isles. (2) It is well known that there is a monastic site on the far south-west rocky shore of the island, even though this is now traditionally called a nunnery. (3) There is a considerable sea inlet between Canna and the tidal island of Sanday, forming Canna harbour and at high tides cutting Sanday off from Canna. (4) The Gaelic (Celtic) Church 'always dedicated its churches to the founder, or the founder of the monastery from which the founder of the

---

* Professor W. J. Watson, who devoted an important chapter of his book on the Celtic place-Names of Scotland to the places mentioned by Adamnan, points out that Adamnan's *Colosus* must = Coll, as Colonsay (pronounced Colo'osai in Gaelic) = Kolbein's island, a Norse post-Columban name.

church came',[6] and the original chapel at Cill or Keill on Canna was dedicated to St Columba.

But to my mind the most compelling reason for identifying Canna with Hinba is that Colum Cille was expecting Baithin to join him there from Eigg, a thing he could not possibly have been expecting Baithin easily to do if Hinba had been Jura or Na h-Eileacha Naomha (= 'the Holy Rocks') in the Firth of Lorne. On the other hand it would have been natural for one of the two monks going north of Ardnamurchan on a mission to have gone to Canna and the other to Eigg with the idea of meeting again on Canna, which has the better harbour of the two islands. Canon William Reeves thought that Canna could reasonably be identified with Hinba.[7]

Colum Cille's mission extended to Skye, where the saint baptized the pagan Artbranan at a place on the sea where there was a river, called thenceforth (at least, until the Norsemen came) 'Dobur Artbranani', i.e. 'The Water of Artbranan'. This place unfortunately cannot be identified now; Professor W. J. Watson says that the only place-name on Skye known to him in which the word *dobur* or *dobhar* ('water') enters is Tot-ardor ('Tobht' ard-dobhar') in the Bracadale district.[8] One could hardly travel between Iona and Bracadale in the kind of boat used in Colum Cille's time without using Canna harbour.

The impression made on Scotland by Colum Cille remains very great. Sometimes it is suggested that St Margaret of Scotland, King Malcolm Ceannmór's queen, should be held in higher honour and devotion by Highland Catholics than Colum Cille. Comparison between the merits of saints is invidious. While one must respect St Margaret for her personal sanctity and the reforms she carried out in contemporary Church discipline and practices, she was working from a position of established regal power in a nominally Christianized country. The fact that Scotland was by the second half of the eleventh century at least nominally Christian was due in no small measure, as far as the Gaelic-speaking half of it was concerned, to the faith, sanctity, physical courage, and endurance of St Columba, who worked amongst pagans in a rough and difficult country, often making dangerous journeys in small boats in stormy Hebridean seas. Colum Cille and Iona will never fade from Scotland's national consciousness.

Nor will he from Canna's, for the present chapel is dedicated to him, and apart from in our minds, his memorials are written in the small carved stone crosses of simple beauty that have been preserved on the island, and above all in Canna's national shrine, the remains of the Celtic nunnery at Sgor nam Ban Naomh, in a place of great natural beauty on a broad grassy ledge between cliffs below and above on the south-west coast of the island.* The National Trust for Scotland will be a most suitable guardian of this holy place, which the inhabitants of Canna do not want to be disturbed. They honoured St Columba by commemorating on his Day, 9 June, in 1963 the fourteen-hundredth anniversary of his coming to Scotland, when Mass was said in beautiful weather in the open air by the famous carved cross and near the site of St Columba's original chapel at Keill, by the late Revd Fr. Donald MacDougall in the presence of a large congregation, many of whom had come from the other Small Isles and the mainland by motor boat.

NOTES

1. Giblin, *The Irish Franciscan Mission to Scotland, 1619–1646*, p. 68. MS translation by Dom Denys Rutledge.
2. O'Donnell, *Betha Columb Chille*, ZCP IX 265.
3. Ibid. ZCP IX 267.
4. Ibid. ZCP IX 269.
5. Adamnan's *Life of St Columba*, trans. Fowler, p. 126.
6. Meisser, *The Celtic Church in England after the Synod of Whitby*, pp. 3, 21.
7. William Reeves, DD, *Life of St Columba, Founder of Hy*, Edinburgh, 1874. Historians of Scotland Series, Vol. VI.
8. *History of the Celtic Place Names of Scotland*, p. 75.

* See the Report of the Ancient Monuments Commission on the Outer Hebrides, Skye, and the Small Isles, p. 217, where 'Sgor' of the name is wrongly translated 'Skerry'. 'Sgor' in Canna place-names is used in the Faeroese sense of a grassy slope between two cliffs. It is pronounced with a short *o*. Presumably this nunnery would have originally been called after the person who founded it. Probably that name was forgotten during Viking times, while memory of the purpose of the foundation survived. 'Sgor nam Ban Naomh' ('Scree of the Holy Women') could be a back-translation into Gaelic of a Norse appellation, something like *Heiligakvinnaskor*.

2 THE COMING OF THE NORSEMEN

In the last decade of the eighth century began the Viking raids on the whole of Britain, including the north and west coasts of Scotland. However much one may admire the navigational feats of the Norsemen, their settling of the Faroes, Iceland, and Greenland (the first two already discovered by Irish monks), and their discovery of America – for there can be no doubt that sailing from Greenland they did discover America, though they were unable to form any permanent settlement there – no effort to romanticize their achievements is ever going to succeed in covering up the trail of death, destruction, rape, and pillage that their barbarous unprovoked raids inflicted on Gaels, Welsh, and Anglo-Saxons alike. Attacks by the 'Gentiles', i.e. pagan Norsemen and/or Danes, are first mentioned by the Irish annalists in AD 793, and for the next two hundred years hardly a year goes by without such an attack being mentioned in these annals.

> Bitter is the wind tonight
> That tosses the ocean's white-capped waves;
> Tonight I fear not the coursing of the Irish Sea
> By the fierce warriors from Norway[1]

That year the Annals of Ulster record that the Norsemen devastated all the isles of Britain. The following year Skye was 'pillaged and wasted' (*Sci doscradh agus do lomradh*). The Norsemen made religious foundations a particular target, no doubt because valuable relics were to be plundered from churches and monasteries, but probably also from a hatred of the Christian religion. Iona was one of the first to suffer; in 797 (*recte* 802) the Annals of the Four Masters* record that the

---

* The Annals of the Four Masters were compiled by four Franciscan friars, Michael, Conaire, and Cúcoigrich ó Cléirigh, and Fearfeasa Ó Maolchonaire, between 1616 and 1636 near their monastery at Donegal, from all the MS sources of Irish history available to them. Their motive for the work was the preservation of Gaelic national traditions threatened by the collapse of the last vestige of Irish independence with the defeat of Hugh O'Neill, Earl of Tyrone, at the battle of Kinsale in 1601, and his flight to Rome in 1607.

monastery of Iona was burned by the Norsemen, '*Hi Choluimb Chille do losccadh la hallmurachaibh. i. la Nortmanoibh*'. In 801 (*recte* 806) the same annals record that the Norsemen plundered Iona and killed sixty-eight persons there, clerical and lay. In 823 (824 according to the Annals of Ulster) Blathmac, son of Flann, was martyred on Iona.

In 985 the Annals of the Four Masters record that 'Hi-Choluim-Chille was plundered by the Danes on Christmas night; and they killed the abbot, and fifteen of the seniors of the church along with him.' The Annals of Ulster also record this. Happily this outrage did not go unavenged; the next year the Four Masters record that 'a great slaughter was made of the Danes who had plundered Hi, for three hundred and sixty of them were slain through the miracles of God and Colum Cille'.

We know nothing about the history of Canna in the period between the mission of St Columba and the beginning of the thirteenth century. Norway became Christian in the first third of the eleventh century under her kings Ólaf Tryggvason and St Ólaf Haraldsson, not without some violence, and Iceland was converted about the same time – the story of that conversion can be read in the Saga of Burnt Njal. Archaeologically and linguistically as well as destructively, the Norse occupation made a deep impression on the islands of the Hebrides, certainly playing a part in the development of Scottish Gaelic as a language distinct from Irish, and affecting the oral traditions and toponymy of the isles deeply.

Practically every feature of the shores of Canna and many other Canna place-names bear appellations of Norse origins; some of these names are easily intelligible today, such as Langanes, a peninsula on the north side of the island (wrongly entered as Langan-innis on older Ordanance Survey maps). Langanes means 'Long Ness' – there is a Langanes in Iceland. Tallaibrig, from Norse *Hallabrekka* ('sloping hill') on Sanday (itself a Norse name, given to islands with a conspicuous sandy beach – there is a Sanday in the Faroes); (Camus) Stianabhaig on Sanday, from *steinna-vík*, ('stony bay' – it is a very stony bay – the Gaelic *Camus* is superfluous). Stéidh, an anvil-shaped little island off the south-west part of Canna, from the Norse *steði*, anvil. Cràcasgor, one of the steep slopes in the same part of the island, from *kráka,* crow, and *skor* – in Canna, *-skor* or *-sgor* in place-names of Norse origin is used in the Faeroese sense of a steep grassy slope between two cliffs, one above and one below. A raven's nest is there today. Làmasgor, a long steep grassy slope on the north side of the eastern part of Canna, suitable for grazing sheep (when one can get them on and off), Norse *Lambaskor.* Geugasgor, further west, the highest cliff on Canna and a great breeding place for puffins and other sea-birds, is possibly Norse *Geiguskor,* 'Dangerous Cliff'. Greòd, a large, very stony field on Sanday, must be Norse *grjót,* 'stones'.

Other such names can be seen in the list of Canna place-names in Appendix IX. The origin and meaning of the name 'Canna' itself is uncertain. It is very interesting that the name *Cana* occurs in the list of British islands in the Ravenna Cosmography, as well as *Scetis,* 'Skye'. The Cosmography was written early in the eighth century, and is therefore pre-Norse.[2] If the identification with present Canna is to be made, this suggests a connection with Old Irish *cana, cano,* 'wolf-whelp, young warrior', Scottish Gaelic *cana* 'porpoise' or 'dolphin' by transference.

Porpoises and dolphins are common around Canna and the other Small Isles, and it is possible that the *Muc* of *Eilean nam Muc,* Isle of Muck, represents *muc-mhara,* 'whale', and not *muc,* 'pig', though Professor W. B. Lockwood informs me that the Norse equivalent *Svíney* has often been given pejoratively to Norwegian islands and skerries that are a danger to navigation.

Though the present second syllable of the Gaelic for Canna, *Canaidh* (rhymes with 'eye'), does suggest the Norse *ey,* 'island', it may be significant that the fort or place of refuge at the far south-western end of the island is called Dùn Chana, not Dùn Chanaidh. The late Revd C. M. Robertson, a good Gaelic scholar, recorded the Gaelic for Canna as *Eilean Chanfhathaich,* three syllables, presumably with hiatus between the last two (the *fh* is silent); but I have not heard this pronunciation, though some speakers do unvoice the final *y* sound to slender *ch.*[3]

The first Norse visitor to Canna of whom there is actual record was an Icelander, Guðmundr Arason, the Bishop-elect of Holar, who sailed from Eiafjorðr in Iceland on 14 July 1202 with Hrafn Sveinbjornsson, to go to Trondhjem in Norway. They were blown completely off course by wild northerly gales, and after running great dangers, found themselves in the Hebrides. 'And it seemed that no man could pilot them through; and most men expected that the ship would be wrecked, and the men drowned.' Hrafn then took over the piloting of the ship, and 'they sailed through the night; and he piloted with great skill and good fortune . . . At the moment when they had come opposite the islands, they saw day-break . . . Next they came into good harbourage, beside an island that is called Sand-ey. And there the merchants raised a harbour mark.'

There can be no doubt that this was Sanday of Canna; there is no other Sanday in the Hebrides having a good harbour.

The Norse king of the Hebrides then was King Olaf, son of Godfrey, son of Olaf Morsel; he was called Olaf the Black. King Olaf's bailiff came to the Bishop and Hrafn and demanded payment of landing-dues in respect of twenty Icelanders, probably the majority of the crew. Knowing landing-dues would be demanded in Norway, and as they were unwillingly in the Hebrides, they refused.

After that, Hrafn and the Bishop-elect, with very many others, went on shore, and to the church; because the Bishop-elect wished to hold services. There was the King come; and he invited the Bishop-elect to table. But when the Bishop-elect wished to go away, the King said that the Bishop-elect must do him right, or else he said he would keep him. But the Bishop-elect refused this flatly. Hrafn said that this was to be looked for, and offered to do the King honour. But he said they must have all that he had.

But when the skippers knew that the Bishop-elect and Hrafn were detained, Botolf bade the men take their weapons, and said that they should not part with so valiant a fighter without his finding out what had become of them, Hrafn and Guðmund. And when they were ready, they sprang into the boat, and rowed to land. They went ashore in battle-order. But the Hebrideans sat under a knoll, with the Bishop-elect and Hrafn.[4]

Peace was made between the parties and as a compromise the Bishop-elect and Hrafn paid six landing dues. It is a vivid picture; the Icelandic bishop going ashore to say Mass in St

Columba's chapel on Canna; being detained with his captain, Hrafn, by King Olaf; the Icelanders coming ashore from their ship to rescue them, and finding the Hebrideans sitting with their captives under a knoll, very possibly the conspicuous knoll known now as Cnoc nan Còrr, 'The Knoll of the Herons', and peace being made between the parties by inter-mediaries – an obscure page of Hebridean history is suddenly brightly illuminated by the story.

With regard to this and the preceding chapter, it should be pointed out that the silting up of Canna Harbour with shell sand carried eastwards from the Tràigh Bàn ('White Beach') on Sanday by rising tides (which come from the West) and prevailing winds, must have been going on over a prolonged period of time; and that in the days of Guðmundr Arason, and still more of St Columba, the deep water in Canna Harbour must have been far more extensive than it is today, justifying Adamnan's description of it as a 'great sea-bay', especially in the days of small boats. Indeed Canna and Sanday may have been joined by sandhills at that time. The Irish Annals record many great storms since St Columba's time, especially one in 744 which drowned many of the Iona community according to the Annals of the Four Masters.

NOTES

1. *Thesaurus Palaeohibernicus*, II. 190.
2. A. F. L. Rivet and Colin Smith, *The Place-Names of Roman Britain*, pp. 214, 296. I am grateful to Dr M. Henig for drawing my attention to this reference. With regard to the comments on the name on p. 296, if the *Cana* of the Ravenna Cosmography is our Canna, it cannot have any-thing to do with the Latin adjective *cānus*, 'white', as the prevailing colours of Canna are the green of the grass and the black of the basalt that composes the island; nor with Latin *canna*, 'reed', as reeds are not con-spicuous here. Canna in fact is dolphin-shaped.
3. In a paper on the Topography of the island of Eigg, *Transactions of the Gaelic Society of Inverness*, xxiii. 200.
4. See A. O. Anderson, *Early Sources of Scottish History*, II. 358–60; A. Sommerfelt, 'Norse-Gaelic Contacts', *Norsk Tidsskrift for Sprogvidenskap*, XVI. 232.

3 CANNA AND IONA

After the beginning of the eleventh century, references to Iona in the Irish annals become less frequent. But there is plenty of evidence of the continued existence of the monastic community; any idea that it was destroyed by the Norsemen and only revived by the Benedictine foundation of 1203 is quite wrong. Queen Margaret of Scotland (St Margaret), who married King Malcolm c.1070 and died in 1093, is said to have restored the monastery, but there is no mention of such a thing in the Irish annals, which refer to the deaths of abbots of Iona in 1005, 1025, and 1099. One striking incident recorded in the Annals of Ulster for the year 1164 is the arrival of a powerful delegation from the monastery of Iona, acting on the advice of Somerled (the founder of the family of the Lords of the Isles) and the men of Argyll and the Hebrides, to try to persuade Flaithbertach ua Brolchain, who was abbot of Colum Cille's foundation of Derry, to accept the abbacy of Iona, 'but the successor of Patrick [at Armagh] and the King of Ireland, that is, Ua Lochlainn, and the nobles of Cenel-Eogain [Colum Cille's clan] prevented him'.

Flaithbertach ua Brolchain died in 1175, and the Annals of Ulster then describe him as 'successor of Colum Cille, tower of wisdom and hospitality, a man to whom the clergy of Ireland gave the chair of a bishop [in 1158 – this probably refers to his having been made a mitred abbot] and to whom was offered the succession of I [Iona], died piously'. In 1188 one Amhlaim ua Daighri died there on a pilgrimage.

The first surviving historical allusion to Canna, as far as I know, occurs in the bull of Pope Innocent III that confirmed Celestinus as abbot of the new Benedictine foundation there, and lists the endowments of the monastery. The endowments included Iona itself, the churches of the Outer Hebrides ('Insegal'), Mull, Colonsay, 'Cheldubsenaig', Chelcenneg (Kilchenzie), and Islay, and the islands of Mull, Colonsay, Oronsay, Canna, and Calvay; the lands of 'Magenburg', 'Mangecheles', 'Herilnean', and 'Sotesdal'; the lands of the

abbey in Islay, of Markarna (Muckairn), and 'Camusnanesre'.*
The foundation was made by Raghnall, son of Somerled, who
succeeded to the Hebrides and Kintyre, and who also founded
a Benedictine nunnery in Iona and a monastery of Grey Friars
at Saddell in Kintyre. The abbey was to pay two bezants
(about the equivalent to two sovereigns if gold, or four old
shillings if silver) a year to the papacy. The bull is dated the
fifth day before the Ides of December, 1203.†

The wording of the bull suggests that the possibility of
trouble with regard both to the succession of the abbacy, and
the abbey's possessions, was anticipated. And indeed trouble
was not long in coming. The very next year, 1204, the Annals
of Ulster recorded that:

a monastery was built by Cellach [blank space follows] in the centre‡ of
Iona, without any right, in dishonour of the Community of Iona, so that he
spoilt§ the place greatly.

The northern Irish clergy were furious. The bishops of Tyrone
and Donegal, three abbots 'and a large number of the Community of Doire [Derry, Colum Cille's foundation] and a large
number of the clergy of the North' went over and razed the
new building 'according to the law of the Church'.
Amalgaidh, the Abbot of the monastery of Derry, was elected
(traditionalist) Abbot of Iona by the Irish and the Hebrideans.

One would much like to know what words were omitted or
illegible after 'Cellach'. It seems very likely that they would
have been *abad Ia* 'Abbot of Iona', and that Cellach must have
been the same person whose name was Latinized as 'Celestinus'
in the papal bull of 1203. It is not difficult to sense the resent-
ment of the clergy of the north of Ireland, which had been the
original country of St Colum Cille and the scene of his early
labours, at a new monastic order being brought in by an
upstart Hebridean half-Norseman to take over the monastery

---

* *Camus nan Eisirean*, 'Bay of Oysters'?

† The bull is printed in full in the *Book of Islay*, pp. 6–8. It is also quoted by Sheriff
J. R. N. MacPhail in Vol. I of *Highland Papers* (Scottish History Society), where the
reference to Canna is not indexed.

‡ *ar lar croí*. Translated 'in the centre of the enclosure', but it is an idiom meaning
'in the very middle'. In *Early Sources of Scottish History* it is translated 'in the middle
of the sheepfold of Iona'!

§ *romhill*, translated 'wrecked'.

of Iona, where the traditional order and discipline of Colum Cille had endured, in spite of Viking raids, for over six hundred years.

The great Benedictine Order, which had done so much for the Catholic religion and European civilization since its foundation at Monte Cassino in the Dark Ages, in 529, had been introduced into Scotland under the patronage and during the reign (1124–53) of King David I. In such cases as that of Raghnall, son of Somerled, and the Benedictine foundation of Iona, one can reasonably look for a woman's influence. It is not very difficult to find here. Raghnall's mother, as has been said, was Ragnhildis, daughter of Olaf, King of Man and the Hebrides; his sister, Beathag or Beatrix, became a Benedictine nun, and was later prioress of the Benedictine nunnery her brother founded on Iona;[1] Raghnall 'was married to MacRandel's daughter, or, as some say, to a sister of Thomas Randel, Earl of Murray'.[2] King David I had brought the Benedictines to Urquhart, near Elgin in Moray.

Raghnall's successors took a characteristic revenge for the Ulstermen's raid on the new monastery of Iona. In 1212 the Annals of Ulster (which never again mention Iona after 1204) recorded that:

Thomas, son of Uchtrach with the sons of Raghnall, son of Somerligh, came to Derry of St Colum Cille with six and seventy ships, and the town was badly damaged by them, and [the peninsula of] Inishowen was completely destroyed by them and the Cenel-Conaill [whose king was Aedh ua Néill].

– Uchtrach or Uchtred (a Norse name) of Galloway had brought Benedictine nuns to Lincluden in Nithsdale, near Dumfries.[3]

In 1214 the attack on Derry was renewed: 'Thomas, son of Uchtrach, and Ruaidhri, son of Raghnall, plundered Derry completely and took the treasures of the monastic Community of Derry and of the Church of [St Colum Cille's] monastery.'[4] To Iona?

Another factor in the situation needs to be considered; the history of the monastery's endowments. A. O. Anderson quotes an entry from the *Liber Censuum* for 1192, where under 'Norway' in addition to the bishoprics of Orkney and the

Hebrides and Man is entered: 'the church of St Columba of the island of Iona; two bezants yearly.'[5]

This is the same amount as the Abbey of Iona was to pay the Vatican under the terms of the bull of 1203 in favour of the Benedictines! In other words, the abbey was already endowed before the Benedictine foundation, usually supposed to have been based on Raghnall, son of Somerled's, generous assignment of the lands described in the bull, was made. It may well be that all Raghnall did was to transfer the already existing endowments from the Irish to the Benedictine foundation; but unless we can ever learn what the pre-1203 endowments were (and the information may exist in some inaccesible document in the archives of the Vatican or of the Archdiocese of Trondhjem), we cannot know. It is quite possible that Canna was part of the endowment of the monastery of Iona before 1203.

There is a remarkable traditional confirmation of what happened on Iona in 1203 in the unpublished report to Rome on the condition of the Highlands and Islands by Fr. John Tyrie, written in 1737. Fr. Tyrie says of Iona that there was once on it a great monastery, built in St Columba's time, but later rebuilt more magnificently, with a fine church. He also says that the misfortunes of the MacLeans of Duart in the seventeenth century were popularly ascribed to their desecration of Iona, which presumably happened in the time of Sir Lachlan MacLean's chiefship, of which we shall hear more later.

The troubles that took place on Iona and at Derry in 1203, 1204, 1212, and 1214 were the last important clashes between the sympathizers with the traditional practices of the old Gaelic or so-called Celtic Church and those of the Roman discipline. The most intransigent followers of the former were always to be found in Ulster, St Columba's native province, so closely associated with Iona. After the coming of St Patrick in the fifth century, they had made Ireland a centre of learning and fervent Christianity, which Irish missionaries had carried all over Western Europe at a time when the Roman Empire had been overrun by barbarians. They had converted a great part of England north of the Thames, including the important kingdom of Northumbria.

But in their remote corner of Europe they had clung to an obsolete system of calculating the date of Easter, on which the dates of all the other church festivals depended, and to an abandoned style of tonsure that marked their clergy out as different; these were matters supposed to have been settled by the Synod of Whitby in 644, when uniformity with the Roman calendar and tonsure (already accepted in southern Ireland) was agreed. But various other forms of disciplinary and organizational practices were also involved, which though well suited to a loosely united rural nation, were becoming more and more disapproved of in cities where political power lay. These differences persisted for far longer. But with its magnificent record of religious and cultural achievement in the sixth and early seventh centuries, it was intolerably galling for the followers of the Gaelic church to be told by new Anglo-Saxon converts from the South of England that they were doing the wrong things. Those of us who deplore the suppression of the Tridentine Latin Mass will have some conception of their feelings.

The Benedictines settled in at Iona, and established (or continued) a magnificent tradition of stone carving. Unfortunately their own records are lost, but some of their letters to Rome survive. They had their troubles. In 1426 Dominicus (Donnchadh mac Coinnich), the same Abbot of Iona who supplicated Pope Martin in 1428 for the excommunication of the raiders who were ruining Canna, was involved in a determined attempt to prevent a scandal at the monastery when he petitioned the Pope to grant the monastery 'the privilege that henceforth no noble be received into the monastery as a monk or brother without the unanimous consent of the Abbot and convent, since certain noble abbots who have presided in the said monastery kept noble women as concubines, had offspring by them and dowered them with the goods of the monastery', which would be 'totally destroyed if such nobles [i.e. Gaelic *uaislean*, near relations of clan chiefs] are admitted as monks, since they wish to enter only that they may receive service from, not that they may give service to, God and man.'

The Abbot was under pressure to admit as a monk one Fionghuin mac Fhionghuin or Finnon MacKinnon, nephew of a former 'noble abbot' and son of the chief of the clan

MacKinnon, who then held lands in Mull (some formerly belonging to the monastery) as well as in Skye. The young man's vocation to the Benedictine order was naturally regarded with scepticism. The papal response was that the Abbot and monastery be not bound to receive anyone through whose reception scandal might arise.[6]

In making this petition, Abbot Dominicus was making a firm stand against a very real evil which in the long run did enormous harm to the Church in Scotland; the persistent attempts, in the fourteenth and fifteenth centuries, of the Scottish nobles and clan chiefs to obtain lucrative clerical situations for their needy younger sons, often in institutions which their pious forebears had founded and endowed in the twelfth and early thirteenth centuries. It can well be asked how obedience to the rules of clerical celibacy under conditions of great temptation could have been expected from the poorer secular clergy in the Highlands and Islands when the kind of example against which Abbot Dominicus protested could come from the great Benedictine monastery of Iona, which certainly violated memories of the earlier asceticism of the Celtic Church.* The ultimate result was that when the sixteenth century came, too often the man who was drawing the emoluments was not doing the work, but instead some poorly paid substitute, ill-learnt and badly equipped to dispute with the zealous followers of Luther and Calvin.

It is necessary to consider how ordinary religious life must have been arranged in the Highlands in medieval times. One gets the impression, from frequent clerical complaints in supplications to Rome of the cost of entertaining visitors at the times of major Church festivals, that on such occasions there was an influx of parishioners to attend the services in the parish church, travelling on horseback, on foot, or in small boats, and having to be fed and sheltered during the periods in

* See the chapter on 'Ecclesiastical Celibacy' in Dom Louis Gougaud's *Christianity in Celtic Lands*. The Church had been willing to ordain married men, provided the ordained and his wife henceforth lived as brother and sister; but not to allow ordained men to marry. Rules were being tightened up everywhere in the eleventh century. Even so, a priest in the remote Highlands and Islands of Scotland who lived with the woman who kept house for him, and had children by her, might in those times be considered guilty of disobedience rather than immorality; but hardly a monk who kept a concubine.

question. Otherwise the priest would be likely to make a regular round of the various small thatched chapels in the remote parts of his parish in the summertime. As Highland and Hebridean parishes were far bigger than Lowland or English ones, and roads other than very rough tracks non-existent, this is really the only way things could have been done.

Nothing is known about what became of Abbot Cellach or of Abbot Amalgaidh – the disappearance of the archives of the Benedictine monastery of Iona is a very severe loss to Highland history. On 22 April 1247 Pope Innocent IV 'granted to the Abbot of Iona licence to use the ring and the mitre, and to give benediction, in absence of any papal legate or bishop; and pronounced that the abbot and convent of Iona . . . were not to be summoned to the general chapter of Benedictines in Scotland'.[7] The isles then still belonged to Norway and Iona was under the archbishopric of Trondhjem (Nidaros). After the annexation by the Scottish Crown in 1263, Pope Nicholas IV wrote to the Bishop of Argyll, on 3 October 1289, declaring that the abbey of Iona, in the diocese of Argyll, was immediately subject to the Roman Church, and not to the diocese.[8]

This explains why on 15 March 1428 'Dominicus' (i.e. Donnchadh, or Duncan) the abbot of Iona sent the following supplication to Rome, the earliest known surviving extended document referring to Canna:

Since in the island of CANNA, Sodor diocese, situated among the islands of Scotland and pertaining to the monastery of ST. COLUMBA, isle of HY [Iona], O.S.B., said diocese, and in the parish of St. Donnan,[9] by reason of wars and other calamities in the past divers homicides, depredations and other ills were perpetrated, so that some strong men [*valentes viri*] of the familiars of the Abbot and convent were slain by pirates and sea rovers [*predones*], and divers farmers [*incole*] and inhabitants of the island were afraid to reside there and cultivate the land, and transferred themselves elsewhere, deserting the island to the no little loss of the said monastery, – therefore DOMINICUS, present ABBOT and the convent of the said monastery supplicate that the Pope would grant them privilege and indult that the said island of Canna and all and sundry the inhabitants of both sexes and of whatsoever condition with their servants and familiars and all who may betake themselves to the said island with their goods movable and immovable may enjoy full and free immunity in all things, as best and most honourably obtains in the kingdom of Scotland; and that the Pope would give mandate to the Bishop of Sodor that he cause the said immunity and everything concerning it to be inviolably observed in perpetuity, and that any violaters and disturbers of the peace should incur sentence of excommunication from which they may not be absolved, except at the point of death, unless they have made due satisfaction and restitution.[10]

These incursions were the consequences of feuds within the Lordship of the Isles in the 1420s which had reduced the monastery of Iona to great financial and personal difficulties. But worse were to come after the Lordship was suppressed at the end of the century and particularly after the Scottish Reformation of 1560.

NOTES

1. *Highland Papers*, i. 11.
2. Ibid. 13. The earldom of Moray is an anachronism.
3. Agnes Mure MacKenzie, *The Foundation of Scotland*, p. 202.
4. *Annals of Ulster*.
5. *ESSH* II. 361, in a footnote, with reference to *Diplomatarium Norvegicum*, vii. 16.
6. *Scottish Supplications to Rome, 1423–28*, p. 139; see also *Highland Papers*, i. 32, 83–92.
7. *ESSH* II. 361.
8. Ibid.
9. The church of St Columba of Canna seems to have been in the parish of Kildonan (St Donnan of Eigg), *Originales Parochiales*, II. i 334–5, 359.
10 .*Scottish Supplications to Rome*, II. 199 (Scottish History Society, third series, XLVIII).

4 CANNA AND THE LORDSHIP OF THE ISLES

The great Somerled, 'Somhairle* mac Ghiolla Brighde', who expelled the Norsemen from the West Highland mainland, died in 1164, murdered by his page (according to MacVurich) or his nephew (according to Hugh MacDonald) at the time when he was confronting Malcolm, King of the Scots in arms at Paisley, the matter at issue being the overlordship of Argyll and Kintyre.† It is quite possible that the outcome of this meeting might have been peaceful. He was buried on Iona.

Somerled had been married to the Princess Ragnhildis, daughter of Olaf the Red, King of the Isle of Man, Islay, Mull, and the Isles south of Ardnamurchan. According to Hugh MacDonald, he had gained his father-in-law's consent to the marriage by rescuing him from his sinking galley – the leak having been arranged by a friend of Somerled, who was a foster brother of Olaf's – boring holes in the galley's hull and stopping them with buttered wooden pins. Somerled and Ragnhildis had a number of children, and important Highland families are descended from two of them, Dugal (Dubhghall means 'dark foreigner', the Gaelic term for the Danes) who was the progenitor of the MacDougalls, an important family and clan in Argyll until they took the wrong side of the Scottish war of independence and fought against Bruce; and Raghnall, then anglicized or Latinized 'Reginald', better Ranald, who was the forebear of the MacDonald Lords of the Isles (Kings of the Isles in Gaelic), who take their clan name from his son Domhnall (Donald).

Ranald, whom MacVurich calls *Rí Innsi Gall agus oirire*

---

* Somhairle has been absurdly given 'Samuel' as an English equivalent in modern times.

† The chief Highland sources for the history of Somerled and his descendants, including the Lords of the Isles, are the *Book of Clanranald*, kept by the MacVurich poet-historians of the chiefs of Clanranald, in South Uist, and Hugh MacDonald's History of the MacDonalds', printed by Sheriff J. R. N. MacPhail in the first volume of *Highland Papers* (Scottish History Society) second series, Vol. 5). The MacVurichs were the last Gaelic family bards in Scotland or Ireland who wrote the classical Gaelic that was formerly common to both countries. Hugh MacDonald was a MacDonald of Sleat.

Gaoidheal ('King of the Hebrides and Argyll'), was he who founded (or imposed) the Benedictine Monastery on Iona in 1203, and his sister Beathag (or 'Beatrix') became prioress of the nunnery there. He died in 1207 or 1208 and was buried on Iona. He was succeeded by his son Donald – it is significant that the MacVurich historian recorded that 'Messages came from Tara in Ireland that Donald, son of Ranald, should take the government of the Hebrides [Innisgall] and of the majority of the Gaels.'* Donald, who made a penitential pilgrimage to Rome in the course of his life, resisted the claim of the King of Scots to the superiority of the isles, pointing out that he held them from the King of Denmark, and would not accept the superiority of the King of Scots. Donald could also claim the isles through his mother, who was the heiress of her father and brothers.[1]

Donald was succeeded by his son Aonghus Mór, who was followed by his son, Aonghus Òg, from whose brother Eóin were descended the MacDonalds of Ardnamurchan. Aonghus Mór died in 1294 on Islay; he had supported Bruce in the war of the Balliols. Aonghus Òg married the daughter of O Catháin in Ireland, who brought with her 'the unusual retinue' of 'twenty four sons of clan families from whom sprang four-and-twenty families in Scotland'.[2] Aonghus Òg died on Islay in 1326; one of his sons was the progenitor of the MacDonalds of Glencoe.

The sovereignty of the Kings of Norway over the Hebrides ended in 1263 when the Norwegians were defeated at Largs after their fleet had been badly damaged by a September storm supposedly raised by Scottish witches. The King of the Scots had professed he would be willing to agree to the Norwegian King Hakon retaining the overlordship of all the islands on the west of Scotland except Bute, Arran, and the Cumbraes, but seeing the stormy season approaching, he procrastinated.[3] The Norwegian expedition had come too late in the summer. Its fate affected Ireland as well as the Hebrides; an appeal from the Irish Gaels to King Hakon for help in expelling the English was under consideration.

The Norwegian kings' overlordship of the Hebrides had been a light one. In 1228–9 Hakon Hakonsson's saga re-

* 'Tara' used figuratively for 'some of the leading men in Ireland'.

marked that 'the kings of the Hebrides, who had come of Somerled's race, were very unfaithful to king Hakon'.[4] The kings of the Scots, nearer at hand, were to become a greater menace to Hebridean independence, and eventually to extinguish it, though only after they became able to achieve naval supremacy on the north-west coasts of Scotland and the isles, and after family quarrels and internal feuds had weakened the Lordship of the Isles. The kings or Lords of the Isles did not hesitate to intrigue with the kings of England in efforts to maintain their independence, something that gave the kings of the Scots an additional pretext for trying to suppress it.

In the fourteenth and early fifteenth centuries the power and influence of the 'kings of the isles' ('Domini Insularum') reached its highest magnitude. John, (Eóin) son of Aonghus Òg, succeeded his father in 1326. John was twice married, the first time to a lady usually known as Amy MacRuairi, though in Gaelic a woman cannot be 'mac' anyone, mac meaning 'son'. In Latin she was referred to as Amia soror Reginaldi; Hugh MacDonald calls her Algive, daughter of Allan, son of Roderick MacDougall; the MacVurich historian refers to her as "Anna inghen Rúaghraidhe mic Ailin ardfhlath Lagurna', 'Anna daughter of Ruairi son of Allan, Lord of Lorne'. Both historians agree in saying that amongst other children John had by her two sons, Godfrey and Ranald. Both historians allege that Amy and John were never actually married; unfortunately for these writers and other MacDonald historians who like to maintain that only the children of John's second marriage, to Princess Margaret, daughter of King Robert II of the Scots, were legitimate, the papal dispensation for the marriage of John and Amy has been discovered. It is dated 4 June 1337 at Avignon.[5]

The fact is that Amy 'MacRuairi', an heiress who had brought John of the Isles the dowry of the lands of Garmoran and the Northern Isles,* was repudiated by her husband on the grounds of some technical irregularity when he had the opportunity to marry a daughter of the King of the Scots. The dispensation for this marriage was dated 14 June 1350. The repudiation is said to have been done with the approval of the

---

* i.e. the districts of Moidart, Arisaig, Morar, and Knoydart, and the Hebrides north of Ardnamurchan.

Council of the Isles but particularly with the encouragement of John's foster-father MacInnes of Ardgour. Amy had her revenge on MacInnes; she reported slighting words spoken by him to her ex-husband, who gave commission to Donald MacLean to kill MacInnes, which Donald did, as well as killing MacInnes' five sons, thus getting possession of Ardgour. Hence the MacLeans of Ardgour.

John of the Isles provided for his sons by Amy by dividing her dowry between them. Godfrey got North Uist, Benbecula, half South Uist, Boisdale, Canna, Sleat, and Knoydart. Godfrey gave Boisdale to MacNeil of Barra, and St Kilda to MacLeod of Harris. Ranald, who became the progenitor of the Clanranald family, got half South Uist, Eigg, Rum, Morar, and Arisaig. Hugh MacDonald goes on to say that Godfrey's four sons never 'enjoyed their patrimony; for Ranald, their uncle, took hold of all their share of South Uist to himself, with the Isle of Canna, in the time of his tutelage [i.e. while he was their guardian], they being young, and not having come to any years of perfection'.[6]

This Ranald was the progenitor of the MacDonalds of Clanranald. Of course he had no complete right to Canna, which belonged to the Abbey of Iona – it would be interesting to know what the Abbot and monks thought of his dealings with his nephews. It must be remembered that in feudal times outright property in land such as developed in times of *laissez-faire* economy and social relationships, did not exist – land was held by vassals from superiors (and ultimately from the Crown or from the Church) in a series of interlocking mutual obligations and privileges. It was a system which, whatever its failings, established personal responsibility throughout the social structure. Ranald's chicanery was the beginning of the Clanranald interest in Canna, but it did not attain technically complete ownership until R. G. MacDonald of Clanranald purchased the superiority of the island from the Duke of Argyll in 1805, whose ancestor Archibald Earl of Argyll had obtained it from the Bishop of the Isles in 1628 – and the Argyll family had lost it temporarily between 1681 and 1690, owing to their act of rebellion in the former year.*

* It appears that the MacDonalds of Sleat had an interest in the superiority of Canna in 1617 and 1633, but the position is obscure.

At this point it may be interesting to picture the administration of the Lordship of the Isles as described by Hugh MacDonald, the seventeenth-century historian of the MacDonalds of Sleat:

At this ceremony [of proclaiming the Lord of the Isles] the Bishop of Argyll, the Bishop of the Isles, and seven priests, were sometimes present; but a bishop was always present, with the chieftains of all the principal families, and a *Ruler of the Isles*. There was a square stone, seven or eight feet long, and the tract of a man's foot cut thereon, upon which he stood, denoting that he should walk in the footsteps and uprightness of his predecessors, and that he was installed by right in his possessions. He was clothed in a white habit, to shew his innocence and integrity of heart, that he would be a light to his people, and maintain the true religion. The white apparel did afterwards belong to the poet by right. Then he was to receive a white rod in his hand, intimating that he had power to rule, not with tyranny and partiality, but with discretion and sincerity. Then he received his forefathers' sword, or some other sword, signifying that his duty was to protect and defend them from the incursions of their enemies in peace or war, as the obligations and customs of his predecessors were. The ceremony being over, mass was said after the blessing of the bishop and seven priests, the people pouring their prayer for the success and prosperity of their new created Lord. When they were dismissed, the Lord of the Isles feasted them for a week thereafter; gave liberally to the monks, poets, bards and musicians. You may judge that they spent liberally without any exception of persons. The constitution of government of the Isles was thus: Macdonald had his council at Island Finlaggan, in Isla, to the number of sixteen, viz.:- four Thanes, four Armins, that is to say, Lords or sub-Thanes, four Bastards, [i.e.] Squires, or men of competent estates, who could not come up with Armins or Thanes, that is freeholders, or men that had their lands in factory, as Macgee of the Rinds of Isla, MacNicoll in Portree in Sky, and MacEachern, Mackay, and MacGillevray in Mull, Macillemhaoel or MacMillan, etc. There was a table of stone where this council sat in the Isle of Finlaggan; the which table, with the stone on which Macdonald sat, were carried away by Argyle with the bells that were at Icolumkill. Moreover, there was a judge in every Isle for the discussion of all controversies, who had lands from Macdonald for their trouble, and likewise the eleventh part of every action decided. But there might be still an appeal to the Council of the Isles. MacFinnon was obliged to see weights and measures adjusted; and MacDuffie, or MacPhie of Colonsay, kept the records of the Isles.[7]

– which, alas have disappeared, an incalculable loss for historians of the Highlands and Islands of Scotland.

This is not the place where the full story of the Lordship or Kingdom of the Isles can be told, of the marriage of Donald, son of John and Princess Margaret, to the heiress to the earldom of Ross, and of his successful defence of his claim to that earldom at the battle of Harlaw in 1411. John of the Isles had died at Ardtornish in Morven in 1380, and the MacVurich historian relates how Ranald above-mentioned, his son by Amy MacRuairi, was steward of the Isles at that time, and called a meeting of the nobles of the Isles and his brothers at Kildonan on the Isle of Eigg at which he gave the sceptre (*slat tighearnais*, the white rod referred to above) to his half-brother Donald 'against the opinion of the men of the Isles'. My understanding of this remark is that as a historian of the Clanranalds, the MacVurich writer of the Book of Clanranald meant to suggest that the islemen would have preferred that Ranald should succeed him. Donald's brother John was the progenitor of the MacDonalds of Islay and Kintyre, and his other brother, Alexander or Alasdair Carrach, 'scald-headed Alasdair', of the MacDonalds of Keppoch.

Donald, who 'gave lands in Mull and in Islay to the monastery of Iona, and every immunity [*gach saoirsi*] which the monastery of Iona had from his ancestors before him; and made a covering of gold and silver for the relic of the hand of Colum Cille', ended his days after taking the brotherhood of the Benedictine order, dying on Islay and being buried in the Church of Odhran, on Iona, around 1420.[8]

He was succeeded by his son Alexander, who in 1427 was treacherously taken, with other Highland chiefs, by King James I of Scots, after an invitation to attend a parliament at Inverness, was imprisoned and humiliated, and after reprisals he took against Inverness, defeated and forced to beg for royal clemency, and then again imprisoned. Alexander, who was married to Elizabeth Seton, daughter of Alexander Seton, Lord of Gordon and Huntly, died in 1449 at Dingwall where he was buried on 8 May, and was succeeded by his son John.

The Lordship of the Isles went out on a note of high tragedy. John of the Isles married Elizabeth Livingstone at an early age, and had no children by her. He is described by Hugh

MacDonald as 'a meek, modest man, brought up at the Scots court in his younger years, and a scholar, more fit to be a churchman than to command so many irregular tribes of people. He endeavoured, however, still to keep them in their allegiance, by bestowing gifts on some, and promoting others with lands and possessions; by this he became prodigal and very expensive.'⁹

This policy of appeasement was resented by the Islesmen. John had illegitimate sons, John and Aonghus. John died young; more and more the MacDonalds came to look to Aonghus, a much stronger character than his father, to lead them and check these dilapidations of the Lordship's wealth. Bitter quarrels resulted; after being humiliated by his son in Islay, John went to Inveraray on an unexpected mission, and bestowed the lands of Knapdale 'from the River Add to the Fox-burn [Allt an t-Sionnaich in Gaelic] on the Earl of Argyll, whom he asked to accompany him to Stirling, where the King, James II of the Scots, then was. At Stirling and at Ayr, where John went with the King, he resigned all his lands, except the barony of Kinloss in Moray, of Kinnaird in Buchan, and Cairndonald in the West, to the King.'¹⁰

Civil war broke out between the followers of Aonghus, mostly MacDonalds, and the chiefs who were willing to submit to the King, MacLean of Ardgour, MacLeod of Harris, and MacNeil of Barra. The action, a naval one, was fought at Bloody Bay in waters off the north-west of Mull. The chiefs were defeated; and an enmity resulted between MacLeod of Harris and MacDonald of Clanranald, that lasted until 1613. Aonghus and his followers continued their struggle for independence. Aonghus was married to Mary, daughter of the first Earl of Argyll, who at this time was on Islay with their three-year-old son, Domhnall Dubh. The Earl of Argyll provided the Earl of Atholl with boats to cross over to kidnap Domhnall Dubh, who was kept prisoner thereafter on Innis Chonaill in Loch Awe 'until his hair got grey'. Later the Scottish government sought to discredit his claim when the Islemen brought him forward as heir to the Lordship by saying he was not legitimate, typical official smear tactics.

Aonghus himself, after having led a raid in reprisal and capturing the Earl and Countess of Atholl by violating the sanctuary of the chapel of St Bride,[11] and imprisoning them on Islay for about a year, was murdered at Inverness c.1490 by an Irish harper from Monaghan named Art Uí Cairbre (Diarmaid Cairbreach according to the Annals of Loch Cé), who had been bribed by one of the MacKenzies to kill him. The harper was killed by being 'drawn after horses until his limbs were torn asunder' after which his head was cut off and exhibited on a stake. Hence the poem by the Dean of Knoydart addressed to the head, *A chinn Diarmaid Uí Chairbre*,[12]

> O head of Diarmaid Uí Chairbre,
> Though great thy spoils and pride,
> Little I deem thy anguish
> Though thou hangest on a wythe.

Without legitimate issue, and predeceased by both his natural sons, John of the Isles, who spent a good deal of his time around court after leaving the Isles, died at Dundee in January 1503. He is usually said to have been forfeited, but as Sheriff J. R. N. MacPhail says, no official record of such a forfeiture exists. Sheriff MacPhail points out that there are many statements in the royal accounts of the expenses of himself and his servants being paid from the royal treasury of King James IV, and that the account of his dying in 1498 in an obscure Dundee lodging given by the authors of *Clan Donald* (who incidentally must have copied it from Dr Dugald Mitchell's *History of the Highlands and of Gaelic Scotland*) misinterprets the facts.*

The Lords of the Isles had gone:

> King's sons who earned not satire,
> Folk of manliness and honour,
> Fierce, well born, of high spirit,
> Liberal in bestowing

— so Giolla Coluim (= 'servant of St Columba') wrote in the *Book of the Dean of Lismore*.[13]

'After the death of Angus', writes Hugh MacDonald, 'the Islanders, and the rest of the Highlanders, were let loose, and

---

* Footnote in *Highland Papers* I. 50–1. Sheriff MacPhail also points out that the tomb of King Robert II which the authors of *Clan Donald* describe as being at Paisley, and where they say John of the Isles asked to be buried, is actually at Scone.

began to shed one another's blood. Although Angus kept them in obedience while he was sole lord over them, yet upon his [i.e. John's] resignation of his rights to the king, all families, his own as well as others, gave themselves up to all sorts of cruelties, which continued for a long time thereafter.'[14] The Scottish Crown had at last succeeded in shooting down the eagle, but had thereby only let loose a flock of kestrels in the western Highlands and Islands. The central government at Edinburgh could not, before achieving naval supremacy on the west coast of Scotland, replace the administration of the Council of the Isles: after 1490, every Government action and every legislation in connection with Gaelic Scotland was to be repressive.

Historians of this period are apt to repeat freely the official complaints of 'rebellion' and 'treason' in connection with the Lordship. The fact is that the Islemen considered their rights derived from Norway, not from Scotland, and their customs and traditions from Ireland, and that they owed the Scottish Crown little in the way of allegiance, especially when their freedoms were threatened. 'Rebellion' and 'treason' cease to be so called when the side invoking them wins, when they become 'glorious revolution' and 'fighting for freedom'.

Many will regret that the Lordship of the Isles did not survive under Norwegian protection in a form that could have led to the Hebrides now possessing the present liberties of the Isle of Man, associated with the Scottish isles in Norse times. That is a 'might have been' that is worth considering.

NOTES

1. *Book of Clanranald*, pp. 156–7 (Reliquiae Celticae II).
2. Ibid. 158–9.
3. *ESSH* II. 627 *et seq.*
4. *ESSH* II. 465.
5. Printed in *Highland Papers*, i. 73–4.
6. *Highland Papers*, i. 27–8.
7. *Highland Papers*, i. 23–5. See also Monro's *Western Isles of Scotland*, ed. R. W. Munro, pp. 56–7.
8. *Book of Clanranald, Rel. Celt.* II. 160–3.
9. *Highland Papers*, ii. 47.
10. *Highland Papers*, i. 48; *Rel. Celt.* II. 163.

11. Hugh MacDonald denies this, see *Highland Papers*, i. 51.
12. W. J. Watson, *Scottish Verse from the Book of the Dean of Lismore*, pp. 56–7.
13. W. J. Watson, op. cit. 92–3.
14. *Highland Papers*, i. 52.

5 AFTER THE DOWNFALL OF THE LORDSHIP

The downfall of the Lordship of the Isles coincided almost exactly with an event which in the long run was to have an enormous effect on the Highlands and Islands of Scotland – the discovery (or rediscovery) by Columbus of America. North America was later to provide a home for many thousands of exiled Highlanders and Islesmen, often compulsorily exiled, as prisoners after the Rising of 1745, or victims of the Highland Clearances; and tropical America was to provide the potato, which was to become a staple part of the diet of Highlanders after the middle of the eighteenth century (and which Canna produces of very high quality).

But in 1500 all this was still a long way off in the future. The Highlands and Islands of Scotland were then one of the uttermost parts of the known world of Europe, together with Iccland and the Faeroes. The good pieces of land, such as Islay, Kintyre, Tiree, Canna, the west side of South and North Uist, were fiercely coveted by the possessors of the rockier and peatier parts, which were and are far larger.

An immediate consequence of the end of the Lordship was a scramble by the leading vassals of the former Lords of the Isles to secure charters from the Crown for the lands they had been holding from the Lordship. One of these was Hugh or 'Austin' (Gaelic 'Huisdein') MacDonald of Sleat, brother of John, the last Lord. Austin, says Hugh MacDonald,[1] took 'his charters from the king for all his patrimony which his father and mother bestowed on him formerly, in favour of his heirs-male, legitimate or illegitimate; which patrimony consisted of North Uist, the parish of Hough [Hógh] in South Uist, Canna, Benbicula, Sleat, Trotternish, and Lochbroom'.

This charter exists, and is printed by Sheriff MacPhail.[2] It is a confirmation of the charter to Hugh from his brother John, 'Comes Rossie et Dominus Insularum', but unfortunately the date of the original charter is obviously wrongly entered in the Record of the Great Seal. The curious thing about the charter is that there is no mention whatever of Canna in it. Hugh MacDonald himself says that Hugh of Sleat's contemporary, Allan MacDonald of Clanranald, 'possessed the lands of Hough, Benbicula, [and] Canna' which his family had wrongfully retained since Ranald, his great grandfather, had filched them from his nephews while acting as their guardian (see p. 24). It is clear enough from a rather confusing passage in Hugh MacDonald's History that Allan of Clanranald refused to give up Hough, Benbecula, or Canna to Austin, even when ordered to do so by his Chief; 'for the lands [sic, read 'lairds'] of Muidort [i.e. the Clanranalds] always kept possession of them tho' contrary to right; neither had they any legal tithe [sic, read 'title'] to their other holdings till King Charles the Second's time'.³ Hugh MacDonald at the end of his History refers to Trotterness, Sleat, North Uist, Canna, Lochbroom, and Kishorn as lands inherited by Donald Gruamach MacDonald of Sleat from his father Donald Gallach (in 1539 or 1540),⁴ but Canna was never in Donald Gruamach's hands. It was of course still officially the property of the monastery of Iona. But Hugh MacDonald was a partisan of the MacDonalds of Sleat.

It is interesting to trace the status of Canna, Rum, Eigg, and Muck as recorded at various times, from Dean Munro's account of the islands in 1549 to Martin Martin's in 1703. Bit by bit the ownership of the bishopric of the Isles and the Abbey of Iona – the two were united in 1499 – becomes eroded, reduced to nominal rents paid unwillingly or not paid at all by *de facto* occupiers whose successors became accepted popularly as the actual owners of the lands. Even as early as 1549 Dean Munro describes Raasay as 'pertaining to McGillichallum [= MacLeod of Raasay] be the Sword, and all to the Bishop of the Iles in heritage. This McGillichallum should obey as vassal McCloyd of Leozus' [MacLeod of Lewis].⁵ He obviously didn't! Ironical that 'McGillichallum' means 'son of the servant of St Columba'! By 1593 the situation of Raasay was that McGillichallum's successor was paying a rent of 16 merks⁶ a year to the Bishop, but enjoying an income of 500 merks a year from 'sundrie tributes' out of the island himself.⁷ This kind of thing was typical. On Mull at the same time the Bishop had 30 merklands, 'but McClane Doward has it in hes possessioun occupiet be his kin'. This was Sir Lachlan MacLean, 'callit Great McClane'.[8]

A distinction is drawn in such accounts; land 'pertains' to the Bishop, but is 'possessed' by Clanranald, and so on. In modern parlance, 'occupied' would perhaps be a more suitable term, if it didn't imply residence. The following is a table of the 'pertainence' and 'possession' of each of the Small Isles over the century and a half between Dean Monro's and Martin Martin's visits.

1549 – Dean Monro[9]

Canna – 'perteins' to the Abbot of Iona.

Rum – 'perteins' to the Laird of Coll 'callit M^{c}ane abrie' [= MacLean of Coll, whose Gaelic patronymic is *Mac Iain Abraich*]; 'This land obeyis to McGillane of Doward instantlie' i.e. MacLean of Coll is MacLean of Duart's vassal for Rum at this moment.

Eigg – not stated.

Muck and Eilean nan Each – 'pertein' to the Bishop of the Isles.

1561 – 'Rentale of the Bishoprick of the Ilis and Abbacie of Ecolmkill'[10]

Canna – described as one of the Abbot's lands within Clanranald's bounds. Rent £20; the parsonage of Cannay is said to pertain to the Abbot of Iona. (By 'parsonage' is meant the proportion of the teinds or tithes then due to the titular holder of the benefice. The parsonage teinds[11] formerly consisted of grain only.)

Rum – not involved.

Eigg – not involved.

Muck – pertains to the Bishop of the Isles, 'possest be M'Aen of Ardnamurchan' (MacDonald of Ardnamurchan).

c.1593 – Description of the Isles of Scotland*

Canna – 'perteins to the Bishop of the Iles, but the said Clan-Rannald has it in possessioun . . . it is six merk land and will raise 20 men.'

Rum (spelt 'Romb') – 'perteins heretablie to ane Barron callit Laird of Challow [Coll], quha is of McClane [of Duart's] kin, but is possest and in the handis of Clan-Rannald.' It is 'ane Ile of small profit, except it conteins mony deir, and for sustenation thairof the same is permittit unlabourit [= un-cultivated], except twa touns [villages].' 'It is ten merk land, and will raise 6 or 7 men.'

Eigg – pertains to the Clan Rannald. 30 merk land. Will raise 60 men to the wars.

Muck – pertains to the Bishop of the Isles, possessed by MacIain of Ardnamurchan. Four merk land. Rent, 160 bolls corn (oats or barley), of which half go to the Bishop and half to the 'laird'. It will raise 16 men 'to the weiris'.

1626 – Bishop Thomas Knox's Report[12]

Canna – pertains to Abbot of Iona, possessed by John MacLeod [of Harris], who has lease of neither land nor teinds.

Rum – unstated. No lease of lands.

Eigg – belongs to Clanranald. No lease of teinds.

Muck – 'belongs to' the Laird of Coll, pays a chalder of four rowed barley.

c.1630 – The Description of the Highlands of Scotland.[13]

Canna – 'pertaining to the Captaine of the Clan-ronnald'.

Rum – 'appertaines to the Laird of Colla'.

Eigg – not stated. 30 merk lands.

Muck – 'appertaines to the Bishop of the Illes'. 6 merk lands.

* Skene, *Celtic Scotland*, pp. 433–4. This is an important document, possibly an official report for James VI. The description of Eigg contains an account of the massacre of MacDonalds suffocated by the MacLeods in the famous cave, dated 1577. There are difficulties about accepting this date, which are discussed later. The account of Rum reveals that the island was being kept as a sporting estate 400 years ago, and that when MacLean of Coll acquired it for a rotten galley later, according to tradition, he was simply buying it back. In 1633 Ranald MacDonald of Benbecula was accused of shooting deer there (*Highland Papers* IV. 227).

1703 – Martin Martin[14]

Canna – Allan MacDonald of Clanranald 'is proprietor'.
Rum – MacLean of Coll 'is proprietor'.
Eigg – Allan MacDonald 'of Moydart' [= Clanranald] and
  Allan MacDonald of Morar, are 'proprietors'.
Muck – not stated.

Some interesting points are revealed by these statements. Canna 'pertains' to the Abbot of Iona in 1549, is described as one of the Abbot's lands within Clanranald's bounds in 1561, is held in possession by Clanranald around 1593. In 1626, however, it pertains to the Abbot of Iona but is temporarily, at least, in the possession of John MacLeod of Harris and Dunvegan (Iain Mór, who succeeded his father Sir Ruairi[15] in the same year). Very shortly afterwards, around 1630, Canna is said to pertain to the Captain of Clanranald, with no mention of the Abbot or of MacLeod. Meanwhile in 1628 the Earl of Argyll obtained a confirmation of a charter of the superiority of Canna from the Bishop of the Isles, making whomever he chose to install there his vassal. This superiority lasted until Clanranald redeemed it in 1805, with only a break of nine years after Argyll's successor's forfeiture for rebellion against the Crown in 1681.

Rum* in 1549 pertained to MacLean of Coll, over whom MacLean of Duart was then trying to assert a feudal superiority, not without violence. Around 1593 it still nominally pertains to MacLean of Coll, but is 'possessed' or 'occupied' by Clanranald. The 1630 account does not mention Clanranald, but Martin Martin in 1703 simply says that Coll is the proprietor. Thus the story that MacLean of Coll bought Rum from Clanranald for a (rotten) galley must be qualified by saying that the island 'pertained' to Coll all the time – he simply got Clanranald out of it in this way. The account from *c.*1593 reveals that Rum was run as a red deer reserve for

---

* The spelling RHUM is bogus and artificial and should be abandoned. It was imposed on the Post Office and the Ordnance Survey by the then proprietor, the late Sir George Bullough, in 1903, though the Post Office did not yield until 1905. Earlier postmarks have the spelling RUM (J. A. MacKay, Island Postal History Series, No. 4: Skye and the Small Isles, p. 70.) In the same way there was an attempt to turn the name MUCK into MONK ISLE in the 18th century.

hunting nearly four hundred years ago. The remains of a medieval deer-trap are a very interesting feature of Rum's archaeology.

The blood-stained sixteenth century was to prove that the Scottish Crown was capable of destroying the independence of the Islanders but incapable of instituting good government in its place. Meanwhile many of the Islanders remained as attached to the memory of the Lordship of the Isles as their eighteenth-century successors were to be to the cause of the exiled Stewarts. In 1502 the imprisoned Domhnall Dubh, son of Angus of the Isles, accepted by Hebrideans as the legitimate heir to the Lordship in spite of governmental propaganda attempts to smear him with the assertion that he was illegitimate, was rescued from his imprisonment on Innis Chonain in Loch Awe by the MacDonalds of Glencoe, to lead a rising backed by MacLeod of Lewis (who was married to Domhnall's aunt), MacLean of Duart, and Cameron of Lochiel, which the government suppressed with difficulty, and Domhnall Dubh was transferred to imprisonment in Edinburgh Castle.

In 1513 came the Scottish defeat at Flodden, when King James IV and many of the best men in Scotland were killed, leaving in their places second-raters. It is very doubtful whether Scotland ever really recovered from Flodden. There followed a rising by Sir Donald MacDonald of Lochalsh, 1514–17, another attempt to restore the Lordship. By 1531 the Argyll family, one whose rise was founded on the eclipse of the Lords of the Isles, overplayed its hand when Cailean Meallach, third Earl of Argyll, attempted to treat the Lieutenancy of the Isles, a position of great power to which his father had been appointed, as a heritable office. This was followed by the suspicion that many of the disturbances in the Isles were being fomented by the Argyll family in the hope of benefiting from the forfeitures that would follow.[16]

In 1540 King James V made the first showing of real naval power on the west of Scotland, leading a powerful sea force there around the north of Scotland, on which he invited the local chiefs on board and then treacherously shanghaied them to Edinburgh, where some of them were liberated after giving hostages for their future obedience, others detained there until after his death in 1542, when the infant Mary Queen of Scots succeeded, and the country was governed by the Regent Arran.

In 1543 Domhnall Dubh escaped from Edinburgh Castle and led what was to be the last desperate attempt to restore the Lordship of the Isles, this time with considerably more support from the islanders, including the chiefs of the MacDonalds of Clanranald, Sleat, Ardnamurchan, Glengarry, and Knoydart, the MacLeans of Duart, Lochbuy, Coll, Torloisk, and Ardgour; MacKinnon of Strathswordale; MacNeil of Barra, and MacQuarrie of Ulva.[17] These personalities formed the last Council of the Isles, which met at Knockfergus (Carrickfergus) on Belfast Lough in the north of Ireland. One cannot help admiring the indomitable spirit and hardiness of Domhnall Dubh, who since the age of three had spent all but three years of his life under duress when he escaped from imprisonment in Edinburgh in 1543. There was some backing from King Henry VIII of England for his attempt, but things went wrong owing to a planning delay, Donald's army dispersed, with quarrels about the distribution of Henry VIII's subsidy, and the venture collapsed – shortly afterwards Domhnall Dubh died of fever at Drogheda. With him went the last hopes of restoring the Lordship.

Scottish historians for the most part seem to be incapable of realizing that the islanders had a point of view and a way of life to defend. They had inherited their language and religion and law from Ireland; their first great leader, Somerled, had expelled the Norsemen from the western mainland of Scotland with no help from the Scottish government; the titles and charters of their chiefs derived not from the Scottish crown but from that of Norway, before 1263. They had a proud and long tradition of independence behind them. The acceptance of charters from the anglicized Scottish Crown in place of their charters from their native Lords of the Isles gave them no additional security, but exposed them both to the rivalries of neighbours and the political jockeyings of families like the Earls of Argyll and the MacKenzies of Kintail who sought to advance their possessions by absorbing those of the Church and the Lordship.

Moreover it must be remembered that the destruction of the archives of Iona and those of the Lordship of the Isles leaves the clan historians of the MacVurichs and of Hugh MacDonald as the only source where the islanders' point of view is stated, apart from what survives of contemporary Gaelic verse – and Scottish historians have never felt knowledge of Gaelic to be indispensable when writing about the Highlands and Islands. This leaves the official records of such bodies as the Scots parliaments and the Scots Privy Council as the main source of information for this period, and their language is continually coloured with official prejudices and only states the official point of view – which may at times be no nearer the truth than what *Pravda* was likely to print about the East German, Hungarian, Czech, and Polish disturbances in 1953, 1956, 1968, and 1981–2.

Even Gregory, whose *History of the Western Highlands and Isle of Scotland* is founded on very assiduous and praiseworthy research in the original records, falls into the style of writing about the Islesmen in the language of official propaganda. This material needs to be read with some insight and not always taken *au pied de la lettre*. As an example we can consider the Scottish Government's arrangements for the administration of justice, introduced in 1504, under which Inverness or Dingwall was to be the seat of the Court of Justice for the islands north of Ardnamurchan, and Tarbert, Loch Fyne, or Campbeltown of that for the islands south of Ardnamurchan. Duror, Glencoe, and Lorne were to attend the court in Perth; Lochaber the court of Inverness. 'The Justice Air of Argyll proper', adds Gregory, 'was to be held at Perth, if the King should desire; so that Highlanders and Lowlanders might have equal facility in obtaining justice.'[18] Presumably he is quoting the official document, an Act of the Scottish Parliament.

Equal facility in obtaining justice! The Gaelic-speaking Highlander or Islesman north of Ardnamurchan was expected to go across Scotland, then for the most part still a trackless forest infested with wolves and bears, to attend a court where laws which he had no part in formulating and which could conflict with the ancient Celtic and Norse customs and traditions he had inherited, were administered in what to him was a foreign language. Imagine the outcry if Scots-speaking citizens had been expected to attend a Gaelic court!

The clan system as popularly visualized really dates from the breakdown of the Lordship of the Isles. At times it resembles a shattered resistance movement defending traditional local liberties in the Highlands and Islands; at others it is reminiscent of the struggles between competing Mafia 'families'* Contemporary Scottish governments entered into this game whole-heartedly. In the second half of the sixteenth century there were particularly vicious feuds between the MacDonalds of Clanranald and the MacLeods of Dunvegan in the north, and between the MacLeans of Duart, led by their chief Sir Lachlan MacLean (c.1540–1598), and the MacDonalds of Islay. Both these feuds could have been suppressed by the old Lord of the Isles; the Scottish Government, which had no objection to Highland clans decimating each other, and the Argyll family, which stood to gain by the MacDonald – MacLean feud, could not or would not stop them.

Canna was involved in incidents connected with these feuds, according to some accounts. One was the suffocation of the followers of Clanranald of Eigg in the famous cave, allegedly by the MacLeods of Dunvegan. In the (apparently official) Description of the Isles written around 1593, a date is actually assigned to this incident, March 1577, the name of the alleged Clanranald leader on Eigg is given, 'Angus John McMudzartsonne',† and the number of people killed is said to have been 395.

The difficulties of accepting this story as it stands are discussed by Noel Banks in his *Six Inner Hebrides*, and by the present writer in his notes to the song *'S trom an dìreadh* in the second volume of *Hebridean Folksongs* (Clarendon Press, Oxford, three volumes, 1969–81). There is an alternative account, from the MacLeod point of view, in the Bannatyne MS quoted at length by Canon R. C. MacLeod of MacLeod in his *The MacLeods of Dunvegan*, according to which the incident took place much earlier, in the time when Alasdair Crotach was the chief of the clan (i.e. 1480–1547). In this, after the MacLeods had been infuriated by the ill-treatment which a party of their people shipwrecked on Eigg had received from

* As has been pointed out by Seán Ó Faoláin in his book *The Great O'Neill*, pp. 12–14.

† This implies he was a son of a son of Iain Mùideartach, eighth chief of Clanranald, who died in 1584; but it is impossible to place him from the genealogies in *Clan Donald*.

the inhabitants, they had vowed to put to death every soul on Eigg, Rum, and Canna, all of whose inhabitants gathered together to hide in the cave. The Revd Donald MacLean, who wrote the account of the parish of the Small Isles for the 1794 Statistical Account of Scotland, attributed the massacre to Alasdair Crotach.

It is hardly necessary to point out that before 1547 Canna was Church land and Rum belonged to MacLean of Coll, so their inhabitants were unlikely to be involved at all. The impression is that the writer of the 1593 Description wanted to include the story as evidence of Highland barbarity, and used it to cover up the incident of 1588 when Sir Lachlan MacLean was accused of having invaded Canna, Rum, Eigg, and Muck with the aid of a hundred Spaniards from the famous Spanish galleon* that limped into Tobermory harbour after the dispersal of the Spanish Armada, and despoiled the said islands, and burnt 'the samen Illis, with the haill men, wemen and childrene being thair intill, not spairing the pupillis [i.e. boys of less than fourteen years and girls of less than twelve] and infantis'.[19] The important thing about this statement is, that it was not made as a complaint by Clanranald and the MacDonalds, but by the King's Advocate.

The matter is made clearer by the report of Sir Lachlan MacLean's trial, when the charges against him are more specific; it is alleged that in November 1588 he had 'burnt with fyre the landis of Canna, Rum, Eg, and Ellan ne Muk, and hereit plundered the same; that he slew and crewillie murdreist Hector M'Cane Channaviche [Eachann Mac Iain Chanaich (?)] and Donald Bayne his brother, with ane grit nowmer of wyffis, bairnis and puir laboreris of the ground, about aucht or nyne scoir of sawles, quha eschapit the fyre, was noch spairit be his bluidie sword'. But his real crime was the fact that he employed the Spaniards, the King's enemies, in his private wars against the MacDonalds, the King's subjects. He was imprisoned in Edinburgh Castle awaiting the King's decision, but got out on bail, which he forfeited.[20]

* R. P. Hardie has established in *The Tobermory Argosy* that the galleon must have been the *Juan de Sicilia*, and that it was not a treasure ship. The traditional Gaelic story of the destruction of the galleon is that it was blown up by the jealous wife of a MacLean gentleman who was interested in a Spanish lady aboard, the bomb being smuggled into the ship by her page.

It is very difficult not to suspect that Sir Lachlan MacLean of Duart was getting some high-level protection. He is known to have been in communication with Queen Elizabeth, who hoped that he would assist her forces against O'Neill and O'Donnell in Ireland, and who had promised him a pension.[21] King James VI aspired to succeed Elizabeth and wanted to stay on good terms with her, even though she had murdered his mother. James also would not have objected to Duart's weakening the power of the MacDonalds, or being a counterpoise to the rising power of the Earls of Argyll. Duart is blatantly guilty of treason and murder in 1588, yet is allowed to escape from Edinburgh Castle, and the only penalty he suffers is the forfeiture of his bail.

The writer of the 1593 account of the Isles must be perfectly well aware of all this yet he says nothing about it, bringing in instead an incident said to have taken place on Eigg in 1577, the suffocation of the population of the island in the cave by the MacLeods. If the MacDonalds on Eigg had all been suffocated by the MacLeods in 1577, they would hardly have been available to be massacred by MacLean of Duart and his Spaniards in 1588!

Religious fanaticism consequent upon the politics of the Scottish Reformation added a very unpleasant ideological tinge to the clan feuds of the second half of the sixteenth century. In the ensuing Scottish 'Cultural Revolution' many of the artefacts and all the library of Iona were destroyed. 'In this Ile vas a great many crosses to the number of 360, which vas all destroyed by one provinciall assembly holden on the place a litle after reformation, their foundations is yet estant . . . the registers and records of this Ile was all written on Parchmen but all destroyed by that Assembly that destroyed the crosses.'[22] Considering that many Scottish and some Norwegian and Irish kings, as well as every person of importance in the Isles during the existence of the Lordship, had been buried on Iona, there must have been a forest of crosses there before the Reformation. This was not written by some recusant propagandist, but by the Revd John Fraser, who was born on Mull in 1647 and who was minister of Coll and Tiree from 1678 to 1704, a man who knew the traditions of his native district thoroughly.

Sir Lachlan MacLean of Duart cannot escape grave suspicion of having been involved in this. He was the most powerful person in the immediate neighbourhood; in the 'Account of the Family of MacLean', written in 1716, he is described as 'the First Protestant Chief of the MacLeans'.[23] His father Hector MacLean of Duart had had a charter of Iona from John Carswell, first Protestant Bishop of the Isles, between 1566 and 1572, renewed in favour of Sir Lachlan's son and heir Hector, by King James VI in 1588.[24] In an unpublished report on the condition of the Highlands in 1739, Fr. Tyrie records the tradition that the subsequent misfortunes of the MacLeans of Duart, who lost all lands except Brolos by foreclosure to the Argyll family in 1679, were considered in the Highlands to be the just consequence of their desecration of Iona.

Truly, in the words of George Thomson's 'Antiquity of the Christian Religion amongst the Scots', written in 1594, 'From that time [i.e. 1560, the date of the Reformation in Scotland] the kingdom was so on fire with civil wars, was so polluted with massacre and bloodshed, that nought else seemed to exist but a perpetual shambles.'[25]

NOTES

1. *Highland Papers*, i. 48.
2. Ibid. 96–9.
3. Ibid. 59–60.
4. Op. cit. 72.
5. Monro's *Western Isles of Scotland*, ed. R. W. Munro, p. 70. Ferquhar, Bishop of the Isles, had brought an unsuccessful action against MacLeod of Raasay over this usurpation, in 1533. See *Collectanea de Rebus Albanicis* (*CRA*), 4, footnote.
6. A Scots merk was two-thirds of a pound, i.e. thirteen shillings and fourpence in pre-decimal coinage. Merklands, penny-lands, and ounce-lands were units of assessment for taxation, of considerable antiquity.
7. Skene, *Celtic Scotland*, III. 433.
8. Ibid. 434.
9. Monro's *Western Isles*, p. 67.
10. *CRA* 1–4. It is interesting that the Abbacie of Iona still owned some of the lands mentioned in the papal bull of 1203, now held from the Abbot by 'Clandonald of the West'. These are 'Mwichelleishe' (1203 Mangecheles), 'Skeirkenzie' (1203 Chelchenneg), 'Camasnanesserin in Melphort' (1203 Camusnanesre), and the penny-land of 'Muckarn' (1203 MacKarna).

11. *Scottish National Dictionary*, under 'parsonage'.
12. *CRA* 122.
13. MacFarlane, *Geographical Collections*, iI. 175–7 (Scottish History Society). This description has something in common with that printed by Skene. The MacIains or MacDonalds of Ardnamurchan lost their lands in the 1630s.
14. Martin Martin, *A Description of the Western Islands of Scotland*, 1716 corrected edition, pp. 273–9.
15. Sir Ruairi or Rorie MacLeod of Harris was one of the chiefs converted or reconciled to Roman Catholicism by the Irish Franciscans in 1625. This well-known family is now called MacLeod of Dunvegan or MacLeod of MacLeod.
16. Gregory, *History of the Western Highlands*, p. 139.
17. Op. cit. 170.
18. Op. cit. 100.
19. *Register of the Privy Council of Scotland*, III. 342.
20. Maitland Club, *Criminal Trials*, I, pp. ii, 230.
21. *Register of the Privy Council of Scotland*, V. 295.
22. MacFarlane's *Geographical Collections*, II. 217.
23. MacFarlane's *Genealogical Collections*, I. 133.
24. *CRA* 18n, 161.
25. Scottish History Society, *Miscellany*, II. 131.

6 THE ISLES AND THE STATUTES OF IONA

At the beginning of the seventeenth century two events affected the Gaelic world profoundly: the first was the defeat of the last independent Irish chiefs, O'Neill of Tyrone and O'Donnell of Tír Chonaill (Donegal), at the battle of Kinsale on 24 December 1601; the second the death of the English Queen Elizabeth on 24 March 1603, and the subsequent Union of the Crowns of Scotland and England. No more could the Hebridean chiefs hope for encouragement from their counterparts in Ireland, no more could they look to the King of England for support in any possible future attempt to revive the Lordship of the Isles. Further, in dealing with the Gaels, the King now had the resources of England as well as those of the Lowlands of Scotland behind him, whereas Gaelic hopes of adequate Spanish or French support were invariably to be disappointed. One thing that did not change: the old Church lands of the Isles remained in the effective occupation of the clan chiefs.

It was shortly after these two events that the notorious plantations of Ulster, the evil consequences of which are only too obvious today, began, driving a wedge between the Gaels of Ireland and of Scotland. Hitherto, Ulster, had always been the most intractably independent part of Gaelic Ireland.

In the summer of 1609 the island chiefs Angus MacDonald of Dunnyveg (Islay), Hector MacLean of Duart (Lochlan's heir) and his brothers Lachlan and Allan, Donald Gorm MacDonald of Sleat, Sir Rory MacLeod of Harris, Donald MacDonald of Clanranald, Rory MacKinnon of Strath (Skye), Lachlan MacLaine of Lochbuie, Gillespie MacQuarrie of Ulva, and Donald MacPhie of Colonsay were captured by Lord Ochiltree and Bishop Andrew Knox of the Isles by a trick (rather against the Bishop's conscience) and forced under duress to subscribe to the so-called Statutes of Iona at a court held by Bishop Knox at that place on the twenty-third of August of that year.

The terms of the Statutes are of great interest.[1] Of course they express the Government's point of view. To get an idea of the Islesmen's or Gaelic point of view it is necessary to do some reading between the lines. The terms begin with the usual propaganda references about Highland barbarity, as if there was not plenty of barbarity in the English-speaking parts of Scotland at the time. The terms are as follows:

1. The Chiefs are to see that the ruinous churches in the isles are to be restored, and that the ministers 'plantit' in them are to be obeyed and to receive their stipends, and church discipline is to be kept.

2. 'marriages contractit for certaine years' are to be forbidden.

3. Inns are to be built to entertain 'passengers and strangers' at reasonable expense, and relieve the inhabitants of the burden of Highland hospitality.

4. No one is to be allowed to live in the Isles without an independent income 'ane speciall revenew or rent' to live on, or a craft to keep him.

5. The Chiefs' households are to be limited as follows: Hector MacLean of Duart, eight gentlemen; Angus MacDonald, Donald Gorm of Sleat, MacLeod of Harris, and Clanranald, six gentlemen (= uaislean) each; MacLean of Coll and Rory MacKinnon, three each; Duart's brother Lachlan, three servants; all to be kept at the charge of the Chiefs themselves.

6. Sorning 'be way of conzie' (coinnmheadh, compulsory billeting as a condition of tenancy) to be forbidden, except for reasonable payments to the Innkeepers referred to in Section 3.

7. The importation of whisky or wine whether obtained from mainland merchants or from local 'trafficquaris' to be forbidden. Any person may apprehend such imports and dispose of it at their pleasure, without payment. The fines for buying illegally imported alcohol to be £40 for the first offence, £100 for the second, and the confiscation of all the possessions of the buyer for the third. But people in the Isles

were to be allowed to 'brew acquavitie [whisky] and uthir drink to serve their aune housis'.

8. Any gentleman or yeoman worth in goods sixty cows must send his eldest son whom failing his eldest daughter to the Lowlands to be educated in English.

9. No person to bear firearms outside his house or to shoot at deer, hares, or wildfowl, in accordance with Act of Parliament.

10. Bards, beggars, vagabonds, jugglers, 'nor profest pleisant pretending libertie to baird and flattir' not to be received in the isles by any of the chiefs, but to be put in the stocks and then expelled from the district.

11. Chiefs to apprehend disobeyers of the statutes, and after trial to seize their goods on behalf of the Crown, and produce the malefactors for justice.

12. No chief, or superior of lands, to receive or maintain any fugitive malefactor disobedient to his own chief and superior.

Reading between the lines of this document, one may say in comment:

1. It must be remembered that the Isles had had no part in the Scottish Reformation. To comply with this clause meant accepting all the harsh personal and political discipline of Calvinist rule. What this involved is easily discernible from the surviving Minutes of the Synod of Argyll (between 1639 and 1651): excommunication, i.e. political and social ostracism, for political reasons; compulsory attendance by everyone at Calvinist services and sermons; control of personal movements between parishes; return of fugitives for church discipline; harassment of Catholics, of all social ranks; the destruction of historic monuments, such as pictures in churches or carved crosses. It is no wonder that 'the gentlemen and heretors of the country' refused 'to give their concurrence to the exercise of kirk discipline' as the Synod of Argyll complained in May 1642.[2] The first clause of the Statutes of Iona complained of 'the contempt of these

[ministers] quha ar alreddy plantit'; the Synod of Argyll in 1643 recorded that there were 'very few that have care to ware and bestow upon [spend money on] the traineing up to their children for the ministery within the bounds' of the Synod.[3]

The religion the people of the Isles wanted was clearly apparent when the Irish Franciscans came to the Hebrides in 1624, when several of the subscribers to the Statutes and thousands of ordinary Hebrideans were speedily reconciled to the Roman Catholic church – the latter mostly from ignorance, not from Protestantism – in numbers that the Vatican found difficult to believe, having the illusion that Scotland was by then totally Calvinist. Amongst the reconciliations were inhabitants of Canna.

2. It is not clear whether this clause refers to contracts governing future marriages, or contracted marriages that turned out to last for only a few years. Certainly feuds between the children of Chiefs by different mothers had caused a great deal of trouble in the Isles. The alleged practice of temporary marriage was called 'handfasting', but as A. E. Anton has pointed out, paraphrasing Cosmo Innes, 'there is no proof, or approach to proof, that handfasting in Skene's sense [trial temporary marriage] or any other peculiar customs of marriage were recognized in medieval Scotland after the introduction of Christianity had given one rule of marriage to the whole Christian world'.[4]

What seems to have happened in the Highlands and Islands was that, owing to geographical or other difficulties, the formal engagement or *réiteach* was considered binding and sufficient for cohabitation pending formal church marriage; after the Reformation the more so if the participants did not want to be married by a protestant minister. But such marriages *per verbo de futuro* were open to abuse if either or both parties later wanted to repudiate them.

5. MacLean of Duart seems to be getting favoured treatment here.

6. Of course it would handicap the movement of a Chief's forces if this obligation on the part of his tenants (derived from Gaelic law) was prevented. It is clear that the prohibition was

aimed at the Chiefs themselves, for in the Caution issued to them in 1619 by the Privy Council it was stated that when they travelled across the country to make their annual appearances they were not to 'sorn' (ask for free hospitality as a service from their vassals).

8. All the principal tenants as well as the Chiefs in the Isles would be affected by this. *Ní math iarla gan Bhéarla* 'no good an earl without English', as the poet Felim MacDougall wrote and the Dean of Lismore recorded in his famous Book more than a hundred years earlier.[5] As long as English was the sole official language of the Highlands and Islands, and the only language used in courts of law, so long was it very advisable that responsible persons in Gaelic Scotland should be bilingual, so that they and their followers be not taken advantage of in official dealings. But that is not the purpose of this clause; the children so sent to the Lowlands would provide useful hostages, and the education they would get would be of course a protestant one.

The Statutes of Iona applied only to the Isles, of course, but they were only the prelude to a long series of enactments aiming at the obliteration of the Gaelic language in the whole of the Highlands and Islands; similar pressure was applied in Ireland by the English government. In 1616 the Privy Council enacted that a school should be established in every parish in Scotland so that 'trew religion [i.e. Calvinism] be advanceit and establisheit' and that the 'vulgar Inglish toung be universallie plantit and the Irische language . . . be abolisheit and removeit'. This was confirmed by the Scottish Parliament on 26 June 1633 and re-enacted on 2 February 1646. So started the plantation of an official educational system in the Highlands and Islands which at the worst actively persecuted and at the best ignored the native language in education until the 1918 Education Act made the teaching of Gaelic officially permissible in state schools in the Highlands.[6]

Socially, the ultimate effect of this legislation was to create an unfortunate class difference of language between Highland landowners and their tenants, accentuated when their sons began to be sent to English 'public schools' to be assimilated culturally to the ascendancy Anglo-Irish gentry's mental atti-

tudes – an achievement of Eton and other such establish-
ments that has not been widely recognized. But historically
the anglicization of Gaelic-speaking Irish and Scottish Highland Catholics has led to the spread of Catholicism in the
English-speaking countries on a world-wide scale, a most
ironical situation when one considers the original purpose
behind the attacks on the Gaelic language in Scotland and
Ireland.

10. Irish kings were complaining about the burden the
entertainment of the itinerant poets and their trains imposed
on their hosts, before and at the time of St Columba. But it
would be naïve to think that the purpose of this clause of the
Statutes had any such altruistic purpose. The poets, *filidhean*,
were the educated intellectual class of Gaeldom, thoroughly
trained in Gaelic history and genealogy and in the composition
of highly wrought classical Gaelic poetry, written in elaborate
metres. Their classification here along with vagabonds and the
like is denigratory propaganda.

Why the Government wanted to suppress the bards is illustrated by the occasion on which Fr. Cornelius Ward
(Conchobhair Mac an Bháird, of the famous Donegal bardic
family) obtained access to Sir John Campbell of Calder, the
Earl of Argyll's right-hand man in the struggle to dispossess
the MacDonalds of Islay, at Muckairn in Argyll in 1624. Ward
obtained access to Calder in the guise of an Irish bard, having
composed a poetic eulogy of Calder (for which a bard would
normally expect to be paid something), accompanied by a
reciter to sing the poem and a harpist to accompany it. Having
obtained this access, which otherwise might well have been
impossible to get, after three days Ward disclosed himself to
Calder, and after a private argument, Ward won Calder over
to Catholicism,[7] a conversion which created enormous
scandal and infuriated the Privy Council of Scotland when it
became known. The incident shows that the Highland nobility in the early seventeenth century understood classical
Gaelic verse, and it makes one wonder whether certain Highland chiefs whose hands had to be led at the pen when signing
legal documents in English or Latin, could not have written
their signature in their own native language and its script.

I have discussed the Statutes of Iona at length because they set the tone of Government legislation towards the Highlands and Islands practically permanently. Their immediate weakness was that in fact there was no one who could administer most of them locally except the island chiefs themselves. The chiefs could call attention to breaches of the regulations by their rivals, or the ministers to be planted in the Isles might act as informers; but not until after the failure of the 1745 Rising could these kinds of regulations be applied systematically. Meanwhile from the civil wars of 1639–45 and the Cromwellian administration, a sympathy developed between the Stewarts and the Highlanders that had been lacking in the days of James VI and I. All this was going to affect the future of Canna.

NOTES

1. *Register of the Privy Council of Scotland*, IX. 26.
2. *Minutes of the Synod of Argyll*, 1639–51, p. 72.
3. Ibid. 73.
4. A. E. Anton, ' "Handfasting" ' in Scotland', *Scottish Historical Review*, XXXVII. 102.
5. W. J. Watson, *Scottish Verse from the Book of the Dean of Lismore*, p. 240.
6. For a detailed account of this persecution, see J. L. Campbell, *Gaelic in Scottish Education and Life*, 1950 edition.
7. Cathaldus Giblin, *The Irish Franciscan Mission to Scotland, 1619–1646*, pp. 53–4.

7 THE COMING OF THE IRISH FRANCISCANS

In 1613 Iain, son of Donald son of Allan MacDonald, heir to the chiefship of Clanranald, married Mór (Marion), daughter of Sir Rory MacLeod of Dunvegan. This marriage marked the final ending of a feud that had disgraced the northern Isles throughout the sixteenth century.

Two years later the last resistance of the MacDonalds of Islay to the Earl of Argyll and John Campbell of Cawdor collapsed with the capture of Dunyveg Castle, the walls of which were unable to withstand the power of artillery. The ablest of their leaders, Coll Ciotach MacDonald, famous in seventeenth-century Highland history, escaped and shortly afterwards captured with his friends an Irish ship, following which they returned to the Hebrides. There are two versions of what happened next. One is the official complaint of Sir Rory MacLeod to Lord Binning (later the Earl of Haddington), dated 18 June 1615,[1] according to which 'Coill Makgillespik' and his band had come to the isles north of Ardnamurchan 'and stoppet the first night at the yle of Camis' (which must be Canna), thereafter gone on to North Uist, where they were entertained and supplied with 'four horse load of meat, in the whitche there wes two swyne, on[e] salted and one vnsalted' by Marjory Mackintosh, wife of Donald Gorm of Sleat, and then persuaded by her, young Donald 'Mackenyees good brother' and 'Clan Neill vaine' (i.e. MacLean of Boreray[2]) to go to Hirta (St Kilda), which belonged to MacLeod. Donald Gorm's wife provided them with two pilots. 'And coming to the ylle they slew all the beastiall of the ylle both kowes and horses and sheepe and took away all the spoolyee of the yle, onlie reserved the lyves of the enhabitants thereof.' Returning to North Uist, says MacLeod, they landed the pilots and gave all the spoils of their raid on St Kilda to the North Uist people.

This is the kind of story that popular writers on the Highlands immediately accept and repeat. Fortunately in this case there is an independent and much more detailed account in the deposition of one Robert Williamson,[3] a sailor and member of the ship's crew, who was shanghaied by Coll Ciotach to help his band work the ship, and who was able to give a first-hand account of the whole affair. The party had gone first to Texa, a little island off Islay, whence Coll and his friends made a secret visit to Islay itself; then to Colonsay, where they did not land; then to Mull for four days; 'from thence to Canna, some xx[tie] [20] milles from Mulley, where they were about viij [8] dayes. There they went ashore and feasted and dranke with there friends, and chiefly with McCallan O'Cahan his wife' [i.e. Clanranald (Mac 'ic Ailein) and O'Cathain's* wife, Mary, who was a daughter of Angus of Dunnyveg; the O'Cathains had been connected with the Lords of the Isles by marriage previously[4]], 'her husband then being in Scotland'.

The journey had continued to 'ile Arte', i.e. Hirta (St Kilda). 'There they landed and took great stoare of barley and some xxx[tie] [30] sheepe for theire provision.' There they stayed for a month. Williamson says that 'there were but tenn men and tenn women inhabiting thereon' (this implies that other St Kildans had hidden themselves). Williamson says that the party sailed over to inspect the small island of Boreray off St Kilda to see if it might be practicable to construct a fortification there. After remaining a month, they returned south calling at all the places they had visited on their way to St Kilda, and thereafter at Rathlin Island off Ireland, where Williamson escaped.

Williamson went on to say that the boat had been a small one of five or six tons, and the party aboard had numbered thirty men and boys and had with them fourteen 'callivers', twenty-three swords, seventeen targes, and every one had a long sgian (dirk) and those who had guns had 'some xx[tie] shott of powder but not much more'. On the way back Coll had also landed at Iona, drunk whisky with Lachlan MacLean, Hector MacLean of Duart's brother, and brought five or six pounds of powder and lead there.

It is obvious from Williamson's account that the boat Coll had could not have taken the carcasses of all the livestock on St

---

* This was probably the wife of Giolla Dubh Ó Catháin, who was a foster-brother of Ranald MacDonald, first Earl of Antrim. His son Mághnus is mentioned in the *Book of Clanranald*, *Rel. Celt.* II. 183.

Kilda away to North Uist or anywhere else. It is very doubtful whether the whole stock of semi-wild Soay sheep there could have been rounded up for slaughter. What obviously happened was that the party requisitioned provisions, mutton and barley meal, to feed on during the month they spent on the island. We do not know how information about this reached MacLeod at Dunvegan by 18 June, but obviously the story reached him in garbled form, or else he was exaggerating in the hope of getting bigger compensation.

Coll Ciotach and his friends can hardly have made an extended voyage around the Hebrides in a small hijacked vessel simply for the purpose of visiting St Kilda and inspecting Boreray. It is significant, although one cannot prove the connection, that the islands which he visited in 1616, Texa, Islay, Colonsay, Mull, Canna, North Uist, and Iona were all likewise visited by the Irish Franciscans in 1624 and 1625, and possibly earlier – the mission began in 1619, but earlier reports are lost. And the Irish Franciscan missionaries were told by the papal nuncio at Brussels in 1623 before they left for the Hebrides that Coll Ciotach MacDonald, by then established in Colonsay, was a Catholic leader who could instruct and direct the missionaries 'per omnes illas insulas', through all these islands.[5]

The Irish Franciscan College of St Antony of Padua was founded at Louvain in 1606 by King Phillip III of Spain at the insistence of Flaithrí Ó Maolchonnaire OFM, known in English as Florence Conroy. Conroy himself belonged to a family of hereditary Gaelic poet-historians, bards of the O'Connors and MacDermots of Connacht. After the Irish defeat at the battle of Kinsale in 1601 and the flight of the Earls of Tyrone and Tyrconnel and their friends in 1607, the College became the great centre of Gaelic learning in exile, producing heroic missionaries to work in Ireland and Gaelic Scotland in the darkest days of their history, as well as a notable number of Gaelic devotional works.[6]

Appeal to the Irish Franciscans for help was made at a time when there was not one priest left in the Highlands and Islands and not a single Gaelic-speaking student at the Scottish exiled seminaries in Rome, Douai, or Paris. Irish Gaelic-speakers at the time could easily make themselves understood in the

Hebrides and on the mainland south of Kintail (probably not so easily in Ross-shire or Sutherland).

The first mission of two Franciscans, Fr. Brady and Fr. McCann, and a lay brother, John Stuart, was sent in 1619, Brady to work in the Highlands and Fr. McCann in the isles. Fr. McCann was arrested towards the end of 1620 and banished in 1622. None of this mission's reports have come down to us. After Fr. McCann's arrest further appeals were made to Louvain for help. This led to the appointment of a larger mission, Frs. Paul O'Neill, Brady, Patrick Hegarty, McCann (again), and Cornelius Ward (Conchobhair Mac an Bháird) in 1623. The mission arrived in 1624.

No praise can be too high for the courage and hardiness of these men, especially Fathers Ward and Hegarty. They were liable to instant capture and imprisonment if recognized by the civil authorities, and in the field they had to live in constant poverty and discomfort both on sea and on land. It is easy to trace the inspiration of the example of St Columba. Partly through the jealousy of Scottish Lowland priests at Rome, partly through sheer incredulity of its success, the mission was miserably supported by Rome, both financially and with regard to necessary faculties. The Roman authorities simply could not visualize the conditions under which it was working.

Fr. Ward worked on the mission from 1624 to 1637, with intervals caused by the need to make journeys to Rome and to Brussels to beg for more support for the mission, and two years of imprisonment in London, where he was caught on the way back to Scotland in 1629. Fr. Hegarty left the mission in 1631 to direct the friary at Bonamargy in County Antrim which had become the headquarters of the mission in 1626, the year when Fr. O'Neill, who had worked in Skye, withdrew.

It is the reports of Frs. Ward and Hegarty that have survived, a source of material for Highland historians that had remained unknown until they were published (original Latin with English précis) by Fr. Cathaldus Giblin OFM in 1964. Their importance as a source for Highland history is beginning to be realized, but the publication of a full English translation with historical notes is badly needed.[7]

The scene the Franciscans found in Kintyre (which they

describe as if it were still MacDonald property) was one of
desolation, desecration, and poverty, the outcome of clan
warfare and government repression. Islay was still Catholic
at heart; it had been described by Archibald Campbell of
Glencarradale in a report to Sir John Campbell of Calder in
1615:

Sence my cuming heir I fand owt a number of images whiche I hawe
caussit to be bruntt: the religioun that the cuntrie pepill hes heir
amongst them is Popishe for yair is newer [there is never] a minister
in the wholle Ille except wan poore man that the bishop did leaue
heir.[8]

The Franciscans visited in turn Sanda, Kintyre, Islay, Texa,
Jura, Cara, Colonsay, Iona (where they said the first Mass since
the Reformation), the Ross of Mull, Caisteal Tioram in
Moidart, the Small Isles, South and North Uist, and Barra.
They met no popular opposition whatever; the only Chief
who was hostile in this area was Hector MacLean of Duart,
son of Sir Lachlan the enemy of the MacDonalds, who had
died a Protestant in 1598.

One or two of the few ministers made immediate appeal to
the military authorities to arrest the Franciscans, but their
protectors were strong enough to frustrate them. Fr. Ward
arrived in the Small Isles on 28 August 1625 accompanied by
some of Clanranald's household and with his approval.
Clanranald, Iain Mùideartach, had been reconciled to the
Church by Fr. O'Neill in 1624. Ward first landed on Eigg,
where, he said, no priest had been since the Reformation. He
found the ancient church dedicated to St Donnan roofless.
Ward spent eight days on the island preaching and teaching.
He found one old woman who remembered having heard
Mass in her childhood. The Eigg people made him swear on
the sacred missal that what he said to them was true – an
interesting example of the Gaelic asseveration *a leabhara, tha*!
('By the Book, it is!') still used in South Uist and Barra. As a
result of his teaching, 'two only short of 200 exchanged their
heresy for the Faith'.* One tenant with his family, related to a
minister, refused to come over.

* A very interesting population statistic and one which hardly suggests that the
true whole population of Eigg could have been destroyed in the cave by the MacLeods
in 1577, or by Sir Lachlan MacLean and his Spaniards in 1588.

Neil MacKinnon, minister of Strath and Sleat in Skye, to whom the Small Isles had been also entrusted by the Protestant Bishop of Argyll – an impossibly large area for one man – got word of what was happening on Eigg. He came to the island at night with soldiers intending to seize Ward: but Ward's armed friends persuaded him to abandon the attempt, and by offering him the teinds of a third part of the island, Clanranald got him to agree to promise to stay out of Eigg and leave the priests and Catholics there in peace.

The Eigg people wanted Ward to reconsecrate their church, but unfortunately Rome had not given him the faculty necessary for such a duty, a serious administrative error. He was joined on Eigg by Fr. Paul O'Neill who had spent eight months with Sir Rory MacLeod working in Skye, until overtaken by serious illness. They both left Eigg to call on Clanranald at Caisteal Tioram, and then Ward crossed to Rum with Clanranald's brother and other gentlemen. Here the wind kept them for four days. One of the two main tenants, and his son, with fourteen others, became converts.

Fr. Ward continued to Canna: His first impression is quoted at the beginning of the first chapter of this book. Ward continued:

I was detained here by an adverse wind for nearly two weeks, and announced to the inhabitants the light of the gospel, alleging that it was the faith to which Columba owed the sanctity he had received and which spreading out over the whole world from the 'apostolic college' fills heaven with saints and the earth with penitents. Finally, without it, it had been granted to no mortal either to escape destruction, or to hope for life.

The sermon was satisfactory but its result was not. For the children of earth as they were, with their hearts on the earth, they were intent on the crops, not their salvation, and paid more attention to the autumn – for it was that season then – than to their souls. However, two gentry with the wife of one and the son of the other, besides four others, were rescued from the night of infidelity. All received the sacrament of penance, but only three, because they alone were fasting, received Holy Communion. Here I baptised one short of twenty.

Fr. Ward continued to South Uist, where he actually converted Ranald MacDonald, the first minister appointed to the island, who went abroad to study for the priesthood and returned ordained – the first protestant minister and the first post-Reformation priest of South Uist were one and the same person! He had the same success in North Uist, where he had 768 converts, or reconciliations, and only fourteen persons, the minister, presumably the 'verie auld man callit Donald Macmillen' named in Bishop Knox's 1626 report, and his family and immediate friends, remaining in the Protestant congregation. Ward had intended to go from Uist to Ireland, but adverse winds detained him, and he took the chance to visit Barra briefly. There he reconciled 116 persons and married the lawful heir of the island, who had been forcibly dispossessed by a usurping younger brother, imprisoned, and not released until he renounced his inheritance. The usurping brother was later converted by Fr. Hegarty.

Ward sailed to Canna on 26 February 1625 and on the next day to Mull. And how, it may be asked, had the distinguished subscribers to the Statutes of Iona reacted to the Franciscan mission? The answer is highly interesting. Angus MacDonald of Dunyveg was dead before the missionaries arrived in Scotland. Clanranald, MacLeod of Harris, and MacLaine of Lochbuie, welcomed them and accepted the Catholic religion. Donald Gorm of Sleat had died in 1617; his son and successor (and nearest claimant by descent to the Lordship of the Isles), Sir Donald MacDonald of Sleat, did nothing to hinder them. Donald MacPhee of Colonsay's successor Malcolm had been eliminated by Coll Ciotach MacDonald in 1623, and Coll, who strongly favoured the Franciscans, was in control of Colonsay in spite of the fact that the Earls of Argyll held a nominal superiority of the island and Coll's acquisition of it was achieved by violence. Colonsay indeed was geographically essential to the mission, now that Islay and Kintyre had been lost to the MacDonalds of Islay. But the greatest and most spectacular achievement of the Franciscans was the conversion of Sir John Campbell of Calder, already described (p. 49).

On 5 February 1626 Clanranald wrote to Pope Urban VIII on behalf of himself and his principal relations and his clan and, as lord of the districts of Moidart, Arisaig, Glenfinnan, and the islands of Uist, Eriskay, Canna, and others adjoining, a letter of great interest, putting as it does for the first time (apart from in Gaelic poetry) the point of view of the Hebridean 'Resistance'.[10] Describing himself and his relations as 'rulers of lands, men of ancient nobility' he refers first to their gratitude to the Pope for the Franciscan Mission:

For His greatness and kindness has deigned to regard us with the eyes of His mercy, redeeming and enlightening our people who for this long time have sat in darkness; the darkness I mean of error, which the turbulent detested followers of the accursed faithless Calvin had introduced, through the violence and tyranny of the Council of Scotland, through lying pseudo-bishops and fraudulent ministers of their error and false religion, exterminating among our predecessors the holy Catholic faith, the one apostolic Catholic Roman faith, outside of which there is no salvation, razing our churches, profaning our cemeteries, tearing down, treading underfoot, breaking up, burning our altars and sacred images, as indeed the memory of aged surviving witnesses bears testimony.

Clanranald went on to praise the work of Fr. O'Neill and Fr. Ward highly, saying that Ward had converted 2,373 in the isles and neighbouring mainland, and baptized 383, within two years. Clanranald said that he believed that his and the other branches of the MacDonald clan together, 'than which there is none more noble in the whole kingdom', could easily conquer the whole of Scotland (this was no idle boast; they very nearly did under Montrose and Coll Ciotach's son Alasdair less than twenty years later) 'but that they would need the help of four ships and sufficient arms for 7,000 of their men, and the help of the Catholic Kings to hold it'. (If any reader is tempted to raise eyebrows at this plea for foreign aid, he should remember that Hanoverian governments in the eighteenth century had no hesitation in using Hessian troups against Prince Charles's rising in 1745, or against the American colonists in the American War of Independence in 1776–82.)
Clanranald went on:

If we receive help of this kind we shall easily reduce the whole of Scotland to obedience to the faith of Christ and of your Holiness, nor do we expect any other reward for this (God is our witness) than His glory, the salvation of our souls and freedom from the miserable yoke and intolerable slavery of diabolical heresy. It is certain and evident (since it is already known in the Council of Scotland that we have received the true faith) that we shall be compelled to the renunciation of it or to the loss of temporal goods and life, or both, as has frequently happened, not only to Scots but also to many Irish. The greatest hope of success is in the fact that this part of Scotland, always accustomed to arms, has become warlike, strong in battle, favoured by victory and at one time fierce and obstinate against the Romans themselves, in the fact that often, smaller in number but superior in strength, we have beaten the Britons, from the fact also that many centuries ago our ancestors crossed from Ireland and drove out the Picts, the first inhabitants of the land, and after that we have never been driven out by anyone, nor have any of us to this day been subject to any external prince of power. Our country and islands are in themselves difficult for an enemy approach bound as by impregnable walls into a fortification, the sea flowing among them and received into their bosom, with safe harbours and anchorages for ships of every kind, small and large, and they are far removed from the incursions and outrages of the English to whom we have never at all [ex toto] given obedience. All the Gaelic-speaking Scots and the greater part of the Irish chieftains joined to us by ties of friendship, from whom we once received the faith (in which we still glory) from whose stock we first sprang, will begin war each in his own district to the glory of God . . . [MS torn] we who after the example of our forefathers have always been expert in arms when necessity arose, so that freed from the power of slavery and our enemies we may be faithful to one God in holiness and in justice constantly, for ever.

This is hardly communication one would have expected from the kind of Highland chief depicted as an ignorant barbarian by the propaganda of the contemporary Scottish Privy Council or the Acts of the Scottish Parliament.

The heroic Fr. Ward, after twice travelling to Louvain during his mission to make his reports and plead for more support and more faculties, was captured in 1629 in London returning from Belgium, imprisoned, and offered a benefice worth £1,000 a year if he embraced Protestantism and preached it in the parts of the Highlands and Islands where he had preached Catholicism, and threatened with death if he refused; eventually he was released after the intercession of the Polish ambassador, and left with ambassador Rakowski for Poland. After various adventures he reached Rome, where he had to engage in argument with various jealous sceptics to prove that the mission really existed and had produced the results claimed. Part of the evidence in his favour was the letter from Clanranald to Pope Urban VIII quoted above.

Meanwhile the mission was continued by Fr. Patrick Hegarty in the Isles. He visited the Small Isles in August 1630, travelling from Mull to the Isle of Muck on the tenth, where he 'converted' three persons and baptized two on the eleventh before having to escape from Calvinists to Eigg. On Eigg on the twelfth and thirteenth he received a hundred converts, baptized twelve persons and celebrated two marriages, besides hearing many confessions from earlier converts. After a brief visit to Moidart he returned to Eigg for four days and received twelve more into the church and celebrated two more marriages. On 26 August he went to Canna for a day and received two persons and baptized one before continuing to South Uist, the next day – there on 9 September he was captured by 'pseudo-bishop' Thomas Knox and his men but rescued by Clanranald's uncle Ranald MacDonald of Benbecula, 'Raghnall Mac Ailein 'ic Iain', an action that provoked a furious letter from King Charles I to the Privy Council of Scotland on 10 December of that year,[11] and cost Clanranald himself the dispensation he had been allowed by the King from the annual attendance at Edinburgh required of the island chiefs.

Ranald mac Ailein mhic Iain was charged by Lord Lorne, heir to the Earldom of Argyll, bitterly anti-Catholic since his father's conversion following a second marriage around 1618,[12] with two murders, wearing firearms publicly, shooting twelve deer on the Isle of Rum in August and September, and having 'thrie mareit wyiffes alive'.[13] The two latter charges correspond to breaches of numbers 9 and 2 of the Statutes of Iona.* Oddly enough, nothing is said about his having rescued Fr. Hegarty from Bishop Knox.

Ranald was charged to appear at Inveraray on 10 January 1634, but had more sense than to do so. It would have been difficult to make the journey from Benbecula in mid-winter in any case. Ranald died peaceably on Canna in 1636. His brother

---

* Lord Lorne was obviously out to get him one way or another. With regard to the last charge, it is not clear how easily an islander could have got a bill of divorcement at the time.

John, from whom the MacDonalds of Kinlochmoidart descended, died on Canna in the same year, and the bodies of both were taken to Howmore in South Uist for burial.[14]

Fr. Hegarty continued working in Uist after his rescue for the rest of September, then went to Barra. In December he was in Benbecula, where he received Raghnall mac Ailein 'ic Iain and his final wife, Margaret MacDonald, sister of Angus of Dunyveg, into the church. Fr. Ward had not been able to do this in 1625 as he lacked faculties for dispensing them from the impediment of being related within the prohibited degrees.[15] In April 1631, after having been in Barra and Uist again, Fr. Hegarty was warned that Bishop Knox was about to make a fresh attempt to arrest him, and advised by the Catholics to leave Uist. He crossed over to Canna on 13 April, where he received fourteen persons and baptized seven; on the fourteenth he left for Colonsay where he spent ten days, and then went to Kintyre, where pursuit became so hot that he had to cross to Ireland by night on 6 May.

It is doubtful whether the people of Canna were to see another priest until Fr. Dermit Dugan of the Congregation of St Vincent de Paul came to the island in 1652, twenty-one years later. Fr. Dugan's reports show scant appreciation, if any, of the labours of the Irish Franciscans before him; leading Highland historians, ignorant of the then unpublished Franciscan reports, believed that the survival of Catholicism in Canna and other districts mentioned was due entirely to Fr. Dugan's mission. With no disrespect to this devoted missionary, a man of entirely different personality from Fathers Ward and Hegarty, there would have been no Catholicism for him to revive in Canna, Uist, Barra, and so on but for the earlier labours of the Franciscans in these places.

NOTES

1. Denmylne MSS, p. 242. Scottish History Society, *Highland Papers*, iii (Second Series, 20).
2. See Campbell and Collinson, *Hebridean Folksongs*, III. 130, 266.
3. Printed in the *Book of Islay*, pp. 263–4n.
4. See MacVurich, *Book of Clanranald*, *Rel. Celt.* II. 158–9.
5. Cathaldus Giblin, op. cit. 24–5.

6. T. F. O'Rahilly, Introduction to Flaithrí Ó Maolchonaire's *Sgáthán an Chrábhaidh*.
7. More than thirty years before Fr. Giblin's book appeared, MS transcripts of some of these reports had been made by the late Monsignor Cameron, who was parish priest of Castlebay in Barra from 1908 to 1921. They were kindly made available to the writer by the late Monsignor Canon MacMaster, Fort William.
8. Denmylne Papers, SHS *Highland Papers*, iii. 185–6.
9. See J. L. Campbell, 'The MacNeils of Barra and the Irish Franciscans', *Innes Review*, V. 33.
10. Original Latin published by the Revd Brendan Jennings in *Archivium Hibernicum*, XII. 117. English translation by Dom Denys Rutledge, OSB, with notes by the writer printed in the *Innes Review*, IV. 110–16.
11. *CRA* 127.
12. Neither the date of this second marriage, nor his conversion to Catholicism, is mentioned in Burke's *Peerage* or in *The Clan Campbell*.
13. *Highland Papers*, iv. 226–7.
14. *Book of Clanranald, Rel. Celt.* II. 173.
15. *The Franciscan Mission to Scotland*, 133, 135. In the index to this work Ranald is wrongly called the son of Clanranald. He was Iain Muideartach's uncle.

8 THE ARGYLL SUPERIORITY AND THE CIVIL WARS

Within three years of Iain Mùideartach the Captain of Clanranald's 'conversion' or reconciliation by the Irish Franciscans, which would not have been known immediately, Archibald, the heir to the Earl of Argyll who had been exiled after his conversion to Catholicism in 1618, had obtained a charter of the superiority of Canna, the bailliery of the islands, and the teind sheaves 'lying in [i.e. vested in] the monastery of Icolmkill in the Sheriffdom of Inverness'[1] from Thomas Knox, 'pseudo-bishop' of the Isles (as the Franciscans called him; not long afterwards the extreme Presbyterian party in Scotland would be using far less flattering terms for bishops). The charter itself does not seem to have survived, but the sasine (legal document of taking possession) is dated 1 November 1627, and it was confirmed on 29 January 1628,[2] where Canna is described as 'extending to £10 of land with houses fishings and mills, garbal [grain] and rectorial tiends never separated *a trunco*, lying under the monastery of Iona'. Archibald and his heirs were to be hereditary baillies of the island, and to pay the bishop £80 plus £3. 6s. 0d. augmentation, double feu-farm on entry of heirs, one penny blench [quit-rent] to the monastery and faithful service'.

The dates of this charter and sasine are significant; Bishop Knox had said in his report of 1626 that neither the teinds nor the land of Canna had been let, that is he was getting no rent for them from whoever was in 'possession' of the island, stated to be Clanranald in the 1593 report, and John MacLeod (presumably of Dunvegan in 1626; there is no confirmation of this MacLeod 'possession'; Sir Rory MacLeod of Dunvegan, John's father, himself a convert of the Franciscans, died in 1626). The Bishop of the Isles was in no position to collect rent for Canna or its teinds from either Clanranald or MacLeod – but Lord Lorne, heir to the Earldom of Argyll and *de facto* head of the Clan Campbell in the absence of his exiled father, certainly was, and could put both political and financial pressure on

Clanranald or any other 'possessor' of Canna as long as the charter was in effect.

This £83. 6s. 0d. (probably £83. 6s. 8d., i.e. 125 Scots merks) was the origin of the Crown feu-duty which was still payable on Canna when the writer became proprietor in 1938; the equivalent in sterling was then £6. 19s. 5d. On 10 June 1968 the writer redeemed this feu-duty for £104. 11s. 3d., the cost then of 2½ per cent Consols sufficient to produce the same income at the time. Provided he could collect rent and teinds, Lord Lorne was making a very profitable bargain with the Bishop; in 1654 he let Canna for six years with all its teinds and pertinents to Allan MacDonald of Morar, a descendant of Dougall VI of Clanranald and therefore a distant relation of our Iain Mùideartach, for 1,200 merks a year, ten times what the bishop (or his substitute) was being paid.[3]

The MacDonalds of Sleat also had an interest in Canna. Sir Donald MacDonald of Sleat acquired – how it is not known – on 26 March 1633, the year of the Scottish coronation of King Charles I, a charter of Canna for £24 a year in feu-farm.[4] In 1641, during a very temporary truce in the Covenanters' war, King Charles I bargained with Sleat and with the MacDonell Earl of Antrim by promising them various lands which the forfeiture of the Earl of Argyll, an ardent covenanter, would produce.[5] These included an offer of Canna, Rum, and Muck to MacDonald of Sleat, whose daughter Janet was to marry in 1655 Iain Mùidertach's son and heir Donald.[6] As can be read in Chapter 3 of this book, the MacDonalds of Sleat felt they had a historical claim to Canna.

Donald, younger of Clanranald, must have been born around 1624 or 1625. As his parents were married in 1613, his three sisters Mór, Catriona, and Anna* were presumably older. Donald's age is given in the *Book of Clanranald* as about twenty at the time of the battle of Kilsyth which took place in August 1645.

A good deal is known about this Donald, younger of Clanranald, from the *Book of Clanranald*, highly favourable,

---

* Celebrated in the famous waulking song *Cha déid Mór a Bharraidh bhrònaich*, 'Mór (Marion) will not go to miserable Barra', a flyting between the bardesses of Clanranald and MacNeil of Barra. See *Hebridean Folksongs* II. 113. In fact Catriona did marry Gill' Eóghanain MacNeil of Barra in 1653.

the *Minutes of the Synod of Argyll*, uniformly hostile, and local oral tradition, which does not portray him in at all a favourable light as chief (1670–86). Probably his health and temper and personal nature had been affected by his experiences in the Montrose wars, which are vividly described in the Book of Clanranald, a manuscript history of the Clanranald family kept by successive members of the MacVurich bardic family, one of whom obviously took part in them for at least part of the time.

As the MacVurich writer says:

I remember that the Scots were the soonest to begin this war of the Three Kingdoms, and not the English or the Irish. For after having made a Covenant or Union against the King and the English for the purpose of setting aside the bishops and appointing presbyters in their stead, they sent for all the Scottish officers in the other Kingdoms beyond the sea, and they made Commander-in-Chief of Alexander Leslie, an old soldier, who had been for a long time fighting in foreign countries. That army marched into England; it was the first army set on foot in the time of King Charles, and it is against him it was. . . .[7]

In Scotland the issue in effect was whether the King or the left-wing Calvinist clergy should govern the country; if the former, an episcopate was necessary. Religion then permeated political thinking; in the years between 1632 and 1651, when the Scots were finally defeated by Cromwell at the battle of Worcester (where the MacLeods suffered very heavily), we are continually reminded of the atmosphere of strife and fanaticism that exists in Lebanon today. In the Western world today political battle-cries arise around themes like fascism, capitalism, Marxism; in the first half of the seventeenth century the political cries were of papistry, prelacy, Arminianism,* malignancy. The left as always was completely humourless and convinced of its heaven-sent rightness, which it was an insult to God on high to challenge. It is something to be said

* Arminius, or Hermann, was Professor of Divinity at the University of Leyden in 1603. He charged the Calvinist theory of predestination with making God the author of sin. He did not deny 'election' but based it on God's foreknowledge of man's merit. For this he and his followers were expelled from the Dutch National Reformed Church. Most Scots, in so far as they have any interest in theological matters today, would now agree with Arminius. Letters on the danger of Arminianism still appear occasionally in the columns of the *Stornoway Gazette*.

for the contemporary, allegedly barbarous Highlanders that most of them never then succumbed to this kind of fanaticism; no doubt the Gaelic language prevented its being easily communicated to them.*

In 1642 King Charles declared war against Parliament, and early in 1644 commissioned Montrose to raise an army in Scotland in his support and create a diversion there. Montrose had originally been a supporter of the National Covenant in 1638 – a document which is couched in language in the highest degrees offensive to Catholics, rhetoric of a kind of which the last surviving echoes can still be heard in the North of Ireland today. Montrose had recoiled from the religious fanaticism and anti-monarchical views of the Covenanters. He reached the Highlands, got in touch with Alasdair, son of Coll Ciotach MacDonald, and raised an army on behalf of the King.

Being technically a vassal of the Earl of Argyll (the Lord Lorne who succeeded in 1638), Iain Mùideartach (Clanranald) was expected to join the forces of the Earl of Argyll besieging Mingarry Castle in Ardnamurchan; Argyll was the leader of the Covenanters in the western Highlands. But Iain Mùideartach instead went back and raised the men of Uist, Eigg, Moidart, and Arisaig, raided Sunart and collected all the sheep and cattle there to feed the garrison of Mingarry;† 'and Alasdair [son of Coll Ciotach] and Donald, son of Iain Mùideartach, met each other, for this was their first acquaintance with one another'.

Iain Mùideartach, chief of Clanranald, and his son Donald and other MacDonald leaders, fought under Montrose and Alasdair Mac Colla at the battle of Inverlochy, 2 February 1645. After the battle of Alford, fought while Alasdair Mac Colla and Iain Mùideartach were away in the western Highlands raising more men, Alasdair returned with all the young men left in Clanranald's country, commanded by Donald. 'When they reached Montrose's camp they were joyfully and gladly welcomed by Montrose and all the rest. Each company of them was presented separately to the General, and the company of the son of Iain Mùideartach, Donald, was brought forward. He was

* For a very fair account of the failings and the virtues of the Covenanters, see John Buchan's *Montrose*, pp. 56–64.

† The rather clumsy translation of the *Book of Clanranald* in *Reliquiae Celticae* does not make it clear when *togbháil creiche* means collecting cattle etc. on enemy territory to feed one's own troops and not looting and raiding; cf. *Rel. Celt.* II.197.

modest, good natured, affable and unpresuming in the presence of friends, but strong and fearless before his enemies. He was in the twentieth year of his age at that time.'

The meeting took place at Fordoun in the Mearns. The MacVurich chronicler says that Montrose said to Alasdair Mac Colla, his second in command, in his tent that it was not much use for the Captain of Clanranald to have come to join him with a force without having rounded up enough cattle and sheep to feed their men,* and that Donald should have done this. Alasdair left the tent and went and told Donald that he must do this next morning, taking only his own men, apart from guides. Donald did this with great success. Some of the other Gaels would try to drive such lifted cattle to their own houses, wrote MacVurich, but not the Clanranalds, who helped greatly in supplying Montrose's army.

While on this errand Donald and his party met an old *seanchaidh* or tradition-bearer who was well acquainted with the history of the district, and who told them that it had not been raided in this way since Donald of Islay, Lord of the Isles, fought the battle of Harlaw in 1411. 'And you, if you are the Captain of Clanranald, must be of his race', said the old man to Donald.

After some manœuvring and retreating, due to the fact that Montrose was facing superior forces, the decisive battle of his campaign was fought at Kilsyth on Lammasday, 15 August 1645. It was a brilliant and decisive victory, in which Donald, younger Captain of Clanranald, and the Gaelic-speaking troops distinguished themselves particularly. Donald was the first man who jumped the dry stone dyke of the enclosure at the head of the glen where the Covenanters had concentrated. After the battle, as the MacVurich chronicler wrote, 'they encamped at Hamilton, and the keys of the great Castle came to them from Edinburgh, and all Scotland submitted to them'.

The rest of the story, and of Donald of Clanranald's subsequent adventures in the Civil Wars, is best told here in the words of the *Book of Clanranald*. I have modified the translation in *Reliquiae Celticae* slightly in a few instances:

* This is what MacVurich means when he says that Montrose had complained that the force had come *gan líon creichthe do tabhairt astech go harm an rí*. Translation of *líon creichthe* as 'a large prey' is quite misleading. It was not booty Montrose wanted for the army but the meat, to feed his men.

As to the Marquis of Montrose, he marched with a part of his army intending to go to England to relieve the King, who was sorely pressed by the English at that time, but he was defeated at Philiphaugh, and was not able to give assistance to the King.

Alasdair, son of Colla, came from the camp at Hamilton to Kintyre and cleared it for himself, and he drove out of it the Clan Campbell, and he erected Dunaverty as a place of strength [in Kintyre]. Donald, son of John Moydartach, came from the camp of Hamilton to his own country. Montrose proceeded to the North from the defeat of Philiphaugh with all those that survived of his men, and they continued so for some time. Montrose was in the north part of Scotland, and Alasdair, son of Colla, was in Kintyre, harrassing Argyle and Cowal and their bounds; and John Moydartach was in the Rough Bounds [western Inverness-shire] near the coast. John Moydartach and his son Donald went to Islay, and their own forces with them, and they drove out of it all the Clan Campbell that were there.

About this time the Earl of Antrim came from Ireland to Kintyre to enquire after the army that he himself had there, and he sent for those that were with Montrose, and they came to him at once. In consequence of this Montrose left the kingdom to solicit assistance from other kings and princes to aid King Charles. On his return from that journey, he was dishonestly destroyed by the Parliament of Scotland by the Covenanters,* together with the Marquis of Huntly, and many other nobles who were on the side of the King.

A good many of the gentry of the Hebrides flocked to the Earl of Antrim, such as the Clan MacLean and the Clanranald, intending to set an army on foot again on behalf of the King; meantime the King's order came to the Earl of Antrim to disband the army, for the King was at that time in the hands of his enemies, *viz.* the Parliament of England and Scotland united against him. The Earl of Antrim disbanded the army, and Antrim went to Ireland.

Alasdair, son of Colla, remained in Kintyre and made a strong-hold in it and in Islay. The other Gaels who were on the side of the King went about to their own lands to protect them against the enemy. They were at length surrounded by a large army. Sir David Leslie and Mac Cailin [the Earl of Argyll†] came to Kintyre, without any notice being obtained of the time they would come till they came to Largie, where Alasdair and his men were separated asunder. Alasdair's party were dispersed; Ranald Og, son of Alasdair, son of Angus Uaibhreach, was

* On 21 May 1650, after every humiliation the Covenanters could heap on him.

† *Mac Cailin Mór* is the Gaelic patronymic of the chiefs of the Argyll family; the meaning is 'The Great Son of Colin'. The original 'Great Son of Colin' flourished in the last quarter of the thirteenth century. Forms of the name such as 'MacCallum More' are perversions.

taken prisoner, and was put to death at Inveraray some time after that.

Alasdair, son of Colla, went to Ireland, and he was killed at Cnoc-na-nDos, with many other gentlemen of the Clan MacDonnell, in the battle which Murchadh O'Brien [Lord Inchiquin, leader of the Parliamentary party in Munster] gave them in the year 1647 [on 13 November].

This great army of David Leslie, and Mac Cailin along with them, came to Islay and to Mull, and all submitted to them except John Moydartach alone and those who joined him.

With regard to John Moydartach, son of Donald, son of Allan, laird of Clanranald, being forsaken by all after Montrose and the Marquis of Huntly had been put to death, and such as lived of the gentry who were on the King's side had been banished to foreign countries, he alone stood out from the [Rulers of the] Kingdom; and the few that lived of the party on the King's side were gathering around him. Messages were constantly sent to him from the Rulers of the Kingdom requesting him to make peace with them, but he did not accept them. However, he sent his son Donald to Ireland, and all those who remained with him of the men of Ireland, and some of his Scottish gentlemen along with them, and he himself and the rest of his men remained to defend his inheritance.

As to Donald, he set off from Uist in a rigged low-country frigate which he had, and in a Highland galley, with about 300 soldiers, composed of veterans, in the year 1648. From thence they went to the Sound of Mull, to Colonsay, and to the Sound of Islay, where they fell in with a large ship, which they captured with her full cargo of seed barley; they took another ship on the sea, found nothing in her, and they let her away. They sailed for Ireland; they were overtaken by a storm on the coast, so that their ships were separated. Some of them reached the harbour of Killybegs in Donegal. Donald and those who were along with him landed on the Magilligan Point in County Derry, and they sent back the ships to Scotland. He went to Achadh Dà Charad where there was a garrison favourable to them. From thence they went to County Cavan, where they met Philip O'Reilly, chief of that country, and a friend of theirs. They went from thence to Mullingar, and he left his men quartered in that town, and he himself went to Kilkenny, where the [Confederacy] Council of Ireland were sitting. He received orders for himself and his men to join the Council's army under the command of General Preston. That is the army in which was Alexander, the Earl of Antrim's son, and those who lived of the Scots and Irish of the MacDonnells and their friends, who went over with Alasdair, son of Colla, to Ireland. This regiment had not less than fifteen hundred chosen gentlemen in it, Donald, son of John Moydartach, being lieutenant-colonel of it, and Angus, son of Alexander, laird of Largie in Kintyre, being the senior captain.

For some time this army were esteemed and honoured for their taking of great towns from the enemy, until they broke away from the army of Preston, but were overtaken in County Wexford. They had a large number of Irishmen with them of the Cavenaghs, who acted as their guides, and when these came to the places they were acquainted with in their own country, and on a border of a wood which was near them, they fled and left all there, so that the enemy rushed in among them and dispersed them. Donald, Chief of Clanranald, and Angus, Chief of Glengarry, were taken and sent prisoners to Kilkenny; they remained there for some time in prison until the Marquis of Antrim found means to release them. Glengarry* came out sooner than the son of John Moydartach, and he went overseas to the King, and left Donald in prison, where he remained for some time until more money was given for his ransom by the Duchess of Buckingham, [first] wife of the Marquis of Antrim. He then went to Wexford; a ship was sent for him by the Marquis of Antrim to convey him to land at Caolas Stadhlaidh in [South] Uist, and Angus the grandson of Alasdair, laird of Largie, came along with him, and his friends were joyful at his return to them. His gentlemen soon came after him in a ship which they took on the Irish coast, namely, Murchadh,† a son of MacNeil of Barra, a great, handsome man, accomplished and well educated; Alexander, son John, son of Allan of the 'Buaile';‡ Donald Gorm, son of Allan; Donald Roy, son of Donald, son of Lachlan MacVurich; John, son of Donald of Benbecula; Angus, son of Alexander, son of Godfrey. John, son of Brian MacVurich, and another part of the men, came another way for themselves.

After Donald returned from that expedition he and his father spent time in defending their district until they obtained peace from the rulers of the Kingdom; their enemies however, held them in debt which increased upon them during that time; this left themselves always in distress, and also their posterity.

The debts referred to were no doubt partly incurred through the cost of supporting their fighting men in Montrose's and

* *Mac mhic alasduir* in the text, and translated 'The grandson of Alaster'; but *Mac 'ic Alasdair* is the patronymic of the MacDonalds of Glengarry, and their representative is involved here.

† Possibly the Murchadh (Murdo) mentioned in an old waulking song, see *Hebridean Folksongs*, II. 164–5.

‡ Reading *na buaillog* of the text as *na buaileadh*, 'of the fold of cattle' implying wealth. *Na buaileadh* was sometimes a family sobriquet, see Dinneen's Irish–English Dictionary. But Mr. R. I. Black confirms MS *na buaillog*.

Alasdair Mac Colla's wars, that is, in support of their legitimate King; and through their naturally withholding teinds and
stipends payable to Argyll (as lessee) or to other enemy lessees
or to the Covenating ministers, payments which the
Clanranalds could feel every moral justification in withholding. In May 1650 the Synod of Argyll ordered the presbytery
of Skye to use every diligence in collecting the stipends of the
vacant churches in Clanranald's bounds, and stated that the
teinds of South Uist, where the churches had been vacant since
1643 (and where in fact there never had been more than one
minister) were now in arrears to the extent of 4900 merks
(£3,266).[8] In 1655 the Synod ordered a letter to be written to
Clanranald demanding payment of the stipends of vacancies in
Ardnamurchan amounting to £100 p.a. for ten years, i.e.
£1,000.[9] In 1656 the Synod recorded that no reply had been
received from Clanranald to a letter regarding kirk vacancies
in Moidart and Arisaig. Small wonder![10]

In 1651 Clanranald is at the head of the Synod's list of
excommunicates, that is to say persons designated for social,
political, and religious ostracism (resistance to the Covenant
being considered as an insult to the Deity) a list which also
includes the names of his son Donald, Angus MacDonald of
Glengarry, and Ranald MacRanald, the minister converted by
the Franciscans in 1625 who had become the first post-
Reformation priest of South Uist. In 1642 the Marquess of
Argyll had been asked to back the Synod's demand that
Clanranald send the priest residing in his family to the Synod
'that ordour may be taken with him';[11] in 1654 the Synod again
asked the Marquess to write to Clanranald to the same effect.[12]
By 1654 the priest referred to was presumably Fr. Dermit
Dugan the Vincentian, who had arrived in the Isles in 1651; the
Synod apparently did not have information of this mission
until 1654. In October 1655 the Synod requested the Earl of
Seaforth, Sir James MacDonald of Sleat, MacLeod of
Dunvegan, the MacLean of Duart heir's guardian, MacNeil
of Barra, the chief of MacKinnon, MacLaine of Lochbuie, and
the Captain of Clanranald to attend the diet to be held at Iona
on the last Wednesday of May 1656 to discuss the menace
presented by 'the many priests and jesuits [typical exaggeration]
come from Ireland and other places'.[13]

None of them appeared, but at that May 1656 meeting the Vincentian mission is named, Fathers Francis White and 'Diarmid o Dovegan, who came over sees in companie of the Laird of Glengarrie the year 1651'; of these, Fr. Dugan visited Canna in 1652. 'Thes preists doe ordinarlie reseid in Uiste, Barra, Mudart, Candort, and Arresag where [covenanting] ordinances are not at all, and hes for the most part perverted these bownds and the chief men amongst them, as Captains of Clanrannald elder and yonger, McNeill Barra and Mc Ien vic Shemis* and Glengaress whole familie, if not himself.'[14] (Actually the elder Clanranald and MacNeil of Barra had been received by the Franciscans.) The Presbytery of Skye was told to summon these chiefs and 'deall earnestly with them to make them sensible of their backslyding from the reformatione contrair to their oath and covenant' (which it is unlikely any of them had signed) and 'if after much paines taken they proove obstinate, that the foresaid persons as chief men there to the example of others be processed with excommunicatione' (Clanranald and Glengarry were excommunicated already). Alternatively the ministers of Edinburgh were to be asked to get Cromwell's English to deal with the priests and excommunicates, who included Donald of Clanranald.[15]

In May 1658 at a meeting held at Dunoon the Synod interrogated or 'posed'[16] the Rev. Archibald MacQueen, minister of Snizort in Skye, about his having married Donald of Clanranald, an excommunicated 'rebel'. The Synod had been informed of this at its previous meeting at Inverary in October 1657. The marriage was to Janet, youngest daughter of Sir Donald MacDonald of Sleat (who died in 1643), in 1655. It was an extraordinarily embarrassing situation. The Revd Mr MacQueen said he had been unaware of the excommunication. This is hardly possible; but the bride was the sister of Sir James MacDonald of Sleat, the laird of MacQueen's parish in Skye, on whose goodwill the Synod depended much in that island – later Sleat was to marry in 1661 Marie MacLeod of Dunvegan, the sister of Donald's second wife Mór MacLeod,

* This is Donald Mac Iain 'ic Sheumais, the famous MacDonald warrior who defeated the MacLeods at the battle of Cairinish in North Uist in 1601. See *Hebridean Folksongs*, III. 94–9, 250–6.

whom Donald married in 1666, then becoming Sleat's brother-in-law.

In October 1658 Donald of Clanranald was still recorded by the Synod of Argyll as excommunicated. The Clanranalds never gave in to the Covenanters. Anyone who reads the Minutes of the Synod of Argyll (1639–60) with an eye on the modern world can perceive at once the operations of a revolutionary minority forcing its ideology on an unwilling majority with the support of the civil power of the State. All the more honour to Glengarry, MacNeil of Barra, and the Clanranalds and their lands, including Canna, that they stood out to the last resisting such pressure.

NOTES

1. Fourth *Report of the Historical MSS Commission of* 1874. I am obliged to Mr Noel Banks for drawing this to my attention.
2. Clanranald Papers. Copy communicated by Mr David Scott Moncrieff, WS.
3. Inverary Papers; kindly communicated by Dr Eric Cregeen.
4. *Inquisitionem ad Capellam Domini Regis Retornatum.*
5. David Stevenson, *Alasdair Mac Colla and the Highland Problem in the Seventeenth Century*, p. 71.
6. *Clan Donald*, iii. 471.
7. *Rel. Celt.* II. 177.
8. *Minutes of the Synod of Argyll (MSA)*, i. 173, 174.
9. Ibid. ii. 104.
10. Ibid. ii. 120.
11. Ibid. i. 38.
12. Ibid. ii. 39.
13. Ibid. ii. 110.
14. Ibid. ii. 121.
15. Ibid. ii. 122.
16. A misunderstanding of this word led the writer of MacQueen's entry in Scott's *Fasti* to suppose that MacQueen had been *deposed* for performing this marriage!

9 'BLACK DONALD OF THE CUCKOO' AND CANNA

Donald MacDonald younger, Captain of Clanranald, is of particular interest to us because he had a closer connection with Canna than any of the other chiefs of Clanranald. He was the first Clanranald to get a charter of the island, in 1672; he is traditionally said to have imprisoned his wife (presumably his second wife Mór or Marion MacLeod) in Coroghon 'castle' on Canna; and he died on the island in 1686.

In view of the long association of the Clanranalds with Canna, first mentioned in 1561, it may surprise readers to learn that actually they had no legal standing with regard to the island until two hundred years later. But having secured the superiority of the island from the Protestant Bishop of the Isles in 1627, a familiar incident in the process of the transference of Church land to what amounted to private ownership, the Earls of Argyll were in a position to choose their own tenants and profit by their feudal superiority. Possibly their first choice was Sir Donald Campbell of Barbreck and Ardnamurchan, who is mentioned in 1635 as being required by the Privy Council to regulate the fisheries around Canna in respect of the lands he held there.[1]

The earliest lease of Canna discovered so far is that by Archibald, eighth earl and first Marquess of Argyll, to a member of a collateral branch of the Clanranalds, Allan MacDonald of Morar in 1654. Argyll's choice of a MacDonald tenant was surprising; but he may not have felt it practicable to try to install another Campbell. As it was, there is nothing more recorded against the 'laird of Moroir' in the Minutes of the Synod of Argyll than that he had intromitted for a time with the teinds of Snizort in Skye.[2] The lease was for six years and comprised everything including the great and small teinds and the offices of Stewartry and Bailliery of the island. Entry had actually taken place at Whitsuntide 1653. The rent was to be 1,200 Scots merks (£800 Scots) a year and Allan was to relieve the Marquess of all forms of taxation on the estate.

Allan is let off 200 merks of the first year's rent. He signs his name 'Allan McRonald', and the witnesses were Patrick MacVicar, J. Campbell, Coline Campbell, and George Campbell. The lease was signed at Inveraray.

In May 1660 King Charles the Second was restored to the throne of the United Kingdom. In February 1661 Archibald Marquess of Argyll was charged with treason, found guilty, and sentenced to execution. Considering his political and military anti-royalist record, there was no chance of any other verdict. He was not a likeable person, and there was poetic justice in his fate after the way he had acted at the time of the execution of Montrose ten years earlier.

His forfeiture gave Allan of Morar the opportunity to try to hold Canna directly from the Bishop of the Isles, a step which would have reduced his rent from 1,200 to 125 merks (£800 to £83. 6s. 8d.) a year. Unfortunately for Allan and anyone else in his position, the executed Marquess of Argyll's heir Archibald (later ninth Earl of Argyll) was restored to the honours and estate of his grandfather in 1663. In a document surviving at Inveraray, Allan of Morar, who says he was given a fourteen year lease of Canna in 1659, renounced 'all pretendeit rights and tacks made in my favours of the samen lands and Ile be the Bishope of the Iles or any other persone whatsumevir' and accepted the feudal superiority of the Earl of Argyll again, having delivered up the Bishop's lease to be destroyed.

This Allan MacRonald or MacDonald of Morar was probably Allan IV of Morar, son of Ailean Mór who *Clan Donald* says fought in the Montrose War; but that work is very uncertain about the dates and the names of the wives of either Allan.[3] At any rate, his lease of Canna expired in 1672, when Donald XIII of Clanranald obtained the following charter from the Earl of Argyll:

Contract between Archibald Earl of Argyll and Donald McDonald of Moydart, Captain of Clan Ronald, whereby the Earl lets to Donald and his heirs male, *etc.*, the isle of Canna with the teind sheaves thereof, to be held in feu of the Earl for payment of seven hundred pounds Scots yearly; and for serving the Earl, when required, with a galley of sixteen oars, sufficiently appointed with men and necessaries for thirty days yearly between the isle of Canna and Icolmkill, and paying to the Bishop of the Isles and his successors, the Earl's superiors in the said isle, eighty three pounds six shillings and eight pence of feu duty, and six shillings and eight pence in augmentation thereof; under an obligation also to exhibit and produce any of the said captain's kinsmen or other possessors of the said isle, who shall happen to be guilty of any crimes, before the Earl, at least to satisfy the party injured within forty days after being required, and to keep them skaithless of all damage they shall incur through any illegal deeds, civil or criminal, that shall happen to be committed by the possessors of the said isle; reserving power to the Earl of winning adamant, silver, or any other mineral in the said isle. Dated 18th March 1672.[4]

Argyll as usual drives a hard bargain; the rent for the island is reduced from £800 to £700 p.a., but on the other hand Clanranald (whose father Iain Mùideartach had died on Eriskay at an advanced age two years earlier) has to undertake to pay Argyll's rent owed to the Bishop of the Isles, and to provide a galley of sixteen oars and crew for a month and a year for sailing between Canna and Iona, presumably to carry rents and teinds of Church lands in money and kind. Argyll was very probably thinking of the foreclosure he meant to exercise in the near future on the lands of the MacLeans of Duart, whose superior he was and whose debts he had acquired: armed resistance on the part of the MacLeans was expected, and very nearly materialized.[5] Argyll would have expected his other vassals to help him. Argyll had already withdrawn the bailliery of Canna from Allan of Morar and given the commission for it to Sir Rory MacLeod of Talisker on 30 October 1665.[6]

After facing Argyll in arms for three years, the MacLeans of Duart gave in in 1679 when they were officially threatened with the use of the Argyll, Bute, and Dumbartonshire militia against them, and Argyll took possession of Mull (except for Brolos and MacLaine of Lochbuie's lands), Iona, and Tiree. But in 1681 Argyll himself was charged with anti-Government propaganda ('leasing-making') over his opposition to the Test Act (which was directed against both Roman Catholics and Covenanting fanatics, but with express exclusion of the royal family), in consequence of which he himself was forfeited, like his father twenty years earlier. Donald of Clanranald was free to make his own terms with the Bishop of Argyll again, which he did with considerable financial advantage to himself; only the Bishop's rent of 125 merks or £83. 6s. 8d. Scots to pay, and no sixteen-oared galley to provide.[7] The confirmation of this charter is dated 25 April, 17 and 18 July of 1684, and its terms were as follows:

Charter of Confirmation and Novodamus by Archibald Bishop of the Isles with consent of his Dean and Chapter to Donald MacDonald of Moydart, Captain or Chief of the family of Clanranald, of the Island of Canna, in the Shariffdom of Argyll, with the office of hereditary bailie, which Island and bailiary thereof formerly pertained heritably to the said Donald, held of Archibald, ex-Earl of Argyll, with confirmation under the Great Seal, and were held by the said Earl of the Bishops of the Isles in feu-farm and are in the hands of the King by the forfeiture of the said Archibald ex-Earl of Argyll, whereupon the Crown presented the above Donald MacDonald as immediate tenant and vassal of the Bishops of the Isles, and for which a single sasine shall suffice, to be held by the said Donald his heirs and assignees, of the Bishops of the Isles heritably in fee, for 125 merks of the old feu duty and 13/8 in augmentation thereof, and payment of taxes, impositions and other public burdens and services, falling on the said Island.'

Donald of Clanranald had rid himself of an irksome financial and feudal burden, but he did not live to enjoy his new freedom for long; he was already sixty years of age, and died two years later on Canna, as will be told.

He had a troubled married life, or lives. His first marriage to Janet MacDonald of Sleat in 1655 had resulted in the Revd Archibald MacQueen being questioned by the Synod of Argyll for having married an excommunicated person (he had been excommunicated by the Synod for his part in the Montrose and Alasdair Mac Colla wars). Nothing seems to be known about this marriage. Alexander MacKenzie[8] and Alice MacDonald of the Isles[9] both say that there was 'issue' from this marriage; *Clan Donald* mentions none. It certainly did not produce an heir who survived childhood.

In 1666 Donald married his first cousin Mór or Marion MacLeod, daughter of Iain MacLeod XIV of Dunvegan (chief 1626–49) and sister of Rory XV and Iain Breac MacLeod XVI of Dunvegan. An abstract of the marriage contract is printed in the *Book of Dunvegan*, i. 57–8, by Canon R. C. MacLeod of

MacLeod, where it is incorrectly stated that Mór was 'the daughter of the late sister of the present John MacLeod of Dunvegan'. The date of the contract is given as 10 November 1666, but it is actually the twelfth.

This contract is No. 9 in the book. Unfortunately it is somehow inextricably confused with No. 8 which is the contract between Sir James MacDonald of Sleat (Donald Clanranald's brother-in-law by his first marriage) and Marie MacLeod, Mór's sister. I am much obliged to Dr Peter Anderson of the National Register House for a complete transcript of Mór's actual contract. In this she is described as 'Mistres Moire* Mackleoid' the lawful sister of 'John Mack-Leoid of Dunvegane'. The use of the title 'Mistres' implies that she had already been married, and *Clan Donald* asserts that she was the widow of Norman, son of Sir Norman MacLeod of Bernera; but this is clearly impossible, as this Norman was the second son of Sir Norman's second marriage, and born after 1661.[10]

Mór undoubtedly did have a son by this Norman, as there is a bond for 500 merks in the Clanranald papers executed by her in favour of Alexander MacLeod 'her son begotten between her and Norman MacLeod, son of the late Sir Norman MacLeod of Bernera'. The bond is dated 11 November 1706, after her second marriage, which was to Ranald MacDonald of Milton.[11] *Clan Donald* says there were no children of this marriage. The probability is that this Alexander MacLeod was born after Mór separated from Donald in 1680. Norman's name is not mentioned in her husband's accusation of adultery.

The marriage contract insists that the marriage is to be *per verba de presenti* and 'in face of Christ his Church and hely congregatioune *per eadem verba*'. In other words it is to be a Protestant marriage in the established (then Episcopalian) church, and not a Catholic marriage *per verba de futuro* with the actual ceremony put off until a priest might be found to perform it. Donald is to infeft his future wife with the rents of

* 'Mór', 'Moir', or 'Moire' (the *i* in Scots spelling denotes that the preceding vowel is long) is today usually anglicized as 'Sarah'. The diminutive 'Mórag' is better known now. There is some risk of 'Moire' being confused with 'Marie' in reading seventeenth-century script.

certain lands in South Uist but subject to the consent of his father, who is still alive (he died four years later). Iain Breac MacLeod of Dunvegan is to provide Mór with a dowry of 13,500 merks (£8,950 Scots) of which 7,000 merks at Martinmas 1667 and 7,500 at Martinmas 1668. The marriage is to take place between the date of the contract (12 November 1666) and the end of that November 'or sooner as the saidis pairtis sall think expedient'. This gives a distinct impression that Mór may have been pregnant at the time of the wedding, which her father was so anxious to expedite.

Mór MacLeod became a Catholic after her marriage; this is stated in St Oliver Plunkett's report on the state of the Hebrides to the Internuncio at Brussels in 1671, where it is said that she and 500 others on the Clanranald estates had been converted by the Vincentian Fr. Francis White. In 1678 Canna was visited by Fr. Alexander Leslie, who gives a touching account of the spiritual hunger of the inhabitants (see Appendix I).

The marriage of Mór and Donald broke up in 1680 with Donald initiating a process of divorce for desertion and adultery, charges which Mór denied. The well-known contemporary Scottish judge Sir John Lauder of Fountainhall recorded in his legal diary in the winter of 1676–7 the rumour that Mór, a Catholic, when ill had got her husband 'tho Protestant' to send for 'Pere Whyte' from Inverness to hear her confession; but some days afterwards Donald, the rumour said, had returned from hunting and discovered Mór and the priest in a compromising situation, and had 'immediatly caused lead out the Priest to his utter gate, and hing him over it, and sent hir some dayes journey into the Hylands, with expresse inhibition not to returne'. The story is quoted from a legal point of view as illustrating Roman law's allowing the killing of a wife taken in the act of adultery.[12]

The place of such an event, if it occurred, would have been Caisteal Tioram in Moidart. Hanging at the castle gate was a customary method of exercising local jurisdiction in Scotland; in July 1685 the Marquis of Atholl wanted to hang Charles, second son of the Earl of Argyll, 'at his father's gate in Inverairay' for having taken part in his father's rebellion (Atholl was stopped from doing so by the Scottish Privy

Council).[13] The place of exile could well have been Canna. But the whole story falls from the fact that 'Pere Whyte', who must be Fr. Francis White the Vincentian missionary who first came to the Isles in 1653, did not die in 1676 or 1677, but on 28 January 1679;[14] his headquarters were in Glengarry, not Inverness; Donald, though nominally a Protestant – '*ipsi domini ob politiam sunt protestantes*', wrote St Oliver Plunkett of the Hebridean chiefs in 1671 – 'the lairds themselves are Protestants for political reasons', adding that Donald of Clanranald '*etsi haereticus multum favet cattolicis*'.[15] Finally there is the character of Fr. White himself, a devoted missionary described by the Prefect of his Mission in 1676 as 'broken down by hard work, his strength reduced by ill-health, greatly esteemed by all, even by the heretics, and much revered by them'.

The story is obviously false, but Sir John Lauder was no bigot; he was an honourable man who deplored the Covenanting 'phanaticks'; refused appointment as Lord Advocate in 1692 because he felt he could not defend the Government's involvement in the massacre of Glencoe; and, as MP for Haddington, took a patriotic stand against the 'unequal incorporating Union' of 1707. In 1686 he said in the Scottish Parliament that 'ther was no man within the House more desirous to have these odious marks of division [i.e. the terms 'Papists', 'heretics', and the like] buried, and that we might all be united in the general name of Christian.'[16] When he privately noted this rumour, never published before 1848, he was not disseminating anti-Catholic propaganda. Any such event as the execution by Clanranald of a missionary priest allegedly caught in a compromising situation with the Chief's wife, would have left an indelible mark on Gaelic oral tradition.

No such story is known. What we do have is memories of Donald's dispute with his wife, of his ill-treatment of her, and of a row Donald had with some priest at a time after Fr. White's death. It is significant that the charge Mór defended herself against in the autumn of 1680 was that of adultery with one Alexander MacRonald, possibly a member of the Morar family; Allan of Morar signed his name 'Mackronald' to the lease of Canna he got from Argyll in 1654. The charge was vehemently denied. Traditionally Donald's reputation as

Chief of Clanranald is far from a good one. The local tradition that attaches to Mór is that she is the Clanranald wife who was shut up in Coroghon prison on Canna to prevent her meeting or joining a lover. Pennant mentions this in 1772, and Edward Daniel Clarke is quite specific about it, apparently having got the story from Hector MacNeill, tenant of Canna since 1782, on his visit to Canna in 1797.

He writes:

This castle was formerly used as a prison for the wife of MacDonald of Clanranald, to secure her from the addresses of MacNeil, an ancient laird of Barra. The lady, however, found means to effect her escape and join her lover; for one night, having sewn together her blankets, she let herself down, and fled.[17]

Fr. Charles MacDonald, in his 'Moidart or Among the Clanranalds', says that 'Donald had immured a native lady in the castle at Coroghon, for what crime no one now knows, and seemed disposed to keep her there for the rest of her life', an injustice against which the local priest preached a vigorous sermon. Hearing of this, Donald returned to Canna with his famous gun, the 'Cuckoo' – Donald's Gaelic nickname was *Domhnall Dubh na Cuthaige* – with the intention of shooting the priest, who had to go into hiding until he could be quietly ferried over to another island.[18]

The Revd William Matheson tells me that in the papers of Alexander Carmichael the tradition is recorded that Mór composed the song *Ged is grianach an latha* after meeting a former lover in Skye from whom she much regretted parting for Uist. In translation the song, which is No. XLIV in the second volume of *Hebridean Folksongs*, begins:

> Sunny though the day may be,
> Little joy its beauty gives me,
> As I wait beside the narrows
> While my loved one sails not over.

– Whoever the loved one was, it is clear from the song that he was a MacDonald.

According to *Clan Donald*, Donald of Clanranald and Mór had six children from this marriage, which ended in separation in 1680. If that is so, she must have been considerably younger than her husband, who was about forty-two at the time of the marriage. In fact she could have been twenty years younger and even so a widow when they married in 1666.

Mór vigorously defended herself against the charges of desertion and adultery brought against her by Donald of Clanranald in July 1680. The charge of desertion she said was 'but a most calumnious and false pretext used by her husband to palliat and cover his unjust deserting her. And since it is not at all relevant and is fully taken off by her offering to adhere, the same merits no answer, but withall that place of the country beeing so remot [?Canna] and far from all loyall assistance and the people beeing so barbarous and easilie influenced by the Captain of Clanranald their master and chief, she therefore humbly craves she may be indemnified.'[19]

The charge of adultery was with one Alexander MacRonald, possibly a member of the MacDonald of Morar family. It was vehemently denied:

The same is a most groundlesse and false assertion and is absolutely denyed nor can it be inferd from the alleged profession elicit from her befor the Commissar of Isles★ since by our law Adulterie cannot be proven but by witnesses *de facto deponentis* And if it were otherways poor women would be in a miserable condition since they may be under such impressions of feare and fire [?] because of their sex and condition as might verie easilie bind the guilt upon them but since no extrajuridicall profession can prove a cryme even *in constanti vivo* much lesse ought this extrajuridicall profession to prove such a horrid cryme of adulterie if she had professed [?] the same qch [= which] she alwayes denyes It beeing notor to the whole Countrey that she was most barbarously used and threated† in order to the eliciting [?] of divorce [illegible] her to please the jealousie and humor of [illegible] of her husband.

As a young man, Donald of Clanranald had been a brave and capable soldier and leader of men; when Prince Charles Edward was in hiding at Corradale in South Uist in June 1746, Alexander MacDonald of Boisdale told him that Donald, who was his grandfather, had fought seven set battles for King

---

★ I do not know who the Commissary of the Isles was in the 1680s. The Commissary had the power to grant divorces. For a reference to abuses from this, see *Minutes of the Synod of Argyll*, i. 37 (Scottish History Society).

† Scots for 'threatened'.

Charles the Second, but there had been no acknowledgement of it at the time of the Restoration.[20] As Chief of Clanranald, tradition both of Moidart and of Canna and Uist depicts him as arbitrary and cruel. No doubt the atrocities of the Civil War had hardened him early. We do not know anything of his medical history, which might also account for that development in his personality. He died in 1686 on Canna. He is sometimes said to have died in the house which is now called the Bothy, and which was inhabited by the MacNeills of Canna before Canna House was built in the 1860s, when its top storey was removed. But there is indisputable evidence that this house must have been built between 1781, when Hector MacNeill got his first lease of the island from Clanranald, which stipulated that he should build such a house, and 1787, when the first report of the British Fisheries Society stated that he had built it; so that the house, now the Bothy, which on the Clanranald map of 1805 is called 'Corrygan', should be referred to as the 'MacNeill House' and not as the 'Clanranald House'.

I quote the account of his death as given to me by the famous Gaelic *seanchaidh*, the late Angus MacLellan, 'Aonghus Beag', Frobost, South Uist on 1 November 1950. The story was also well known on Canna, and is told in a more prolix form by the Revd Fr. Charles MacDonald in *Moidart or Among the Clanranalds* in 1889.

This Black Donald of the 'Cuckoo', one of the Clanranalds, lived at Caisteal Tioram;* and I understand that he was not a very good man. He had a gun, which he himself called the 'Cuckoo'; and he would say to anyone who did anything to him 'I'll put the "Cuckoo" to you'. That's how he was called 'Black Donald of the "Cuckoo".' He hanged an old woman at Caisteal Tioram for stealing a snuff-box; and the spot has been called Tom na Caillich, 'the Old Woman's Mound', ever since.

Once Black Donald heard that there was a priest on Canna who wanted to go to Uist. Black Donald went with his boat to Canna. It seems there was an animal† that followed the Clanranalds – it followed him, Black Donald, anyway – its picture is on the stone on their grave at Howmore. The animal was following the boat, and the

---

* In Moidart, on the mainland.
† i.e. a familiar spirit, said to have been a giant toad.

day became very bad. The animal was on the top of each wave that followed the boat. One of the crew said it looked as if they wouldn't manage, that they would be lost. Black Donald himself was steering, and the animal came alongside the boat. At last Black Donald beckoned to it, and it came on board. The sea improved then, and they got to Canna.

Black Donald made a plan to remove a plank from every boat on Canna, so that the priest could not get away to Uist. He kept the priest seven weeks on Canna. One day, when the priest was down on the shore, he saw a boat going past, and he began to beckon to it. The boat kept in to the shore, and the priest got into it, and where it was going to but Loch Eynort! When the boat took off from the land, the priest turned and looked back and said:

'I am not asking torment for your soul, but that your body may be kept here unburied as long as you've kept me.'

When Black Donald was dying on Canna, he was in terrible distress. People were going in to see him. There was a widow's son there, a brave, strong fellow. A whistle was heard outside the house, and the man who was in his death-throes on the bed got up to go out. Everyone who was there cleared out but the widow's son, who caught hold of Black Donald and put him back on the bed. Then they heard another whistle, and he tried to get out. The widow's son caught him at the door, and put him back on the bed. There was someone standing on a knoll opposite the house, and he was so tall that they could see the island of Rum between his legs. This person went away, and they saw him walking on the surface of the sea over to Rum. This has been the worst piece of sea ever since, the sea between Rum and Canna.

As long as Black Donald was alive, he was thanking God and the widow's son that the widow's son had kept him in the house; and when he died, there came bad weather; and his body was seven weeks on Canna, before they got away with it to Howmore* and the day they went with it, there came such a gale that they had to land at Peterport in Benbecula, and take the body from there overland to Howmore. Black Donald is buried there along with the other Clanranalds, and I understand that he was not the best of them.

Versions of this story were also told to the writer by Angus MacDonald on Canna ('Aonghus Eachainn') and by Angus MacKinnon, from Eigg, at Clydebank, on 15 December 1949. Mr Angus MacKinnon said that the house where Domhnall Dubh died was called 'Taigh na Dòirlinn' and that a big

---

* The ancient burial place of the Clanranalds in South Uist.

strange dog, unknown on the island, had come into the house and gone out again before the unnatural whistling outside began.

NOTES

1. *CRA* 111.
2. *MSA* i. 175.
3. *Clan Donald*, iii. 253–4.
4. *Report of the Historical MSS Commission, 1878*, p. 480.
5. See Sheriff J. R. N. MacPhail, 'Papers Relating to the MacLeans of Duart, 1670–80'. Scottish History Society, *Highland Papers*, i. 242–337.
6. Clanranald Papers.
7. There is a discharge to Donald of Clanranald by Bishop Archibald of the Isles for 'the soume of on hundreth and forty-five [merks] as of due [? feu] duety payable be him to me out of his lands and island of Canna for the cropt and year 1682' printed in the paper by the Revd Archibald MacDonald, DD, 'Gleanings from Charter Chests of the Isles' in *Transactions of the Gaelic Society of Inverness*, xxxviii. 402–3.
8. Alexander MacKenzie, *History of the MacDonalds*, p. 215.
9. Alice MacDonald of the Isles, *The House of the Isles*, p. 89.
10. The Revd Dr Donald MacKinnon and Alick Morrison, *The MacLeods*, ii. 30.
11. I am grateful to the Revd William Matheson for drawing my attention to this Bond.
12. Sir John Lauder of Fountainhall Bt., *Historical Notices of Scottish Affairs*, pp. 142–3 (*HNSA*).
13. Ibid. 655.
14. See David MacRoberts, 'The Death of Father Francis White', *Innes Review*, XVII. 186–8, and Dom Odo Blundell, *The Catholic Highlands of Scotland*, II. 161–77.
15. Cathaldus Giblin, 'St. Oliver Plunkett, Francis MacDonnell O.F.M., and the Mission to the Hebrides', *Collectanea Hibernica*, XVII. 100.
16. *HNSA*.
17. Otter's *Life of E. D. Clarke*, in which Clarke's journal of his Hebridean trip is reproduced, pp. 321–40. The reference to MacNeil of Barra suggests local tradition confused Mór MacLeod with her collateral ancestor Mary MacLeod who did go to Ruairi an Tartair of Barra in the 16th century.
18. *Moidart or Among the Clanranalds*, pp. 88–9.
19. *Dunvegan Papers*, No. 11.
20. *Lyon in Mourning*, ii. 97.

10 CANNA AND THE SPCK IN SCOTLAND

After the forfeiture of Archibald, ninth Earl of Argyll, in 1681, and his execution on 30 June 1685 in consequence of the unsuccessful rising he headed in the west of Scotland in support of Monmouth's rebellion, Donald of Clanranald and the other island chiefs who had been the unwilling vassals of the Argyll family, must have hoped that their delivery from the political and economic thraldom of Argyll's superiority might be permanent. Had that been so, the whole subsequent history of the West Highlands and Islands and of Scottish Gaeldom might well have been very different. It was not to be.

On 12 February 1687, James VII, 'King of Scotland, England, France, and Ireland', who had ascended to the throne two years earlier, issued his famous proclamation of religious liberty. 'We having taken into Our Royal Consideration the many and great inconveniences, which have happened to Our Ancient Kingdom of *Scotland* of late years through the different persuasions in the Christian Religion, and the great Heats and Animosities amongst the several Professors thereof, to the ruine and decay of Trade, wasting of Lands, extinguishing of Charity, contempt of the Royal Power, and converting of true Religion, and the fear of GOD, into Animosities, Names, Factions, and sometimes into Sacriledge and Treason' – how true it all is. The proclamation goes on to announce toleration for Moderate Presbyterianism and the Quakers; and relief for Roman Catholics* from the crushing burden of the Penal Laws – not always invoked, but always there – the Government itself, of course, was then Episcopalian. Only the extremist Covenanters, who had been preaching justification for the murder of bishops and civil authorities, were excluded, 'seeing [that] from these Rendezvouzes of Rebellion, so much Disorder hath proceeded, and so much Disturbance to the Government, and for which after this Our Royal Indulgence for tender Consciences, there is no excuse left'.

* James VII's own statement of his reasons for becoming a Catholic can be found in the *Celtic Magazine* IX. 439–442.

One man's terrorist is another man's freedom fighter; James VII's attempt to secure freedom of conscience in Scotland failed, so he has been vilified and the Covenanting fanatics of his and his brother's reign have been canonized, metaphorically speaking. James might as well have been the late Shah of Iran urging moderation and tolerance on the followers of Ayatollah Khomeini. His attempt was generations before its time, not realized until the foundation of the American Constitution, with its clause forbidding the establishment (originally in the European sense) of any particular form of Christianity, in 1787; and the repeal of the Penal Laws in Britain in 1829. James was a naval man, and not a natural diplomat or a politician; it would have taken the highest degree of political skill to have made his proclamation officially effective at that time. Better perhaps to have bided time and allowed the anti-Catholic legislation of past years to become a dead letter.

Archibald, heir of the ninth Earl of Argyll, returned from exile in Holland with Dutch William in November 1688; his father's 1681 forfeiture was speedily reversed, and in 1701 his support for William and Mary was rewarded by his being made Duke of Argyll and Marquess of Kintyre and Lorne. All his father's former vassals became again subject to the Argyll superiority. In 1696 Argyll assigned Lt. Daniel Calder of Sir John Hill's regiment, then occupying Clanranald's main residence of Caisteal Tioram in Moidart, to collect for him his rents from Eigg and Canna.[1] It is significant to find the military at Argyll's service for the collection of rents from his feudal vassals at such a time.

To their great credit the members of the Scottish (Protestant) Episcopate refused to accept William of Orange as their legitimate monarch, which he certainly was not. As for the Catholic clans of the Highlands and Islands, their loyalty to the exiled successors of the Stewarts, their only hope for relief from political and economic bondage, grew firmer than ever. On 27 July 1689 the Royalist forces under Grahame of Claverhouse won a victory over the forces of William of Orange at Killiecrankie that could have been decisive but for the death of their commander at the moment of victory. Repression quickly followed. On 16 January 1691 Dutch

William signed the order for the massacre of the MacDonalds of Glencoe, an event that provoked a scandal which forced William to appoint a commission of inquiry, which covered up for him by deciding that Stair, his Secretary of State for Scotland, had exceeded his instructions. Stair was not prosecuted.

Next William granted the rents of the suppressed bishopric of Argyll and the Isles to the Synod of Argyll for the purpose of 'erecting of English schools for rooting out the Irish language, and other pious uses' (*sic*). Highland tenants of the bishopric who were unwilling to pay their rents for what was, in fact, an attack on their language and religion, were to be punished by having soldiers quartered upon them until payment was made – a penalty against which the Covenanters, who had had to endure no comparable oppression, had cried to high heaven when it had been inflicted upon *them*. In 1696 the Education Act of 1646 was re-enacted. By 1698 the rents of the bishopric of Argyll and the Isles were financing twenty-five fixed English schools, thirteen peripatetic English schools, and five grammar schools. The Act of 1696 placed the financial burden of the new parochial schools upon the proprietors and their principal tenants. In this way the attack on the Highland language and Highland traditions was to be financed out of Highland rents.[2]

Not unnaturally there was opposition to this policy in the Highlands and Islands that began to draw Highlanders of whatever religion – and the now established Presbyterian Church still had very few ministers in the western and insular Gaelic-speaking areas – together in support of the Jacobite cause. To counter this opposition, in 1709 a number of wealthy subscribers in Edinburgh and the south of Scotland were incorporated under the title of 'The Society in Scotland for Propagating Christian Knowledge'. The object of this Society was to remedy any deficiencies in the application of the 1696 Education Act by the provision of charity schools in the Highlands and Islands supported by private subscriptions and the interest on the Society's capital. These schools were to be manned by schoolmasters of proven loyalty, and they were to teach the English language, the Presbyterian Calvinist religion, Church music, and arithmetic only.

The policy of the SPCK was summed up in its Memorial to the Court of Police in 1716:

Nothing can be more effectual for reducing these countries [i.e. the Highlands and Islands] to order and making them usefull to the Commonwealth than teaching them their duty to God, their King and Countrey [sic], and rooting out their Irish language, and this has been the care of the Society so far as they could, for all the schollars are taught in English, and none are allowed to be masters of the Societie's Charitie Schools, but such as produce sufficient certificats of their piety knowledge and loyalty.[3]

The unattractive school-books provided for the SPCK's Gaelic-speaking pupils included the *Westminster Confession of Faith*, the *Shorter Catechism*, *Vincent's Catechism*, *Protestant's Resolution*, Pool's *Dialogue*, and Guthrie's *Trials*, all in English. It was a travesty of an education – simply politico-religious indoctrination in Calvinism and the English language. Objections were indeed made against the banning of Gaelic in these SPCK Schools by sensible ministers and schoolmasters on the spot in the Highlands, but they were brushed aside in the Edinburgh Offices of the Society.

It has never been suggested before, but it may well have been the case that the remarkable book on St Kilda that Martin Martin published in 1698 and his even more remarkable *A Description of the Western Islands of Scotland*, first published in 1703 and reissued as a second edition in 1716 with a dedication to Prince George of Denmark, very probably had a profound effect in awakening the douce Whigs of Edinburgh to the fact that (from their point of view) the Highlands and Islands were still very 'imperfectly reformed'. It is highly significant that the very first schoolteacher dispatched to the Highlands and Islands, Alexander Buchan, was sent to St Kilda, where the inhabitants, though described by Martin Martin as 'of the Reform'd Religion', still observed the festivals of Christmas, Easter, Good Friday, and All Saints', and 'swore decisive Oaths' by a nine-inch brass crucifix that stood or lay upon the altar of their chapel[4] (and which thereafter quickly disappeared). Martin's information on religion in the other Isles can be summarized as follows:

Islands entirely or nearly entirely Catholic:
Benbecula, South Uist, Barra, Canna, and Eigg. To which
should be added Rum, which Martin wrongly describes then
as Protestant.

*Islands where Catholic customs and festivals survive, and there are a
few Catholics:* Mull, Trotternish in Skye.

*Islands entirely Protestant nominally, where Catholic customs
and festivals survive:* Lewis, Harris, North Uist, Coll, Tiree,
Colonsay, Jura, and Islay.

The Presbyterian establishment of William and Mary made
their ascendancy permanent through acquiescence in the ending of Scottish independence by the 'unequal incorporating
Union' of 1707. It is not surprising that there was a Jacobite
rising in 1715 against this and other aspects of their policy,
during the course of which Allan MacDonald of Clanranald,
Donald Dubh's heir and successor, lost his life at the battle of
Sheriffmuir, killed, it was popularly said, by a silver bullet that
negatived the charm he used to wear.[5] The Rising put the
whole future of the SPCK's educational policy into jeopardy.
In 1725 the General Assembly of the Church of Scotland had
no difficulty in persuading 'German Geordie', King George I,
to give the SPCK in Scotland an annual grant of £1,000 for its
purposes, as described above. The same year the male inhabitants of Rum were forced into the Presbyterian church there
by the proprietor, MacLean of Coll, in an incident recorded in
the *Register of the Actings and Proceedings of the Committee of the
General Assembly of the Church of Scotland for Management of the
King's Bounty for Reformation of the Highlands and Islands of
Scotland*, on 10 May 1726. The British Fisheries Society party
that visited Canna in August 1788 was given a vivid traditional
account of the incident, printed in a later chapter here.

The Minutes of the Committee and of the General Meetings
of the SPCK are of the greatest interest – religious, political,
social, and economic – for the history of the Highlands and
Islands between the Union of 1707 and the accession of King
George III in 1760. They show what the majority of the
Highlanders were rebelling against in 1715 and again in 1745 –

a calculated, well-financed attempt, backed by constant political pressure, to destroy their language and their religion. The Minutes of the SPCK were only placed in the National Register House in Edinburgh in 1933. Since then no Scottish historical society had ventured to publish them; presumably they are still politically too embarrassing.

The members of the Committee of the SPCK first decided to look into the matter of sending a schoolmaster to the Small Isles when their Clerk was asked to look into their books and report what had been decided previously regarding schools 'and whether any of the masters or their allowance may be given to some of these places'.

The Clerk reported on 22 June that 'there is a design of setling [a minister] in the said four islands above mentioned where there are many papists, as likewise that preachers and catechists are going to these places sent by the Committee for Reformation of the Highlands and Islands, the Committee [of the SPCK] are of opinion this may be a fit season of sending Schoolmasters thither, seeing the Ministers, preachers and Catechists may very much encourage the School Masters, and because the Societies funds cannot allow schools to all these places [other situations, including Coll and Tiree, were also under consideration] without sinking schools in other places'.

The Committee decided to allow £100 a year, half the salary of the demitted schoolmaster at Corgraph (Aberdeenshire), for an itinerant schoolmaster for the Small Isles. Subsequently, however, SPCK schools were started in each of the four islands, though not immediately. On 23 May 1728 the Committee agreed that one James Wright should have a commission to be schoolmaster at Eigg and Canna. Meanwhile the Revd Donald McQueen had been appointed Minister of Sleat (in Skye) and the Small Isles, in 1727; on 5 September 1728 the Committee's Minutes recorded that

As also the Committee had a letter from Mr Donald McQueen Minister shewing that he visits the School frequently, and finds some of the schollars advance but slowly, being often taken from the school on account of the poverty of their parents, others read the scriptures and other books tollerably, are writing, do repeat the Catechism and a part of the Protestants Resolution, that the Master reads, prays and sings Psalms with the people on the Lord's

Day in his absence, and in his spare hours catechises the people, and craving payment of the Masters salary, and recommending Kenneth McCaskell for being Schoolmaster and Catechist at Muck, who has already sixteen schollars there, and John Stewart to be Schoolmaster and Catechist at Egg who entered to his work the twelfth of June last, and his schollars are yet but few; he desires that if the Society had not already appointed one for Cana they would provide one for it against Martinmess next, and craves books to these schools, that the number of persons past five years in his Parish is Eight hundred fifty six of which three hundred and fourty at Egg all papists, ten persons excepted, at Muck one hundred and twenty eight, sixty of whom are Protestants, at Rum One hundred and fifty two all Protestants, six women excepted, at Cana Two hundred and thirty six all papists sixteen persons excepted; the Committee having considered the premisses found that they had upon the twenty first of August last given a Commission to the said Kenneth McCaskell to be Schoolmaster in the Isles of Egg and Muck, and finding by their Minute the eighth of June 1727, that they had only allowed one school for Egg and Muck, and another for Cana, ordered a letter to be written to Mr McQueen, desiring him to send up, a certificate in favours of the said John Stewart, and resolved then to give him a Commission to be Schoolmaster at Cana, but found the Society's funds will not allow another school to these Islands, and that the Schoolmaster of Muck may serve the Island of Egg by turns.

In fact there was very little chance of the SPCK making any progress on Clanranald's islands, Eigg and Canna. On 1 April 1731 the Committee reported that there was

Produced a letter from a privat hand* giving a full account of the state of the Isle of Rum, Muck, Egg and Cana with respect to religion, particularly that the inhabitants of Egg and Cana being much addicted to popery and under the management of Priests and the awful power of Popish chiefs, there was not any probability of the means of instruction being entertained by them, and therefore the author is of opinion that the continuing a school in Egg can be of no benefite to the Protestant cause, but rather promote the direct opposite interest, and as to Rum and Muck enhabited mostly by protestants he proposes that one Schoolmaster might sufficiently serve both, who might be at Muck in Summer and Harvest, and at Rum in Winter and Spring, the passage betwixt the two being short; and that if the Society would bestow what money might be spared

* MacLean of Coll's?

by this settlement upon such schollars as would punctually attend, whether Protestant or Popish parents, there might be hopes of gaining some at least, being boarded in Protestant families and following the school in its motion, and this would more endear the people and forcibly enclose them to yeeld to right measures of instruction, than tho' there were a school placed in every town . . . .

The population statistics are very interesting; but the report shows that there was no hope of gaining Canna or Eigg for the Whig cause. It was not until the early nineteenth century that the Gaelic language was utilized in Highland education, by the Gaelic Schools Society, founded in 1812; and its existence was simply ignored in the Scottish Education Act of 1872, that initiated compulsory education in Scotland. Implicit in the SPCK's Highland educational policy was the preparing of the average Highlander to take a none too exalted place in the emerging capitalist system that was soon to supersede the last remains of Highland feudalism.[6]

NOTES

1. *The Clan Campbell*, i. 17–18.
2. See Audrey Cunningham, *The Loyal Clans* (Cambridge, 1932), p. 429; also William MacKay, 'Education in the Highlands', *Transactions of the Gaelic Society of Inverness*, xxvii. 250–71.
3. SPCK General Meeting Minutes for 2 June 1716.
4. Martin Martin, *A Description of the Western Islands of Scotland*, pp. 287–8 (1716 edition).
5. Fr. Allan McDonald recorded this tradition in South Uist in 1887.
6. Cf. *The Rise and Progress of the S.P.C.K.*, p. 33.

11 CANNA, 'MAC MHAIGHSTIR ALASDAIR', AND THE FORTY-FIVE

In the spring of 1751 a small book was published in Edinburgh bearing the title:

AIS–EIRIDH
NA
Sean Chánoin Albannaich;
NO,
An nuadh Oranaiche Gaidhealach.
Le Alasdair Mac-Dhonuill, Bailli Chana
Ris am bheil coimh-cheangailte
EIDER–THEANGAIR am mineachadh ann
am Beurla gach cruaigh fhacall a tharlas
anns an leabhar so.
Clo-bhuailt' ann
DUNEIDIUNN
Go feim an Ughdair
MDCCLI

That is, 'The Resurrection of the Ancient Scottish Language, or, the new Highland Songster. By Alexander MacDonald, Baillie of Canna. To which is added a Glossary in which every hard word that occurs in this book is explained in English. Privately printed in Edinburgh, 1751'.

Alexander MacDonald, 'Alasdair mac Mhaighstir Alasdair' as he is called in Gaelic, is today far the best-known personality connected with Canna historically.

How he came to be appointed Baillie of Canna, and by whom, is uncertain. The Clanranald estates were not forfeited after the Forty-five, though it was expected they would be, and in fact they were included in the forfeited estates surveyed for the Government by David Bruce. Their escape from forfeiture – which presumably would have been in favour of Clanranald's superior, the Duke of Argyll – was due to a lucky combination of circumstances. By an arrangement made in 1726 and put into effect in 1727, Ranald MacDonald XVII of Clanranald was in fact only the life-renter of the estates, of

1. Canna Harbour, 1787. Print of sketch by Lt. Pierce of the British Fisheries Society visit, obviously drawn from memory.

6. The Celtic Cross at Keill, the situation of the pre-Clearance village on Canna. One of the representations of the cross may be the Adoration of the Magi.

7. The Punishment Stone, *Clach a' Pheanais*, an ancient pillory; the offender's thumb could have been wedged in the small hole in the stone.

8. The late Hector MacDonald, farm manager, with a prize Highland heifer, 1961.

9. Highland cattle at Tarbert, Canna. The Isle of Rum is in the background.

10. Sheep on Canna.

11. Razor-bills on Geugasgor.

12. A Guillemot colony near Sloc a' Ghallabhaich, 1966.

13. Sea-birds feeding on sprats north of Canna, 1966.

14. Ringnet boats working under the cliffs of Canna, 1968.

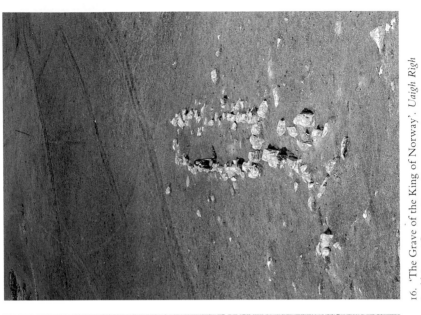

16. 'The Grave of the King of Norway'. *Uaigh Rìgh Lochlainn*, at Langanes.

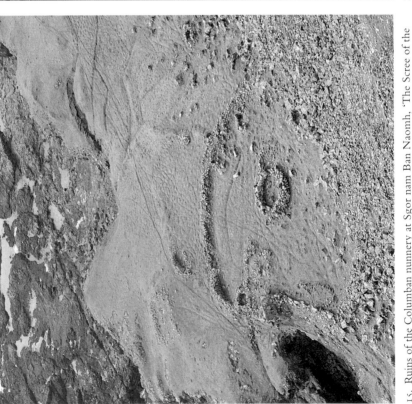

15. Ruins of the Columban nunnery at Sgor nam Ban Naomh, 'The Scree of the Holy Women'.

which his son Ranald, the 'Young Clanranald' of the Forty-
five, was fiar or outright owner.[1]

The older Ranald, 'Old Clanranald', did not take part in the
Rising, through after it was over, he was taken with other
leading Jacobites to London and kept prisoner until July 1747.
His heir Ranald, on the other hand, was involved in the Rising
up to the hilt, but was wrongly named 'Donald' in the Bill of
Attainder of 4 June 1746. Consequently when the survey of the
forfeited estates was projected in 1748, a legal protest was
made on behalf of the Clanranalds on the grounds that 'Old
Clanranald' had not been involved in the Rising and that there
was no such person as 'Donald MacDonald younger of
Clanranald'. This protest was sustained by the Judges of the
Court of Session in Edinburgh, who decreed on 21 December
1751 that the Sheriffs of Argyll and Inverness should put
Ranald MacDonald, Elder of Clanranald, life-renter, and
Ranald, younger of Clanranald, fiar, in possession of the lands
and heritage claimed by them.[2]

But this was after the publication of Alexander MacDonald's
book – earlier in the same year. It is strange that no one has so
far discovered any documentary reference to the appointment
or to the duties he carried out while he held it. Although the
tradition of his sojourn is very strong on Canna, no building or
ruin or piece of land is pointed out now as having been
occupied by him. His name is not mentioned in the 1749 rental
of Canna, where his predecessor James MacDonald is entered
as the tenant of Keill and Coroghon.[3]

His book contains thirty-two Gaelic poems. It was the first
book of Gaelic poetry printed in Scotland, and for many years
the only one to be prepared for the press by its author. Hardly
any of the seventeenth- and eighteenth-century Gaelic poets
could write their own language, (not surprisingly considering
the education policy of the Scottish and British Governments)
and their poems were nearly always taken down from their
own recitation or from the rich memory of oral tradition.

MacDonald's book, like his own personality, is an unusual
mixture of contradictions and opposites. It begins with a poem
in praise of the Gaelic language which was obviously written
under the influence of a very similar poem written in praise of
the great Welsh polymath Edward Lhuyd[4] by the Revd John

MacLean, Presbyterian minister of Kilninian in Mull, who had succeeded the Revd John Beaton, last Episcopalian minister of that parish in 1702, where he officiated until his death in 1753. MacDonald's book also contains nature poems, love poems, drinking songs, translations of poetry of the great Montrose, satires (some obscene), a poem on the coming of venereal disease to Ardnamurchan (presumably brought by the English workers in the York Company's lead mines at Strontian in the 1720s) that is of great interest for the medical history of the Highlands, but which has been suppressed as immoral since 1802, and two poems, one on old age and the other on a dialogue between the friend and foe of whisky, which are attributed to the North Uist bard John MacCodrum.

But the most important poems of the book consist of rousing appeals to the Highlanders to unite and rise again in support of the Stewarts Prince Charles and James VIII, and in bitter denunciations of the usurping Hanoverians who had deprived the Highlanders of their natural garb and of the guns they used to hunt the deer, executed some of their natural leaders, and imprisoned and banished others. In the words of the Gaelic proverb, he wrote (in a poem preserved elsewhere in manuscript) of King George II that his love and care for the Gaels was 'but the love of a raven for its bone'.[5] In his elegy on Lord Lovat he said (the translation is the writer's):

> We are beneath oppression's heel,
>   Ashamed we are, and weary;
> The remnant that remains of us
>   Is scattered 'midst the mountains
> With terror filled before our foes
>   Who hunt us 'midst the islands;
> They've made of us but wretched thralls,
>   O Charlie, come to help us!

and elsewhere, in manuscript:

> O Gaeltacht! if thou'rt asleep
>   Lie not for long in dreams;
> Bestir thyself, I beg of thee,
>   Ere stolen is thy fame.
> O, waken up full mightily
>   Kindled with wrathful fire,

And show them that thy steel's still keen
In one more battle dire.

There was a possibility of a new rising in the summer of 1751, and it is very likely that MacDonald's book was published (with the printers wisely withholding his name from the title-page) to help to promote this. The book is excessively rare today, only about a dozen copies existing. The usual story is that the stock was burnt by the common hangman in Edinburgh in 1752; but no official order for the book's destruction has ever been found.

In the light of this poetry, and MacDonald's career in the Forty-five as the first officer commissioned by Prince Charles, whose unofficial Gaelic tutor he became – he had raised fifty 'cliver fellows' in Ardnamurchan for the Jacobite army in July 1745★ and fought in the Clanranald regiment throughout the campaign, later giving Bishop Forbes a considerable amount of information about it – it is astonishing to find that for at least fifteen years before that date, Alexander MacDonald had been employed at a salary never more than £18 a year working as a catechist and schoolmaster for the very anti-Jacobite SPCK at various times at Kilmory, Islandfinnan, Kilchoan, and Coirivulin in Ardnamurchan. There was a proposal in 1742 to send him to South Uist in this capacity. One can only suggest that this situation arose in consequence of some personal quarrel with his chief Donald of Clanranald, who succeeded his cousin Ronald, son of Donald Dubh, in 1725. This Donald, then of Benbecula, married his predecessor's sister Janet. If so, the breach must have come after February 1727, for there is a document in the Clanranald papers written and witnessed by 'Alex^r MackDonald second son to the Deceased Mr Alex^r MackDonald Min^r of Islandfinan' on 28 February 1727, regarding a debt due by the Clanranalds to Roderick MacLeod of Contullich.[6]

Alexander MacDonald's father was, according to *Clan Donald*, the fourth son of Ranald MacDonald of Milton, South Uist, who himself was a grandson of Raghnall mac Ailein 'ic

★ *Lockhart Papers*, ii. 479, 'Journall and Memoirs of Prince Charles' expedition into Scotland, etc. 1745–6., by a Highland Officer in his Army'. There can be no doubt whatever that, as was first pointed out by Compton MacKenzie, MacDonald was the Highland officer in question.

Iain of Benbecula who had supported the Irish Franciscans in the 1620s and 1630s. He graduated MA at Glasgow University in 1674, was ordained by the then established Episcopal Church, and became minister of Islandfinan in Moidart, where he remained for the rest of his life. He was married to a MacLachlan lady. He remained in his parish as a Non-Jurant minister after the revolution of 1690.

'Alasdair mac Mhaighstir Alasdair', his second son, is said to have been born in 1690, to have been a student at Glasgow University, and to have left without taking a degree owing to an imprudent early marriage. It is also said that he went there to study for the ministry, but left for lack of funds.[7] These assertions cannot be maintained: had he been born in 1690 and made a student marriage, say around 1710, his children could not have been described as 'my weak family' as he called them in a letter of 5 December 1730 to Sir Alexander Murray of Stanhope,* nor could his wife have been pregnant in 1746, as he told Bishop Forbes she was when they were on the run after Culloden. In any case Glasgow University has no record of Alexander MacDonald, son of 'Maighstir Alasdair', as a student. The likeliest date for Alexander MacDonald's birth is around 1700; there is nothing in his poems about the 1715 rising, but plenty to suggest that he was acquainted with the account of the Montrose wars in the Book of Clanranald, which I have quoted in an earlier chapter.

He was well educated; there are classical and biblical references in his poems, and when the SPCK decided on the production of an 'English and Irish Vocabulary', 'as a means to extirpate the Irish Language' on 4 November 1725, he was the person ultimately charged by the Presbytery of Lorne with its production. In which he had undoubtedly had the help of the Revd John MacLean of Kilninian, the informant of Edward Lhuyd, a very sympathetic personality and himself an excellent Gaelic poet. The work, 'A Galick and English Vocabulary', really a translation of Latin word-lists, was finished in 1738, when the SPCK paid MacDonald £10 for his labour; it was printed by R. Fleming for £45. 10s. 0d. and sent to the SPCK's schools in 1741.

* I am obliged to Dr B. S. Megaw for drawing my attention to this letter. Murray of Stanhope was interested in the lead mines at Strontian.

Meanwhile MacDonald's official salary as an SPCK school-master and catechist had been reduced from £18 to £15 in 1738, to £14 in 1740, and to £12 in 1743. In April 1745 it was reported that he had been absent for most of the preceding summer, though the school had been supplied by his son. Two months later the Committee of the SPCK recorded that 'It's repre-sented . . . that Alex^r MacDonald Schoolmaster at Ardnamurchan is an offence to all Sober Well inclin'd persons as he wanders thro' the Country composing Galick songs, stuffed with obscene Language.' Probably this refers to his Rabelaisian song on the subject of the libidinous behaviour of two old fellows in Ardnamurchan; his political satires were composed later. The Committee recommended that the Synod of Glenelg should be asked to look into the matter. Three weeks later, on 4 July 1745, the Committee decided to dismiss MacDonald, who they had been told had left his school at Coirivulin. On the eighteenth MacDonald was aboard the *Du Teillay* at Loch nan Uamh along with his brother Angus, his cousin Alexander MacDonald of Glenaladale, and the son and heir of his chief, Ranald MacDonald of Clanranald, welcoming Prince Charles. In the interval it is believed he had become a Catholic.

After the disaster at Culloden, where it is not true that the MacDonalds refused to charge because they were placed on the left wing of the Prince's army,[8] MacDonald was on the run until the Act of Indemnity was passed in June 1747. After that he became an important informant of the Revd Robert Forbes, an Episcopalian clergyman and ardent Jacobite who later became Bishop of Ross and Caithness, and who made it a life's work to collect all the reminiscences of participants in the 1745–6 rising that he could.* On 10 July 1749 Forbes wrote to MacDonald:

You know well how I employ much of my time, and how anxious I am to make up as compleat and exact a collection as possible of some certain memorable events, etc. And therefore I hope I need not to use many words to prevail with you to give me all the assistance in your power. You told me you intended to take up your abode in Egg or Canna, which if you do, then it will be in your power to make up

* Published by the Scottish History Society in three volumes, 1895–6, under the title of *The Lyon in Mourning*, and probably their most popular publication.

an exact account of the severe pillaging and plunderings that were committed in these islands. You know I like much to have everything minutely and circumstantially narrated. Forget not then to give the names of those who were principally concerned in pillaging Egg and Canna, such as officers of sogers, commanders of ships, sloops, or yachts. Be mindful likewise to make as exact a calculation as you can of the damages sustaind by the inhabitants of these two islands. In a word, send me an account of everything you can have well vouched. I need not point out particulars to you; for well do you know what I want and what will suit my taste.

Remember me to Dalely and Laig when you happen to see them. It will at all times add to my happiness to hear of your welfare and that of your family, to whom I wish everything that is good. I ever am, Honest Allaster, your most affectionate friend and very humble servant,

ROBERT FORBES.

On 22 April 1751, when on a visit to Edinburgh probably in connection with the publication of his book, Alexander MacDonald called on Forbes and gave him a statement of the Hanoverian atrocities in Eigg and Canna. The part of that statement connected with Canna is reproduced here:

Upon the 3d of April 1746, Lieutennant Thomas Brown, an Irish gentleman with a command of 80 men, did sail with a tender from the *Baltimore* man of war by Captain Fergusons order, which layed then at the harbour of Lochnadaal at Sky, at whose end Lord Loudon had a camp then, came to the haven of Canna, and after sending for James M'Donald, bailie of the Island, and uncle to Glenaladal,* told him he was sent by Captains Ferguson and Dove for some fresh beef and mutton, vizt., 20 fat cows and so many wedders. The gentleman asking his orders was answered he would show him noe commission of that kind, but if he would not present his demands without further controul he would take them *brevi manu*. He had 60 armed men at his heels; the flower of the Islanders was with the Prince; soe that the bailie judged it safer both for himself and inhabitants to grant his request, and consequently sent off to the meadows for the above number of cattle, and took them up in proportion to the number of the tenements the Isle consisted of.

But being wind-bound for 4 days in Canna harbour, behold! they complained to the said bailie the beef of the cattle slaughter'd stunk, and that the country should give them the same number over again.

* And Alexander MacDonald's cousin. He held Coroghon and Sanday from Clanranald at a rent of 178¹/₃ merks (£266. 14s. 4d. Scots).

The bailie reckoned this both unjust and cruel, and that it was enough for the poor inhabitants to gratify him of what they received already. Upon which the officer was petted and said with a rage he knew where and by whom he woud be served. He meant Laaig's cattle, whom he heard was in the Prince's army. So he hurls away his 60 armed men, gathers all the cattle of the Isle into a particular creek, shot 60 of the best dead, threw the old beef overboard and woud not allow the poor distressed owners to finger a gobbet of it, no, not a single tripe of the first or former. 40 of the last cattle belonged to Laaig,* 20 to the tennants.

Captain Duff and Captain Ferguson aboard the *Commodore* came again a little, or about the 15 of April, harrass'd all the Isle, and at a certain night when they became fully acquaint through all the country, they (I mean all the young luxurious men among them) combined to make ane attack upon all the girls and young women in all the Isle marryed or otherwise. But a certain marine who had some grains of Christian principles about him advertised the whole, and was obliged to climb to hide themselves in grottos and in the hollow of hideous precipices that were somewhat unaccessable, which rescued them from the unhumanity of those libidinous hounds.

A certain company of them came to execute their sensuality into a certain family, Evan More MacIsaac, his house, from which fled two girls, the landlord's daughters. Their mother who was fifty years old, worn with sickness and within a mouth of her time, stayed at home as dreading noe danger of that sort. But they missing their aim and geting none of the females within a houseroof but that poor creature, they setts a strong guard with drawn swords upon the door of her house, fettered her husband in order to quench their concupiscence on his spouse. Providence favourd the creature so far that she wonn out through the guard, and the darkness of the night concurrd to make her rescue. For they got out in pursuit of her a great hurry, and 12 of them was at her heels, when she meeting and sinking down into the very depth of a quaggmire, they leaps over her believing she was still before them. The poor woman contented herself to continue their all the night, till she understood they were all back to their ships. But when she was so much afflicted with the rigour of the cold, and she being bigg with child, turned ill, aborted and died next night. The rest continued their sculking in a starving condition till the men of war sail'd off.

After the battle of Culloden was hard fought, Captain Dove and

---

* John MacDonald III of Laig in Eigg. He held the 'town and lands of Tarbet' in Canna from Clanranald at a rent of £223. 6s. 8d. (335 merks). He was descended from Alexander II of Morar. He was succeeded in Laig by Alexander MacDonald's son Ronald around 1770.

Captain Fergusone went to Canna successively and committed several branches of cruelty upon the poor people, wanting them to inform them of the Prince or any of his officers. After General Campbell* turned back from the search of his Royal Highness from the Western Coast, he calls at Canna, and hurls away the honest bailie prisoner into his ship without allowing him to speak for himself, or as much time as to shift himself or take leave of his wife. At this stretch he was brought the length of Horseshoe† in the shire of Argile, from Horseshoe was brought back to Canna. Then he believed he would be liberate, but instead thereof they caus'd 40 of his cows to be slaughtered, would not permit him as much liberty as goe ashore to take leave of his wife or children, or to bring his cloaths with him, but brought him prisoner to London where he continued upwards of 12 month, notwithstanding of Loudon's protection in his pocket.

This 'Loudon' was John Campbell, fourth Earl of Loudoun, who fled with Cope from the battle of Prestonpans, and later commanded the forces raised in the north for King George I by Forbes of Culloden, which were ridiculously repulsed by Lady MacIntosh at the 'Rout of Moy'.

Of the 'flower of the islanders' from Canna, we only know one name, that of Hugh MacDonald from Tarbert, described in the 'Prisoners of the Forty-Five' as a labourer, in 'Fairback's' regiment, captured at Duddingston on 6 November 1745 and gaoled in Edinburgh on 25 January 1746. He was afterwards discharged.

Alexander MacDonald undoubtedly must have composed some of his poetry while Baillie of Canna. There is a strong local tradition that at least part of his famous epic on the Galley of Clanranald and its voyage through a storm from Loch Eynort in South Uist to Carrickfergus in Ulster was composed in Canna, while he was lying under an upturned boat at the head of Canna Harbour near the spot known as 'Lag nam Boitean'. The same tradition exists in South Uist about Loch Eynort.

In the course of this long poem the assigning of various members of the crew to various tasks is described, and two stout fellows from Canna, Donald MacCormick and John Johnston, are given that of attending to the mainsail halyard.

* General John Campbell of Mamore, afterwards fourth Duke of Argyll.
† Horseshoe Harbour in the island of Kerrera, off Oban.

In the 1749 rental of Canna, there is a Donald Johnston mentioned as holding a half-pennyland in the Kirktown of Canna; and in 1818 there was a P. MacCarmic and a John MacCarmic among the tenants of Sanday, where the former tenants of Lag a' Bhaile at Coroghon had been moved to make kelp between 1788 and 1805.

Alexander MacDonald mentions Canna twice in his *Aiseiridh*. The first time is in his famous poem in the form of a waulking song, addressed to Prince Charles under the penning of 'Mórag', a song which is still popular.

> *Mo chion a dheanadh leat éirigh,*
> *Do Chaiptin fhéin Mac-Mhic-Ailein.*
>
> *Gun theann e roimhe roimh chàch riut,*
> *'S nì e fàs è, ach thig thairis.*
>
> *Gach duine tha 'n Uidhist 's am Mùideart,*
> *'S an Arasaig dhùbh ghorm a' bharraich.*
>
> *An Canaidh, an Eige, 's am Móror,*
> *Réisimeid chòir ud Shìol-Ailein!*
>
> *An am Alasdair is Mhontròis,*
> *Gum bu bhòcain iad air Ghallaibh!*

> My friend would rise with you,
> Your own Captain of Clanranald.
>
> He adhered to you before all others,
> And will do so yet, but come over.
>
> Every man in Uist and Moidart
> And in dark-green Arisaig of birch-woods.
>
> In Canna, in Eigg, and in Morar,
> The true regiment of the MacDonalds!
>
> At the time of Alasdair [Mac Colla] and Montrose,
> They were terrors to the Lowlands!

The other occasion is in his political poem called 'The Ark', in which he designates at great length the fate in store for various Campbell lairds and their adherents for their behaviour in 1745–6. Some are to be left to drown in the ocean for their political crimes, some are to be given a dousing in the brine but pulled aboard the Ark when purged of their

Whiggish taints, and some are to be welcomed on the Ark immediately as true royalists. The last group includes the Campbells of Inverawe, Carwhin, Airds, and Lochnell. It is very evident that the Clan Campbell was not the monolithic Whig organization in 1745 that it is sometimes described as being.

A particular object of detestation to Alexander MacDonald was Mrs Campbell of Barr, a poetess who had composed what is probably the only known Whig Gaelic poem connected with the Forty-five. It is lost now, but from Alexander's replies to it we know it questioned the legitimacy of King James VIII. In the Ark Alexander MacDonald wrote of her:

> *Ma thig a bhan-bhárd na d' líonamh;*
>   *Ostag mhío-narach an Obain,*
> *Ceangail achdair r'i do bhrandi,*
>   *Go bi toirt dram do'n a rónamh:*
>
> *Ach ma chinnis i na Jonah*
>   *'S a sluggadh beo le muic-mhara:*
> *Go meal i a cairstealan fheólain;*
>   *Ach a sgeith air córsa Chana.*[9]

> If the poetess comes into your nets,
>   The shameless little female pub-keeper from Oban,
> Tie an anchor of brandy to her
>   To give a dram to the seals.
>
> But if she becomes a Jonah,
>   And is swallowed alive by a whale,
> May she enjoy her fleshy quarters
>   Provided she be spewed up on the coast of Canna.

– where, no doubt, Alasdair mac Mhaighstir Alasdair would have dealt with her.

There is a tradition that he addressed an opprobrious quatrain to some Canna men fishing from the rocks of Rubha Cairinnis on Canna when leaving the island on a little boat for South Uist. I heard this anecdote from Angus MacDonald (Aonghus Eachainn 1863–1948) not long after I first came to Canna. Later Dr Calum MacLean recorded it for the Irish Folklore Commission. I give my translation of his transcription:

Alexander MacDonald was for a time living in Canna. He was bailie for one of the Clanranalds when they had Canna. One fine day he was going over to Uist in a rowing boat, and some old men of the island were down at the place called Gob a' Rubha, the point past the pier. When Alexander was going past, one of the old men who was fishing for cuddies said to him: 'Won't you give your opinion of us now, Alasdair?.' 'I will do that', he said; and he said to them:

> *Thug sibh ur cùl ris na creagan*
> *Buidheann fhiata nan glùn giobach;*
> *'S olc an dream sibh, ge nach trod sibh,*
> *Na fir mhóra, ròmach, ghiobach!*

You with your backs to the cliffs
A wild crowd with hairy knees;
You're a bad tribe, even if you aren't quarrelling,
Big shaggy hairy fellows!

Just how long Mac Mhaighstir Alasdair remained as Baillie of Canna is unknown. In fact for a person who is well known as the leading Gaelic poet of the Highlands and as the former officer in the Jacobite army who was an important informant of Bishop Forbes, extraordinarily little is known about his life after 1751. After he left Canna he was for a time tenant of the farm of Eigneig in Moydart; after leaving Eigneig, from which he said in one of his poems he was summarily evicted by the factor, he went to Inverie in Knoydart, which in the same poem he praises to the skies by comparison with Eigneig. The same song[10] makes it clear that he had also quarrelled with the local clergyman, presumably the priest Fr. William Harrison, who is said to have disapproved strongly of Alasdair's ribald songs.[11] From Inverie he went to Arisaig, where he died around 1770, and is buried. His ghost has been seen in South Uist a number of times this century.

There is a strong aura of a man whose career had gone wrong about him, such as might attach to a spoilt priest or minister. A bitter quarrel with his parents is hinted at in the poem on the flyting between himself and the Mull plough-man. But we know no details. Alasdair was certainly a remarkably well-educated man, who left a very strong mark on Highland history and Scottish Gaelic literature. We may well wish we knew more about his sojourn on Canna.

NOTES

1. A. MacKenzie, *History of the MacDonalds*, pp. 427–8.
2. *Clan Donald*, ii. 358–9; *Forfeited Estates Papers*, p. 312.
3. See Appendix X.
4. *Archaeologia Britannica*, Preface. See also Campbell and Thomson, *Edward Lhuyd in the Scottish Highlands*.
5. A considerable amount of MacDonald's Jacobite verse can be found in the writer's *Highland Songs of the Forty-Five*, published in 1933, second edition in 1983.
6. Reproduced in the 1924 edition of Alexander MacDonald's Gaelic poems.
7. John MacKenzie, *Sàr Obair nam Bàrd*, p. 101 (1865 edn.); Revd Charles MacDonald, *Moidart or Among the Clanranalds*, pp. 152–3.
8. Agnes Mure MacKenzie, *The Passing of the Stewarts*, p. 434.
9. 1751 edition, p. 180.
10. 'Iumairich Alaistir as Eignaig do dh Ioibhir-aoidh', *Eigg Collection*, pp. 143–6.
11. Revd Charles MacDonald, op. cit. 156. Alasdair may very well have disapproved of Fr. Harrison's not supporting the Jacobite cause in 1745.

A note in Bundle 117 of the Dunvegan Papers proves that Alexander MacDonald the 'Famous Composer of Morack' (i.e. the well-known Gaelic poem in praise of Mórag) was installed on Canna by 10 April 1750.

The researches of Mr Ian Stewart, past President of the Kintyre Antiquarian Society, on the MacNeill families of Kintyre, have revealed that the 'Black Lachann of Balligrogan' denounced as a Hanoverian informer by Alexander MacDonald in his poem 'The Ark' (1751) was a Kintyre MacNeill possibly related to Hector MacNeill who came to Canna in 1781 (see Chapter 14).

12   THE COMING OF THE EARLY SCIENTISTS

In the last quarter of the seventeenth century men in Britain and abroad were beginning to get weary of politico-religious controversy and the civil disorders and conflicts that arose from it, and began to turn their minds to natural philosophy and to take an interest in the survivals of antiquity and the curiosities of nature; except in Scotland, where the Revolution of 1688, the 1690 settlement, and the Union with England in 1707 revived sectarian politics for another two generations[1] – not without later relapses.

Early accounts of the Isles, beginning with that of Dean Monro, are written from what can be called an old-fashioned aristocratic point of view. That is, they are interested in the identity of the superiors and the occupiers of the islands, in game animals and birds and fish, such as red deer, falcons, and salmon; in the quality of land for cultivation and/or grazing; in the number of fighting men an island can produce; and in rents, teinds, and church buildings. Occasionally unusual features are mentioned, such as Coroghon 'castle', used as a place of refuge and later as a prison on Canna. But on the whole things like archaeological and natural history features, and local Gaelic folklore and traditions, are not treated as of any great interest.

Martin Martin's great books on St Kilda and the Western Isles instituted an entirely new approach. They were, of course, written under the influence of the late-seventeenth-century scientific awakening. They awoke the learned world to the fact that the Highlands and Islands of Scotland were a repository of remarkably archaic survivals. Previously Robert Kirk, the Episcopalian minister of Aberfoyle who published a transcription of Bedell's Irish Bible in Roman lettering for the Highlanders in 1690, had written his account of Highland folk belief – *The Secret Commonwealth or a Treatise displaying the Chief Curiosities among the People of Scotland as they are in use to this Day* – for the interest of his friends Bishop and Mrs

Stillingfleet, in 1692.* Highland Second Sight became an object of intense interest to these enquirers; was it or was it not a gift acquired through a pact with Satan? If it was, the possessor was in considerable danger; the last burning for witchcraft in Scotland occurred as late as 1722. J. Aubrey's *Miscellanies*, published in 1696, contain twenty-nine pages of 'second sight' stories transmitted from the Scottish Highlands. The greatest of all these antiquarians was the Welsh polymath, Edward Lhuyd, 1660–1709, Keeper of the Ashmolean Museum at Oxford, who undertook a four-year survey of the Celtic countries in 1697, collecting an enormous amount of archaeological, geological, botanical, and linguistic information, and many Welsh and Gaelic manuscripts; but his tour in the Highlands was confined to Argyll, Mull, Iona, and Kintyre in the autumn and winter of 1699–1700.† Research on all these subjects still continues, though nowadays tending to become statistical and depersonalized as compared with that of the earlier authors.

Martin Martin's account of Canna² is brief. The dimensions he gives of the island, in Scots miles, suggest that his information was at second hand, and his orientation suggests that he was relying on Andrew Johnston's map, published in 1695. *Tarsin* (*Tarsainn*, 'across-wise') for Canna would be the sea-kenning for the true name of the island, unlucky to be uttered while at sea; similarly Rum was called *Rìoghachd na Forraiste Fiadhaich*, 'the Kingdom of the Wild Forest', and Eigg was called *Eilean nam Ban Móra*, 'the Island of Big Women', by the islanders when at sea. Heiskeir, also called *Heisgeir nan Cuiseag*, 'Heiskeir of the Rushes', is the fifty-acre island six miles south of the west end of Canna, still the property of the writer. Allan MacDonald was the son of Donald Dubh of Clanranald, having succeeded in 1686. Martin gives the earliest description of the magnetic properties of Compass Hill.

---

* Edward Stillingfleet was Dean of St Paul's 1678–89 and Bishop of Worcester 1689–99. See Mario M. Rossi, *Il Cappellano delle Fate, con Testo Originale e Traduzione del Regno Segreto di Robert Kirk*, Naples, 1964.

† See Campbell and Thomson, *Edward Lhuyd in the Scottish Highlands, 1699–1700*. Lhuyd's diaries unfortunately were lost in a fire, but his rough notes, some written in Welsh, his sketches of monuments on Iona, and most of the Irish MSS he collected, have survived, as well as letters he wrote to other scholars about his survey.

Isle CANAY.

THIS Isle lies about half a Mile of *Rum*; it is two Miles from South to North, one from East to West. It is for the most part surrounded with a high Rock, and the whole fruitful in Corn and Grass: The South end hath plenty of Cod and Ling.

THERE is a high Hill in the North end, which disorders the Needle in the Compass: I laid the Compass on the stony Ground near it, and the Needle went often round with great Swiftness, and instead of settling towards the North, as usual, it settled here due East. The Stones in the Surface of the Earth are black, and the Rock below facing the Sea is red; some affirm that the Needle of a Ship's Compass, sailing by the Hill, is disorder'd by the Force of the Magnet in this Rock: but of this I have no Certainty.

THE Natives call this Isle by the Name *Tarsin* at Sea; the Rock *Heisker* on the South end abounds with wild Geese in *August*, and then they cast their Quills. The Church in this Isle is dedicated to St. *Columbus*. All the Natives are Roman Catholicks; they use the Language and Habit of the other Isles. *Allan Mack-Donald* is Proprietor. There is good Anchorage on the North-East of this Isle.

But the classical early scientific account of Canna is that made by Thomas Pennant on his second tour in 1772, after the dust raised by the 'Forty-Five' had finally settled down, and printed in his *Tour in Scotland and Voyage to the Hebrides*, published in 1776, and dedicated to Sir Joseph Banks, the great botanist who accompanied Captain Cook on his expedition around the world in the *Endeavour*, 1768–71; this is illustrated by the first drawing of Coroghon 'castle', made by Moses Griffiths:

FISHERY.   At seven o'clock in the evening [of July 11th, 1772] find ourselves at anchor in four fathom water, in the snug harbour of the isle of CANNAY, Formed on the N. side by *Cannay*, on the South by the little isle of *Sanda*: the mouth lies opposite to *Rum*, and about three miles distant: the Western channel into it is impervious, by reason of rocks. On that side of the entrance next to *Sanda* is a rock to be shunned by mariners.

As soon as we had time to cast our eyes about, each shore appeared pleasing to humanity; verdant, and covered with hundreds of cattle: both sides gave a full idea of plenty, for the verdure was mixed with very little rock, and scarcely any heath: but a short conversation with the natives soon dispelled this agreeable error: they were at this very time in such want, that numbers for a long time had neither bread nor meal for their poor babes: fish and milk was their whole subsistence at this time: the first was a precarious relief, for, besides the uncertainty of success, to add to their distress, their stock of fish-hooks was almost exhausted; and to ours, that it was not in our power to supply them. The rubbans, and other trifles I had brought would have been insults to people in distress. I lamented that my money had been so uselessly laid out; for a few dozens of fish-hooks, or a few pecks of meal, would have made them happy. The *Turks* erect *caravansaras*. Christians of different opinions concur in establishing *hospitia* among the dreary *Alps*, for the reception of travellers. I could wish the public bounty, or private charity, would found in fit parts of the isles or mainland, magazines of meal, as preservatives against famine in these distant parts.

CROPS.   The crops had failed here the last year: but the little corn sown at present had a promising aspect: and the potatoes are the best I had seen: but these were not fit for use. The isles I fear annually experience a temporary famine: perhaps from improvidence, perhaps from eagerness to encrease their stock of cattle, which they can easily dispose of to satisfy the demands of a landlord, or the oppressions of an agent. The people of *Cannay* export none, but sell them to the numerous busses, who put into this *Portus Salutis* on different occasions.

CATTLE.   The cattle are of a middle size, black, long-legged, and have thin staring manes from the neck along the back, and up part of the tail. They look well, for in several parts of the islands they have good warm recesses to retreat to in winter. About sixty head are exported annually.

Each couple of milch cows yielded at an average seven stones of butter and cheese: two thirds of the first and one of the last. The cheese sold at three and sixpence a stone; the butter at eight shillings.

HORSES.   Here are very few sheep: but horses in abundance. The chief use of them in this little district is to form an annual cavalcade at *Michaelmas*. Every man on the island mounts his horse unfurnished with saddle, and takes behind him either some young girl, or his neighbor's wife, and then rides backwards and forwards from the village to a certain

SINGULAR
CUSTOM.

cross, without being able to give any reason for the origin of this custom. After the procession is over, they alight at some public house, where, strange to say, the females treat the companions of their ride. When they retire to their houses an entertainment is prepared with primæval simplicity: the chief part consists of a great oat-cake, called *Struan-Micheil*, or St. *Michael's* cake, composed of two pecks of meal, and formed like the quadrant of a circle: it is daubed over with milk and eggs, and then placed to harden before the fire.

Matrimony is held in such esteem here, that an old maid or old batchelor is scarcely known; such firm belief have they in the doctrine of the ape-leading disgrace in the world below. So, to avoid that danger the youth marry at twenty, the lasses at seventeen. The fair sex are used here with more tenderness than common, being employed only in domestic affairs, and never forced into the labors of the field. Here are plenty of poultry and of eggs.

Abundance of cod and ling might be taken; there being a fine sand-bank between this isle and the rock *Heisker*, and another between *Skie* and *Barra*; but the poverty of the inhabitants will not enable them to attempt a fishery. When at *Campbeltown* I enquired about the apparatus requisite, and found that a vessel of twenty tuns was necessary, which would cost two hundred pounds; that the crew should be composed of eight hands, whose monthly expences would be fourteen pounds; that six hundred fathom of *long-line*, five hundred hooks, and two *Stuoy* lines (each eighty fathoms long) which are placed at each end of the long-lines, with buoys at top to mark the place when sunk, would all together cost five guineas; and the vessel must be provided with four sets: so that the whole charge of such an adventure is very considerable, and past the ability of these poor people.

RENTS.

The length of the island is about three miles; the breadth near one: its surface hilly. This was the property of the bishop of the isles, but at present that of Mr. *Macdonald* of *Clan-Ronald*. His factor, a resident agent, rents most of the island, paying two guineas for each *penny-land*; and these he sets to the poor people at four guineas and a half each; and exacts, besides this, three days labor in the quarter from each person. Another head tenant possesses other penny-lands, which he sets in the same manner, to the impoverishing and very starving of the wretched inhabitants.

The *penny-lands* derive their names from some old valuation. The sum requisite to stock one is thirty pounds: it maintains seven cows and two horses; and the tenant can raise on it eight bolls of small black oats, the produce of two; and four of bear from half a boll of seed; one boll of potatoes yields seven. The two last are manured with sea-tang.

The arable land in every farm is divided into four parts, and lots are cast for them at *Christmas*: the produce, when reaped and dried, is divided among them in proportion to their rents; and for want of mills is ground in the quern. All the pasture is common, from *May* to the beginning of *September*.

It is said that the factor has in a manner banished sheep, because there is no good market for them; so that he does his best to deprive the inhabitants of cloathing as well as food. At present they supply themselves with wool from *Rum*, at the rate of eightpence the pound.

MANU-
FACTURES.
All the cloathing is manufactured at home: the women not only spin the wool, but weave the cloth: the men make their own shoes, tan the leather with the bark of willow, or the roots of the *tormentilla erecta*, or *tormentil*, and in defect of wax-thread, use split thongs.

About twenty tuns of kelp are made in the shores every third year.

Sickness seldom visits this place: if any disorder seizes them the patients do no more than drink whey, and lie still. The small-pox visits them about once in twenty years.

All disputes are settled by the factor, or, if of great moment, by the justices of the peace in *Skie*.

This island, *Rum*, *Muck*, and *Egg*, forms one parish. *Cannay* is inhabited by two hundred and twenty souls; of
RELIGION.
which all, except four families, are *Roman Catholics*; but in the whole parish there is neither church, manse, nor school: there is indeed in this island a catechist, who has nine pounds a year from the royal bounty. The minister and the popish priest reside in *Egg*; but, by reason of the turbulent seas that divide these isles, are very seldom able to attend their flocks. I admire the moderation of their congregations, who attend the preaching of either indiffe-

rently as they happen to arrive. As the *Scotch* are œconomists in religion, I would recommend to them the practice of one of the little *Swiss* mixed cantons, who, through mere frugality, kept but one divine; a moderate honest fellow, who, steering clear of controversial points, held forth to the *Calvinist* flock on one part of the day, and to his *Catholic* on the other.* He lived long among them much respected, and died lamented.

The protestant natives of many of the isles observe *Yule* and *Pasch*, or *Christmas* and *Easter*, which among rigid presbyterians is esteemed so horrid a superstition, that I have heard of a minister who underwent a censure for having a goose to dinner on *Christmas* day; as if any one day was more holy than another, or to be distinguished by any external marks of festivity.

In popish times here was probably a resident minister; for here are to be seen the ruins of a chapel, and a small cross.

Much rain and very hard gales the whole night; the weather being, as it is called in these parts, broken.

JULY 12. Bad weather still continues, which prevented us from seeing so much of this island as we intended, and also of visiting the rock *Humbla*. Go on shore at the nearest part, and visit a lofty slender rock, that juts into the sea: on one side is a little tower, at a vast height above us, accessible by a narrow and horrible path: it seems so small as scarce to be able to contain half a dozen people. Tradition says, that it was built by some jealous *regulus*, to confine a handsome wife in.

COMPASS-HILL. To the North-West above this prison, is the *Compass hill*, in *Erse* called *Sgor-dhearg*, or the red projecting rock. On the top the needle in the mariners compass was observed to vary a whole quarter; the North point standing due West: an irregularity probably owing to the nature of the rock, highly impregnated with iron.

COAL. In the afternoon some coal was brought, found in the rocks *Dun-eudain*, but in such small veins as to be useless. It lies in beds of only six inches in thickness, and about a foot distant from each other, divided by strata of whin-stone.

* Sir James Campbell of Ardkinglas (1745–1831) records that in the church which he and his wife attended while staying in Basle (around 1818) 'in the morning high mass was performed with all the insignia of Popish worship. In the afternoon, the crucifix and the altar-piece were concealed by a curtain, and the Protestants assembled in their simpler fashion to say their prayers and hear a sermon.' (*Memoirs*, ii. 292.)

> Fuel is very scarce here, and often the inhabitants are obliged to fetch it from *Rum*.

JULY 13   A continuation of bad weather. At half an hour after one at noon, loose from *Cannay*, and after passing with a favorable gale through a rolling sea, in about two hours, anchor in the Isle of RUM.

Dr Samuel Johnson and James Boswell, most famous of all the visitors to the Hebrides, arrived at Armadale in Skye on 2 September 1773. Dr Johnson's interest in the Isles was literary, historical, and sentimentally Jacobite. The literary aspect of it was due to the publication of the first volume of James MacPherson's alleged translations of the poems of Ossian, which had appeared ten years before, creating a literary sensation. Dr Johnson denied both the authenticity and the merit of the poems, but was interested enough to investigate their background and the possibility of ancient Gaelic manuscripts surviving in the Highlands and Islands. He did not allow ignorance of the Gaelic language to embarrass him; English-speaking writers and historians seldom do. Still less was he conversant with the concept of a traditional oral literature. For two generations the Ossianic controversy was to continue, creating an enormous amount of heat; one side arguing that the poetry published by James MacPherson could not possibly be authentic, the other arguing as passionately that they were the real thing. Neither was right; the fact was that MacPherson had woven themes from the old traditional ballads connected with Fionn Mac Cumhail and his band, into a fantastic epic poetry of his own.*

Had this explanation been put to Dr Johnson, he would have probably demanded proofs, which might not have been easily forthcoming; what is surprising is that he seems to have been utterly ignorant of his famous fellow-Oxonian Edward Lhuyd's Celtic tour, manuscript discoveries, and book *Archaeologia Britannica*. Dr Johnson was familiar with Pennant's *Tour* and Martin Martin's *Description of the Western Islands*. He had a great admiration for Pennant's book, which he defended against its islander critics.[3] He had read Martin's book when a young man, and it had aroused his interest in the Hebrides.

* The reader should consult D. S. Thomson, *The Gaelic Sources of MacPherson's Ossian*, on this matter.

What was very much to Dr Johnson's credit was the stinging rebuke he gave the SPCK privately through William Drummond, the Edinburgh bookseller, when he heard that some political members of the Society had opposed the project of publishing the New Testament in Scottish Gaelic on the grounds that doing so would tend to preserve the distinction between Highlanders and Lowlanders.[4]

Unfortunately Dr Johnson and Boswell never reached Canna on their tour. Dr Johnson regretted this himself; 'if we had travelled with more leisure, it had not been fit to have neglected the Popish islands. Popery is favourable to ceremony; and among ignorant nations ceremony is the only preservation of tradition. Since Protestantism was extended to the savage parts of Scotland, it has perhaps been one of the chief labours of the Ministers to abolish stated observances, because they continued the remembrance of the former religion. We therefore who came to hear old traditions, and see antiquated manners, should probably have found them amongst the Papists.'[5]

Dr Johnson had the idea that 'the Romish religion is professed only in E[i]gg and Canna, two small islands into which the Reformation never made its way'. It is odd that no one told him about South Uist and Barra, but perhaps he was thinking in terms of the orbit of his tour. 'If any [Catholic] missionaries are busy in the Highlands, their zeal entitles them to respect, even from those who cannot think favourably of their doctrine', he went on to write.[6] He and Boswell got no nearer to Canna than Tallisker in Skye, an estate they much admired, from where they would have been able to see Canna.

At Armadale, where they landed in Skye, Dr Johnson and Boswell, who were guests of Sir Alexander MacDonald of Sleat, met at his house one Donald MacLeod, 'a very genteel man', who had previously held a farm on Canna, and who acted as their guide on Skye for the next fortnight. Boswell says that he was the son of one of MacLeod of Dunvegan's ministers, and that the late laird had educated him.[7] It is not possible to say from Scott's *Fasti* which MacLeod minister Donald's father was. Donald himself may have been the Donald MacLeod to whom Ranald MacDonald of Clanranald gave a lease of Keill and other lands of Canna for three 19-year terms from Whitsuntide 1760, on 22 June 1761; if not, he was almost certainly connected with him. Boswell says he had been a tenant in Canna, but had been dispossessed of his farm.

Their acquaintance ended on a rather sour note when, short of money at Dunvegan, Boswell gave Donald MacLeod a bill for £30 drawn on Sir W. Forbes and Co. to cash at Bracadale on 15 September 1773. Donald MacLeod did not reappear for twelve days, eventually turning up when they were at Coirechatachan, with only £22 of the money. He had used the other £8 to pay some debts for poor emigrants; however, he gave Boswell a good bill on MacLeod of Ose for the remaining £8 on 3 October.[8]

These early travellers were the forerunners of many others, most of whom were inspired by an interest in geology, or by general curiosity. James Anderson (1785); the heads of the British Fisheries Society in 1787 and 1788; George Dempster (1792); E. W. Clarke, the discoverer of cadmium (1797); Necker de Saussure (1807), the Swiss geologist who left an interesting account of Ranald MacDonald – Alexander MacDonald's son who had the farm of Laig on Eigg; Robert Jameson, mineralogist (1813); John MacCulloch (1824), the geologist and correspondent of Sir Walter Scott, who himself had visited Eigg in 1814; James Wilson (1842); Muir, author of *Ecclesiological Notes* (1856); Robert Buchanan (before 1871); Gordon Cummings (1876); R. G. Collingwood (1906); Thomas C. Lethbridge, the archaeologist (1924); Professor Alf Sommerfelt, the famous Norwegian linguist, in 1943; Dr Calum MacLean, the well-known folklore collector, in 1947; Dr Jedrzej Giertych, the Polish author, in 1951. Besides the earlier Italian of Catholic Church reports, Canna has been written about since 1800 in French, Norwegian, and Polish.

Right up to 1929, when MacBraynes's then new ships, the first *Lochmor* and the *Lochearn*, superseded the tiny *Plover* and *Cygnet* on their regular Hebridean schedules, visiting Canna and islands like it was still something of an adventure and a journey into the past, only to be attempted by travellers who could endure discomfort and seasickness, or by intrepid yachtsmen who ventured north of Ardnamurchan without the help of radar or radio-telephones, and often without auxiliary engines. The first yachtsman to call at Canna was John Scott of

Halkshill, the Greenock shipbuilder, with the *Frame* on 23 July 1796; an anonymous account of the tour was printed in the *Imperial Magazine* in 1819. A large number of yachts, including even American and Canadian ones, call at Canna nowadays.

NOTES

1. There always is this time-lag, e.g. the Irish Folklore Commission was founded in 1926; the School of Scottish Studies was not founded until 1951.
2. 1716 edition of Martin's *Description of the Western Islands*, p. 275.
3. Boswell, *Journal*, 182–3.
4. Ibid. 345.
5. Johnson, *Journey to the Western Islands*, 175–6.
6. Ibid. 145–6.
7. Boswell, *Journal*, 172.
8. Ibid. 225, 245.

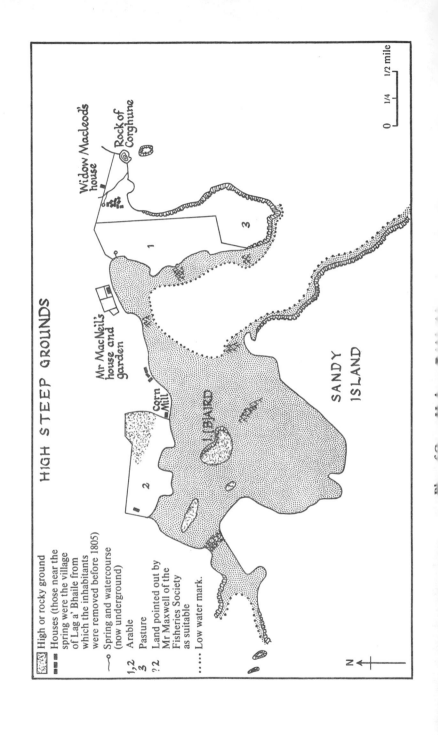

HIGH STEEP GROUNDS

Widow Macleod's house

Rock of Corghune

Mr MacNeil's house and garden

Corn Mill

LUBHARD

SANDY ISLAND

High or rocky ground

Houses (those near the spring were the village of Lag a' Bhaile from which the inhabitants were removed before 1805)

Spring and watercourse (now underground)

1,2 Arable
3 Pasture

?2 Land pointed out by Mr Maxwell of the Fisheries Society as suitable

.... Low water mark.

N

0   1/4   1/2 mile

13 CANNA AND THE BRITISH FISHERIES SOCIETY

The British Fisheries Society was incorporated with a capital of £150,000 in 1786 with the title of 'The British Society for Extending the Fisheries and Improving the Sea Coasts of this Kingdom'. It devoted itself largely to the establishment of fishery settlements. Although the headquarters of the Society were in London, the first settlements made or considered by the Society were in the north-west of Scotland, and there was a strong Scottish element in its directorate, which included the Duke of Argyll and the Earl of Breadalbane, first Governor and Deputy Governor of the Society, and MacKenzie of Seaforth, Lord Gower, the Earl of Moray, the Marquis of Graham, Sir Adam Ferguson, and George Dempster.* John MacKenzie of Arcan, near Dingwall, the Secretary of the Highland Society of London, was made the first Secretary of the Fisheries Society, which was moved by a genuine zeal for the good of the Highlands and Islands. There is a distinct suggestion of the atmosphere of the National Trust for Scotland about the British Fisheries Society in its early days.

The Society was responsible for founding fishing villages at Tobermory, Ullapool, Lochbay in Skye, and Wick. Canna with its excellent harbour was under its very serious consideration immediately. Hopes in that respect were unfortunately to be frustrated, as will be seen. The accounts of the Society's visits to Canna in the summers of 1787 and 1788 are of exceptional interest, and are reproduced here in their entirety. The 1787 Hebridean tour of the Society's directors was reported in serialized form in the March, April, and May 1792 numbers of the magazine *The Bee*:

5th July [1787] . . . Reached Cannay at four o'clock P.M. and were joined at eight by captain Macleod of Herries in his brig. A ling brought on board 5½ feet long, weight 44 lib.; – 3 shilling asked for it, because we were strangers to the price of fish there. Foggy and

* Dempster later wrote an account of 'The Magnetic Mountain of Cannay', published in the first volume of *Archaeologia Scotica* in 1792, p. 183.

rainy all day. Visited by Mr Macneal tacksman of Cannay, at whose house some of the party slept.

Cannay island.

July 6. Were informed repositories for salt must be on the ground-floor paved with brick. Cannay harbour is one of the finest in the Hebrides, about half a mile in length, shelving from eight to fourteen feet, and from thence to the beach the ground is good sand and clay, mixed. It is capable of containing about fifty sail of all kinds of vessels. It has an outlet to the east and west, so that fishers can go out in all seasons. The sea round abounds with cod, ling, and mullet; herrings are frequent round it, and a considerable quantity of fish are actually caught here now. Mr Macneal thinks a fishing station might be advantageously placed here, and would have no objection to co-operate with the society in establishing one. Beside the larger fish and herrings, without the harbour, the harbour itself swarms with a smaller kind of fish, about the size of haddocks. They are called *scythes* or *whiting pollock*, very useful for the maintenance of the people. They are often taken in small bag-nets; and, after taking out the livers for their oil, the rest of the fish are carried to the dunghill. Two hundred of them were taken last night by the cutter's boat; but the larger fish of the same kind carried off all their hooks. Seaforth strongly of opinion a society's fishing station should be established here, where a small embankment would suffice for unloading boats, which, with a few houses for holding salt, and huts for the fishers, and lots of land for farther building round the harbour, would be all the expence the experiment would cost the society.

A great many sun-fish or basking sharks are taken in these seas. The liver is oily, and the only part of the fish that is made use of. Went to see one which they said is small; – it is twenty feet long, – a very strong fish, much the shape of the shark, except the head and mouth; but not of its disposition, being far from voracious or dangerous; – its skin rough like shagreen. When cut to the bone, the outward part seemed like fish, but the inward, near the bone, like flesh, – certainly eatable. In Iceland ropes are made of the skin which is tough and strong. In the evening went a syeth-fishing with rods, lines, and hooks. The bait a white feather. Took in half an hour about 100, hooking them as fast as we could throw in the lines. Some as large as twelve or fifteen pounds; the medium about one pound and a half. They come to the surface, put their heads above the water, and make what is called a *play* of fish. The water bubbles as if it boiled, and this is the fishers guide. The herrings make a *play* of the same kind. On Sandy Island, which forms one side of the harbour, the party discovered a seam of coal cropping out to the surface, it did not exceed an inch in thickness; – gathered a basketful of the coal, – it burnt very well. Encouragement to try for a better vein of coal, or to pursue the same. Heard also coal had been discovered in Mull. It would probably be easier to find coal here, than to get the coal tax repealed or commuted: Natural difficulties are sometimes easier to overcome than political ones, especially of the tax kind.

7th July. In Cannay there are about three hundred inhabitants, all Roman Catholics, a sober, quiet industrious race, and not contemptible fishers, especially of the sun-fish*. The island, above six miles round, beautiful to the eye, abounding with good land, and exquisite pasture, very improveable. Mr Maclean [Macneal] has built a neat house of four rooms on a floor, two stories high. Its situation, facing the south and fronting the harbour, very pleasant; – is building a corn mill to go by water. The corn hitherto all ground in quearns. He is sole tacksman. Many of the inhabitants must leave the island.

Memorandum.

To make Cannay important, 1. The Society to accept of Clanronald's offer of a grant of land near the harbour.

2. To carry out a little pier, and to build a few warehouses for salt and stores.

3. To provide lime, slate, and wood.

4. To advance these articles to all persons intending to build houses; the interest of their price to be added to the yearly rent of the houses. The lots for houses, thirty feet front, three hundred deep.

The day fine till the evening. All night it rained hard. Wind due N.

8th July. Wind all contrary but the day fine. Walked out, – examined magnet rock. A compass placed upon it veers to the east and stops there. In passing it in a boat, the compass veers and shifts, at last fixes to the east. The rock extends from the harbour half a mile into the island; said, ridiculously, to be the biggest loadstone in the known world. Ruins of a considerable old castle behind the harbour. At a little distance from thence the rocks are all columnar, like Staffa, and very curious were they not so near Staffa.

The account of the 1788 British Fisheries Society tour, written by Lord Mount Stuart, is MS 9587 of the National Library of Scotland. It was kindly brought to the attention of the writer by Mr Ronald Black, and is printed here by the permission of the authorities of the Library.

---

* The first sun-fish that was ever caught on these coasts was by a native of Cannay, on the shore of this island, about twenty years ago. An adventurous undertaking at that time, when they were ignorant of every thing that respects this fish, but its bulk and strength. *Edit.*

. . . for tomorrow we anchored at Canna at 8 p.m. on Sunday 17th August.

Monday 18th August. Went with two compasses to examine the new magnetic rock lately discovered by Mr. MacNeil on the east entrance of the harbour. Found the compasses point from East to West instead of North and South. From thence went to the top of Compass Hill, so called; where the compass points South instead of North. From thence walked to Mr. MacNeil's house by the cluster of houses called a town.[1] Mr. MacNeil had married a sister of [Colin] MacDonald of Boisdale, and we found him with three daughters and a son, another boy was gone to Mull,* two of the girls were grown up. He had with him a Mr. MacDonald, a brother in law,[2] who had served in the army in America, they came aboard and dined. We returned with him to the house to tea. The house had a neat outside but miserable interior, for the first time I perceived the inside of a room not plaistered but roughcast, the room was in addition paved with stone. He had laid out a good large kitchen garden with a wall round it, not indeed high enough, he had also built a mill though it is doubtful whether a constant supply of water can be obtained; a wind mill was never once adverted to, and on my mentioning it he owned it would have been better.

MacNeil has likewise built an inn, and proposes placing a good tenant in it;[3] he by degrees will apportionate the quantity of cattle to the quality of the soil and extent of the island, which bids fair to enhance the value, and will consequently benefit both Landlord and Tacksman; upon the whole Mr. MacNeil's conduct seems highly meritorious.

Canna belongs to MacDonald of Clanronald who holds the Duke of Argyll as Superior, this is the case also of South Uist and Benbecula. It is by far the prettiest island we have visited, beautiful views, romantic rocks, fine rich verdure. The extent three miles of their computation by one and ½. The produce Bear [four-rowed barley] and Black Cattle. Though a country calculated for sheep, none are to be seen. It seems so many disputes had arisen when flocks were kept up that the under tenants unanimously joined in a petition to the Tacksman to take them away; and they afterwards bound themselves under a heavy penalty not to keep more; a custom prevails throughout the northern Hebrides, that all the produce of the Dairy, the goats and the sheep belongs to the wife, hence on enquiring whether no sheep remained I was answered 'Mrs. MacNeil has a few'; from these wool sufficient is usually obtained

* Where Colin MacDonald of Boisdale, Hector MacNeill's brother-in-law, had bought the estate of Ulva in 1777. Presumably this son was the eldest, Donald, then (1788) nineteen.

for making the plaid, hose etc. that may be wanted in the family; for no stock of sheep is seen anywhere amongst the Hebrides. The pasture of Canna is so inviting however Mr. MacNeil will probably turn his thoughts to this species of farming and besides the meat passes for being uncommonly delicious.

He is the first Tacksman ever employed on the spot, heretofore the small tenants governed or rather quarrelled amongst themselves. His lease is 24 years five of which are expired, and upon this only security the house, the garden, the inn, the mill, have been reared. He pays Clanronald £206 and talks of putting still more into his pocket, his own profits are doubtless at least equivalent to the Proprietor's otherwise the banishment he undergoes would be intolerable, he being the only person of education in Canna; he maintains however that they are never one week alone throughout the year.

30 ton of kelp joins in forming no inconsiderable part of the Canna resources. We saw the people busily employed in collecting and burning it. The number of souls amounts to 320 – the oldest 86 – they are all fishers and of course fish hooks become a valuable present which together with tobacco, not less in esteem, we took care to bestow. The inhabitants seem to have divided themselves into 4 townships the largest containing 30 families, but in these much useful ground is thrown away by the houses being scattered here and there without any regularity, nor can cabbage gardens be brought forward as an excuse for this wantoness because according to the laudable custom of the Hebrides, none are to be discovered; the buildings are similar to those of their neighbours, formed of loose stones and in every sense mean.

In the center [?] of this principal town the old chapel appears quite in ruins with a curious shaped cross at a small distance the top broken off, what remains is carved with figures, you distinguish the lamb [?] very plain. Till lately they buried here and considering that they are all Papists I was astonished to view the little care taken of this consecrated spot which is suffered to remain in rubbish and to grow over with weeds, nothing to excite attention is perceptible amongst the ruins of the Chapel. The shape of a window pleased me a good deal.

The inattention before noticed extends to the new burying ground so covered with dockens etc. the mouldering heaps are nowhere discernible, nor are crosses or any exterior mark of their worship to be seen. A particular spot is reserved for sailors and strangers who die or who are cast away, for they will not allow their bones to mix with others. Near this spot a hut no better has been erected by way of Mass house, where the priest officiates, who resides in the Island of

Egg and who comes now and then for that purpose bringing with him the necessary ornaments. The present Priest's name is MacDonald bred at the Scots College at Paris.[4]

Of holydays they have only 12, and their worship is [so]* primitive that no relicks of any sort are discoverable, although I purposely sent a Roman Catholic servant to search their houses. In Barra the altar is constructed of earth in the open air. When they fall sick an express is instantly despatched for the Priest for they are all extremely attentive in their last moments. At their funerals the old superstition of carrying the body round towards the sun mentioned by all Hebridean authors still prevails.

The custom of riding on the Michaelmas day is broken through owing to Mr. MacNeil, who thinking a fine day lost perhaps in the middle of harvest was not to be counterbalanced by superstition forbade his servants to attend, and most of the people being employed by him, the mandate controled the procession. He might perhaps have acted as well in giving way, without the smallest trifle of superstition myself I respect the uninformed weakness of the poorer man and when unattended with essential mischief either to the mind or to the mass [,] for God sake secure for him an additional moment of comfort when you have it in you power . . . .
. . .† superstitious comfort we are told is happiness supreme.

The annual temporary famine proclaimed by Pennant exists no longer, kelp and fishing has introduced a sort of intimacy with the mainland that never more will be lost sight of. A common rowboat is not afraid to fight its way to the very center of Glasgow, the return of such a one was hourly expected with a supply of various little conveniences amongst which fish hooks would not be omitted.

Two Taylors reside in the island, but no other workmen, but MacNeil undertakes the establishment of both Smith and Carpenter, and should a fishing town be establish'd as a temptation to which Clanronald has offered the Society a present of the necessary land.

It seems close to the shore there is a superior bank for Ling fishing. The Harbor is fine, beautiful and safe and the aspect thoroughly agreeable.

The summit of the Compass Hill offers a most extensive prospect. The magnetic power appartaining to this rock is well known and has been often described, the magnet points due south. A similar rock has been discovered by Mr. MacNeil on the east entrance of the harbor, here the compass points East. I should suspect that this extraordinary quality prevails throughout most of the island, a mixture of iron is everywhere perceptible in the Brooks and the

---

* Word blotted out.   † 'for surely to the' deleted in MS.

valleys: but on tasting the water in a variety of spots I discovered no impregnation, nor was I lucky enough to procure any specimen of the rock that would of itself affect the magnet.

The New Mill is built of a stone which would seem to form the basis of the island, it is hard and resists the pick-axe, when left exposed to the air upon the ground, you may break the largest mass with your fingers, you then perceive a mixture of iron and small stones resembling volcanic matter. The rocks above are the same only you discover amongst them beautiful zeolites. Columnal rocks present themselves throughout full as perfect as Staffa although not in such large still especially fine. Many pretty shells ornament the shores. They have most kinds of fish, plenty of rabbits, no hares, no moorfowl or blackcock, numerous wild fowl. Moorfowl abound in the adjoining island of Rume, though every man keeping a gun that species as well as the deer will soon be at an end.

The hatred to the Rum people ever since they left the Popish persuasion is something remarkable. When a child misbehaves the mother cries 'I'll send you to Rum', a threat from anyone upon any occasion concludes in Rume and Mr. MacNeil told me in one of the sermons the Priest said 'if you commit such crimes the Lord will turn his back upon you then what will you do, where can you go etc?' Upon this a poor man got up and said seriously 'if there be amongst us any such wicked person, let them be sent to Rum'. The change of religion in Rume was literally occasioned by the violence of the Grandfather of the present Maclean of Coll though not exactly as related by Johnson. He had a child at nurse in Rume and happening to go and see it of a Sunday, it occurred to him to ask a friend of his, a clergyman, who chanced to accompany him, to preach.

A Roman Catholic man present went out of the room, the Nurse also a Roman Catholic followed him with the Child, this circumstance enraged Maclean to such a degree that running after the man he beat him most unmercifully with a stick adding 'get back you rascal to the Kirk'. This drubbing frightened the inhabitants so much they none of them ventured more to go to Mass. People in Canna continue to marry as early as mentioned in all the Authors, before the age of 20.

A Greenock sloop laden with kelp from Barra to Liverpool lay alongside of us.

Mr. MacNeil related this trait of Flora MacDonald coming back from America the end of last war with her husband, a Privateer appeared which rendered it necessary to clear for an engagement, she helping with all her might fell over a cannon and broke her arm when she immediately exclaimed 'the Devil has now got hold of me for fighting in defence of George'.

Old leases to small tenants will all expire in two years when MacNeil's plan of a sheep farm will certainly cause emigration. Ruins of old castle still in being where Clanronald confined his wife.*

Tuesday 19th August. Mr. MacNeil and Mr. MacDonald came on board to take leave brought milk, greens etc. Weighed anchor at 9 a.m. wind at S.S.W.

Unfortunately soon afterwards things started to go wrong. First of all, Clanranald offered the Society, whose directors dined with him on Benbecula on 12 July, a site for a fishery station on Canna, and also 'any quantity of land' at Loch Skipport in South Uist. He renewed these offers to the directors before they left Benbecula (where they had earlier on the same day a very interesting interview with 'Macmuirish Clanranald's blind bard'). The Society however did not immediately respond to the offer of a site on Canna. Then they were told that it had a large fishing population that 'was on the eve of being removed by an engrossing tenant unless the Society came to their aid'.[5]

This looks very much like a concerted argument put up in order to force the Society's hand. The 'engrossing tenant' was the Hector MacNeill mentioned, who had obtained a twenty-four year lease of Canna from Clanranald in 1781. Hector MacNeill was married to a daughter[6] of Alexander MacDonald of Boisdale by his third wife Anne, daughter of MacNeill of Barra; she was thus related to Clanranald, whose great grandfather, Donald of Benbecula and XVIth of Clanranald, was her grandfather. In 1789 Clanranald offered the Society fourteen acres of land on Canna free of rent or feu-duty, and this was accepted. At the time it could not be really said that the Canna people or more than a few of them were full-time fishermen: they were nearly all involved in kelp-making and agriculture. They did not have the necessary capital to take to fishing.

The contemporary plan of the Harbour of Canna and the two pieces of ground offered by Clanranald shows that the land consisted of Rubha Cairinnis and the adjacent ground of Lag a' Bhaile, where the plan shows nine existing houses, and

---

* This paragraph added later. In fact with the price of kelp rising the clearance of Canna for sheep did not take place until 1851.

part of the field called Druim an Uistrich at Coroghon, and a piece along the shore at the head of the harbour between Rubha nan Corr, which became later the site of the 'Square', and Lag nam Boitean. The plan was made by George Langlands in 1788. Clanranald said he was ready for the Society's scheme to go ahead at once; Hector MacNeill started to argue over terms. MacNeill wanted £400 in return for surrendering the lease of the fourteen acres, and appointment as the Society's local agent; the Society was prepared to pay him £100, but not to give him the agency.

It then became obvious that two small pieces of land amounting only to fourteen acres would be quite inadequate for a fishery settlement. An attempt was made to get Clanranald to agree to something like 500 or 600 acres at 'full present value'. The additional land was at first refused and then offered 'for an enormous sum', which the Society refused to pay. So the plan of making Canna, the best place of all the islands around the Minch, a British Fisheries Society station, came to nothing, greatly to the Society's regret, and its inhabitants were condemned to another three generations of poverty and emigration. 'Farewell bonny Cannay, the best fishing station in the Highlands and the most tempting spot for a settlement – farewell poor inhabitants', wrote George Dempster to John MacKenzie, secretary of the Society on 15 June 1790.[7]

John MacDonald of Clanranald himself was only a fairly young man and probably not in good health, for he died in 1794 in his early thirties. He had to think of what it would cost his estates to support his widow from a second marriage to Colin MacDonald of Boisdale's daughter Jean, who in the event survived him by fifty-three years, and two aunts, one of whom lived until 1816 and the other until 1838. Marriage settlements could become grievous financial burdens on Highland estates – a matter which has not received due attention from social historians and economists, such settlements being considered entirely private and confidential by the lairds.* As

---

* The only great Highland family that has been candid about its financial history is the MacLeods of Dunvegan, see *The Book of Dunvegan*. In fact the financial pressure of injudicious marriage settlements on heirs to estates must have had a lot to do with the Highland Clearances.

for MacNeill, he probably disliked the idea of a competing employer on the island, and wanted as much labour as possible at as low rate as possible for making kelp, for which the inhabitants of Lag a' Bhaile were removed from their fertile sheltered valley to exposed Sanday before 1805 – their dwellings at Lag a' Bhaile are not shown on the map of Canna made for Clanranald's successor that year.

Kelp-making for the production of soda in any case was more profitable than fishing at that time. It had been introduced into the western Highlands around 1755 by Hector MacNeill's father-in-law, Alexander MacDonald of Boisdale (an additional influence). Thirty years later, many thousands of tons of kelp were being made, and in 1787 the British Government put a duty of five guineas a ton on barilla (the Spanish equivalent of kelp), so that the price of Highland kelp was rising just at the time a fishery station at Canna was being considered. As the average cost in wages of making kelp was £2. 5s. 0d. a ton and freight charges south were £1. 5s. 0d. a ton while selling price was going as high as £22 a ton,[8] the profits to the landowners and their principal tenants like MacNeill were enormous – and some disastrous marriage settlements and family legacies were made on the illusion that they would be permanent. In fact the industry was killed in the 1820s by the development of the Leblanc process of making soda from salt, and by the free-trade policy which was coming into favour with the Government.

The Highland fisheries on the other hand were hamstrung by the Government's duties on salt, designed to protect English salt-makers. Attempts to allow fishermen a drawback of duty on salt used for curing fish, while making sure none was directed for any other kind of use, led to a fantastic web of bureaucratic red tape, completely frustrating to the Highland fisherman. The case was very well put to E. W. Clarke in 1797 on Rum by Mr MacLean, brother to the Laird of Coll who owned the island:

A slight alteration in the excise laws, respecting the article of salt, would produce a very rapid change in favour of the Highlanders. For want of this necessary article, some hundreds of them, during the present year, will be compelled to manure their lands with the fish they have taken; if they were permitted to manufacture it themselves, all Europe might be supplied from these islands, with the fish they would be able to cure. But, as the law now stands, the natives are constantly in perplexity and distress. If salt is to be had, the regulations respecting it are so complicated, that none of them understand them; by which means they are continually involving themselves in law-suits and difficulties. Add to this the great distance to which they are obliged to go, in order to procure the salt; the expense attending which, together with the trouble, and the danger of trusting their crazy boats to the uncertainty of the seas, discourages them from attempting to cure their fish, and checks the progress of industry.

The nearest custom-house to the island of Rum is Tobermorey. When they arrive there, they are under the necessity of entering into a bond with regard to the salt they purchase, and make oath, under heavy penalties, that every grain of salt they take home is to be altogether and entirely appropriated to the curing of fish. When the operation of curing the fish is completed, if a single gallon of the salt remains, they must make another voyage to the custom-house, with the salt and the fish they have cured; display both before the officers of the customs and take up their bond. But if any part of the salt thus purchased is found afterwards in their houses, they become immediately subject to penalties, sufficiently burdensome to ruin men entirely, or effectually to put a stop to their future industry. If the year proves unfavourable and scarcity of salt prevail, as is the case at present, they are not only deprived of the means of pursuing their fishing to advantage, but even deprived of sustenance for their families during the winter; although Providence has blessed their shores with every necessity, even to abundance, and the power of preserving the plenty thus bestowed is constantly within their view.

Of the kelp industry, Clarke, himself a chemist, wrote:

The inhabitants of Canna, like those of the neighbouring islands, are chiefly occupied in the manufacture of kelp. Cattle and kelp constitute, in fact, the chief objects of commerce in the Hebrides. The first toast usually given in all festive occasions is a 'high price' to kelp and cattle. In this, every islander is interested and it is always drunk with evident symptoms of sincerity. The discovery of manufacturing kelp has effected a great change among the people; whether for their advantage or not, is a question not yet decided. I was informed in Canna, that if kelp keeps its present price, Mr. Macdonald, of Clanranald, will make £6,000 sterling by his kelp and Lord MacDonald will make not less than £10,000.

But the neglect of tillage, which is universally experienced since this discovery was made, is already sensibly felt; and promises to overbalance the good which is derived from it. The lands lie neglected and without manure; and if naked rocks are to succeed corn fields and the labourers desert the pursuits of husbandry to gather sea-weed, the profits arising from kelp to individuals will ill repay the loss occasioned to the community at large, by the defect of those necessaries they are accustomed to derive from their lands.

The best kelp is usually supposed to be that which is manufactured in the island of Barra. Mr. MacNeil, the laird of that island, informed me he got last year twelve guineas a ton for his kelp. The rainy season has this year damaged vast quantities of that which he is preparing, not with standing which, as far as I could learn, he will be able to send 300 tons to the Liverpool markets.

The great scarcity of barilla, arising from the war with Spain, has considerably augmented the speculations of all the western islanders, with regard to their kelp, which is expected to bear a very high price.

The manufacture of kelp is conducted by the following process:– the sea-weed is first collected and dried. The usual mode is to cut a portion of kelp annually from the rocks, taking it from the same place only once in three years. After the kelp has been dried, it is placed in a kiln prepared for the purpose, of stones loosely piled together, and burned. After it is consumed, and the fire is to be extinguished, a long pole pointed with iron is plunged into it and it is stirred about; the result of the burning being, by this time, a thick glutinous liquid, which runs from the kelp in burning. As soon as this liquid cools, it hardens and the operation is at an end. It is then shipped off to market. The usual expense of manufacturing kelp is about two guineas a ton for the labour; if it is sold on the shore, which is generally the case, and estimating the kelp only at eight guineas a ton, the proprietor clears six.

More recent developments of the kelp industry, first for iodine and latterly as a source of alginic acid, have passed Canna by. It has been used for manuring hay fields here regularly, until it became so polluted with the cast-off plastic artefacts of modern civilization, that it could no longer be put on the ground.

NOTES

1. These homes are shown on Lt. Pierce's drawing published in 1789, which must have been made on this expedition. They no longer exist, but the place where they were is called *Lag a' Bhaile*, 'The dell of the town'.

2. This would have been Major James MacDonald of Askernish (in S. Uist), 'who served in the MacDonald and other regiments'. He married Christina, daughter of Donald MacLeod of Bernera (*Clan Donald*, iii. 293). He died at Inverness.

3. The Changehouse, which must therefore have been built between 1782 and 1788.

4. 'In 1783 the number of Catholics in Canna is given as 322, and in Eigg 450, their priest at that time being Mr James MacDonald.' Dom Odo Blundell, *The Catholic Highlands of Scotland*, II. 195.

5. Jean Dunlop, *The British Fisheries Society*, p. 90.

6. Called Janet in Hector MacNeill's will, though no daughter of Boisdale's of this name is mentioned in *Clan Donald*, which says the name of Hector's wife was Margaret.

7. Jean Dunlop, *The British Fisheries Society*, p. 91.

8. J. P. Day, *Public Administration in the Highlands and Islands of Scotland*, p. 85.

14 THE COMING OF
THE MACNEILLS

Hector MacNeill, the first member of this family to obtain the lease of a holding on Canna, came from Kintyre, where his surname was a common one. The Chiefs of the southern MacNeills, who are not to be confused with the MacNeils of Barra, were the MacNeills of Taynish and Gigha, an old family whose representative, heavily burdened with debts, had sold his ancestral home of Taynish in 1779 to Colonel, later Sir Archibald Campbell, and Gigha to John MacNeill of Oakfield, near Ardrishaig in Knapdale.

Among the leases in the Clanranald papers is a missive dated 18 June 1781 from tutors (guardians) of John MacDonald of Clanranald, who must still not have come of age, to continue Alexander MacDonald for ten years in the eight penny-lands of 'Island Ganich', i.e. Sanday, 'at £4 sterling [a] penny [land] yearly of rent on his resigning his right of the Change House of Canna and two penny land of Corgoun in favour of Mr Hector MacNeill, sr., merchant in Campbeltown. At Kilbride'. This is the first reference to Hector MacNeill in the Clanranald papers.

Kilbride, in South Uist, was the residence of Hector MacNeill's brother-in-law Colin MacDonald of Boisdale. The next day a lease of the eighteen penny-lands of Tarbert of Canna, held by Mrs MacKinnon, junior, of Coirechatachan* was also signed, a total of twenty penny-lands at a rent of £4 per penny-land, plus £6 for the changehouse (inn). MacNeill was to be allowed £90 towards the cost of building a slated change-house of stone and lime and a garden on Coroghon, and the estate was prepared to advance him a further £110 at 5 per cent towards the expense of this improvement. In return for these rents and improvements, Hector MacNeill was to get a twenty-four year lease of Coroghon and Tarbert, provided

* In Skye. Dr Johnson and Boswell were very agreeably entertained there by Mr MacKinnon senior and his family in 1773.

that any one or two more of the guardians of John MacDonald of Clanranald in addition to the two, Flora and Colin MacDonald, who signed the lease, approved.

The lease continued: 'And as there are no houses of any kind on the farms you are to get (belonging to the Master) to accommodate the incoming tennant we therefore approve of your Building to the amount of one hundred and fifty or two hundred Pounds Sterling for which you are to have a Milleration* at the Expiry of your Tack, you being obliged to deliver said houses in sufficient and Good Order at the time of delivery.'

The terms of this interesting lease seem to show that Hector MacNeill must have built the house still called the Changehouse on Canna, and the house on the shore now called the bothy since Hector's grandson Donald the second built Canna House in the 1860s and removed the top storey of the old house; but it is possible that there may have been a changehouse on Canna before Hector MacNeill built the slated one – now the oldest inhabited house on the island – between 1781 and 1788.

Hardly anything is known of his antecedents. According to what Angus MacDonald 'Aonghus Eachainn', the last Canna *seanchaidh*, told the late Dr Calum MacLean in 1946–7, the family had a farm at the Mull of Kintyre, and the first of them was called 'Iain Ìleach' – 'John from Islay' in Gaelic. According to a family tradition communicated by Harry MacNeill, Hector's great grandson, who lived for most of his life in Winnipeg, the family had been earlier connected with Kilarrow in Islay.

We know the identity of Hector MacNeill's former residence in Kintyre, Dalintober near Campbeltown, from the fact that when he went to Canna in 1781 or 1782 he left unpaid the rent due to the Duke of Argyll for part of 1779 and all of 1780 and 1781 for a 'park' or field in the Whitehill of Campbeltown. The rent amounted to £3. 5s. 2d. sterling (£39. 2s. 0d. Scots) a year, and there was £2. 11s. 6d. outstanding for part of the year 1779. Hector had given Alexander Campbell, Chamberlain of

---

* Compensation for improvement.

Argyll, a bill of exchange for the £6. 10s. 4d. owing for 1780 and 1781, dated 17 January 1782 and payable on 16 March of the same year. It had not been paid by 1785, and on the 30 September of that year, Commissary Duncan Campbell, lawyer in Inveraray, wrote to Robert Campbell, Sheriff Clerk of Inverness, asking that a process be set on foot in the Inverness-shire Court for the recovery of the sum in question.[1]

The fact that such an inconsiderable sum became the subject of a legal action, suggests strongly that there had been some kind of a quarrel between Hector MacNeill and the Chamberlain of Argyll, leading to Hector's pulling up his roots in Kintyre and taking the opportunity of acquiring a lease of part of the Isle of Canna, doubtless with the help of the influence of his in-laws, the Boisdales, with Clanranald.

Almost everything else that is known about Hector MacNeill's personal life is to be found in the two British Fishery Society reports reproduced in the preceding chapter, that is, details of his family and accounts of actual or projected improvements he had made or meant to make on Canna. The house he is said to have built before 1787 must be what in its altered form is now called the 'Bothy'. As he is also stated to have built an inn (p. 122) it may be that what Alexander MacDonald gave up in 1781 was an unexercised right under a former lease. There are still substantial traces of the mill-dam Hector made, and the millstones still exist; the mill can only have worked by filling up the mill-pond and then opening the sluice, for there is not nearly a sufficient head of water to work a mill at all times.

Being a merchant married to a daughter of an important MacDonald laird, Hector MacNeill should have been in possession of some capital when he came to Canna. His position is of course unknown, but a guess can be based upon the 1798 rental of Canna printed in C. Fraser Mackintosh's *Antiquarian Notes* with the aid of the information provided by Pennant that in 1770 a penny-land cost £30 to stock and was supposed to carry a soum of seven cows and two horses. A penny-land, it may be said, was an old unit of land based on taxation in Norse times. In some places it was considered as equivalent to eight arable acres. In 1718 the rent of a penny-land in Keill, Canna, was 26 Scots merks (£17. 6s. 8d. Scots;

£1. 5s. 6⅔d. sterling). By 1749 it had risen to 30 merks a penny-land.*

In the 1798 rental, which of course is stated in sterling, Hector MacNeill is said to have held the 12 penny-lands of Keill, 7 of Coroghon, and 18 of Tarbert, paying £60 rent for Keill, £28 for Coroghon, and £72 for Tarbert, a total of £160. He was also paying a rent of £6 for the Changehouse and making 14 tons of kelp a year. Four other tenants survived on Sanday, Donald MacDonald and two others holding the four penny-lands of Upper (west) Sanday for a rent of £21, and making a ton of kelp a year, and Alexander MacDonald holding the nine penny-lands of Lower (eastern) Sanday for £5. 5s. 0d. per penny a year (£47. 5s. 0d.) but only paying £42. 2s. 0d. a year, because there was a dispute about the number of penny-lands; and he was making three tons of kelp a year.

If the stocking of a penny-land was seven cows and two horses, then MacNeill could have had 239 cows and 74 horses, and the stocking would have cost him £1,110 sterling at Pennant's figure; Donald MacDonald and his two fellow tenants could have had 28 cows and 8 horses, and Alexander MacDonald could have had 63 cows (or slightly fewer) and 18 horses. But allowance would have to be made, especially in Hector MacNeill's case, for a small number of cows and horses possessed by subtenants whose names do not appear on Clanranald's Canna rental. On the basis of Pennant's figures, the stock on Canna in 1798 would have been 330 cows and 100 horses, or rather ponies. This fits in with the statement of the Revd Donald MacLean, minister of the Small Isles, that in 1794 the total number of cattle in the four islands was 1,100 cows, besides 540 stirks, and 500 two-year olds.[2] There was only a very small number of sheep, kept to provide wool for homespun clothing and mutton for household consumption. There was no sheep on Muck. There were wild rabbits (obviously introduced) on Canna. Mr MacLean noted that the distance from public markets forced the farmers of the Small Isles to sell their cattle to private dealers 'who in general think it their interest to appreciate advantages arising from the local

---

* Scottish currency at the time of the Union of 1707 had one-twelfth the value of English.

situation'. He said that the horned cattle of Canna and Muck grew to a considerable size, owing to the good quality of the grazing on those islands, but were liable to the disease called 'bloody urine' (now 'red water') when taken to mainland markets; this indicates the freedom of Canna from the ticks that carry this ailment, to which the local beasts would not be acclimatized. Canna is still tick-free.

MacLean gives the population of Canna then as 304, increased from 233 as numbered by his predecessor the Revd Mr McAskill in 1768. Early marriages were a cause of this kind of increase in the Small Isles, leading to the subdivision of holdings (sometimes a very small portion of a farm) with consequent poverty. The 1805 map of Canna, made as a part of the survey of Clanranald's estates (possibly the Clanranald at that time, Reginald Gordon MacDonald, already had sales in view, as the same year he redeemed the superiorities held by the Earl of Argyll at a cost of over £5,000[3]) is of great interest at this point. It shows the boundaries of the old farms of Coroghon, Keill, Tarbert, and Garrisdale on Canna, and Upper and Lower Sanday, and gives the total arable acreage as 459.03 (Scots acres) and the pasture as 1,794.95; 2,253.98 acres in all.

The map shows the following number of buildings: at Coroghon, the old mansion house (with a row of trees behind it), the Changehouse and barn, and a building and a barn at 'Corra-dhùn thall', 'yonder Coroghon'; the nine houses in Lag a' Bhaile have disappeared. Keill has thirty-two buildings and a sign which appears to designate the medieval carved cross, and fourteen enclosures; Tarbert has a house and a barn at the present site, and eleven houses west of the Sgrìob Ruadh, one with an enclosure. Garrisdale has three houses, in the glen above the shore cliffs. Upper Sanday has five buildings, and Lower Sanday twelve, one with an enclosure. Four other buildings on Upper Sanday, near the Tràigh Bhàn are only indicated in outline.

These buildings, apart from Hector MacNeill's on Coroghon, and the Changehouse, total sixty-eight but not every one of them was necessarily an inhabited house. On the other hand, some may have been double houses. The Revd Donald MacLean gives the average number of persons per inhabited house in the whole parish at 5.33. On that basis, there were approximately fifty-seven inhabited houses in Canna in the late 1790s. Today the number permanently inhabited is only six; seasonally inhabited are another seven.

Hector MacNeill died in the winter of 1809–10; this can be surmised from the fact that the agreement of R. G. MacDonald of Clanranald to let Canna to his son Donald is dated 26 April 1810. With the prices of kelp and cattle steadily rising owing to the Napoleonic Wars, Hector had done well out of Canna. By his will, dated 19 April 1802, a very business-like document, he left 'all the sundry lands and heritages Tacks Rooms Steadings and possessions belonging to me' with all debts due to him and all his livestock and gear to his eldest son Donald. To his widow Janet he left £500, all the sheep and goats and half the household furniture and plenishing of his house on Canna, and an annuity of £20 from a bond already executed by him. To his second son Alexander he left £100, remarking that he had already provided for him and put him in a situation of doing for himself. To his third son John and six daughters Jean, Elizabeth, Margaret, Janet, Mary, and Ann he left £500 each. The legacies to his potential widow and children were made subject to their resignation of *jus relictae* and bairns' right respectively.

His eldest son Donald was to be executor and residuary legatee. In case of any of his children being under age at the time of his death (which implies that some were so at the time he made his will), their tutors or guardians were to be Ranald George MacDonald of Clanranald, Roderick MacNeil of Barra, Captain James MacDonald his brother-in-law, and Hector MacDonald Buchanan, WS. Socially, naming the chiefs of Clanranald and Barra as tutors was flying pretty high, but no doubt their position would have been merely nominal; the effective guardians, if needed, would have been Hector's brother-in-law, James, and his wife's nephew Hector MacDonald Buchanan, WS, a person then very well-known in Edinburgh.

The mystery about Donald MacNeill, son of Hector, whom we shall call Donald I of Canna, is what he was doing before he succeeded his father in the lease of Canna at the age of more than forty in 1810. In *Clan Donald* there is no mention of a marriage between Hector MacNeill of Canna and any

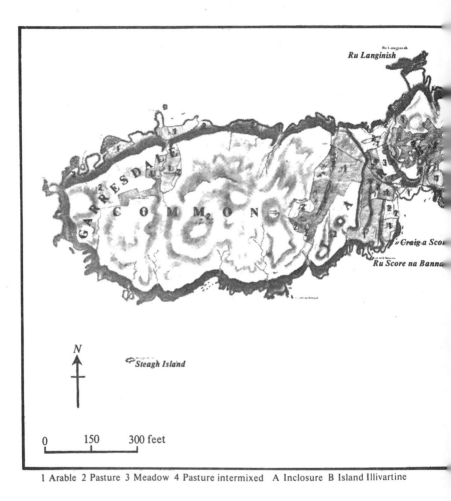

1 Arable 2 Pasture 3 Meadow 4 Pasture intermixed   A Inclosure B Island Illivartine

Canna, showing arable and pasture.

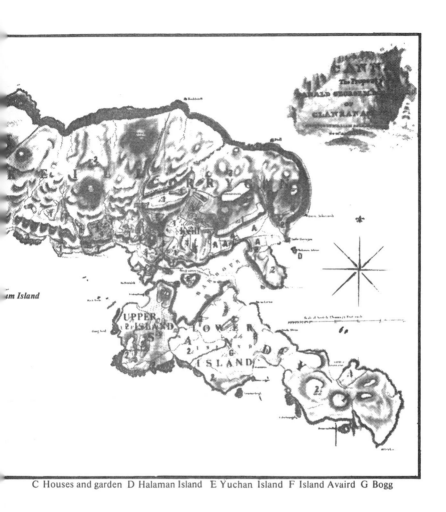

m Island

C Houses and garden D Halaman Island E Yuchan Island F Island Avaird G Bogg

daughter of Alexander MacDonald of Boisdale; on the other hand it is asserted there that Margaret, Boisdale's youngest daughter by his third wife Anne MacNeil of Barra, married 'Donald MacNeill of Kenachreggan, afterwards of Canna, with issue'.[4] R. L. MacNeil of Barra goes further, and asserts that Donald was born in 1800![5] (It is known he was seventy-nine when he died in 1848.)

So far as is known, Donald was never married. He certainly had no legitimate children. The most rational explanation for the misstatement in *Clan Donald* is that somehow his name has been substituted for his father's there. What interest Hector MacNeill had in Kenachreggan, now Inverailort, is unknown; but it is significant that in 1798 the tenant was Lt. Angus MacDonald, of the Dalilea family, subtenant and son-in-law of Colin MacDonald of Boisdale, Hector's wife's half-brother, while the neighbouring farm of Alissary was held by the same Angus MacDonald and Alexander MacLean, the latter very probably related to John MacLean who became tenant of Canna after the Clearance of 1851, and whose daughter Isabella Donald I's natural son Donald II was to marry in 1854.[6]

NOTES

1. *Inverneill Papers*, Letter-book of Commissary Duncan Campbell, WS, 28 Apr. 1784–31 Jan. 1787, pp. 89–90. The researches of Mr Ian Stewart, Campbeltown, have revealed that Hector MacNeill of Canna was connected with the MacNeills of Carskey, Lossit and Balligrogan in Kintyre, and that after 1766 he owned a ship with which he traded on the west coast of Scotland, an enterprise in which his son Donald probably took part.
2. *Old Statistical Account of Scotland*, XVII. 274.
3. I am indebted to Dr Eric Cregeen for this information.
4. *Clan Donald*, iii. 294.
5. *The Clan MacNeil*, p. 88.
6. C. Fraser-MacKintosh, *Antiquarian Notes*, pp. 251–2. See also *Tocher*, 10. 53.

15 DONALD MACNEILL I AND THE GAELIC SCHOOLS

When Hector MacNeill died in the winter of 1809–10 he was a well established man. Having made a socially advantageous marriage some years before coming to Canna, he had entered at the right time to gain the fullest advantage from the steady rise in the prices of kelp and cattle during the troubles that started with the French Revolution and continued with the Napoleonic Wars. Wars which, incidentally, had sent the press-gang round the Hebrides, including Canna, to press young men into what were then the hardships of naval service. On Canna it is well remembered how young men sometimes escaped the press-gang by hiding in a cave in the cliff at the south-west end of the island to which they obtained access by being lowered down the cliff by ropes handled by their friends;* and how the big carved medieval stone cross was deprived of one of its arms by being used by the press-gang as a target for one of their cannons.

The press-gang† would not have affected Hector MacNeill greatly. From coming to Canna in 1781 as the tenant of the Changehouse and two penny-lands of Coroghon, he had grown to be the tenant of all three farms on Canna (as distinct from Sanday). He had at his command a large number of subtenants and cottars whose small rents would have been partly paid in bonded labour, and who would have been available for the kelp harvest at low wages. Speaking only Gaelic, they would have been unable to find work anywhere outside the Highlands, if they had wanted to leave Canna, which only those prepared to emigrate to Nova Scotia did. That was the world Hector MacNeill lived in, and of which a man wanting to get ahead in the Highlands had to take advantage. Otherwise, everything depended on personal relation-

* The Revd Donald MacLean wrote in 1794 that the people of the Small Isles 'seldom enter the navy, unless campelled', (*Old Statistical Account of Scotland*, XVII. 289.)

† 'Press-gang' is apparently the origin of the Scottish Gaelic word *prasgan* meaning a low, scummish rabble.

ships. Some lairds and tacksmen in the Highlands were loved by their tenants and sub-tenants, others were hated.

Finally, Hector had made a sensible will in 1802 and had not burdened his heir with excessive settlements in favour of his potential widow and younger children. He had not tried to cut a social figure anywhere in the South, which his landlord, R. G. MacDonald of Clanranald, was doing in London, with disastrous results to his family fortunes. He had started a dynasty of what became owner-occupiers when his eldest son Donald bought Canna from Clanranald in 1827, which lasted a hundred years; their successors, Robert Thom and his heirs, made another one that lasted for fifty-six years, and the writer, who bought Canna from the representatives of Allan Gilmour Thom in 1938, was owner-occupier for forty-three years before making a gift of the island to the National Trust for Scotland. In 200 years Canna had only seven different occupiers, all of whom farmed the island, from only three different families.

Donald his heir, whom we shall call Donald Senior or Donald I of Canna to distinguish from his son and successor of the same name, succeeded in a very favourable situation. At the same time the Small Isles Church of Scotland parish, consisting of Eigg, Rum, Canna, Muck, and Heiskeir, got a new minister, the Revd Neil MacLean, in 1811. The parish had only existed as a separate entity since 1726; previously it had been united with the parish of Sleat in Skye, under a post-Reformation arrangement that reveals the great shortage of ministers in the Highlands in the sixteenth and early seventeenth centuries – the first Protestant minister of Sleat was only appointed in 1609. The Revd Neil MacLean followed two outstanding ministers, the Revd Malcolm MacAskill (minister from 1757 to 1787) from Rubh' an Dùnain, the part of Skye nearest to Canna, who was known as *Am Ministear Làidir*, 'the Strong Minister', and who wrote a letter on 29 July 1763 to 'Theophilus Insulanus', author of *A Treatise on Second Sight, Dreams and Apparitions*, in which he remarked that he wished 'from the bottom of my heart, that some of my cloth would carry themselves with more decency towards their superiors in most branches of literature, and call to mind that they are only sacred while in the pulpit'.[1] He was writing of ministers who would not help in the second sight enquiry. The Revd MacAskill was followed in the Small Isles by the Revd Donald MacLean (1787–1811) whose article on the Small Isles in the Old Statistical Account of Scotland has already been mentioned. It is one of the classics of that very interesting series.*

The appointment of the Revd Neil MacLean, who was presented by George, Prince Regent, on 13 February 1811 and admitted on 20 June of the same year, coincided with the foundation of the Gaelic Schools Society, the first Annual Meeting of which took place in the New Rooms of the Royal Exchange Coffee House in Edinburgh on 29 November 1811. The Society had been called together by a circular letter dated 10 December 1810. The Society was founded to supplement the 290 SPCK schools then operating in the Highlands and Islands. The SPCK had long since dropped the anti-Gaelic policy of its 1709 founders, and the Highlands and Islands were now producing ministers who were making names as Gaelic scholars. The new Society was founded for the express purpose of teaching children in the Highlands and Islands 'to read their native language'. The Society was financed by private subscriptions, and was non-sectarian and non-political. It was a most happy change from the bad old days of repressive anti-Gaelic legislation and sectarian attempts to 'extirpate the Irish language' from the Highlands.

'The Elementary books shall consist of a Spelling Book in Gaelic, and the Gaelic Psalm Book – to be succeeded by the Sacred Scriptures of the Old and New Testament.' The New Testament in Scottish Gaelic had been published in 1767 in 10,000 copies and reissued in 1796 in 21,500 copies; the translation of the Old Testament was issued in parts from 1783 to 1801 in 5,000 copies, and in a revised edition of 20,000 copies in 1807, in Edinburgh. An edition of 20,000 copies of the whole Bible in classical Gaelic was published by the Episcopalian Revd Robert Kirk in 1690; and as late as 1725 the same kind of Gaelic was used in a translation of the Westminster Confession of Faith of 1643, but this classical Gaelic was familiar to only a

---

* A later well-known minister who was very popular with all denominations in the parish of Small Isles was the Revd John Sinclair, a native of Kilninver, Argyll, who was the minister of the parish from 1864 until his death in 1908.

very few readers by 1800. Gaelic Catechisms had regularly been appearing in print since 1702; seventeen pages of the standard bibliography, the Revd Donald MacLean's *Typographia Scoto-Gadelica*, are taken up with short notices of these.

Otherwise, there were only a very few Gaelic books in print in 1811, mostly books of poetry, like the collection of poems published by A. and D. Stewart in 1804, the poems of Alexander MacDonald and Duncan Ban MacIntyre, unsuitable for elementary reading. James MacPherson's alleged 'Gaelic original' of his bogus translations of Ossian did not appear until 1818, and in spite of its doubtful provenance was defended by various admirers and became a source for questionable entries in Gaelic dictionaries. The literary tradition of the language was still largely an oral and manuscript one. Nevertheless, it is really rather odd that it was only two hundred years after the Reformation that Scottish Protestantism produced a vernacular Gaelic translation of the New Testament.

The Society's Gaelic schools were to be peripatetic and not to stay less than six nor more than eighteen months in any one situation. The Revd Neil MacLean reported on Canna on 7 September 1812. He said that the island was 'most destitute of instruction' and the islanders 'as to book knowledge' 'in a deplorable state'. He wrote that 'all the inhabitants [392] with the exception of seven or eight families, profess the Roman Catholic religion' and were 'remarkably tenacious of their own opinions' – which argues favourably for the teaching of Fr. Anthony MacDonald, who had studied at the Samalaman seminary and at Douai, and who was parish priest of the Small Isles from 1790 till not long before his death in 1843. However, although the Revd Neil MacLean had doubts about it, the school on Canna which was started on 1 December 1813, with William Walker as the teacher, was able to proceed on ecumenical lines. Travelling from Breadalbane, Mr Walker was shipwrecked on Ardnamurchan on his way. On 8 December he reported to the Society that:

The Roman Catholics here make no scruple in learning any thing I request – any portion of Scripture. I am greatly obliged to Mr [Donald] MacNeill for his kindness in every respect; and also to the

Priest, who lives at Eigg, you know, and came to this island some days since. He has been admonishing both old and young to attend. I have heard him saying, (while talking about me,) that he should be greatly displeased, if they should not attend, 'for (addressing them) you see he came here, not for his own interest, but for yours; therefore, I hope you'll consider that.' And there is a prospect of a large attendance. The first day I opened the School there attended 12 people; the second day I had 16, and have increased to the number of 30.

In 1814 Mr Walker reported:

10th February, 1814 – You know before I proceeded to this Station, I entertained some dubious thoughts about what progress I should make among the inhabitants, but I have been happily mistaken: indeed they are mightily pleased to see the progress my Scholars are making in their mother tongue, and I have great pleasure in seeing them so diligent – My *night* School is daily increasing. I had thirty attendants last night; two of whom are married men. One of these did not know a single letter a few days ago, and has got the Alphabet very rapidly. There is another School in the other end of the same building (i.e. the Romish Chapel, both Schools being taught under the same roof,) in which about thirty boys are taught to read English: a few of the people having employed a young Man to do so. I have often observed some of these boys running in among my Scholars (unknown to their Teacher) to steal a lesson from them; and if, on discovery, they were asked what they were doing there? they replied, they were learning to read what they understood. I teach till eight o'clock in the evening, at School, and on returning to my lodgings, there are several persons longing for my return; these I continue to teach till eleven o'clock, and often later.

4th April, 1814 – There was not a Gaelic Bible in the Island, when I came in December last; only two Testaments and one Psalm-book, from whence any person may judge of their state as to book knowledge. Among the population of 400, there were only three or four that could read any Gaelic, and these very imperfectly; now there are thirty that can, so as to be understood by the hearer; ten of these, who have been supplied with Testaments, will read with accuracy. Both the English Teacher, and the Scholars that I mentioned in a former letter, are attending our School four hours a day; upwards of eighty attend occasionally; sixty of these are constant attenders.

15th August, 1814 – I hope the inhabitants of this Island have profited by my teaching. The Scholars are getting a portion of the New Testament by heart every Lord's day, so as to be able to repeat it on the Monday – They are getting so fond of their task, that they very often have double what I request, and I have the pleasure to see every one striving to have more than the other.

3rd September, 1814 – I was really very sorry to part with these young children. Truly it was a very affecting scene to me. When I intimated my going to leave them, tears were evidently seen in many eyes, which brought some from my own, and left an impression to this very moment. On my taking leave of the Priest, (who was then in Cannay,) he expressed his sorrow at my going away, and that it gave him great pleasure to see the progress my Scholars made in the Gaelic.

In 1815 the number of inhabitants of Canna is given as 400, all Catholics except one family,* of whom 62 boys and 34 girls were attending the school. In 1816 Canna is on the Society's list of schools, with a total of 36 scholars taught by William Walker in the year ending 31 October 1816. In 1817 and 1818 there is no mention of the Small Isles in the Society's reports. In 1819 Canna is simply mentioned as one of the places from which the Society's schools had been removed before November 1821. This occurs again in the Appendices to the 1821 and 1822 reports. In the 1821 Census return and in the Appendix to the 1823 report, the population of Canna is given as 206 males and 230 females, total 436. In the twenty-third report, 1834, Canna is mentioned in this (or any other way) for the last time. Meanwhile the King had become Patron of the Society, R. G. MacDonald of Clanranald, MP, a Vice-President from 1823 until 1836. An unusual foreign and corresponding member was 'Sultan Alexander Katte-Ghery Krim-Ghery, Caucasus', mentioned amongst the office bearers in the 1820 report. Clanranald had chaired the annual meeting on 26 January 1824, and in acknowledging a Vote of Thanks had 'noticed the intense interest which the Gaelic schools had excited in districts under his own observation, and the universal cordiality with which they were received and encouraged by the Roman Catholic Clergy'.

It was too good to last; there were always potential difficulties. The 1830 Report quotes from a letter from the Revd Dr MacKay, Minister of Laggan, complaining that in Glenturret in Brae Lochaber, the priest had started his own

* Possibly Donald MacNeill's household; he was not married.

'Sabbath School' and had forbidden Catholic children to attend the Society's school there, as in the case of the Society's school founded two years earlier at Laggan Achdroma in the same district. (The priest was Donald Forbes, a native of Strathglass, who had been appointed to Brae Lochaber in 1826.) Some Catholic priests would be bound to be suspicious of any signs of proselytizing, some Protestant schoolmasters and ministers might find it difficult to maintain a completely neutral position in their approach to teaching.

In the event, the Gaelic Schools Society foundered with the Disruption of 1843. But towards the end there is plenty of evidence that the schools, which had done so much good in removing Gaelic illiteracy and improving local morals, were in some cases becoming involved in stimulating an emotional Calvinist religious revivalism which was getting out of control. The 1837 (twenty-sixth) Report of the Society quoted a long letter referring to the 'awakening in Skye, under the ministry of Mr Shaw' (the Revd John Shaw, who was minister of Bracadale from 1813 till his death in 1823) which relates how in two parishes 'where they [the Society's schools] have not been admitted and no awakening has taken place . . . the bagpipe may still be held at their funerals'. Drinking and brawling at such occasions are rightly reprobated; but here is also an example of the attack the movement developed on the secular music and literature of the Gael. There are fine moving laments played on the bagpipes very fitting for playing at funerals; fortunately they still survive. The Report of 1844 tells how 'in Eig[g], where the revival continued for the greatest length of time, many adults, from forty or fifty years of age, were induced to go to the school' and 'brought to deep anxiety regarding their eternal welfare'. At Loch Carron 'the awakening began toward the close of April. Scenes of deep emotion ensued whenever anyone addressed the children. The voice of the speaker would sometimes be drowned in the general sob of anguish and contrition that pervaded the whole meeting.'

The minister of the Small Isles at that time was the Revd John Swanson, a former grocer and schoolmaster. He was presented to the parish by Queen Victoria on the 26 March 1839, and admitted on 27 August of the same year. His parish church was on Eigg. He was notoriously anti-Catholic. In

1843 he published a Gaelic pamphlet against Popery, in Inverness, and in the same year he went over to the Free Church. Previously, in June 1836 the parish priest of the Small Isles, the Revd Fr. Donald MacKay wrote to Bishop Andrew Scott of the Western Vicariate that the Gaelic schoolmaster on Eigg had been consistently hostile to him and his hearers, and had tried to prejudice the proprietor, then Professor Hugh MacPherson, against him. Professor MacPherson's grandfather had been minister of Sleat in Skye.[2]

However, the thirty-second Report of the Gaelic Schools Society (1843) referred to the 'excellent minister of the parish, the Reverend Mr Swanson' and to a letter from their schoolmaster Donald MacKinnon on Eigg, referring to the population of the island as half Catholic 'and the Protestants were almost papists at heart', a state from which he and Mr Swanson, he said, had rescued them – thus introducing a sectarianism into the island's social life, which was to influence it for a considerable time.

The fact is that Scotland unfortunately was not ready for ecumenical religious schoolteaching in the 1820s and 1830s. Another thing that militated against the Gaelic schools was the hard fact that, as has been said, 'Gaelic alone is not enough to keep a man alive'. The people needed schools where, besides learning to read their own language, they could learn English in order to be better qualified for practical life. The pity is that when they got them through the Education Act of 1872, there was no provision in them for the teaching of the Highlanders' native language and literature at all.

NOTES

1. *Miscellanea Scotica*, iii. 100–1.
2. Noel Banks, *Six Inner Hebrides* (1977), p. 86.

16 THE MACNEILLS BECOME LANDOWNERS

Surviving rentals of Canna show Donald MacNeill senior as tenant of the whole of Canna in 1813, 1814, and 1815 at a rent of £405. 10s. 0d., John MacDonald as tenant of Lower Sanday or 'Kininellan' (Ceann an Eilein, 'the end of the Island') at a rent of £39. 10s. 0d., and crofts (no details) paying a total of £121. 12s. 10d. to Clanranald. Rentals for 1816 and 1817 are missing. The rental of 1818 shows Donald MacNeill's rent had been reduced to £373. 10s. 0d. a year, John MacDonald had disappeared and Lower Sanday had ceased to exist as a separate farm, while thirty-one tenants on Sanday were now paying a total of £166. 6s. 2d. The largest rent of these, £16. 6s. 6d., was paid by Mrs Ann MacDonald, possibly the widow of John MacDonald; on the other hand, ten tenants were paying no more than 16s 8d. each. Their holdings must have been miserably small. The total rent had fallen from £567. 9s. 6d. in 1815 to £539. 16s. 2d. in 1818. Of course the rentals make no mention of subtenants.

In 1820 and 1821 the rents were the same as in 1818, except that another tenant paying only 16s 8d. had been added to the Sanday list. The 1821 rental is the latest available; changes were coming. In 1813 Reginald George MacDonald of Clanranald, who was born in 1788, and who succeeded in 1794, the first member of his house to be educated at an English 'public school' (Eton), with the effects already described (see p. 48), started selling his estates to meet the expenses of the English social and political life in which he had become involved shortly after coming of age in 1810. He had married Lady Caroline Anne Edgecombe, daughter of the second Earl of Mount Edgecombe, in 1812, and the same year became MP for the rotten borough of Plympton, near Plymouth, in his wife's family's part of the world. He remained MP for Plympton until her death in 1824. Some time after this, he married Anne, the widow of Richard Dunning, second Baron Ashburton; she died in 1835.

Such a career was not going to improve his inherited financial position, and surviving letters in the Clanranald papers amply attest financial embarrassment.* In 1813 Lochans, Dalilea, Island Shona, and Muck were sold. In 1826 Arisaig and the superiority of Bornish in South Uist went. In 1827, Eigg. Donald MacNeill must have seen what was coming. He would either have to buy Canna and become an owner-occupier, or risk its being sold over his head and becoming an insecure tenant. He bought, for £9,000 in December 1827 (not in 1826 as is stated in *Clan Donald*). In the Clanranald papers there is a letter from Clanranald's solicitors dated 1 October 1827 referring to the possible sale of Canna and Kenachreggan to Lady Ashburton, and an offer for Canna from a Mr Johnson. Clanranald went on to sell Moidart and Kenachreggan and the Shiel fishings in 1827, and finally Uist and Benbecula to Colonel Gordon in 1838 (for £96,000). Only the stronghold of Caisteal Tioram with its little island was retained out of all the ancestral Clanranald lands.

The proceeds of the sales of the Clanranald estates came to £214,211. 11s. 7d. in all.[1] From a purely selfish financial point of view, he was lucky to get out of them so well. The kelp industry which had been so lucrative had collapsed since the duty on barilla was reduced from £11 to £8 in 1822 and from £8 to £5 the next year,[2] the same year that the Leblanc process of making soda from salt was introduced into Lancashire by James Muspratt at Liverpool. Leblanc had invented his process in 1787, when the British Fishery Society visited Canna for the first time, but its development had been impeded by the French Revolution and the Napoleonic Wars.

It was during the times of the MacNeills that emigration to Canada became an important aspect of life on Canna. An early record of it is that of six Kennedy brothers who emigrated to Nova Scotia in 1791,[3] landing at Parrsboro; two of them went on to Broad Cove in Cape Breton and the other four to Antigonish. But emigration from the Small Isles is not mentioned in the Revd Donald MacLean's report written in

* This Clanranald must have been one of the absentees whom Sir John Sinclair had in mind when he wrote of Scotland that 'the misfortune of being without resident proprietors is greatly aggravated, when they wantonly expend, in foreign countries, the income derived from the labour of their tenantry'. (*Analysis of the Statistical Account*, 1825, p. 236.)

1794 for the *Old Statistical Account of Scotland*. He does say that young women from the parish went to the Lowlands to work at the harvest, and significantly that

In this parish, a spirit of discontent seems much to prevail. Many complain of their rents, and many of their want of schools, besides other inconveniences already suggested.[4]

– which were, difficulties of transport; want of a post office nearer than Fort William; the absurd salt laws (see p. 129); the great distance from public markets, which forced the farmers and crofters to sell their cattle (there were then very few sheep) to dealers on very disadvantageous terms. Other grievances in the Hebrides were excessive personal services exacted by proprietors, the fees demanded by millers to whose mills farmers were restricted for the milling of their grain, and the duty charged on sea-borne coal.

Nevertheless, we find the Revd Donald MacLean writing to Sir James Grant of Grant, Baronet, on 1 January 1803 from Eigg complaining in bitter terms of the activities of emigration agents, some of whom he broadly hints were inspired by the republican principles of the French and American revolutions, whose activities in promoting emigration were now threatening to deprive Great Britain of able soldiers.

In these Isles and along the neighbouring Coasts of the Main-land, an Emigrant Spirit is come to an alarming pitch. It must grieve every lover of his Country and its happy Constitution, to see these fine fellows, who during the late troubles, volunteered for the National Defence – who were trained to the use of arms, and were very capable of doing essential Service to their Country – now determined to quit their Native Land forever.[5]

In the light of this statement it is startling to find Clanranald's factor D. M. Shaw writing from Benbecula to Clanranald's legal agent in Edinburgh only twenty-four years later saying that the estimated population of Clanranald's estates, including Eigg and Canna, was 5,364, of which he recommended the deportation of 2,000 from South Uist and Benbecula and another 200 from Sanday and 150 from Eigg to Cape Breton, at Government expense – estimated at £2 a head – if possible, the Estate to have the selection of the emigrants. Of Sanday, Shaw wrote:

The population of Sand Island of Canna is at least 200. You will see from the plan in your possession the extent of this spot. The people neither fish nor do anything else. I cannot imagine how they live. They are most miserably poor. They make one year 9 tons and the next 15 tons of kelp which I sell for them and credit them the price. This is all the rent they ever pay. Their whole efforts would not pay the fourth part of their arrears. The evil here arises entirely from excess of population. The people were sent to the island* with a view to the fishing to which however they never attended. They can contribute nothing towards payment of their freight to America.[6]

Throughout this letter and earlier and subsequent correspondence and official reports, one can trace the official attitude to the Highlanders and Hebrideans as that of considering them as non-persons only suitable for evacuation to the colonies once they had ceased to be needed as soldiers, statute labourers, or kelp-gatherers. In the event, Canna was sold by Clanranald to Donald MacNeill I in the same year, and this removal was not immediately carried out.

Movements of population on Canna can be traced through maps and, later, through census returns. The British Fisheries map of Canna Harbour of 1788 shows nine houses above Coroghon Bay in the flat valley still called Lag a' Bhaile, 'the dell of the township'. There is no sign of them on the Clanranald map of 1805, but there are seven houses shown on this map to the south of Creag Liath on Sanday which may very well be those of the Lag a' Bhaile crofters shifted over to Sanday to fish or make kelp. The 1805 map shows approximately thirty-six houses at the east end of Canna, including Keill, the chief village, eleven at Tarbert, three at Garrisdale, and twenty-one on Sanday, of which four near the Tràigh Bhàn entered faintly on the map may either have been ruinous or uncompleted.

The 1821 Census shows a total population of 206 males and 230 females on both islands, total 436, and 73 inhabited houses. In the 1831 Census the figures are 124 males and 140 females, total 264, inhabited houses not recorded. A drop of 172. So there was certainly a substantial emigration between 1821 and 1831. Its exact circumstances are uncertain. According to a reply given by Robert Graham to Lord Teignmouth of the

---

* From the main island of Canna, when Coroghon farm was cleared.

Committee on Emigration, the first thing done by Donald
MacNeill I after purchasing the islands (of Canna and Sanday)
had been to emigrate 200 of the inhabitants at his own expense,
and reorganize the remaining community, prohibiting squat-
ting and the subdivision of holdings.[7]

The 1841 Census gives the figures for what can be called the
last traditional distribution of population on Canna and
Sanday. The details are very interesting. On Canna there is
Coroghon house, inhabited by 'Donald MacNeil proprietor of
land, aged 70, maidservants and farm-servants'. In Keill there
were twenty-two inhabited houses, 'crofters, spirit dealer,
tailor, smith, carpenter, poor cottager'. At Tarbert, eight
inhabited houses, 'crofters, agricultural labourer, herdsman'.
(The 1805 map showed the greater part of the hill land west of
Tarbert as 'common'.) One inhabited house at Garrisdale, at
the far west of Canna, was occupied by a herdsman. Twelve
inhabited houses on Sanday were occupied by crofters.

The 1851 Census, which apparently was taken before the
removals of that year, which would have been done at the
usual time of Whitsuntide (late May), reveals that since 1841
there had been a startling redistribution of population. Two
houses are entered for Coroghon, occupied by John MacLean,
born at Allisary (in Moidart), the big drover and prospective
father-in-law of Donald MacNeill II, whose households included a 'governess, servants, shepherd, cook, chambermaid,
[and] dairymaid'. There were only six occupied houses at
Keill, inhabited by 'innkeeper and miller [presumably the
same person], teacher, paupers and [one] crofter'. Six houses
at Tarbert, occupied by a 'labourer, cottars, paupers, mason
and a superintendent of works (builder)', possibly the man
from Tobermory in charge of the workers building the stone
dykes between the hill and the arable ground. One house at
Garrisdale occupied by 'cottars'. But now thirty houses on
Sanday, occupied by 'crofters, carpenter, weaver, paupers,
tailor, fisher [and] blacksmith'.

The inhabited houses on Sanday have increased by eighteen,
those at Keill and Tarbert have decreased by sixteen and two
respectively. At six to a family, there would have been 180
persons on Sanday, an island where under modern conditions
the water supply available for five inhabited houses is hardly

sufficient in dry spells in summer. The total population was 125 males and 113 females, 238.

The 1861 Census, which reflects the consequences of the 1851 removals, more about which in the next chapter, shows the inhabited houses at Coroghon and Keill together as six, except for one pauper, occupied by the 'landed proprietor' and his family and domestic and farm servants. At Tarbert there were six houses occupied by cottars. On Sanday, seventeen houses occupied by 'crofters, boatman, domestic servants, paupers [and] blacksmith'. The total population was down to 55 males and 72 females, 127 persons.

What had happened to change the Hebrideans from 'the fine fellows, who, during the late troubles, volunteered for the National Defence' described by the Revd Donald MacLean in 1803, into the unwanted impoverished small tenants and cottars, non-persons considered suitable only for removal to Canada, in 1827? A combination of causes, of which undoubtedly the prime one was the failure of the labour-intensive kelp industry from which the proprietors had benefited so greatly,* and on which many of them had built testamentary dispositions that their heirs or their trustees could only realize by removing small tenants to make way for big sheep-farmers. Existing land laws made this very easy. As General MacNeil of Barra wrote to Fr. Angus MacDonald, the parish priest of the island, on 30 July 1825, 'if one set of servants (tenants at will are nothing else) won't do, the master must try others'.[8]

In case the reader may be tempted to think, from Shaw's account, that the people sent to Sanday from Canna were too idle to fish, the salt duties and their administration, to which reference has already been made, had produced the effect that 'the poor were totally debarred from ever having it in their power to obtain one bushel of salt, essential for preserving their catches and that the inhabitants of the Isles and of such parts of the coast as were remote from a Customs House were in great measure, excluded from any share in the Fisheries'.[9]

* Up to 1840 in Scotland the foreshore where kelp was to be found was the property of the adjacent landowner, whereas in England it was the property of the Crown. In Scotland the rights of proprietors to the foreshore were undermined by a decision of the House of Lords in that year, and since then Scottish law on the point has been assimilated by legal judgements to that of England.

A striking example of Highland maladministration by Westminster. When the salt duties were at last reduced, in 1817, the Hebridean people had no capital that would allow them to take advantage of the new situation, and far greater part of the benefit of it went to strangers.

No properly organized system of poor relief existed; it was left to the charity of individual proprietors or of volunteer societies in the mainland cities.

The 1830s were particularly bad years in the Highlands and Islands. The harvest of 1835 was poor and that of 1836 worse. As early as 1822 the Revd Alexander Simpson, minister of Uig in Skye, wrote to the Gaelic Schools Society that 'in winter, the Scholars can make little or no progress from want of light, the people being so wretchedly poor that they cannot furnish glass for a single window. The holes that in summer are open, must necessarily be filled up in winter to keep out the cold.' In the same Report of the Society, the Revd Donald Fraser of Kirkhill, who had examined fifteen schools in Kintail, Lochalsh, Skye, Strathspey, Strathdearn, and Strathglass, is quoted as saying that if anything seen during the course of his inspection could be described as painful, it was 'the manifest proof . . . of the existence of extreme poverty and wretchedness . . . In one district, just before the potato crop was ready . . . hundreds of inhabitants had no other subsistance than shell fish, principally the kind called limpets.'[10]

J. P. Day wrote of the London Government neglect of the situation of the Highlands in scathing terms:

It is of interest to note that though the State was largely responsible for the condition of affairs in the Highlands and Islands, it had done little or nothing to rescue the people from the hopeless position into which they had been allowed to drift. The Government had abolished the fishery bounties, it had killed the kelp industry, its soldiers had helped to clear the people from their hill farms. On the other hand, it had not exerted itself for the benefit of the people, except by promoting certain public works, and it had no power of control over the administration of the local poor law authorities. The latter, adhering steadfastly to their abhorrence of a legal assessment, had proved incapable of averting the crisis, and it was only by the action of private benevolent agencies from outside that the people were saved.[11]

However, in its twenty-sixth Report, in 1837, the Gaelic Schools Society was able to quote with approval an anecdote from the journal of its Superintendent, regarding his visit to Coll in 1830, 'Happy people! for although you are deeply sunk in poverty, you are rich in faith and good works. The spirit of God and your Bible have taught you that it is your duty, in whatsoever station of life you may be placed, to be there with content.'[12]

NOTES

1. *Clan Donald*, ii. 304.
2. J. P. Day, *Public Administration in the Highlands and Islands*, (*PAHI*), p. 85.
3. John A. MacDougall, *History of Inverness County*. The 1788 British Fisheries Society report of 1788 noted that the old leases of small tenants were due to expire in two years. See p. 126.
4. *Old Statistical Account of Scotland*, XVII. 292 (1796).
5. Scottish Record Office (SRO) GD 248/656.
6. SRO GD 201/–/354(3). See also J. L. Campbell, 'The Clearing of Clanranald's Islands', *Scots Magazine*, Jan. 1945, where this letter is printed in full.
7. Letter of Mr R. Graham to Mr Fox Maule, 6 May 1837. *Appendix to the First Report from the Select Committee on Emigration: Scotland*, 1841, p. 218.
8. Letter of General Roderick MacNeil of Barra to Revd Fr. Angus Macdonald, 30 July 1825, *Book of Barra*, p. 183.
9. *PAHI* 245–6.
10. *Twelfth Annual Report*, pp. 21–4.
11. *PAHI* 88.
12. Gaelic Schools Society, *26th Report*, p. 37.

17 DONALD MACNEILL II AND THE CLEARING OF CANNA

Donald MacNeill senior, as we have seen, bought Canna in 1827 on a falling kèlp market, probably to secure his position as occupier at a time when Reginald George MacDonald of Clanranald (1788–1873) was selling all his estates. On 2 May 1837, nine and a half years later, Donald MacNeill made a will under which he left the estate of Canna, Sanday, and the Island of Hysker and all his livestock, money, and movable gear to his natural son Donald, then living on Canna, on condition that Donald paid all his lawful debts, and also paid to Donald senior's natural daughter Jean the sum of £3,000, and to Donald senior's nephew Hector Archibald MacNeill, WS, then living in Edinburgh, the sum of £1,000, and to Donald senior's second natural son Archibald the same sum of £1,000. Donald junior was to be his father's sole executor. In the event of his not being of age at the time of Donald senior's decease, the following curators were appointed under the will: 'Captain Archibald MacNeil of the Ninth Royal Veteran Battalion residing in Edinburgh; Hector Archibald MacNeill, Writer to the Signet; Alexander Thomas Esquire, Banker, Greenock; [blank] McSwan Collector of Poor Rates, Greenock; and Dr. Alexander MacDonald residing in Inverness.' In the event of Donald junior's decease before marrying or coming of age, Hector Archibald MacNeill was to inherit Canna.

Donald MacNeill junior was very far from being of age in 1837; in fact he was only about three or four years old. According to his description in legal documents in the early 1850s, of which more later, Donald junior was born on or about 18 June 1833 or 1834. It is odd that there was no knowledge of the exact year, but the confusion that existed after his father's death on 10 November 1848 revealed that written records were not kept on Canna. This gave rise to some tiresome uncertainty about the date on which Donald junior really came of age, a matter of considerable legal importance. There was also the matter of his illegitimacy. Under an Act of 1696 of the

Scottish Parliament, curators of an illegitimate child could not be legally appointed by will, a fact which Donald MacNeill senior and his solicitor must have overlooked. Also, it was questionable for one of them to be a legitimate relative of the testator named in the will as his alternative heir.

One can only speculate on how this situation arose. My theory is that once Donald MacNeill senior felt obliged to buy Canna in 1827 to protect his security, he found himself a landowner without a direct heir. It is doubtful if any of his nephews, established on the mainland, would have wanted to return to Canna to become island farmers. At the same time Donald senior was on the verge of sixty years of age by 1827, and the prospect of going looking for a bride from the families of the small lairds and tacksmen in other islands, who would be young enough to produce an heir, must have been a discouraging one. Possibly an arrangement was made whereby some young woman on Canna was willing to do so without wedding lines. We do not know; such things can well have happened in the old Highlands. Neither the mother of Donald senior's daughter (who was considerably older than Donald junior) nor Donald junior's mother is mentioned in Donald senior's will, nor is Donald junior's mother's name on his memorial plaque in the Canna graveyard.

No doubt there was some independent provision for these ladies. What strikes one about the will is the generous provisions made for the other legatees at a time when Island estates were much less profitable than they were a generation earlier. Donald senior's total money legacies exceeded his father Hector's.

The sky fell in when Donald I died on 10 November 1848, at the age of seventy-nine. Utter confusion followed with regard to his affairs. All the curators he nominated for his young heir refused to act, with the exception of Hector Archibald MacNeill, WS (described as a Captain in the Edinburgh County Militia), who was however informed that his appointment was invalid, because as has been said, the Scots Act of Parliament of 1696 authorized a father only to appoint curators for his legitimate children. It was necessary for Hector MacNeill to petition the Court to appoint him as curator; they refused to appoint him as sole curator because under Donald senior's will he would succeed to the estate should his ward die before coming of age or marrying. To get over this difficulty, Major Archibald MacNeill, formerly of the Royal Veteran Battalion, agreed also to act, whereupon both were appointed curators on 8 March 1849.

Very fortunately the letter book containing the correspondence for the years of 1849 and 1850 between Donald senior's solicitors, the now extinct firm of Nisbet and Sproat, and Hector Archibald MacNeill and others over the future of Canna, had been preserved in private ownership. This reveals that Donald MacNeill senior had kept hardly any written records; no one knew what rents were payable by his small tenants; rents had been paid in kind, usually in the form of young cattle given at various times to the laird, who clearly had been generous to the people of Canna in the hard years of the 1840s. In the Census return of 1841 there is a note by the Small Isles parish schoolmaster in which he states that 'notwithstanding the proprietor of this island [Canna] acted with much generosity and liberality towards his poor people, a good many families in this island would readily follow their friends to America provided that they had the means to do so'. There had been voluntary emigration from Canna to Cape Breton after 1821, and by 1841 the population had fallen to 264. In 1850 Henry Nisbet wrote to Hector Archibald MacNeill that 'the islanders are without gratitude and expect the proprietor to feed them as if they were his own children'. Since 1841, the disastrous potato blight had struck the Isles.

At this time, a big grazier from Moidart, John MacLean from Glenforslan, born at Alissary, was established on Canna, though not resident apart from visits. When he first got a lease from Donald MacNeill is unknown, but he must have had the grazing of a substantial part of the island (except Sanday), for in Nisbet and Sproat's letter book there is a 'Note of Sumes due by John MacLean, Esq., of Canna, to Curators of Mr Donald MacNeill' dated 8 November 1849, amounting to:

1. Half a year's rent of the Island,
   due at Martinmas 1849 . . . . £ 150/0/0
2. Interest of [= on] £1519/18 being valuation
   of sheep stock and black cattle at entry . . . . £ 38/0/0

3. Interest of Mr MacLean's promissory note of
    £700 to late Mr MacNeill, payable at
    Martinmas 1846, for three years . . . . £ 105/0/0
4. Price of cattle bought from Sanday island . . . . £ 27/12/−
5. Price of two feather beds . . . . £   3/0/0
6. Price of Delf bought by Mrs MacLean . . . . £   1/16/1

                                                        £ 325/8/0

N.B. The crop will also have to be paid when
the price is fixed by the Valuators.

Mr MacLean denied that interest on the promissory note
was outstanding, claiming he had already paid this to Donald
MacNeill senior. In the absence of written records the
executors were unable to disprove this, though they had their
doubts. At Whitsuntide 1850 the interest due on crop and
stock at a rate of 5 per cent was stated to be £75. 19s. 6d. At this
rate, the sum stated to be due at Martinmas 1849 as interest
shows that he must have entered on the grazing two years
earlier.

In the existing circumstances John MacLean was in a very
strong position to make an offer for the lease of the whole of
Canna. This he did, offering a rent of £400 p.a. on the following conditions:

1. That the dwelling house was put into good order.
2. That Canna was cleared of small tenants.
3. That a stone dyke 5½ feet high was built between the
    arable ground and the hill grazing. He also wanted sheep
    fanks built.

He also wanted a pier and a proper road made on the island.

Nisbet & Sproat wrote to Hector A. MacNeill on 12 July
1849 that they had already performed the formality of taking
Decrees of Removal against all the Canna people, who of
course were tenants-at-will. 'It is not imperative for you to
remove them though the Decrees were obtained . . . a good
many of them are disposed to emigrate of their own free will
and consent.' On 17 July 1849 Nisbet and Sproat wrote: '. . .
there is no doubt that Mr MacLean expects that all the Tenants
are to be removed from the Main Island, and I am fully aware
that only the Keill tenants are mentioned in the Lease. When

Mr MacLean was signing the lease, he wished the Tarbert tenants to be also inserted for being removed, but this I would not consent to.' The letter added that Mr MacLean was best qualified to be the farming tenant.

In the event, the house was repaired; the stone dykes were built under the direction of a foreman, James Cumming from Tobermory, the workers being paid with charity meal, some of the stones coming from the deserted cottages of emigrants (a later farm manager is said to have broken up carved stones from the old graveyard at Keill and used them in building; two particularly fine ones were hidden by local patriots who buried them in some spot that is now unfortunately forgotten); and the township of Keill, was cleared of small tenants in 1851.

And what of Donald MacNeill junior, on whose behalf, and on behalf of the interests of whose half-sister and brother his curators Hector Archibald MacNeill, WS, and Nisbet and Sproat were acting? The Clearing of Canna cannot be imputed to Donald junior personally. He was only fourteen or fifteen years old at the time of his father's death and only seventeen or eighteen when the people were evicted in 1851. (In those days twenty-one was the time of coming-of-age.) His mother was one of the Canna people.*

Donald junior had lived on Canna for the first seven years of his life, to 1840 or 1841. He had then been sent to an aunt who lived at Oban, to go to school there, and he remained there until he was fourteen or fifteen, that is until 1848, when he had been sent for a time to a school at Irvine; possibly another relative lived there. This seems to have been all the education he had, and it was obviously inadequate for the responsibilities he would have when he succeeded his father as laird of Canna. As a young man Donald MacNeill junior was obviously naïve, unsophisticated, and badly in need of paternal guidance, especially in his dealings with women.

On 29 June 1850 Nisbet and Sproat wrote to Hector A. MacNeill at Haughead Cottage, Innerleithen, saying that Donald had come back from Canna to Tobermory with Mr Sproat, but left the next day to spend another week on the

---

* His half-sister's mother's name was Jane MacDonald. The identity of Donald's mother is not certain.

island, saying that the weather had been so bad before that he wanted to spend another week there to go over the Island, as he did not intend to visit it again for four years. This must refer to the plan for him to study farming in the Borders. But he must have been on Canna again in the summer of 1851 at the time of the great Clearance, probably for farewells, because there is a very strong tradition on Canna that as he was watching the people go, an old woman turned to him and said *Thig an latha fhathast gum fàg sibh Canaidh cho bochd ruinn fhìn* – 'The day will come yet that you'll leave Canna as poor as ourselves'. The day did come, as will be seen. Keill, which must have been inhabited continuously since at least the time of St Columba, was left empty, its well blocked up with stones.

The census figures for 1841, 1851, and 1861 give a good picture of the internal and external population movements connected with Canna and Sanday.

Population

Year	Males	Females	Total
1841	116	139	255
1851	125	113	238
1861	55	72	127

Inhabited Houses

Year	Coroghon	Keill	Tarbert	Garrisdale	Sanday	Total
1841	1*	22	8	1	12	44
1851	2*	6	6	1	30	45
1861	6		6	–	17	29

The 1851 Clearance clearly took place in May, after the 1851 Census, the usual time for terminating tenancies in Scotland. This is borne out by the fact that Fr. Coll MacDonald, who was stationed on Canna in 1850, was moved to Knoydart in June 1851. It is unfortunate that no record of the names of the emigrants, nor of the *immediate* effects of the Clearance, survives, but even ten years later the drastic reduction of population is obvious.

* Occupied by Donald MacNeill senior 'aged 70' in 1841, and by John MacLean 'farmer, b. Alisarry' in 1851.

1. 'The Witches' Home' (Coroghon). Sketch by Dickey Doyle, 1875. Doyle visited Canna in 1875 on Viscount Sherbrooke's yacht.

2. Robert Thom, Laird of Canna from 1881 to 1911.

3. Canna House around 1885. The white building just above the shore was the original laird's house, and had two storeys. The part of the wall painted white shows its full original length. It was called Coroghon; the stack with the building shown in Doyle's sketch was known as *Corra-dhùn thall*, 'Yonder Coroghon'.

4. Robert Thom and a Porbeagle Shark caught off Canna.

5. Yachts and fishing boats in Canna Harbour around 1890.

6. Herring Curing at Canna Pier. Presumably taken between 1892, when the pier was built, and 1905, when the West Highland Railway reached Mallaig, and curing operations were transferred there. Canna Harbour was much used by Barra fishermen at this time.

7. Canna Estate employees and crofters, 1885. Back row, left to right: Mr Hayne, factor; Archie MacLeod; John 'Grieve' MacKinnon; a man from Oban (?); Charles MacInnes; Hector MacDonald (father of Angus MacDonald, see illustration 21). Malcolm MacKinnon; Joseph MacKinnon; uncertain; Donald MacKinnon. Middle row, left to right: Malcolm MacArthur; Mary MacLeod (MacKinnon); Angus MacLeod (whose early memories are printed in Appendix X); Peter MacLeod; Mary MacKinnon; 'Smith' Campbell; Kate MacLeod; Donald MacKinnon; Mary MacInnes. Front row: a Campbell boy (?); Duncan MacArthur; uncertain. The identifications are from Mrs MacGregor's annotated copy.

8. Filling wool bags in the old days. Nowadays shearing and bag-filling are done in a shed, the shearing by electricity.

9. The builders of the Bute Memorial RC Chapel on Sanday.

10. Barra fishing boats in Canna Harbour.

14. Aerial photograph of Canna Harbour, 1981. Shows the footbridge between Canna and Sanday. The RC Chapel can be seen on the upper right, the Presbyterian Church below the stacks on the upper left.

15. (*left*) The Snake Stone. For its possible symbolism, see C. G. Jung, *Symbols of Transformation,* pp. 438–9. The lower two pieces of this most interesting stone were found by the late Allan G. Thom in the stone wall of the present graveyard around 1900; the top piece was found by Margaret Fay Shaw embedded in the soil beside the wall, in 1939.

16. (*below left*) The Canna Celtic Cross, front side.

17. (*below right*) The Celtic Cross, obverse side.

18. Salving timber after storms. Left to right: uncertain; Donald MacKinnon; Tam Campbell; Charles MacArthur; John MacIsaac (1947).

19. Shearing at Canna fank, around 1950.

20. The Haymakers, 1981. Left to right, Geraldine MacKinnon, Ian MacKinnon (farm manager), Donald John MacKinnon.

21. (far left) Angus
MacDonald, 'Aonghus
Eachainn', 1863–1947, the
island's chief tradition bearer.

22. (left) The late Hector
MacDonald, 'Eachann
Aonghuis Eachainn',
bringing blackface sheep
from the west end of Canna
for shearing at the farm
steading.

23. The author and his wife at the front door of Canna House.

24. Lester Borley, Director of the National Trust for Scotland, presents the Royal Highland and Agricultural Society's Long Service Medal to Ian MacKinnon, Farm Manager, Isle of Canna, on 19 August 1983.

Beginning of the formation of basalt columns. Vesicles (gas bubbles) are still abundant at the base of the columns.

Fine-grained, vesicular lava. This zone has cooled suddenly (being the base of the lava flow), so that gas bubbles were "frozen-in" when the lava cooled.

Coal seam. This shaley coal probably represents peat marsh which has been compressed and heated by the overlying lava flow, producing an irregular seam.

Fine-grained volcaniclastic sediment.

Medium to coarse grained volcanic sand, with some current bedding.

Coarse, current-graded, volcanic pebble conglomerate, irregularly interbedded with coarse and medium sand. This suggests vigorous erosion and high current-activity in a beach/intertidal-stream type of environment. Earlier lava flows were the source for this sediment.

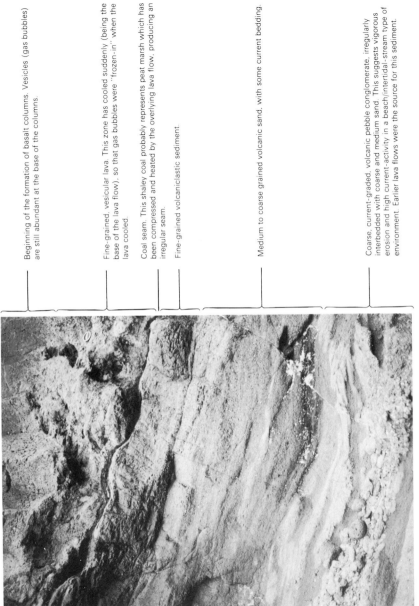

25. Cliff Section, Langanes, Canna, 1983. Section height approx. 2 metres.

Regarding the Canna Clearance of 1851, it is an interesting fact that apart from the Tobermory firm of Nisbet and Sproat, the chief actors in the drama – John MacLean the big grazier and drover, and Hector A. MacNeill, WS, the curator of the young heir – were Highlanders themselves, indeed Hector MacNeill was closely connected with Canna, and the young heir for whom they were acting was the son of a Canna woman (who, if still living, was probably not sent away with the evicted emigrants). The situation illustrates the economic conditions that often produced clearances in the Highlands; an over-optimistic will leaves an heir burdened with legacies that the estate finances cannot afford; the trustees of a marriage settlement or of an heir not of age, usually Edinburgh lawyers, feel obliged to act wholly in the interest of the beneficiaries of the settlement; the practical way to do this is to evict tenants-at-will and let the land to a big farmer, whose sheep and cattle will benefit from the accumulated fertility of many generations of arable land worked with the caschrom, and fertilized with seaweed carried to the riggs on the backs of ponies – or even of women.

T. S. Muir the ecclesiologist, who visited Canna in July 1856, two years after Donald MacNeill junior had come of age, gives a melancholy picture of the desolation of de-populated Keill:

In this island are two places of sepulture, close to each other, one of them ancient, the other modern. Both are lying open, and in a shocking condition. Standing in the older one, and formed of a hard pale-red coloured stone, said to have been brought from the neigh-bouring island of Rum, is a cross six feet six inches in height, the upper and south arms broken off. Like the pillar of Soroby, Tiree, both faces present a double plane, the outer one covered with worn carvings of grotesque human figures, hybrid animals, and braided work. In the other burying ground there are two or three slabs, on one of which is a raven; also a tall red-coloured pillar worn bare. Of the church, which was dedicated to St. Columba, only slight traces remain.[1]

All would have gone well with the big farmer John MacLean for a while. He had the advantage of the fertility of land cultivated and manured for many generations, for his sheep. But land deteriorates under the intense grazing of sheep introduced in such numbers. The late Angus MacDonald, born in 1863 and formerly grieve of Canna, told the writer that parts of the hill that were now covered by heather or bracken, had been green in his young days.

With the failure of the kelp industry in consequence of Government fiscal policy, and the refusal of Clanranald and Hector MacNeill to allow the British Fisheries Society to establish a proper fishing settlement on Canna after 1788, it is clear enough that the island was over-populated in 1851. But there had been voluntary emigration before 1851 and there would have been more, with a little official help, after that date. What is so highly objectionable about the Highland Clearances is the complete lack of security of tenure and compensation for improvements for small tenants before the Crofters' Act of 1886. Under such conditions there were immense opportunities for petty tyranny on the part of the factors and ground officers of absentee landowners in the Highlands, who in those days had the entire force of the law behind them. To a Norwegian or an Icelander, accustomed to a free peasant society, the agrarian conditions that existed in the Highlands and Islands in the eighteenth and nineteenth centuries are quite incredible, something like the conditions that still prevail in Sicily and the southern half of Italy.

In September 1851 Donald junior went to stay with a farmer, William Gibson, at West Bold farm near Innerleithen in order to learn farming, and remained until May 1854, when, as he was (on the earliest calculation) about to come of age on 18 June, Canna was made over to him, but not his money, which remained under the care of his curators. His stay at Innerleithen was punctuated by visits to his half-sister and brother-in-law Mr and Mrs George Melville at Campbeltown, and by occasional trips to Edinburgh, which is about thirty-two miles from Innerleithen.

In the summer of 1853 Donald had the misfortune to fall in with a bunch of rogues at Campbeltown who did their best to entrap him in a situation where money could be extracted from him by threats of a breach-of-promise action. This crowd of shysters consisted of Alexander MacMillan, WS, Keeper of the Minute Book of the Court of Session, and his two brothers-in-law David Cormack and Colin Galbraith, and Colin Galbraith's son and daughter, Edward and Jane. The two Galbraith men were clerks of Cormack's and Cormack was in partnership with MacMillan in Edinburgh. By means of carefully arranged parties and the free use of whisky, the MacMillan–Cormack–Galbraith combine was able to manœuvre Donald into what could be called a compromising situation with Jane Galbraith in Edinburgh in the autumn of 1853, although they were perfectly aware that he was then already engaged to Isabella, the daughter of John MacLean, the drover-tacksman of Canna.

Towards the end of 1853 Donald MacNeill informed MacMillan and the Galbraiths that he could not marry Jane Galbraith, being under this previous engagement to Isabella. But Cormack and Edward Galbraith went to West Bold and got Donald to agree to a meeting at the Crown Hotel in Edinburgh on 30 December. At this meeting, with the liberal use of whisky, Cormack and Galbraith got Donald to sign a deed formally written on stamped paper, which the plotters later extended into the form of a promissory note for £1,000 in favour of Miss Galbraith and her family, and a bond for £3,000 in Miss Galbraith's favour, to bear interest from 1 June 1854. The witnesses to this deed were two waiters employed at the hotel.

On top of this involvement with Jane Galbraith and her rascally relations, Donald junior, apparently unable to resist the attractions of young women or the machinations of their designing relations, had managed to involve himself in the spring of 1854 with Joanna, the daughter of George Black, the Tobermory merchant who had had dealings with Donald senior; Donald met Joanna while attending her sister's wedding. An attachment ensued, followed by a promise of marriage to take place in the middle of July 1854. But by the end of June it was being rumoured that Donald was going to marry Isabella MacLean. George Black decided to ask for an explanation.

The first fortnight of July, 1854, must have been a remarkably tense period in Canna's history. First Edward Galbraith turned up at Canna without warning on the second, with a stamped bill for a promissory note for £1,000 payable to his sister Jane in Edinburgh at Martinmas, which Donald signed, believing that the deed of 30 December 1853 was binding on him, which it was not, since he was not then of age and was acting without informing his curators. Edward Galbraith also brought an extended bond for £3,000 in favour of Jane which Donald agreed to sign at a public house in Edinburgh on 14 July. Donald in due course left for Edinburgh; hardly had he done so than a smack arrived at Canna from Tobermory with a messenger sent by George Black to demand an explanation of Donald's intentions: Donald was not there, and the messenger could not find him at John MacLean's residence in Moidart, or at Fort William, where it was said Donald and Isabella were to be married. All these parties must have believed Donald to be much richer than he actually was.

Donald arrived at Edinburgh and met Edward Galbraith at the Ship Hotel on 14 July, and signed the £3,000 bond in favour of Jane Galbraith. On 15 July Donald married Isabella MacLean, presumably in Edinburgh or not farther away than Glasgow or Stirling. All this flurry went on, obviously, on the assumption that Donald had come of age on 18 June 1854, though that was not absolutely certain. On 22 November Cormack addressed a letter to Donald stating that he had advanced cash to Jane Galbraith on the security of Donald's promissory note and had thus become the owner of the note. This letter was brought to Canna by a messenger-at-arms on 30 November 1854.

The upshot of this business was that on 8 June 1855 claims were presented in the Court of Session by Jane Galbraith and David Cormack for sums totalling £6,000, and by George Black and his daughter Joanna, who asked for £4,000, totalling £9,000, against which the Curators only held a current account for £197. 15s 0d. and a deposit account for £5,447. 9s. 11d. at the Bank of Scotland. Against the latter account the Melvilles and Hector Archibald MacNeill, WS, had claims for £3,000 and £1,000 respectively under Donald MacNeill senior's will. There was an immediate petition against the Black and Galbraith claims. Joan Black in the event accepted £150; and there was, of course, a good defence against the Cormack–Galbraith claim, which according to local tradition was heard before Duncan MacNeill, Lord Colonsay, President of the Court of Session.

In fact, no record of the arguments or discussions that followed the Petition of Recall of 12 June 1855 has been found, but the outcome was that the Arrestments were recalled on Donald MacNeill's finding caution for £1,000, which was paid on 18 September 1855. Taking into account his legal expenses, Donald had started his career as owner of Canna with a financial disaster.

We do not know the date when Donald MacNeill II took over the management of Canna and the ownership of the farm livestock there from his father-in-law, nor what he paid for the livestock, nor whether his wife Isabella got any legacy from her father's property after his death on Eigg in 1866. We do know that by 1857 John MacLean and his family were established in a tenancy of Kildonan farm on Eigg, and were living there, and that in that year and in 1858 the MacNeills were coming over from Canna to pay them visits; on 18 August 1858 they came over with their two eldest children, Jean aged four and Donald aged two, both children speaking only Gaelic.[2]

It follows that Donald MacNeill must have taken charge on Canna before 1857. In 1953 Mr David Fox, who had read an article by the writer about Canna in the *Scots Magazine*, wrote from Innerleithen telling how Donald MacNeill had persuaded his great grandfather, who was steward of the home farm on the nearby Traquair estate, to come to manage Canna 'about a hundred years ago'. Samuel Fox is remembered on Canna; it is believed he was responsible for building the farm steading called 'The Square' at Rubha nan Còrr ('the Point of the Herons').

The only known contemporary description of Donald MacNeill and his family is that contained in Robert Buchanan's account of Canna in his book *The Land of Lorne*, published in 1871, which includes the story of the Hebridean cruise he made in his small yacht the *Tern* several years earlier (no dates are given). He visited Canna in fine weather, saw it at its best, and romanticized it and its owner, as such visitors sometimes do. Buchanan remarks that the laird's house was a 'solid modern building, surrounded by the civilized brick wall [it is stone] . . . a recent erection, strangely out of keeping with the rude cabins and heather houses in the vicinity', and he describes Donald MacNeill as a 'shrewd, active, broad shouldered' man, and still young.[3]

There were eighty people on the island, Buchanan said, and:

Each cottar or shepherd pays his rent in labour, and is permitted a plot of ground to grow potatoes and graze a cow. The fishermen are supplied in the same way. Both sexes toil out of doors at the crops and take part in the shearing, but the women have plenty of time to watch the cow and weave homespun on their rude looms. All on the isle, excepting only the Laird himself, belong to the old Romish faith, even the Laird's own wife and children being Catholics. There is no bickering, civil or religious. The supreme head of the state is universally popular, and praised for his thoughtfulness and generosity – a single example of which is as good as a hundred. It is said to be the custom of many Highland proprietors, notably those of Islay, to levy a rent on those who burn the sea-weeds and tangles on their shore, charging the poor makers about a pound on every ton of kelp so produced. Not so the Laird of Canna. 'He charges nothing,' said our informant.

This idealized account hardly accords with what Mr R. V. G. Thom was told by old men on Canna, that in their young days they were always hungry, and that the shores of the island were scoured for limpets from end to end.

The fact is that by 1871, when Buchanan's book was published, Donald MacNeill must have been a worried man. The 'solid modern building'* which according to tradition his wife had insisted on his constructing for her, after she had visited a wealthy relation in the Kelvingrove district of Glasgow who had one, had to be paid for, and there is evidence that suggests strongly that it was being paid for with borrowed money. Donald's financial history can be traced in broad outline from the list of Discharged Security Writs in the title-deeds of Canna. On coming of age he became liable to pay £1,000 to Hector Archibald MacNeill and £3,000 to his half-sister Mrs Melville. (His brother Archibald who was left £1,000 under their father's will must have died before 1853.) The £5,675. 4s. 11d. left by his father must have been considerably diminished by legal expenses connected with the Jane Galbraith and Joan Black claims. In June 1857 he borrowed £2,000 on bond from

* The house, which is now called Canna House, was originally called Coroghon (Gaelic *Corra-dhùn*, after the farm and castle), later, after Robert Thom built Tighard ('High House' in Gaelic) it was often called the 'Low House'.

Henry Nisbet, WS, of Tobermory, possibly to pay for cattle and sheep taken over on Canna from his father-in-law. There was a further bond in favour of Henry Nisbet dated 23 July 1861 for £1,500.

In 1865 some money must have been available, as the bonds in favour of Hector MacNeill and Henry Nisbet were then discharged, and the Melvilles were paid their claim, all in the month of July. But these payments had been made by borrowing a month earlier £1,000 from the marriage contract trustees of F. F. Bankhardt and Jane Duncan, and £5,000 from those of Malcolm MacNeill of Southland, New Zealand, and Clara Buchanan. These bonds were not discharged until, after several assignations and reassignations, they were met from the proceeds of the sale of Canna to Robert Thom in 1881. Donald MacNeill's progress as a bonded debtor may be summarized as follows:

Date	Debt		Renounced or discharged	Total bonded indebtedness
18 June 1854 (coming of age)	Owed	£4,000		£4,000
8 June 1857	Borrowed	£2,000		£6,000
23 July 1861	Borrowed	£1,500		£7,500
June 1865	Borrowed	£6,000		£13,500
July 1865			£7,500	£6,000
Aug. 1868	Borrowed	£2,000		£8,000
July 1871	Borrowed	£4,000		£12,000
Sept. 1878	Borrowed	£3,000		£15,000
Dec. 1880	Borrowed	£3,150		£18,150

The last two borrowings were £3,000 from the Scottish Amicable Life Assurance Society, and £3,150 from John MacLean at Kenigharair, in Mull. In the case of the first, John MacLean of Gometra is named as Donald's cautioner (possibly the same person). More of these bonds contracted after 1861 were discharged after the sale of Canna.

Donald's wife Isabella died on 25 January 1877, aged forty-eight. They had had five children, Jean, Donald, John, Harry, and Peter, but Jean had died young. All their sons were educated as lay-students at Ushaw College, between 1874 and 1880. The first word of the sale of Canna to Robert Thom came to the outer world with a party of tinkers who crossed in a small boat to Rum, and is recorded by Edwin Waugh in his *The Limping Pilgrim*, published in 1883. Rumours of a sale of Canna had been going round for some time. 'The old man had hardly time to get ashore before he was met with the question "Is Canna sold?", "Canna is sold", replied he; "Canna is sold; it was sold last Thursday to a gentleman of the name of Thom, a Glasgow shipowner. It was sold for £23,000 – the island and all the stock upon it".'

So passed from Canna one of the last, if not the last Highland laird to be a native Gaelic speaker. It is said that the price he got for the island was insufficient to meet all his debts, fulfilling the prophecy the old woman made in 1851 at the time of the evictions. Donald MacNeill, who is said to have become very stout by 1881,* left Canna for Tobermory, and his sons John, Harry, and Peter, emigrated to Manitoba, where Harry, who in 1876 had been a student at Ushaw, later established himself successfully and had a distinguished career as a socially prominent lawyer in Winnipeg. He had some correspondence with the present writer. John died young in a drowning accident in Lake Winnipegosis; Donald went to Australia where he died in Brisbane in 1945.

* He had probably developed a dropsical condition.

NOTES

1. T. S. Muir, *Ecclesiological Notes*, p. 32. It is the 'Punishment Stone', not the Cross, which is of red sandstone.

   The late T. C. Lethbridge was told by Allan MacIsaac, crofter on Sanday, in September 1955, he had been with his father when they were shown, around 1900, the site of St Columba's chapel by an old man who had gone there, and who had told them that the MacNeills had not been responsible for its destruction. In fact, the British Fisheries Society's report of 1788 shows that the chapel was in a ruinous condition nearly 200 years ago (see p. 123). Allan MacIsaac said that Hector MacNeill was buried under slabs of Portland stone ballast near the carved cross, and that he had been a smuggler and was married to a daughter of Clanranald who had brought part of Tarbert, Canna, as a dowry. (We know that his wife was in fact a daughter of MacDonald of Boisdale.)

   Allan MacIsaac told T. C. Lethbridge that the chapel had stood north-west of the cross on a line between it and the neighbouring mound, and that the original MacIsaac croft had been due north of the cross to the east of the Mound.

2. Information kindly supplied by Mr Noel Banks from the diaries of Michael Pakenham Edgeworth, who was married to the then laird of Eigg's sister.
3. *The Land of Lorne*, p. 18.

18   CANNA IN MODERN TIMES

When Canna was bought by Robert Thom in 1881, it acquired an owner who had adequate capital behind him for effecting considerable improvements. Capital from outside the island was not brought in, to any appreciable extent, until Hector MacNeill's entry in 1781. Hector MacNeill, with the help of the Clanranald estate, made considerable improvements, building Coroghon house (now the bothy) and garden, the present 'Changehouse' and barn, Coroghon barn,* and a water-mill near the present chapel. The water-mill has disappeared though part of the mill-dam remains. The other buildings are substantial and in very good taste, though Coroghon house lost its upper storey when Donald, Hector MacNeill's grandson, built the present Canna House or 'Low House' in the 1860s with borrowed money. Before he came of age, his curators had had the fanks and the stone dykes, between the arable land and the hill, built for their tenant, John MacLean. The farmsteading and house were built by Samuel Fox, Donald MacNeill's manager, in the 1850s. Also in his time the public authority erected the schoolhouse on Sanday, which opened in 1874.

The improvements made by Robert Thom were substantial. The pier was built, of green-heart oak, under the Canna Pier Order of 1892. This was a very substantial improvement indeed, and one which led to the development of Canna as a herring curing station much frequented by Barra fishermen, up to the 1914 War; but later Mallaig, with its railhead, took away this business. A steam-driven mechanical grain mill superseded the water-mill, where a smithy was erected. The boiler blew up around 1926. The Sanday crofters were helped to improve their houses. The writer was told that the present crofts on Sanday were created by Donald MacNeill II in lieu of

---

* Coroghon barn is not on the 1788 British Fisheries Society map, which shows Coroghon House and garden, the Changehouse and the Changehouse barn, and the Corn Mill. Coroghon barn however is shown on the 1805 Clanranald map of Canna. 'Coroghon' is a corruption of the Gaelic *Corra-dhùn*, meaning 'Peculiar Fort'.

wages owed to his men at the time of the sale of Canna, and that prior to the coming of the Thoms, money had hardly circulated on Canna at all.

The Thoms built up a fine herd of pedigree Highland cattle, and latterly imported Galloways. They also planted trees behind Canna House and at the foot of its garden. Ninety-five rings were counted in an elm that blew down there in late 1981. In 1905 Robert Thom built Tighard up the hill from Canna House, and planted more trees behind and around it. It is now occupied by the National Trust for Scotland and used for their summer project parties. Later a fine plantation of Corsican pines was made by the ravine of the Haligary burn below Compass Hill. Robert Thom died in 1911 and was very worthily commemorated by the erection of a Presbyterian parish church on Rubha Cairinnis, apparently a copy of an early Irish church building in Glendalough. (The statement in Scott's *Fasti Ecclesiae Scoticanae* that Alan G. Thom restored the ancient church of Canna dedicated to St Columba is wrong; this stood at Keill, more than half a mile away.) The church built in 1913 as a memorial to Alan G. Thom's father Robert was an entirely new building. There is no resident congregation, but the church is much used by East Coast fishermen when in Canna harbour, and there are occasional services for visitors in the summer. Regrettably an interesting carved collection plate was stolen from the church in 1981; a foreign yachtsman was strongly suspected. A fine ornamental wrought-iron gate, presented by Wallace Menzies Esq. for the churchyard enclosure, was dedicated at a service held by the Revd W. Grant Anderson on 27 August 1969.

The original Roman Catholic chapel on Canna was the small building near the former graveyard at Keill of which no trace now remains; it was described by Pennant as being in a ruinous condition as long ago as 1770. A building near the 'Square' was used in the nineteenth century until Robert Thom of Canna in 1886 allowed the Marquess of Bute a site for a Roman Catholic chapel on Sanday, on the opposite side of the harbour from Canna House, where it would be a landmark to shipping. The chapel was built by Lady Bute in memory of her father, Edward, Lord Howard of Glossop, completed in 1890, and dedicated to St Edward the Confessor. The architect was William Frame, and the carvings were by Thomas Nicholls. There was a much larger community on Sanday then, and the harbour was also much used by fishermen from Barra and Eriskay, who were all Catholics; but conditions changed, and when the majority of the population came about to be living on the Canna side of the harbour, reversion was made to the use of the former church building, which during the interval had served as a post office.

An important event in the story of Canna was the construction by the Northern Lighthouse Board of the important lighthouse on Heiskeir or Hyskeir in 1904. Heiskeir, which is still, along with the isolated rock Humla, the property of Dr J. L. Campbell, is a low (thirty-two feet highest point) rocky island of about fifty acres, about twenty of them grass, with many dangerous submerged rocks to the south and south-west; it is a little surprising that a lighthouse was not made there earlier.[1] It is manned by three men, whose families are stationed at Oban; and was provided with a helicopter landing pad in 1973. Landing is easy in calm weather, and a day's outing to Heiskeir, with the chance of seeing basking sharks, killer whales, dolphins, and seals, as well as shipping, has always been a popular expedition. In 1907 the Northern Lighthouse Board added an automatic light at the east end of Sanday, 'Ceann an Eilein'. Anyone who has sailed on these waters in the dark knows how absolutely essential to navigation in the Minch these lighthouses are.

After the island changed hands in 1938, further improvements were made. Central heating was installed in Canna House, and Calor gas lighting there and in some of the other houses. Water was laid on to the Changehouse and the cattleman's house at the farm steading, and indoor plumbing installed. The galvanized iron roofing of the latter was replaced by slates, and the upper storey converted from a granary to second-floor bedrooms and bathroom. Eventually water and electricity (with no help from the North of Scotland Hydro-Electric Board) were laid on to all the farm workers' houses. Electric shearing and oxy-acetylene welding were introduced at the farmsteading. Samples of soil from the arable fields were sent to the MacAulay Institute, and the recommended portions of lime and superphosphates were applied. Tile drainage was done on the Strath at Tarbert, and in the field above Coroghon called Liana Mhór, 'Big Meadow', and a good deal of hill drainage and fencing. Tractors superseded horses, not without some regrets.

On Sanday the right of the proprietor to winter hoggs (ewe lambs kept for breeding) on the crofters' in-bye land was given up in 1942 and the rents of the crofts adjusted by the Land Court in 1943, after which the crofters were able to fence their in-bye land and keep what stock on it they wished. In 1953 water was brought to the crofts with the aid of a Department of Agriculture 50 per cent grant, and the crofters and the school authorities were able to connect their houses to the supply. No more carrying buckets to the spring! The Land Court adjusted the rents again.

Wind-breaks were planted above the shore at Coroghon, and later mixed plantations were planted in several places, beginning with the steep brae east of Canna House, called Bruthach nan Eoill, in the winter of 1956–7; soon afterwards at Calbhach, east of the ridge behind the Canna graveyard, and at Guala nam Fàd, west of Keill. A lake was made on Sanday, and a small plantation beside it, and water-lilies and bulrushes were planted in the lake. The pedigree herd of Highland cattle was restarted in 1946. The Crown Feu-duty, representing the small sum first paid annually by the Earl of Argyll for Canna to the Bishop of the Isles in the early seventeenth century, and the teind charge, an unequal burden imposed in favour of the Church of Scotland in the early eighteenth century, were redeemed.

But the largest post-war improvements were the broadening of Canna pier from forty-two to ninety-six feet in the spring of 1971, necessary owing to the employment by the shipping company Caledonian MacBrayne of larger and larger vessels for the transport of sheep and cattle from the isles to Oban. This improvement was constructed by F. J. C. Lilley (Marine) Ltd. and was carried out with complete success, at less than the estimated cost, and without any kind of Government assistance. The improvement has been greatly welcomed by Caledonian MacBrayne's captains, and has also been extremely useful to fishermen, who have not always appreciated that it was done by the Estate, and not by any

Fishery Board or public body. The same year a new modern Weir-Oliver house was built, originally for a farm worker, on the field called Caslum between the farmsteading and the fank. Mention should also be made of a fine new house built by Mr Angus MacKinnon on his croft on Sanday in 1973–4.

But, with all the improvements that have been made on Canna since 1781, it must be admitted that the final lay-out of the estate is not a good one. This has been due to the pressure in the first half of the nineteenth century on the population to move from Canna to Sanday to become kelp-makers and fishermen. Sanday has only a limited water supply, is some distance from the pier, and is exposed to northerly winds. It would have been far better to have made a single farm, with the crofting population of Canna concentrated at Keill, where there is plenty of water, good shelter, and easy access to general facilities and to transport; Tarbert (the west end of the island) used for livestock raising, and Coroghon kept as a home farm. Were Canna a Norwegian island, it certainly would have a fishing community of about 200; but in that case the fishing in the Minch would have been reserved for local fishermen in the same way as that of the Vestfiord and the Varangerfiord.

So far as livestock is concerned, half the stock of Cheviot ewes had been replaced by blackfaces a considerable time before the change of ownership in 1938. If the original 2,000 Cheviot sheep brought in by John MacLean or his son-in-law Donald MacNeill were all ewes, it is probable (considering that Donald MacNeill was trained in farming at Innerleithen) that they were South Country Cheviots, considerably smaller than the North Country Cheviots now on Canna. At any rate, the present sheep stock on Canna is 500 North Country Cheviot and 500 blackface breeding ewes, with approximately 150 ewe hoggs (year-old ewes kept as breeding replacements) of each breed, the Cheviots being on the east and the black-faces on the west end of the island.

A brief account of the Highland hill-farming year may be of interest here. Financially it runs from 29 May of one year to 28 May of the next. The reason for this is that it is much easier for farm and farm workers' flitting and removals to take place at the end of May, when weather is more likely to be good, and the hours of daylight are many. Under the old Scottish system too, agricultural workers were hired by the six-monthly 'term', beginning on 29 May or 29 November, and paid on 28 November or 28 May.

But the hill-farming year in the Highlands and on Canna can best be described as beginning with the release of the rams after the winter dipping and counting of the sheep stock in mid-November. On Canna the rams, three per hundred ewes, are let go with the ewes on 21 November, so that lambing will not start before 21 April, which is quite soon enough on a Hebridean hill farm. A few more are let go later. In January, the 'dead month', *'mìos marbh'* in Gaelic, the sheep are gathered, and the exhausted rams taken in and given some special feeding, which the weaker ewes also receive before lambing time.

When February comes – spring is supposed to begin on St Bride's Day, 2 February, although a more practical computation is expressed by the Gaelic saying *'Foghair gu Nollaig is Geamhradh gu Là'ill Phàdraig'* – 'Autumn till Christmas and Winter till St Patrick's Day' (17 March) – and that extended by the belief that if St Patrick's Day was fine, the second half of winter was still to come. In 1982 St Patrick's Day was comparatively fine, and no one will ever forget the bitterly cold first four days of May, accompanied by fierce northerly gales, snow and hail.

February and early March are the months for putting manure on the fields kept for hay, mending dykes and fences, working on hill drains, planting or felling trees. An important part of the manure used to be seaweed, bladder-wrack driven ashore by the winter gales and loaded on tractor trailers for carriage to the fields. Modern plastic civilization has put an end to its use; the beaches are so polluted with plastic in every imaginable form that one cannot risk using their seaweed as fertilizer on the hayfields.

As March draws on, ploughing begins for the arable crops, now only oats and potatoes, though formerly rye, barley, turnips, and kale have been grown. Ploughing is likely to be interrupted by bad weather. The truth is we don't like March to be too dry. The soil of Canna, especially on the hill, is shallow, and the growth of grass is slow if spring weather comes when the land is too dry.

Before lambing, the ewes are gathered and dosed for internal parasites, and the weaker ones are kept on in-bye land to lamb. Half are blackfaces and half North Country Cheviots. There is a black strain in the Cheviot flock that produces a small number of sheep with naturally coloured black or dark brown wool. The sheep are gathered again in June for the counting and marking of the lambs, after which the eild sheep – ewes without lambs and year-old females kept for breeding, called 'ewe hoggs' in Scotland – are sheared, the rams have been sheared already. There follows a second gathering in July, when the ewes with lambs, 'milk ewes', are shorn. Then in August the sheep are gathered again and given their summer dipping (which is compulsory, to control sheep scab) and the lambs are weaned, and put over to Sanday to await being sorted for the annual sheep sales in Oban.

There are three such main sales held by Messrs. Thomas Corson and Co. in Oban every autumn, the first in August, the second in early September, and the last in late September. We always try to send the sheep and lambs for sale to the second of these sales, because if storms should prevent their transport, there would still be the late September sale to fall back on. The sheep and lambs are sorted according to breed and quality into a number of groups for sale in the auction ring.

The only market to which we can now take stock in numbers is Oban, and the only suitable ship now available is the *Pioneer*, the car-ferry vessel running between Mallaig and Armadale (Skye) from the middle of May until early October, which is only free to take on stock for Oban at Canna on Sundays. This ship is eminently suitable for the purpose, being a side-loader; but it could not have lifted livestock at Canna had the pier not been widened from forty-two to ninety-six feet in the spring of 1971. Wool of course can be sent to the mainland by the ordinary mailboat, the small *Lochmor*. Rams are bought and sold at the Ben Nevis mart in November.

As for cattle, there are two herds, the pedigree Highland one on the western half of Canna, and the crossing herd, which summers on the eastern part of Sanday, where the ewe hoggs are put to winter. The crossing herd is built on cross-Highland heifers, and the bulls used on it have been from time to time red shorthorn, white shorthorn, Aberdeen Angus, and Highland. The pedigree Highland herd is registered with the breed society. The cattle are fully attested as free from tuberculosis and brucellosis. Being hill cattle, the cows winter and calve outside, feeding after November on hay taken to them by Landrover in the parks; only the bulls and the young stirks are wintered indoors. The cattle for sale go to Oban on the *Pioneer* early in October.

It is to be regretted that for the first time in its history Canna is now without either milk-cows or horses. This is due to lack of milkers, and the present supremacy (which may not last) of the tractor.

It is interesting to compare the prices of sheep and farm wages over a considerable period of time. A fragment of the Day Book of Tallisker left on Canna reveals that in 1859 lambs were selling for around eleven shillings and sixpence (57½ new pence), cast ewes for nineteen shillings and ten pence (99 new pence), wethers (probably three years old) for £1. 10s. 0d. (£1.50) and shearling tups for £2. 10s. 0d. (£2.50). Wool was fetching £1. 2s. 0d. a stone (14 pounds, i.e. 6.35 kilograms). The sheep were presumably blackfaces. The highest farm workers' wages were £14 and 6½ bolls of meal in the half-year. Of course the money pound in those days was a gold sovereign, worth now around £45.

In 1938 at the outgoing valuation of the Canna sheepstock, stock Cheviot ewes with lambs were valued at £3. 11s. 0d. (£3.55 today), eild ewes (ewes without lambs) at £2. 8s. 0d. (£2.40), and three-shear rams at £5. 10s. 0d. (£5.50), all subject to a discount of one-sixtieth. The implied value of lambs was thus £1. 3s. 0d. (£1.15) but the best price received at the autumn sales was no more than 16s. 0d. (80 new pence). Blackface stock ewes with lambs were valued at £3, eild ewes at £2, and the best rams at £6. 5s. 0d. (£6.25). Hill cows with calves, mostly Galloways, were valued at between £14 and £23; a white Shorthorn bull was valued at £26 and a Galloway at £16.

The highest wage paid was £78 a year, without allowances; employees with lower rates of pay got four or five tons of coal (then costing about £2 a ton), a ton of potatoes, and keep of a cow and stirk. All had free houses (tied cottages) on the estate. By 1938, of course, Britain had come off the gold standard, and a gold sovereign was then worth £2. 10s. 0d. in paper money.

The first compulsory Agricultural Wages Order applying to the islands appeared on 23 November 1940. It decreed a minimum wage for shepherds of £2. 12s. 0d. a week (£135. 4s. 0d. a year), for cattlemen £2. 13s. 0d. a week (£137. 16s. 0d. a year), and for other farm workers over twenty years of age, £2. 8s. 0d. a week (£124. 16s. 0d. a year). The District involved, Number 11, included areas such as Argyll and the Highland parts of Perthshire, that are far better favoured than the islands, particularly in the matter of transport. Wages have risen over fifty times whereas the returns from the sheep and store cattle that are the produce of hill farms have risen only about fifteen times in the case of sheep and thirty times in the case of cattle, as compared to the writer's incoming valuation in May 1938. Since then there has been a continual rise in nominal money wages until a shepherd now receives more pounds in a week than he was getting in a year in 1938; but one must compare prices then with those of today, for example whisky at 15 shillings (£0.75) a bottle, against over £6 today.

The Canna – Sanday Footbridge

If Canna has owed many improvements to its tenants and proprietors since 1782, it must be said that it owes very few indeed to any public authority. No house has ever been built (apart from the schoolhouse), no water supply or electricity has ever been installed, no road has ever been improved, no pier has ever been built by any local authority here. The only improvement of this kind ever made was the footbridge between Canna and Sanday. This was made in 1905 by the old Parish Council, which ceased to exist in 1929. At a meeting held in Eigg on 26 July, the Revd J. Sinclair in the chair, it was agreed to spend a sum not exceeding £130 on erecting this footbridge across the tidal channel between Canna and Sanday with the main purpose of making it easy for children on Canna to attend the school on Sanday no matter what the state of the tide. The bridge was built the same summer, for the contractor, a Mr Fletcher from Tobermory, presented his account for £130, which was before the Parish Council on

8 November. It was ordered that the money should be paid out of the Parish Council Fund direct to Mr Fletcher.

This was the beginning of bureaucratic trouble connected with the bridge, which has recurred at intervals ever since. In May 1906 the Parish Council's Accounts, containing this item of £130 for the Canna–Sanday footbridge, were, as statutorily required, submitted to the Auditor of the Local Government Board in Edinburgh. The item in question met with instant official disapproval. After correspondence and a plea of the difficulty of getting legal advice in a remote situation, the Parish Council was told to establish a special Parish Fund to meet such claims as the erection of the Canna–Sanday footbridge, and was told that the Auditor had been instructed to strike the account for £130 out of the ordinary Poor Rate account and transfer it to the Special Parish Rate account and to levy a special parish rate for the current year to meet the debit balance thus created. The Parish Council had no choice but to impose a special rate of threepence in the pound (which was then 240 pence), on an assessed parish rental of £3,188. 16s. 0d., one-half payable by proprietors and one-half by tenants. The enthusiasm with which this order would have been received on Eigg, Rum, and Muck is not recorded, but it can be imagined. The fact is, of course, that the central Government had made school attendance compulsory in Scotland in 1872, and it should therefore have accepted the responsibility for making it possible for children in the Highlands and Islands to get to school under reasonable conditions.

In due course the bridge became the responsibility of the Inverness-shire County Council when parish councils ceased to exist after 1929, and then of the Lochaber District Council after the reorganization of Scottish local government in 1975. But it was far from being a responsibility that was willingly admitted. The bridge had been built over the narrowest part of the tidal channel between Canna and Sanday. Unfortunately this situation is dangerously exposed at times when high spring tides coincide with westerly storms; a much better situation would have been between Rubha nan Còrr (the site of the farmsteading) and the little island called Eilean a' Bhàird, with a short causeway connecting that island with Sanday.

While on the subject of access to the school on Sanday, mention may be made of the blow dealt to small island communities by the centralization of secondary education when the school-leaving age was raised a few years after the 1939–45 War, forcing parents living on islands like Canna to send their children to live in places like Mallaig or Fort William as soon as the children reach the age of eleven, and where the children have to live in hostels unless they are fortunate enough to have relatives who can board them. Forced with this prospect it is not surprising that few if any newcomers to such islands will ever think of putting down permanent roots there; there is a constant tendency amongst such families to look for a mainland job as soon as the eldest child is approaching the age of eleven, if not earlier. This regulation, which is unpleasantly reminiscent of the clause of the 1609 Statutes of Iona that decreed that Highlanders of over a certain economic standing must send their children to be educated in the Lowlands, is and has been acting surely and steadily to promote rural depopulation and the destruction of the Gaelic language and local tradition in the remoter parts of the Scottish Highlands and Islands.

Once shortly before the writer's time on Canna, and twice during it, the bridge has been severely damaged by winter storms, and on the latter two occasions at least, responsibility for its repair was only accepted by the local authority with the greatest reluctance.

The story of the roads on Canna is not very different. Originally the public part of the road was that between Canna pier and Canna Post Office, which was then beside the farmsteading, the 'Square'. For its upkeep the proprietor was allowed a rates rebate of £29 on total rates of £39. 8s. 7d. in 1938. This was acceptable in the days when there was only horse-drawn traffic on the island and wages were only (in modern terms) 7p an hour. It became quite unacceptable once tractors and motor vehicles were introduced and when wages were being raised annually under compulsory agricultural wage orders.

An additional complication came about in 1947 when the island was examined by officials of the Department of Agriculture with a view to the possible rehabilitation scheme under the Hill Sheep Farming Act. Such schemes were required to be comprehensive, and one of the items the Department wanted improved was the two miles of road between the farmsteading and the middle of the island, to Tarbert. This involved ascertaining whether the part of the road in question was the responsibility of the Inverness-shire County Council or not. The disclaimer was immediate.

The rehabilitation scheme was not proceeded with, since it was found preferable to make improvements separately and not as a comprehensive plan. But in 1951 the Estate gave up trying to find shepherds who would live in such an isolated spot as Tarbert, Canna, and decided to work the western hirsel of the island by Landrover from the east, populated end. *Then* the Inverness-shire County Council decided to reverse its 1947 decision that the road between the farmsteading and the shepherd's house at Tarbert was private, and started demanding payment of road fund licence on the vehicle to be used. In fact the local authority played 'heads I win and tails you lose' as hard as it possibly could. Confrontation was resolved by an agreement that the whole road system on Canna should be regarded as private, and that no licence should be needed on any vehicle used there and confined to the island.

Previously, while that part of the road was still public, the local authority had refused any responsibility for repairs of gale damage to the retaining wall holding the road near the pier – without which, approach to the pier would have been impossible – on the pettifogging grounds that the wall was part of the pier work and not of the road, which it obviously wasn't.

Storms and Strandings

As the Hebrides lie in the east Atlantic storm-track, weather varies from extremes of glorious days of natural beauty in calm sunshine, to the wildest kind of stormy weather, sometimes winds of hurricane force.* Here are some personal recollections of such incidents:

On 30 October 1940 my diary records that there was a 'Very

* The strongest winds coming from the south-west, and the Minch being now the rubbish-bin for every piece of plastic discarded by a multitude of yachts, fishing boats, and other vessels, these storms are now unfortunately polluting agents, depositing great quantities of this vile mess on Canna's shores. Visitors unaware of this sometimes blame us for it, absolutely unjustly.

wild southerly storm and rain. Eight man crew of the salvage vessel 'Attendant' came ashore at Tarbert in the morning, having been five hours in their lifeboat after their vessel had gone ashore a hundred yards east of An t-Each. Brought them by lorry to Canna House.'

The vessel had been sheltering just outside Canna's inner harbour, had dragged its anchor in the dark in the wind and rain, and coming forward to recover its position had run on the rocks below the cliffs at Tialasgor, a point actually access- ible by foot along the shore from Coroghon. The Captain and crew, from Northern Ireland, had landed by ship's lifeboat at Tarbert to the alarm of the shepherd of the time, George MacLean, who feared that they were Germans landing off a submarine! They were in Canna House until 4 November. Later there were visits from insurance agents and salvage officers. Most unusually there were no more violent gales that winter, and the *Attendant* was actually repaired, got off the rocks at high tide, towed back into Canna Harbour on 15 March 1941, and eventually taken to the Clyde.

On 30 December 1951, the Hebrides were hit by a hur- ricane. My diary records:

100 mph hurricane blew from west from early morning till after- noon, shifting to NW. No-one could remember the like. The harbour was white with spray like a mist, sea like mid-Minch, seaweed and sand flying in the air. Roof of 'Square' (the farmstead) damaged and at one time in danger of being blown away. Stone parapet beside pier badly damaged: road covered with seaweed. Marine Hotel, Mallaig said to have lost roof. It was hardly possible to walk against this wind and the journey to church was only made with the utmost difficulty. No-one could remember anything like this gale. Fir trees behind Tighard snapped in two. Two large hawthorns blew down blocking both gates into the hen run. Dinghy swamped. *Gille Brighde* filled with salt water, blown up on the beach which had to be siphoned out. Chimney blew off Annie MacKinnon's cottage. Slates loosened everywhere.

That morning the writer had walked with the Revd Fr. John MacLean, now Canon MacLean, from Canna House to the church on Sanday. The wind was so strong that it was barely possible to walk against it in unsheltered spots, and we did not care to try to walk across the footbridge, preferring to stumble in the seaweed below. Nobody else came to Church. It was not an experience either of us would now care to repeat.

Another storm, in 1959: This time the writer had caught the train for Mallaig at Fort William on the morning of Monday 26 October:

Morning slightly better. Drove to Ft. Wm. and left car in garage. Went to station. Train 1 hour late and ran out of steam 3 times between Fort William and Arisaig. 2½ hours late!!! Mallaig, Lochmor left 3,30 p.m., arr. Rum 6 p.m.. Started for Canna but returned and anchored in Loch Scresort to ride out first part of hurricane. 27th Tuesday. Lochmor left Rum 3 a.m. arr. Canna 4 a.m. in calm spell centre of cyclone. 5 a.m. wind started to blow violently and I came down to close windows and I saw that the glass had been at the very bottom of the chart, lower than I'd ever seen it. The hurricane continued violently all day with very severe gusts.

We learned later that the *Lochmor* had never been able to call at Lochboisdale or Lochmaddy owing to the strength of the wind, and only made Tarbert – Harris after having been fourteen hours continuously at sea, the passengers having suffered very severely.

In 1962 there was another stranding. My diary for Saturday 29 September reads:

Severe gale developed in p.m. At 11.30 p.m. distress signals were observed from Corroghon Bay. The 'Widder' of Bremen ashore near cliffs on E. side and in danger from SE gale. 5 members of crew taken off by breaches buoy, and taken to 'Square' and Mrs Mac-Lean's. Captain, mate and engineer remained aboard. Phoned lifeboat which came over and towed 'Widder' out of Corroghon Bay on Monday a.m. 8.00. She then proceeded to Rum to examine damage. Lifeboat returned to Canna to fetch the landed crewmen. Gales continued all day. Those working the breaches buoy here were Ian MacKinnon, Angus MacKinnon and Michael MacLean.

The owners being bankrupt, nothing was paid to the Canna people who had boarded the *Widder's* crew over the weekend. The stranding of the *Widder* made the Coastguard service aware of the necessity of storing adequate equipment on Canna, and of improvement in the very poor local telephone service. These things were done in September 1965 and October 1966 respectively.

NOTES

1. See R. W. Munro, *Scottish Lighthouses*, Thule Press, 1979; R. A. Redfern, 'Lighting up the Western Isles', *The Lady*, 17 Apr. 1980; Noel Banks, *Six Inner Hebrides*, pp. 25, 134.

19 TRANSPORT AND COMMUNICATIONS

Not only ships, but also trains on the West Highland line could be involved in strandings. A famous instance occurred on 17 February 1951. In this case both the writer and his wife were aboard. The writer described the incident in a letter written on 19 February to Lord Malcolm Douglas Hamilton, then MP for Inverness-shire:

As my wife and I were passengers in the famous Lost Train this weekend I thought an account of the incident might be of interest to you in case any questions are asked in the House. The events were as follows:-

3.46 p.m. 17 Feb. Train left Glasgow Queen St. It was snowing lightly at Glasgow and must have been snowing in the hills since midday as snow was thick at Crianlarich station.

About 7.00 p.m. on Saturday the train finally stuck in a drift at Corrour siding.

Early on Sunday morning a gang of men arrived from Ft. William to dig the train out. This was completed by about 3.30 p.m. Sunday. At approx. 4.30 p.m. an engine arrived from Ft. William indicating the line was then clear. It was then fine and sunny and passengers expected the train to proceed to Ft. William at once. Much to our surprise this was postponed for hours to enable a detached luggage van to be coupled to the same train. Meanwhile it started snowing again heavily and we had real reason to fear we would have to spend another night in the frost, as the relief train sent from Glasgow stuck in the snow a mile and a half behind between Corrour and Rannoch. It was nearly midnight when we did leave, water and beer being by then exhausted and everyone cold and hungry, although great praise is due to the kitchen staff of the train's restaurant car for the way they made things go round and their cheerful obligingness.

We were told that the salvage operations were being conducted under the guidance of Perth!

We felt that (a) if it is true this train had no snow plough on the engine it should not have left Glasgow without one as snow was forecast for Saturday and it must have been snowing in the hills by midday.

(b) Not enough provisions and water are carried to meet an emergency of this kind.

(c) Facilities for reversing engines on this line are badly needed. By Sunday afternoon several engines had collected at Corrour but they were all pointing the wrong way and there was no way to turn them round so the snowploughs could be in front. A special snow-clearing machine with plough fore and aft seems needed for this line.

(d) The line is inadequately protected from snowdrifts. Where palisades of sleepers exist there are gaps in them through which the snow was blowing. These holes could at least be closed.

I am afraid I must add that this line possesses the unenviable distinction of being served by the worst and dirtiest passenger coaches I have seen in Britain. This applies to both Ist and IIIrd classes. Also lighting is very bad and lavatory accommodation disgusting. No towels or soap even in Ist class w.c.s., and water provided in cans! In view of the importance of this line (Glasgow–Mallaig) to the inhabitants of Inverness-shire, and seeing that it passes through incomparable country, this should not be so, as tourists are going to get a very poor impression of British Railways from it. We hope very much that this state of affairs can be permanently altered for the better before the Festival of Britain begins.

I would like to add our appreciation of the courtesy and good humour of the railway staff in the incident described above.

Communications – Telephone Service

The state of the telephone service in the parish of the Small Isles in 1938 was vividly described by John MacNair Reid, resident on Eigg, in a letter to the *Glasgow Herald*, reproduced in the *Sea Leaguer*, which was edited by the writer, in September 1938:

A private post office telephone, connecting Eigg, Rum, and Canna, has been used for many years for telegrams only, and only the doctor, on urgent occasions, has been allowed to use that phone, which, in any case, worked merely within the ambit of these three islands, having its connection with the mainland via Skye. It was a private line owned by the Post Office, and no one was allowed use of it, surely a dog-in-the-manager attitude, at the least. Now the public are to be allowed to use this phone. That is the mangificent concession on the part of the Post Office. That is what is called 'linking up the islands with the mainland'.

People on this island, therefore, can telephone Mallaig, or Glasgow, or London. But under the following conditions:-

A subscriber will have to go to the Post Office and ask for the use of the telephone. The instrument will be handed to him at the public counter, and he will enjoy his conversation with the person he calls up, what time customers are buying stamps or sending off telegrams at his elbow. He will, moreover, have to do his telephoning before 7 p.m., for the Post Office closes then. And that is the hour when cheap rates come into force. As can be readily understood, the cheap rates are the only attractive thing about the telephone in a remote area like this.

The same summer the Post Office's publicity department had issued a statement to the Press claiming that the agitation for improved communication was exaggerated, alleging that 'owners of several of the isles, and others who reside on them, are expressing the view that part of the charm and lure of these remote places is their solitude, and therefore they do not look with favour altogether on any agitation to bring all the public advantages of the mainland to such places'. Investigations suggested that in fact this statement represented the views of only a single resident proprietor; it could also have conveyed the opinion of some absentee 'summer holiday Highlanders', in those days notoriously uncooperative in supporting movements for the improvement of public facilities in the islands.

A telephone service is essential for any inhabited island which has no resident doctor or medical nurse. Notwithstanding this, it was actually proposed by a penny-pinching government in 1913 to close down the whole Small Isles telegraph service in order to save about £300 or £400 a year at a time when the Post Office was making a profit of £4,000,000 a year! Luckily the proposal, which aroused vehement protests, was defeated.[1]

In fact, the whole position regarding Post Office services in Canna in 1938 was ludicrous. The island had been ceded by Argyll to Inverness-shire in 1892, before Mallaig was developed, and the local head post office was at Tobermory in Mull; the Canna post office had no direct means of communication with it. Later, when the absurdity of this situation was recognized and Fort William became the Head Post Office for all the Small Isles, the move involved Canna's coming into the Aberdeen postal administrative area rather than that of Glasgow. This simply meant a transfer from one indifferent authority to another, with superb opportunities for buck-passing between them.

Pressure for an improvement did result in the provision of a booth inside Canna post office in which private conversations were possible. But the antiquated type of submarine cable in use reduced voice volume by 50 per cent, and contact with Mallaig could only be made by first cranking a hand-operated bell system, which the postmaster or postmistress at the other end could – and sometime did – ignore if he or she did not feel like bothering to answer and make a connection. Until an outside kiosk was built, the telephone could only be used in Post Office hours. The whole system compared miserably with contemporary telephone facilities on remote islands in the north of Norway. It was not surprising that when representatives of the Coastguard service visited Canna in connection with the stranding of the *Widder* in 1962, they were appalled to find such a primitive telephone system in operation on an island like Canna, situated centrally in the Minch, with a harbour continuously used by fishing vessels and yachts. Whatever may be said (or denied) publicly, local opinion is strong in believing that the improvement in the telephone service when the radio link system was introduced in 1966, was due in no small part to pressure from the Coastguard service.

Not that the radio link service was impeccable from the start; in fact, it was for a considerable time hardly more than experimental, although charged for at the full post office rates. But bit by bit it was improved, and the invention of an ingenious automatic call-recording system enabled individual telephones to be at last installed. Since then telephone conversations have taken place between Canna subscribers and friends in the United States, Canada, New Zealand, France, Spain, and Sweden, something quite unheard of until a few years ago.

Transport

Sea transport is the life-blood of island communities, so it is not the least surprising to find that it is always a matter in the forefront of Hebridean politics. Before the development of a road system in the Highlands, communications between different islands were much easier, at least in the summertime, than they were over the rough tracks between Highland villages and the few towns in the Highlands. In those times there were always plenty of strong young men available to man small boats with sails and oars, while cattle dealers visited the Isles in their own smacks.

Regular sea communications were not possible until after the development of steam ships. The full story of West Highland sea transport still has to be written. Even as late as the 1920s roads in the Highlands were still quite primitive, and journeys by ship could be made all the way from Gourock to Inverness, passing through the Crinan and Caledonian canals. According to Noel Banks, who has compiled some useful information on the subject,[2] the first scheduled service calling at Canna was from Glasgow, by the *Clansman II*, a ship of 600 tons. This started in 1870. The service was mainly for cargo. Mallaig of course did not then exist as a port. David MacBraynes's *Summer Tours in Scotland* of 1895 shows that at that time Eigg was on one schedule and Rum and Canna on another, the ship leaving Oban at 6.00 a.m. on Mondays, Wednesdays, and Fridays for Barra, the Uists, and the west of Skye ports, and calling at Canna at 5.30 a.m. on Tuesdays and Thursdays, arriving back at Oban at 2.00 p.m. the same days.

On Tuesdays, Thursdays, and Saturdays the run was made in the reverse direction, also leaving Oban at 6.00 a.m., and calling at Canna after Tobermory (then the nearest town to Canna) and Rum and arriving at Canna at 11.00 a.m. on Tuesdays and Saturdays, but passing Canna and Rum of Thursdays. The fare from Canna to Oban by these summer season trips was 10s. 0d. (50p) first class and 5d. 0d. (25p) second class, while return tickets were sold at one and a half times single fare. Breakfast, lunch, and high tea aboard cost 2s 0d. (10p) in each case, dinner 3d. 0d (15p). Between then and 1930 the Small Isles were served by a variety of small uncomfortable vessels, first from Arisaig and after 1921 from Mallaig, the most notorious of which were the *Plover* and the *Cygnet*, each of only 191 tons. The writer, who has lived long enough in the Hebrides to have travelled on the *Plover* when it was relieving on the Oban–Barra run, can testify personally to its shortcomings. What it was like to make the sea journey in such a ship from Oban to South Uist in 1890 can be read in the first chapter of Frederic Rea's *A School in South Uist*.

In 1930 Hebridean sea transport was greatly improved by the introduction of the sister ships *Lochearn* and *Lochmor* (I), each of 452 tons, the former sailing out of Oban for Tobermory, Kilchoan, Coll, Tiree, Barra, and South Uist (Lochboisdale) on Mondays and Wednesdays, calling at Canna instead of Lochboisdale on Friday evenings, and returning to Oban; while the *Lochmor* operated out of Mallaig and Kyle of Lochalsh, sailing from Mallaig for the Small Isles, Lochboisdale (where she connected with the *Lochearn*), Lochmaddy, Tarbert-Harris, and Kyle, spending Tuesday nights at Kyle and leaving to make the same journey in the reverse direction on Wednesday mornings, connecting with the *Lochearn* again at Lochboisdale, and arriving at Mallaig on Thursday mornings after calling again at the Small Isles. The *Lochmor* then continued to Kyle, spending Thursday night there, and made another trip in the same direction around Skye, meeting the *Lochearn* again at Lochboisdale, and returning to Mallaig again on Saturday, and continuing to Kyle, where the ship spent the weekend.

This was the fundamental schedule of these ships until April 1964, though there were variations from time to time, as when the Friday evening call of the *Lochearn* at Canna was dropped early in the 1939–45 War in the interests of Uist servicemen going home on leave; or by various arrangements made to provide the Small Isles with calls on Saturday mornings – producing a round trip which almost invariably arrived in Mallaig about ten or fifteen minutes too late to connect with the 1.00 p.m. train leaving Mallaig for Glasgow.

Apart from some deficiency in speed, and limitations in draught and excess height of superstructure due to the exigencies of approaching small island piers and the immense rise and fall of Hebridean spring tides, at least fourteen feet, these boats were thoroughly practical and suitable. They provided good meals, bars, and cabins where passengers could sleep; they had adequate cargo space, and could carry cars or agricultural machinery, and take in sheltered space reasonable consignments of sheep or cattle between the islands or to the markets of Oban, Dingwall (via Kyle), and Corpach (via Mallaig). All these facilities were lost in 1964 when, after about five years of discussion and argument, this was abandoned in favour of large car ferries between the mainland and the principal islands, that is to say in favour of summer visitors coming in their cars (for the charges for carrying cars were too high to encourage local residents to make frequent crossings with their cars to the mainland).

The smaller islands which either had no piers, or where, as in the case of Canna, the piers were too small to be approached by the new giant car ferries, were to be left to get on as best they could with small and inferior vessels. In the case of the Small Isles, a converted wooden minesweeper, the *Loch Arkaig*, 179 tons, with only second class accommodation, no cabins, no sheltered accommodation for livestock, and very poor facilities for carrying or handling anything like cars or agricultural machinery, was put on the run, connecting Canna and the Small Isles with Mallaig alone. This was a reversion to the bad old days of the *Plover* and the *Cygnet* with a vengeance. The former inter-island social and commercial life was completely destroyed; everyone on Canna for instance, had relatives or friends in Barra or South Uist with whom contact was now virtually lost; trade in cross-Highland heifers, rams, and potatoes had existed between Canna and the Outer Hebrides; small quantities of livestock could be sent to the mart at Oban at any time (and brought home if prices bid were unfavourable); from 1964 livestock had to be dispatched by special cattle ship only, all the cattle in one consignment and all the sheep and lambs in another, with no chance of bringing anything home again, however unsatisfactory the prices.

By the end of 1974 the *Loch Arkaig*, which was far from being a new ship when converted by MacBrayne's in 1963 for passenger service, was coming to the end of its natural life, and early in March 1975 MacBrayne's convened a meeting of Small Isles representatives in Inverness to discuss their plan for a replacement vessel. This showed a thoroughly practical type of ship, a medium size ferry of 120 feet capable of carrying six cars or equivalent agricultural machinery or over 100 sheep, with facilities, including a cafeteria, for up to 160 passengers in summertime, and 50 in winter.

Incredible as it may now seem, this gift horse was looked in the mouth and rejected by two of the Small Isles representatives (one a newcomer), in favour of a *smaller* ship, and this with the backing of the Highlands and Islands Development Board. A so-called 'small boat scheme' was developed by these parties, with the backing of the Highlands and Islands Board, involving the idea of serving the Small Isles (Eigg, Muck, Rum, and Canna) and of Armadale in Skye in winter, with a small fast motor boat, a landing craft, and an eighty-foot mailboat, in place of the very adequate vessel MacBrayne's had suggested. This plan originally seemed to have the acquiescence of the Scottish Office on the ground that it would cost less than the subsidy for MacBrayne's vessel; but when it was fully revealed (which was not until early in 1977) its disadvantages were obvious.

These included the facts that whatever good the plan might have done to Eigg and Muck, it could not have done anything but harm to Rum and Canna; it would not have produced a boat adequate to provide winter service for Armadale in Skye; it would be highly questionable for a Government body like the Highlands and Islands Development Board to be supporting a private operator competing with a nationalized shipping company like MacBrayne's; should the private operator decide to give up the service, which at present MacBrayne's was obliged to undertake under the terms of its Contract with the Government, there was no guarantee that MacBrayne's would resume it again.

The dispute came to a head at an official meeting held at Fort William in May 1977, by which time the Scottish Office had come to realize that the 'small boat scheme' would cost very little, if anything, less to run than the MacBrayne's service, and that it would not be adequate for the needs of the whole community and its visitors. This conviction was reinforced when an unofficial plebiscite of the Small Isles, organized by the Chairman of the local Community Council, Mr Fergus

Gowans, resulted in a vote of more than 80 to 11 against the 'Small Boat Scheme', following which the intervention of Mr Russell Johnston, MP, finally secured its rejection.

But unfortunately the time wasted in discussing this impractical idea publicly and behind the scenes between March 1975 and May 1977, resulted in the fact that the money that could have built an adequate ship for the Small Isles service in 1976 was insufficient, with inflation, to do more than pay for the construction of a considerably smaller and less comfortable one, the new *Lochmor*, in 1978. This can only carry 100 passengers in summer and 40 in winter and has no facilities for handling cars or agricultural machinery.

During the controversy over this transport question, and on other such occasions, several propositions could be regarded as axiomatic:

1. No official connected with decision-making on matters of Hebridean transport appears ever to have resided in the Hebrides.

2. On practical sea transport questions the opinions of the newest incomers are preferred to those of senior inhabitants or even the opinions of MacBrayne's experienced skippers.

3. The seas around the Isles are officially believed to be always calm in summer, and passengers can be expected to travel happily for several hours on open decks, or packed like sardines on benches in the saloons, no matter what the weather.

4. Hikers and campers never lie down on these benches, nor put equipment on them.

Anyone who travels on the new *Lochmor* under crowded conditions on a windy wet day, will know that actuality is very different. Caledonian MacBrayne's are not to be blamed for the shortcomings of this ship; it was imposed on them by the tergiversation over its construction. Every summer its inadequacy becomes more and more obvious; the fact is that the population of the Small Isles and the volume of summer passenger traffic compares with those of Colonsay, and the Small Isles should be served by as good a ship as Colonsay's.*

* Nothing said about the deficiencies of any of the ships mentioned in this chapter is to be taken as criticism of the officers and crews of MacBrayne's ships. Their skill in maintaining services under very difficult weather conditions deserves the highest praise.

Certainly, when one considers Canna's transport as a whole, over the years, it is very difficult to find any evidence of improvement, rather the reverse. The Fort William–Mallaig railway line, so heavily used by passengers in the summer, remains continuously under the threat of closure, the paint of its stations peeling, its passing place at Inverailort torn up, its observation car and camping coaches vanished. The sleeper car service from Euston to Fort William has also been threatened. The one solid transport improvement is the greater availability of helicopters to take serious medical cases from the Isles to Fort William or Inverness, a service to which it is certainly essential that island residents should have equal access with visiting hill–climbers who injure themselves.

High sea freight and fare charges mean in effect a tax on all island imports and exports. In this respect it is absolutely essential that Road Equivalent charges should be introduced to free the islands from an intolerable burden, that is, that mile for mile the cost of travel and the transport of goods should be the same for the Isles as it is for the mainland.[3] The present concession of special residents' tickets for the Small Isles is certainly an advance, but it is not enough. If the Minch were filled up with peat the cost of building and maintaining roads to the island communities would probably match the cost of maintaining a sea service. But in any case it is part of the thesis of this book, that historically the Hebrides were integrated with the mainland against their will, and if they are not going to have the fiscal liberties of the Isle of Man and the Channel Islands, they have every right to claim the same facilities and the same standard of living as those that exist on the mainland.

NOTES

1. *Oban Times*, 1 Feb. 1913.
2. *Six Inner Hebrides*, p. 191. The information is admittedly not complete.
3. Since these words were written, the present Government has gone back on its promise to introduce Road Equivalent Tariff for transport to the islands. (February 22nd, 1984).

EPILOGUE

The Coming of the National Trust for Scotland

On 29 May 1981, under a Deed of Gift and with the aid of a generous grant from the National Heritage Memorial Fund, Canna became the property of the National Trust for Scotland, while the former proprietor remained in occupation of Canna House as farming tenant of the islands of Canna and part of Sanday, and owner of the little islands of Heiskeir and Humla. The ownership of the Trust should ensure that Canna's amenities, its archaeology, bird life, plantations, and natural history, and the literary remains of the former proprietor, are preserved and protected; that the island community should have behind it a sympathetic landlord in possession of an adequate endowment not subject to estate duties, and therefore not liable to the frequent changes in ownership that can be so upsetting to island life. In the past two hundred years, Canna has been possessed by only three families, if one counts Hector MacNeill's tenancy in 1782 as practical possession. The National Trust for Scotland, moreover, should have better means to advance the island's interests in the matter of official amenities, than can be exercised by any individual owner. In its efforts to preserve and extend the island's amenities its friends at home and abroad will wish it well. Its success or otherwise in maintaining Canna as a happy Hebridean community will be scrutinized with much attention.

It is hoped that difficulties which have arisen since 1986 owing to the Trust's natural lack of experience in dealing with Hebridean people and Hebridean farming problems will soon be satisfactorily solved.

APPENDIX I SOME EARLY ACCOUNTS
OF CANNA

Dean Munro (1549)

Kannay

Be twa myle of sea, towards the Northwest, towards the Isle of Ronin [i.e. Rum] layes ane Ile callit Kannay, faire maine land foure myle lang inhabit and manurit with a paroche kirke in it, guid for Corne, fisching and grassing, with a Falcon Nest in it, pertines to the Abbot of Colmkill.

> MacFarlane's *Geographical Collections*
> (Scottish History Society) liii. 281.

The miles in these early accounts are Scots miles, about a third longer than English ones. 'Manurit' means cultivated. 'Grassing' means grazing.

'The Description of the Isles of Scotland', Skene, *Celtic Scotland*, iii. 434.

Canna c.1593

This Ile is gude baith for corn and all kind of bestiall. It perteins to the Bischop of the Iles, but the said ClanRanald hes it in possessioun. It is thric mile lang and ane braid. It is six merk land and will raise 20 men. In this Ile is ane heich craig callit Corignan well braid on the heicht thairof, and but ane strait passage, that men may scairslie climb to the heid of the craig, and quhan the cuntrie is invadit the people gadderis thair wives and geir to the heid of the craig and defend thame selfis utherwayis the best thay may, and will not pass to the craig, because it may not be lang keepit onlie fault of water.

'Bestiall' – cattle. 'Hes it in possessioun' – occupies it. 'Merk land' – an old Norse measure of land value. 'Raise 20 men' – produce 20 fighting men, implying a population of about 120. 'Corignan' – Corra-dhùn, Gaelic for 'peculiar fort', now usually written Coroghon in English. This passage shows what was certainly its original use, as a place of refuge or 'maiden castle', see W. G. Collingwood, *The Antiquary*, 1906, p. 376.

Anonymous (c.1630)
MacFarlane *Geographical Collections* (SHS) LII. 177.

Cainna

Cainna ane Illand pertaining to the Captaine of the Clanronnald being nixt to the Illand of Rum, on the westsyde of Rum betwixt it and Wist. This Cainna is verie profitable and fertill both of corne and milk with abundance of all kynd of seafishes And there is verie manie of these foulls and birds aforsaid which are found in Rum, are found in this Illand. There is ane little Illand on the Southwest end or syde of this Illand called Haysgair ne quissag. And when scutts boats or gallys cannot land in Cainna nor in Haysgair nor yet in Tiry The ancient Inhabitants and principall of these Countries do say that saids Gallies boats nor scutts can nowayes land neither in Scotland England nor yet in Ireland.

'Foulls and birds' – Manx Shearwaters

Heisgeir nan cuiseag, 'Heiskeir of the rushes'. Heiskeir is Norse, 'high skerry'.

Fr. Dermit Dugan,
Papers of the late Monsignor Cameron

Canna in 1652

I also worked amongst the people of the Isles of Eigg, Rum [?] and Canna, in which God converted eight or nine hundred persons so little instructed in the matters pertaining to the Christian religion, that amongst them hardly fifteen could be found, who knew any mystery of our holy faith; I hope that the others will quickly follow the example of the first, and will give glory to their Creator; seeing that the greatest thought which they have is to learn the elements of our holy faith, and that with so much ardour, that when I taught the Christian doctrine the gentry and the married ladies were asking (keenly) that I should catechise them publicly.

Fr. Alexander Leslie's Visitation

Canna in 1678

From Rum we arrived at another island, very beautiful, called Canna, all the inhabitants of which are Catholics; they were overcome with joy to see us because they had not seen a priest for more than a year. Their spiritual needs, and their incredible zeal impelled us to stay some few days amongst them, the more because besides other needs they had many children for baptizing, and though certain heretical preachers had passed a little before, and had offered to baptize their said children by assuring them moreover that the priests would consider the baptism valid, by no means would they consent to let them be baptized by heretics saying that God would send them their priests in due time. This same thing nearly all the Islanders do.

On his way back from Uist

The sea having become calm, and the wind turned favourable, we sailed to Canna, where it was fitting to stay to aid the Catholics, who as usual surrounded us with weeping, tears, and lamentations beseeched pity and help. And the more we tried to console them the more difficult it was to escape from them, so that many times I thought to stay with them, and to die in their service, and but for the fact that I did not know the language, and that I had to complete the visit, I would not have gone away from those holy souls, not only to serve them, but to profit myself from their examples of Christian piety, just as one reads of the Christians of the early Church. How many times have I heartfully desired that the Cardinals and Bishops, or some Italian would be in my company who could represent truthfully the condition, the necessities, the zeal, and the piety of these Catholics.

Papers of Monsignor Cameron. Translated from the Italian by Mrs Delia Lennie.

The Synod of Argyle
Miscellany of the Maitland Society, Vol. III, p. 424

A Representation of the most deplorable state of severall Paroches in the Highlands both in the Western Isles and Continent within the bounds of the Synod of Argyle in which places the Reformation never obtained, 1703.

The Isles of Canna, Rum, Isle of Muck within the Sheriffdom of Argyle, and Egg within the Sherifdome of Inverness consisting of about five hundred examinable persons are all popish except fourtie persons that are protestants. There is one Patrick O Haran a priest that frequents here and endeavours to pervert the feu poor protestants in these Isles. The Lairde of Moror is a receiter and abettor of priests heire Witnesses Lauchlan McDonald somtyms Chamberlan of Egg John McDonald his brother John McCannanich all living in Egg . . . .

It is to be noted that the most of the forsaids places ar within the bounds of the Presbytery of Sky where theire are but five ministers and yet sex priests as saide is.

APPENDIX II THE MACDONALDS OF CLANRANALD AND THE MACDONALDS OF BOISDALE

The MacDonalds of Clanranald

The MacDonalds of Clanranald are so constantly in the background of Canna's history, even while having no legal standing with regard to the island, that a brief account of their succession is worth giving. The authorities for this are the *Book of Clanranald*, compiled by the MacVurichs of Stadhlaigearraidh, South Uist, the poet-historians of the family, edited and translated (not always impeccably) by the Revd Alexander Cameron, LL D, in the second volume of *Reliquiae Celticae*; Hugh MacDonald's *History of the MacDonalds*, edited by Sheriff J. R. N. MacPhail, with some relevant Vatican documents, in the first volume of *Highland Papers*, published by the Scottish History Society; Alexander MacKenzie, *The History of the MacDonalds and Lords of the Isles*, Inverness, 1881; and *The Clan Donald* by the Revd A. MacDonald, Killearnan, and the Revd A. MacDonald, Kiltarlity, Inverness, 1904.

There is not always unanimity between these sources, particularly as regards dates. There is a good deal of personal flattery in the MacVurich *Book of Clanranald*.

I The name of the clan and title of its chiefs derives from RANALD (Raghnall), son of John (Eóin), great great great grandson of Somerled founder of the Lordship (in Gaelic always called Kingdom) of the Isles, and his fourth cousin and first wife Amy MacRuairi (whom MacVurich calls Anna inghen Rúaghraighe). This Ranald became High Steward of the Isles. He and his brothers were passed over in the Succession to the Lordship in favour of John's sons by his second marriage to Princess Margaret Stewart, whose father became King of Scotland in 1370 as Robert II. Ranald himself died not long after July 1389, at Caisteal Tioram in Moidart. He was married to a daughter of the Earl of Atholl.

II He was succeeded by his son ALLAN (Ailean), from whom the Chiefs of Clanranald derived the patronymic of MAC 'IC AILEIN, 'Son of the Son of Allan'. This Allan fought at the battle of Harlaw in 1411. He died at Caisteal Tioram in 1419. He was married to a daughter of Stewart of Appin.

III   He was succeeded by his son RODERICK (Ruairi) who died in 1481. He was married to Margaret, daughter of Donald Balloch MacDonald of Islay.

IV   He was succeeded by ALLAN (Ailean), described by Alexander MacKenzie as 'the dread and terror of all neighbouring clans'. This ALLAN is the subject of a bitter Gaelic satire by Fionnlagh the Red Bard in the Book of the Dean of Lismore, where he is accused of sacrilege and incest, and called 'the prime devil of the Gael' – 'aon diabhal na nGaoidheal'. He died at Blair Athol in 1505 (executed there in 1509 before King James IV, according to MacKenzie) and was buried there. He was married to Florence (Flora) MacDonald of Ardnamurchan.

V   He was succeeded by his son RANALD (Raghnall Bàn), who MacKenzie says was executed at Perth in 1513 (1514?) for some unrecorded crime. The Book of Clanranald does not say who his son's mother was; Hugh MacDonald says he was married to a daughter of Roderick MacLeod called 'The Black', Tutor to the heir of MacLeod of Lewis.

VI   He was succeeded by his son DUGALD (Dubhghall), who MacKenzie says was detested by his clan for his cruelties to his own kindred, and assassinated by them. His descendants became the MacDonalds of Morar, with the patronymic 'Mac Dhubhghaill Mhórair' – 'Son of Dugald of Morar'. Succession Dugald–Allan–Alexander–Allan (Ailean Mór), who had a tack of Canna from the Marquess of Argyll (himself the nominal tenant of the island under the Bishop of Argyll) in 1654.

VII   Dugald was succeeded as Chief of Clanranald by his uncle, ALEXANDER (Alasdair) brother of Ranald (Raghnall Bàn). Alexander died at Caisteal Tioram in 1530. He was succeeded by his eldest natural son by 'Dorothy' (Derbhfáil).

VIII   JOHN MOYDARTACH (Eóin Múideordach, 'John of Moidart'), who defeated the Frasers, who were championing the interests of Ranald (Raghnall Gallda, 'Foreign Ronald') the son of Allan IV by Isabella Fraser of Lovat, at the battle of Blàr Léine in 1545. He was much involved in the 16th-century conflicts in the Highlands. He erected a church at Kilmorie in Arisaig and another at Kildonan in Eigg. He died in 1584 (MacVurich says 1574) and was buried at Howmore in South Uist. He was married to Margaret, daughter of MacIan of Ardnamurchan.

IX   He was succeeded by his son ALLAN, who MacVurich says would fulfil any promise he made, drunk or sober. He died in 1590 (?1593) and was buried on Island Finnan in Moidart. Allan was married to a daughter of Alasdair Crotach MacLeod of Dunvegan, whom he repudiated, starting a bitter feud between the MacLeods and the MacDonalds of Clanranald. He was accidentally killed by a slingshot.

X   He was succeeded by his son ANGUS, who only ruled the clan briefly; according to MacVurich he was killed by Angus Og, son of James, while his prisoner at Dunyveg.

XI   He was succeeded by his brother DONALD (Domhnall) who died at Caisteal Tioram in 1617. Two of his brothers, Ranald and John, died on Canna in 1636. This Ranald, 'Raghnall mac Ailein mhic Iain', held Benbecula and was involved in matrimonial troubles; he supported the Irish Franciscan Mission to the Isles. Donald XI married Mary, daughter of Angus MacDonald of Dunyveg.

XII   He was succeeded by his son the second JOHN MOYDAR-TACH (Eóin Múideordach), who married Marion, daughter of Sir Rory Mór MacLeod of Dunvegan in 1613, putting an end to the feud between the Clanranalds and the MacLeods. Both John Moydartach and Sir Rory MacLeod supported the Irish Franciscans. John Moydartach, who played a distinguished part in the Civil War under Montrose, died in 1670 on Eriskay.

XIII   He was succeeded by his son DONALD (Domhnall Dubh na Cuthaige, 'Black Donald of the "Cuckoo" '), who was born about 1625, fought in Montrose's army in the Civil War, married his first cousin Marion MacLeod, who may have been the wife traditionally imprisoned in Coroghon Prison, in 1666; got a charter of Canna from the Marquess of Argyll in 1672; died on Canna in 1686, and was buried in Howmore on South Uist.

XIV   He was succeeded by his son ALLAN who was killed fighting on the Jacobite side at Sheriffmuir in 1715. He was married to Penelope MacKenzie, but had no children.

XV   He was succeeded by his brother RANALD, who died unmarried in Paris in 1725.

XVI   He was succeeded by DONALD MACDONALD OF BENBECULA, a direct descendant of the Ranald who died on Canna in 1636, the brother of Donald X of Clanranald. Donald XVI married his cousin Janet, sister of Allan XIV and Ronald XV. He died in 1730, and was buried at Nunton, Benbecula.

XVII   He was succeeded by his son RANALD, who was born in 1692, and died in 1766. He was married to Margaret, daughter of William MacLeod of Bernera.

XVIII   He was succeeded by his son RANALD, the 'young Clanranald' of the Forty-Five, the subject of a eulogy in Alexander MacDonald's book of Gaelic poems published in 1751. He was born about 1721, and died at Nunton in 1776.

XIX   He was succeeded by his son JOHN by his second marriage, to Flora MacKinnon of MacKinnon, born around 1760. John married his first wife Katherine, daughter of Robert MacQueen of Braxfield, Lord Justice Clerk of Scotland, in 1784. (His second wife, by whom he had no children, was Jean, daughter of Colin MacDonald of Boisdale.) He died in Edinburgh in 1794, and was buried at Holyrood.

XX   He was succeeded by his son RANALD or REGINALD GEORGE, born 29 August 1788, who married first Lady Catherine Anne Edgecombe, second daughter of the Earl of Mount Edgecombe, who became MP for the rotten borough of Plympton; sold all the Clanranald estates in the 1820s and 1830s, and died in London where he is buried in the Brompton Cemetery , on 11 March 1873.

The MacDonalds of Boisdale

This family, very closely connected with the Clanranalds, became one of the most important Hebridean families in the eighteenth century. Its founder was Alexander MacDonald, second son of Donald MacDonald of Benbecula, who succeeded as sixteenth chief of Clanranald on the death of his cousin Ranald in Paris in 1725, by his second wife Margaret, daughter of George MacKenzie of Kildun. He was thus a first cousin of 'Old Clanranald' and uncle of 'Young Clanranald' of the Forty-Five.

Alexander was born in 1698, and obtained a 499-year lease of Boisdale and other lands at the south end of South Uist from Clanranald in 1741; in 1758 he obtained a charter of the lands of Bornish, Smerclet, Kilbride, and the islands of Eriskay and Lingay in Barra Sound. The ruins of his great house with its high stone garden wall can be seen at Kilbride above the southern shore of South Uist.

He is best known for the part he played in 1745, first trying to persuade Prince Charles not to persevere in his venture without the help of Sir Alexander MacDonald of Sleat and MacLeod, which Boisdale knew would not be given; then dissuading the young men of South Uist from joining the Jacobite army; and finally for his helping the Prince, when on the run, to elude his pursuers, for which he was taken prisoner and brought to London along with Old Clanranald and MacNeil of Barra. He was one of the companions of the Prince while the Prince was hiding at Corradale in South Uist. His prowess as a whisky drinker was famous.

By his three marriages he established his family socially; the first to Mary, widow of Sir Donald MacDonald of Sleat, the second to Margaret, daughter of MacLean of Coll, and the third to Anne, daughter of MacNeil of Barra. By these three marriages he had no fewer than nineteen children, ten of whom died young. A daughter of this last marriage, Janet, married Hector MacNeill, the future tenant of Canna, around 1765 – the marriage was *not* between his daughter Margaret by this marriage and 'Donald MacNeill of Kenachreggan, afterwards of Canna' as is asserted in *Clan Donald*. How Hector MacNeill met Janet and married into the Boisdale family is unfortunately unknown; the Boisdale family papers have disappeared. It is significant that his lease of Canna from Clanranald was signed at the Boisdale residence at Kilbride in 1781.

Alexander of Boisdale died in 1768 and was succeeded by his son Colin, who also prospered. He was first married to Margaret, daughter of Donald Campbell of Airds, and secondly to Isabella, daughter of Robert Campbell of Glenfalloch, who was connected with the Earls of Breadalbane. By these two marriages he had in all fourteen children. Thus Colin and his father between them were connected by descent to the Clanranalds and the MacKenzies, and by marriage to three important Hebridean landed families, and two important mainland ones. They also played a considerable part in the affairs of their Clanranald cousins. In the 1770s Colin purchased the estate of Ulva in Mull.

An allusion in the *Lyon in Mourning* (second volume, p. 96) to MacDonald of Baileshear's being the only Protestant in the little company with Prince Charles at Corradale, proves that Alexander of Boisdale was then a Catholic. If the date of his death, 1768, is correctly given in *Clan Donald*, it must have been his son Colin who launched an odious attack on the religion of his tenantry in 1770, described in Bishop Hay's Memorial, issued at Edinburgh in 1771. In consequence of this persecution, which was backed by threats of eviction, 100 emigrants left Uist for Prince Edward Island in 1772. The matter was raised by the Vatican at a high level, and the persecution ceased.

The descent of Boisdale in the senior line ended with Colin's grandson Hugh who sold the estate in 1839 to Col. Gordon of Cluny, and disappeared into obscurity. However, Colin's descendants by his second marriage, the eldest of whom inherited Ulva on Colin's death in 1802, prospered.

APPENDIX III CHARTERS, RENTALS, AND LEASES

Charters

Clanranald Papers

29 January 1628. Confirmation of Charter made by Thomas Bishop of the Isles, etc., to whose bishopric the monastery of Iona and the Priory of Ardchattan are joined, in favour of Archibald Lord of Lorne, in feu-farm the Isle of Canna.
Quoted verbatim on p. 63.

30 October 1665. Commission of Bailliery by Archibald Earl on Argyll to Sir Rorie MacLeod of Tallasker constituting him 'bailie depute' at pleasure within the Isle of Canna. At Inverary.

18 March 1672. Charter by Archibald Earl of Argyll in favour of Donald MacDonald of Moydart, Captain of Clan Ronald.
Quoted verbatim on p. 75.

25 April, 17 and 18 July 1684. Charter of Confirmation and Novodamus by Archibald Bishop of the Isles with consent of his Dean and Chapter to Donald MacDonald of Moydart, Captain or Chief of the family of Clanranald, of the Island of Canna.
Quoted verbatim on p. 77.

Précis of Leases to Allan MacRonald or MacDonald of Morar

At Inverary, 21 January 1654. Lease by Archibald, Marquess of Argyll, Earl of Kintyre, Lord Campbell and Lorne, to Allan Makranald of Morror, his heirs, assignees, and subtenants of no higher degree than himself, of the whole lands and isle of Canna with the teind sheaves, parsonage, vicarage, great and small teinds of the same included, together with all the houses, buildings, yards, tofts, and crofts there, and the mills, multures, fishings, and pertinents of the same, lying within the Sheriffdom of Argyll and pertaining heritably to the noble Marquess. Together with the office of Stewartry and Baillierie of the island and all fees pertaining to these offices.

This for the space of six whole years and harvests following the said Allan's entry, which entry began at the term of Whitsunday 1653 to the land and offices described, including courts, plaints including local jurisdiction and herezelds.* For all of which the said Allan is to pay yearly at Martinmas at Inverary to the said noble Marquess or his chamberlain the sum of 1,200 merks Scots (£800 Scots), making the first payment thereof at Martinmas last (1653).

During the tenancy, the said Allan is to relieve the said noble Marquess of all taxation and public duties that have or will be imposed upon the island of Canna, and Allan and his subtenants are to do for the Marquess all the usual services that may be asked or required outside the Isle of Canna. Allan Makranald is relieved of 200 merks of his first year's rent without prejudice to the Marquess's getting the remaining 1,000 merks.

Written by Patrick McVicar, servitor to George Campbell, and signed by the parties personally. Witnesses, George Campbell, Patrick McVicar; James Campbell, Colin Campbell, servitors to the noble Marquess, who witnessed the signature by Allan McRonald on 7 March 1655 at Carrick.

Declaration of Laird of Moror anent his Possession of Canna, May 1667

Refers to a fourteen-years lease of Canna given him by the late Marquess of Argyll at Whitsuntide 1659, dated at Fyart on the island of Lismore 24 August 1657, and acknowledges Allan MacRonald's occupation of Canna since that time, and that now the noble Earl Archibald Earl of Argyll is his rightful master and superior to whom he owes rent and service for the Isle of Canna. Renounces any pretended rights or lease made in his favour by the Bishop of the Isles or anyone else, and his delivered up to the noble Earl of Argyll the lease made by the Bishop for destruction, the present declaration to be legally recorded. Written by Duncan Fisher, servitor to John Yuill in Inverary, on 31 May 1667. Witnesses, James Mainzies of Couldaires, Archibald Campbell, servitor to the said noble Earl, and the said John Yuill and Duncan Fisher.

(The Marquess of Argyll was forfeited and beheaded in 1661, following which his superiorities of church lands in the Hebrides would have reverted to the Bishop of the Isles, from whom Allan of Morar would have at once asked for a formal lease of Canna.)

Proposed Lease of the Lands of Moidart, Arisaig, and Canna to Donald MacDonald of Kinlochmoidart, 1744

In the course of a long letter written to Clanranald (Ranald XVII) on

---

* Herezeld: the former right of a proprietor or tacksman to take the best beast belonging to a deceased tenant or subtenant; usually a horse, hence Gaelic *each-ursainn*.

21 September 1744 from Kinlochmoidart by his man of business, Roderick MacLeod, WS, MacLeod says it has been agreed that Donald of Kinlochmoidart shall take a lease of Moidart, Arisaig, and Canna for seven years at a rent of 5,100 merks (£3,400) 'over and above the annual rents [interest] of any debts owing by the family to persons within these countrys' (SRO G0201/4/47).

The lands in question had previously been possessed by the Lady Dowager of Clanranald, presumably as her marriage settlement. This would have been Margaret, daughter of George MacKenzie of Kildun, second wife of Donald XVI of Clanranald, and mother of Alexander MacDonald of Boisdale. She must have died recently. The letter states that the purpose of the lease would be to devote 4,000 merks annually towards clearing the Clanranald family debts, and 1,100 merks a year for the maintainance of Clanranald's son (Ronald XVIII) while he was still unmarried, 'this considering the situation of your family and the great debt left upon it by the Lady Dowager, is thought to be a necessary measure'.

This lease is referred to in *Clan Donald*, ii. 358, where the date is wrongly given as 1747, due to a misreading. Clearly Kinlochmoidart could not have taken a lease of these lands in 1747, having been executed for his part in the Forty-Five in 1746, when his house was burnt by Butcher Cumberland.

The reference to the lands in question having been possessed by the Lady Dowager of Clanranald, who had been widowed in 1730, is revealing as it shows that her decease must have taken place in 1743 or 1744, and it helps to explain the interest that her oldest surviving son Alexander MacDonald of Boisdale and his heir had in Canna, which presumably led to his son-in-law Hector MacNeill getting the tenancy of the greater part of the island in 1781.

I am much obliged to Mr D. M. Abbott of the Scottish Record Office for drawing my attention to the correct date of this letter, and providing me with a photocopy of it.

Rentals

The surviving rentals are printed here verbatim, in view of their economic and genealogical interest. Owing to the involvement of the Clanranald family in the Jacobite Rising of 1715, their estates, including Canna, were temporarily forfeited along with others belonging to Highland chiefs and proprietors who were involved in this attempt. Allan MacDonald of Clanranald was killed at the battle of Sheriffmuir in 1715. Hence the payments in 1716 to the Duke of Argyll as Superior and in 1717 to MacLean of Coll as claimant, though what adjudication his claim was based on is unknown at present.

As has been explained elsewhere in this book, owing to legal technicalities the Clanranald estates escape forfeiture after the Rising of 1745.

1696, October 30th. Factory by Archibald, Earl of Argyle, to Lieutenant Daniel Calder of Sir John Hill's regiment, to uplift the rents, etc. of the Islands of Eig and Canna, dated at Inverary 20th May 1696; witnesses, Ronald Campbell W.S. and Mr John Campbell W.S.

The Clan Campbell, i. 17.

Clanranald Papers

5 May 1713. Tack for five years by Allan Mackdonald of Moydart Captain of Clanranald to James Yong in Heill in Minginish in the Isle of Skye, of the fourth part of the Kirktown in Canna, within the shire of Argile and parish of Kilmore in Sleatt; and obliging himself to allow to James the annual rent of 1000 merks [£666. 13s. 8d. Scots] out of the rents, James paying 80 merks for the first year, and 100 merks for the four following years. At Corgun in Canna. Witnesses Archibald Macdonald son of Mr Aeneas Mackdonald and Ronald Mackonald brother german to Clanranald. [Young died within three years; his widow was Margaret MacLeod, see No. 60 in the 1718 rental.]

Rental in 1718

Judiciall Amount or Rentall of the Reall Estate which pertained to the Late Capt. of Clanranald Taken upon the depositions of the tennants of Isle of Canna by Sir Patrick Strachan of Glenkindy Surveyor Genll. of the forfeited Estates in North Britain. In presence of Archibald Campbell of Achatinie One of the Iustices of peace of Argyleshire This thirteenth day of August 1718 years as follows viz.

59   Appeared Angus M'donald in Tarbet and paroch of Slate being deeply Sworn and Interrogate Depons that he payed yearly – to Ranald M'donald Late Capt. of Clanranald for his possession of the Lands of Tarbet, the Sum of Eighteen pounds Sterling and two Sheep. – But that this Late Capt. of Clanranald owed him by bond five hundred merks Scots money and that he has allowance of the Interest of that money in the first end of his rent And a Tack of the Lands till the money was payed And depons he payed the three Last years as follows. Viz Cropt 1715. to the Late Capt. himself, – 1716, to Archibald Cameron of Dungallon as factor to the Duke of Argyle

and 1717, to the Laird of Coll, as having right by Adjudication to the Lands and this is the truth as he shall answer to God.

Ang M'Donald

Arch: Campbell I.P.

60   Donald M'Leod in Keill for Margaret M'Leod his Mother Makes Oath, That She possesses a part of Keill worth One hundred merks yearly which She is obliged to pay, And that She has allowance yearly from Clanranald Out of the first end of the said rent Off the Interest of One thousand merks Scots due to her and her Late husband by bond by the Late Capt. of Clanranald Depons that She payed the balance of her rent Cropt 1715. to the Lady Clanranald, 1716 to Dungallan and 1717 to the Laird of Coll & So is not in arrear, Which is the Truth as he Shall answer to God. And further depons his mother hes a Tack of these Lands as the other deponent has untill her money is payed up.

Donald M'Looud

Arch: Campbell I.P.

61   Malcolm Campbell in Keill and paroch aforesaid Makes oath That he payed yearly to the Late Capt. of Clanranald for one pennyland of Keill TwentySix merks Scots and One Sheep, Depons he is in no arrear having payed Croft 1715. to the Captain of Clanranald himself And the Last two years as above Which is the truth as he shall answer to God depons he cannot write –
Arch: Campbell I.P.

62   Ranald M'donald in Keill & paroch aforsd. Makes oath That he payed yearly to the Late Capt. of Clanranald Ninteen merks – and a half Scots for three farthing Land of Keill, And one Sheep, And payed the two Last years rent As above and was not in the possession Cropt 1715. Which is the truth as he shall amswer to God & depons he cannot write

63   The Said Angus M'Donald in Tarbet for Angus M'donald in Corgown Absent Makes Oath That the said Angus M'donald in Corgown payed yearly for his possession of the said Lands to the Late Capt. of Clanranald, The Sum of two hundred & Seventy one merks Scots, And is obliged further to pay yearly to Clanranald's officer Ten Shillings Sterl. for a half pennyland of his own possession, Depons the said Angus is but ane Intrant tennant and payd. the Last years rent to the Laird of Coll And that the deponents brother who was possessor of the Said Lands formerly payed the two preceeding years as above to the Capt of Clanranald and Dungallan, Which is the truth as he shall answer to God.

Ang: M'Donald

Arch: Campbell I.P.

64   Ewen M'kinnan, Finlay M'arthur, Iohn M'Leod, Donald M'Leod all in Keill & paroch aforsd. That Each of them payed yearly to the Late Capt. of Clanranald for a half pennyland which each of them possess of the said Lands, The Sum of thirteen merks Scots money and a Sheep Each, & no more, And payed the three Last years rent as above, Which is the truth as they shall answer to God & depons they cannot write –
Arch: Campbell I.P.

65   Angus M'ormet in Keill aforsaid Makes oath That he payed yearly to the said Late Capt. of Clanranald for his possession of three fardens of the Said Lands and Sum of Ninteen merks and a half Scots, And payed the bygone rents as above, Which is the truth as he shall answer to God & depons he cannot write, And further depons he pays a sheep yearly. –
Arch: Campbell I.P.

66   John M'donald in Keill, and Allan M'donald yr. Make oath That they payed yearly to the Late Capt. of Clanranald for a pennyland of the Said Lands which each of them possess, The Sum of Twenty Six merks Scots Each, and one Sheep, And depone they payed the Last three years rent as the Last deponent did, Which is the truth as they Shall answer to God & depone they cannot write.
Arch: Campbell I.P.

67   Donald M'donald alias Iohnston in Keill for himself and Angus M'ilirevich there Makes oath that they possess a pennyland of Keill Whereof the deponent three fardins and the said Angus one fardin ffer which they pay yearly Twenty Six merks Scots – and a Sheep each, And that they payed the three bygone years rent as above Which is the truth as he shall answer to God & depons he cannot write –
Arch: Campbell I.P.

68   Hector M'kinnan in Keill Makes oath that he payd. yearly to the said Late Capt. of Clanranald for a half pennyland of the said Lands The sum of thirteen Merks Scots and a Sheep. And payd. the three bygone years as above Which is the truth as he shall answer to God & depons he cannot write
Arch: Campbell I.P.

69   Iohn M'kinnan in Keill & paroch aforsd. Makes oath that he possesses two pennyland of the said Lands of Keill Worth fifty two merks yearly, Which he is to pay in time coming but is any intrant tennant, He believes the bygone rent was payed as above Which is the truth as he shall answer to God and cannot write.
Arch: Campbell I.P.

Rental of Canna in 1749

(David Bruce, Surveyor of Forfeited Estates in Scotland)

Tenant	Possessions	Money Rent	Sheep
Alexander MacLeod	Three farthing land of Kirktown of Canna	£15	1
Roderick Macdonald	Three farthing land of Kirktown of Canna	£15	1
Mary Macdonald	Three farthing land of Kirktown of Canna	£15	1
Angus MacArthur	One penny land of do.	£20	1
John MacArthur	and one farthing	£ 5	1
Donald MacIsaac	One penny land of do.	£20	1
Donald Edmond	One half penny land of do.	£10	1
Donald Johnston	One half penny land of do.	£10	1
Donald McDougal	One half penny land of do.	£10	1
Donald Edmond elder	One half penny land of do.	£10	1
Neil MacKinnon	One half penny land of do.	£10	1
Neil Campbell	One half penny land of do.	£10	1
Mary MacDonald	One half penny land of do.	£10	1
Mary Macdonald younger } Mary MacInnis }	jointly for one half pennyland of do.	£10	1
Angus Macdonald	One half penny land of do.	£10	1
John MacKinnon	One penny land of do.	£20	1
Donald MacLeod	One penny land of do.	£20	1
Neil MacNeil	One penny land of do.	£20	1
Katherine MacDuffie	One half penny land of do.	£10	1
Donald MacAlpin	One half penny land of do.	£10	1
Archibald MacArthur	Three farthing land of do.	£15	1
John Macdonald	Town and lands of Tarbet	£223:6:8	–
James Macdonald*	Korghoun and Sand Island of Canna	£266:13:4	–
Waste	Kirktown of Canna	£30	2

* James Macdonald was baillie of Canna. (See p. 100) He and John Macdonald, the tacksmen, had of course many subtenants who are not mentioned in this list.

Rental of Canna as collected or paid to Boisdale* during Bruce's
Factory.   *Undated.*
Canna ....£1250 – –

2 April 1755. Contract whereby Ranald Macdonald yr of Clanranald
sets in tack to Magnus and Donald MacLeod, merchants in
Glasgow, the lands of Corrogin and Island Gainich [Sanday] in the
Island of Canna, for three periods of 19 years from Whitsunday 1756
with provision that if Ranald shall not prevail to have the tack of the
estate of Clanranald set to Alexander MacDonald of Boystill (dated
5 September 1749) and to David Bruce, late surveyor of Forfeited
Estates, reduced, the present tack is not to take place till the expira-
tion thereof, and that either party may break the tack at the end of
each 19 years.
And Ranald binds himself to make the first offer of the lands of Keil
or Kirktown in Canna and any other farm therein possessed by John
MacDonald of Laigg after his decease, with power to build houses
thereon; and Magnus and Donald MacLeod obliged themselves to
pay £33:6:8 sterling yearly with £40 sterling in name of gressum in
the first year of each 19 years, and to pay cess and other public
burdens and to build all necessary houses, and particularly a con-
venient public house on the lands of Keil or Corrogin. At
Edinburgh. [With note that before subscription both parties have
liberty to break the tack at the end of each 19 years.]

23 June 1761. Registered tack by Ranald Macdonald to Donald
MacLeod in Canna of the lands of Keill and others for three 19 year
terms from Whitsunday 1760, all previous tacks being renounced.

*Account of the Valued Rent of the Isle of Canna
the property of Ronald McDonald of Clanronald*

Maill
Lands.
16. Kilchannich Fourteen pounds seven shill[6]
    & eight pence   £14 7 8
16. Corghoun & Ellangannach Eleven pounds
    two shill[s] and two pence 11 2 2

* Alexander MacDonald of Boisdale, later to become Hector MacNeill's father-in-
law.

18. Tarbert Ten pounds .... 10 – –
       Total Valued Rent of Canna Is Thirty five
         pounds nine shillings & ten pence Sterling   £35 9 10
                                    Inveraray 20th November 1767

That the above is a Just and Exact Acco$^{t.}$ of the Valued Rent of the Isle of Canna comprehending the ffarms above specified conform to the Roll of Valuation of the Shire of Argyll made up and compleated by the Commissioners nominated and authorized by Act of Parliament for that effect upon the Thirtieth day of April One thousand seven hundred and ffifty one years Is Certified & Attested by me Deputy Sheriff Clerk of the said Shire.

                                          (Signed) Peter Lindsay

18 June 1781. Missive by the Tutors of John Macdonald to continue Alexr Macdonald for ten years in the eight penny lands of Island Ganich [Sanday] at £4 sterling penny yearly of rent on his resigning his right of the Change House of Canna and two penny land of Corgoun in favour of Mr Hector MacNeil, sr., merchant in Cambeltown. At Kilbride.

Missive – Clanranald & Curators for the lands of Tarbert etc. at Canna To Mr Hector McNeill, Merchant, Campbeltown, 1781

                                          Kilbride, 19th June, 1781
Sir
    WHEREAS you have agreed to pay us the Sum of four pounds Sterling for every penny of the Eighteen pennylands of Tarbert as possessed by Mrs MacKinnon Junior of Coriechattachan & two pennies of the farm of Corrogown all in the Island of Canna & that yearly as Rents amounting in whole to Eighty Pounds Sterling P. annum – And as You have undertaken to Build a Changehouse & Garden on the Farm of Corrogown of Stone and lime & Slated for which we allow you now about Ninety Pounds Sterling towards helping of the same & that whatever Sum more will be advanced for Building Said house not exceeding ONE HUNDRED & TEN pounds Sterling you will be obliged to pay us at the Rate of five per cent P. annum for money so advanced as also the ordinary Sum of Six pounds Sterling formerly paid as Rent for said Changehouse, & in consideration of the above Rents and other Conditions we bind & oblige us to give You a Lace of twenty Four years of the above mentioned lands & Changehouse commencing at Whitsd? & Eighty

live years with speciale provision that any one or two more of the
Tutors & Curators for John MacDonald Esq. of Clanranald agree or
concurr with us in giving you this Lace on the terms above
mentioned – AND as there are no houses of any kind on the farms you
are to get (belonging to the Master) to accomodate the incoming
tennant we therefore approve of your Building a house & Offices of
stone & lime Slated to the amount of one hundred & fifty or two
hundred pounds sterling for which you are to have a Milleration at
the Expiry of your Tacks You being obliged to deliver Said houses in
sufficient & Good Order at the time of delivery, n⁵ proviso that this
Clause is agreeable to the rest of the Tutors & Curators which it is
hoped will be –

& we are   Sir

To Mr Hector MacNeill

Your most Obed⁵ Servants

Merch⁵ Campbeltown

John MacDonald
Flora MacDonald Consents
Collin MacDonald Consents

I have   the above and accept of the same place & Date
above written   Hector MacNeill

From C. Fraser Mackintosh, 'Antiquarian Notes' 1897.
The source of this information is not given.

The modern parish of Small Isles comprehends the four islands of
Canna, Rum, Eigg and Muck, whereof, by the will of Lord Lorne of
ever profane memory, all but Eigg are in the county of Argyle.
Canna and Eigg belonging to the Clanranalds, and upon these
islands I desire to make some observations. In 1798 the rental of
Canna was as follows:-

1. Tarbert, an 18 penny land – Hector Macneill   £ 72 0 0
2. Corrogdan, a 7 penny land – said Hector
   Macneill 28 0 0
3. Keil, a 12 penny land – said Hector 60 0 0
4. Change House of Canna – said Hector 6 0 0
5. Heisker Island – said Hector. No rent mentioned.
6. Sandy Island – Alex. Macdonald, a 9 penny
   land at £5 5s per penny 47 5 0
   There is a dispute as to the number of
   pennies, tenant in use to pay only
   £42 2s 0d.

7. Upper Island, a 4 penny land – Donald
   Macdonald and others 21 0 0
   Macneill makes 14 tons of kelp, Alexander
   3 tons, and Donald Macdonald 1 ton of kelp.

Duncan Macarthur was ground officer, and Macneill factor, of
Canna. It was reputed a fertile island and, now practically un-
inhabited, contained in 1772 a population of not less than 220 souls.

The valuations on the Clanranald estates were all penny-lands, sub-
divided into halfpenny and farthing lands. To stock a penny-land,
according to Pennant's information (see p. 112) required a sum of
£30 sterling, and it carried seven cows and a horse.

An Informal Record of the 1810 Lease of Canna

Canna 26 April 1810

I as Commissioner for R. G. MacDonald Esqr. of ClanRanald Do
hereby agree to let you the ferms of Keil Coragon and Tarbet in
Canna with the Island of Hysker all as Presently possesed by you as
also the Sea Ware of Island na Bard but reserving the liberty of fuel
and divot from the Hill of Keanatyh [?] to the tenants of the upper
Sandy Island of Canna with the necessary roads for carrying of the
same And that for the space of Eleven Years from and after Whitsunday first you and your heirs and executors paying yearly at
Martinmass to Clan Ranald or his Factor or others a Rent of Four
hundred Pounds yr. you to be entitled to full Meliorations for your
houses and stone dykes in case of your removal at the foresaid term
of years in terms of the Different Missives from the late John
Mac Donald Esqr. of ClanRanald to the late Mr Hector Mac Neill of
Canna your Father and that in terms of a Comprisement [?] to be
made by men mutually chosen You are to pay as formerly at the Rate
of 5 pCent for the £110 of Clan Ranald in your hands during this
agreement – You are not to Assign or Sublet the Premises now let to
you –
A Regular Tack containing the usual and necessary clauses as
generally adopted at this time on the ClanRanald estate to be entered
into with you – J A M [?]
N.B. You are to be continued in possesion of Sanday during the
foresaid space at a Yearly Rent of Thirty five Pounds sterling but
reserving to ClanRanald liberty to inclose and plant.*

(SRO GD 201/2/63)

* The reference to 'fuel and divot' suggests that the inhabitants of Upper Sanday,
the west end of Sanday, were getting their peat from the main island of Canna; but the
place-name 'Keanatyh' is a puzzle. 'Island na Bard' is Eilean a' Bhàird, a tidal island in
Canna harbour. Keanatyh = Beinn Taighe?

Rental of Canna delivered up by Mr Brown to Mr Campbell
at Whitsunday 1813

Names of Farms	Names of Tenants	
Island of Canna	Mr Donald MacNeill	£405 10 –
Crofts of Do.	Sundries	121 12 10
Keninellan	Mr John MacDonald	39 10 —
	Total	£566 12 10

Rental of Canna for Mart[s.] *1814*

Farms	Tenants	
Island of Canna	Mr Don[d] MacNeill	£405 10 –
Crofts of Do.	Sundries	121 12 10
Keninellan	Mr John Macdonald	39 10 –
		£566 12 10

Rental of Canna for Crop 1815

Island of Canna	Mr D. MacNeill	£405 10 –
Crofts of do.	Sundries	122 9 6
Keninellan	Jo. Macdonald	39 10 —
		£567 9 6

Rental of Canna Mart^{s.} 1818

Donald MacNiel Esqr.		£373	10	–
Mrs Ann MacDonald	Sand Island	16	6	6
John Jameson	Do.	9	7	8
Niel MacIntosh	Do.	10	6	6
Hugh Jameson	Do.	9	2	4
Malcolm MacArthur	Do.	5	15	5
Finlay MacArthur	Do.	5	10	–
Widow Niel MacKinnon	Do.	5	1	10
Donald MacLean	Do.	5	10	–
Donald MacIntosh	Do.	5	10	–
John MacArthur Senr.	Do.	5	10	–
John MacIsaac	Do.	5	12	6
Allan MacArthur Junr.	Do.	5	12	6
Alex. MacArthur	Do.	5	12	6
John MacInnes	Do.	5	12	6
William Jameson Senr.	Do.	5	16	3
Niel Jameson	Do.	6	0	6
Mrs Alexr. MacDonald	Do.	14	6	0
William Jameson Junr.	Do.	6	2	–
Malcolm and Widow Campbell	Do.	9	16	–
Alexr. MacLeod and John MacArthur	Do.	9	16	–
Lachlan MacArthur	Do.	5	12	6
Angus MacLeod	Do.	–	16	8
Don^d Campbell	Do.	–	16	8
P. MacCarmic	Do.	–	16	8
Finlay MacCaskill	Do.	–	16	8
Malcolm MacArthur	Do.	–	16	8
Christian MacDonald	Do.	–	16	8
Lachlan Jameson	Do.	–	16	8
Edward Jameson	Do.	–	16	8
Lachlan MacIsaac	Do.	–	16	8
John MacCarmic	Do.	–	16	8
		£539	16	2

Martinmas 1820 and Martinmas 1821

Same as Martinmas 1818, except for one more tenant on Sanday, Lachlan MacInnes paying 16s. 8d., total rent £540. 12s. 10d.

Clanranald's Debt to Donald MacNeill

Edinburgh 1 November 1823

Upon the 17th, 18th and 22nd September 1823 appeared Donald MacCarmic on behalf of Donald MacNeill Esq. of Canna.

John MacIntyre (for the Trustees of R. G. MacDonald) and holding in his hands a trust deed [which *inter alia* bound them to pay MacNeill the accumulated sum of £4,500 sterling with annual rent of £225 and penalties] furth of all and haill the lands fishings teinds and others under written *videlicet* [here follows a long list of Clanranald's lands in Moidart, Arisaig, Eigg, South Uist, and Benbecula as well as Canna itself] extending to a ten pound land [this refers to an ancient assessment] with all and singular houses . . . woods fishings . . . mills built or to be built . . . along with the heritable office of bailiary. . . .

General Register of Seisins, Reversions & c (GR), Vol. 1290, p. 55. I am obliged to Sir Archibald Ross for drawing my attention to this and also to the leases of 1781 and 1810. It appears that Clanranald's Trustees are making the rents of the whole of Clanranald's estates a security for the repayment of this loan. It was only one of Clanranald's many debts. In 1820 his estates had been put under trustees, Canna had been pledged to a firm of London jewellers for £10,000, to Hagart of Bantaskine for £5,000 and to William MacDonald of St Martins, advocate, for £18,000; and in 1823 in November it was also pledged to a firm of London silversmiths for £10,000. (GR 1185. 250, 1186. 10 and 33, 1289. 45).

The loan was liquidated when Donald MacNeill was 'scizcd' as proprietor of Canna on 15 January 1828. The agreed price was £8,000, with MacNeill claiming £1,000 for improvements executed during his tenancy. MacNeill paid (in separate transactions) £7,600 for the property and £400 for the feudal superiority (which Clanranald had earlier purchased from the Duke of Argyll). MacNeill was simultaneously admitted to the heritable office of bailliery of Canna. the witnesses to the 'seizing' or sasine were Malcolm MacIsaac, innkeeper, and Hector MacIsaac, fisherman. (GR 1487. 272).

APPENDIX IV EARLY CANNA EMIGRANTS TO NOVA SCOTIA

KENNEDY

In 1791, six Kennedy brothers came from Canna (Scotland) and landed at Parrsboro (Nova Scotia). They remained there seventeen years.

Two of them, Donald and John, afterwards came to Broad Cove, Inverness Co.; the other four went to Antigonish.

In 1812, Murdoch and Alexander from Antigonish came to Loch Ban and Light Point.

MACDONALD

Allan and Alexander MacDonald – two brothers – settled at Foot Cape from Canna (Scotland) – date not given. Each took a farm of 200 acres and married.

Alexander's family – five sons and two daughters – all dead.

Allan's family – seven sons and one daughter – all dead except Roderick and James (1922).

Roderick has son, Neil, a schoolteacher.

Both families noted for their wit and pleasantries. Allan from Canna was well educated and had some medical skill. He often acted as doctor; he was also a fiddler.

MCISAAC

About the year 1812 Allan McIsaac arrived from Canna and settled on 400 acres of land at Broad Cove, Inverness Co. He had three sons, John, Alexander, and Donald. Alexander had six sons and three daughters, namely:

John died a lay brother in the Monastery of Petit Clair-vaux, Tracadie, Antigonish.

Donald became a priest and was parish priest of Great Narrows and River Inhabitants. He is buried in Stella Maris Cemetery at Inverness on his father's old farm.

Angus and *Allan* were both schoolmasters in Inverness County.

Aeneas – simple-minded and harmless – lived and died with James.

James only member who married. Wife was Ann

McDougall, daughter of Alex. McDougall, carpenter of Broad Cove Banks. They had a large family. The Inverness railway and coal company took over a lot of their land at Inverness at a good price.

Donald (son of Allan McIsaac from Canna) had five sons and five daughters: of whom

Allan was father of Dr J. A. McIsaac of New York, and of Daniel McIsaac who was Mayor of Inverness Co. in 1922.

John (son of Allan McIsaac from Canna) settled at Broad Cove Intervale. He married Sarah Beaton and had six sons and five daughters. He occupied a vast tract of land there. His sons were Angus, John, Alexander, Donald, Allan, Neil.

Alexander was Canon McIsaac of Halifax.

John settled in Mabou – large family.

Donald (miller) and *Allan* settled at Foot Cape. Donald married Mary Gillis – family: John, Angus, Allan, Stephen, James, Anthony, Sarah. He did a lot of farming and business. John, James, and Sarah married.

Allan – twice married. First family – all left the place, second family – Joseph and John A. still there in 1922.

Along with Allan McIsaac (mentioned as coming from Canna in 1812) there came from Canna his sister Ann (who married a Roderick MacLean who came from Rum about 1810 and settled in Broad Cove). Also his brother Angus McIsaac. Angus settled at the head of the Pond – now Inverness harbour (first settler) – five boys, Archibald, Donald, Roderick, Angus 69, James. (Angus, from Canna, is referred to as Aonghas Mac Neil.) Archibald's family moved to Newfoundland (Codroy) after his death.

Donald Ruadh, son of Angus (from Canna) married M. MacDonald – farm sold for debt. Acquired later by his sons Angus and John who were still in occupation in 1922.

Roderick (son of Angus from Canna) married Mary Rankin of Sight Point – large family. Eldest son Rory still lives there in 1922.

Angus Òg (son of Angus from Canna) – large family of boys – moved to Codroy, Newfoundland.

One of John (son of Allan who came from Canna) McIsaac's daughters – Margaret McIsaac – married Hugh MacDonnell, son of Thomas MacDonnell (Ban) from Strathglass, Scotland. Thomas had settled in Judique and John McIsaac in Broad Cove Intervale.

Archibald Kennedy from Canna settled in 1819 in Glenville (formerly Black Glen). Family of five sons and one daughter. Ronald, the eldest, married Margaret McIsaac, daughter of Allan McIsaac (from Canna) of Broad Cove.

JAMIESON   Many years ago a family of Jamiesons came from Canna. One of them, Lauchlin, settled at Piper's Glen, and married a MacIntyre. They had two sons and four daughters. The eldest son, Neil, was a piper.

MACDONALD   John MacDonald came from Canna, and was an early settler at Glencoe (Cape Breton). He was twice married, first to a daughter of Angus Archibald MacDonald, secondly to Sarah Stewart. He had six sons and four daughters.

MACINTOSH   The MacIntoshes of Post Hastings are descended from Neil MacIntosh, from Canna, Scotland. Neil's son Norman came from Canna when a boy, and settled at River Denys. He married Margaret Black of River Inhabitants. They had eight daughters and three sons. [There is a Neil MacIntosh amongst the tenants of Sanday in 1818, see p. 220.]

Information from J. L. MacDougall's *History of Inverness County, Nova Scotia*, 1922.

APPENDIX V POST-REFORMATION
CATHOLIC CLERGY

Missionary Priests

(a) Irish Franciscans

Fr. Cornelius Ward (Conchobhair Mac an Bháird), October 1624; February 1625.
Fr. Patrick Hegarty, August 1630; April 1631.

(b) Vincentians

Fr. Dermit Dugan, 1652.
Fr. Francis MacDonnell, 1671.

Papal Visitor to the Mission

Fr. Alexander Leslie, 1678.

Episcopal Visitations

Bishop Nicholson, 1700.
Bishop Gordon, 1707.

Secular Priests

Fr. Patrick O'Haran (?O'Hara), 1700, 1703.*

After 1715, the Catholics of the Small Isles were probably served from Arisaig, Morar, or Moidart. The first priest specifically mentioned as stationed in the Small Isles was Francis MacDonald, who went to Eigg in 1742. He left the Church in 1743, and became a Presbyterian catechist at Strontian, but early the next year was accused before the Presbytery of Mull of gross immorality, the

---

* *Miscellany of the Maitland Society*, III. 424. Information regarding the post-1715 priests to 1791 is derived from F. Forbes and W. J. Anderson 'Clergy Lists of the Highland District, 1732–1828', *Innes Review*, XVII. 129–84; later names and dates kindly supplied by the Revd Fr. R. MacDonald, Dunoon.

prosecutors being Catholics, Bishop Hugh MacDonald and MacDonald of Kinloch Moidart, and the 'information' being drawn up by John Stewart, drover in Mull, and Alexander MacDonald (see Chapter 11). The case was dealt with by Francis MacDonald's being sent to Skye.

Alexander Kennedy, 1769–72.
Austin MacDonald, Small Isles with Knoydart and Moidart, 1773–5.
Allan MacDonald, 1776–80.
James Hugh MacDonald from Morar, 1784–91, went to Prince Edward Island.
Anthony MacDonald, 1791–1834. Remained on Eigg in retirement, died 1843, aged seventy-three.
Donald MacKay, from South Uist, 1834–42.
Alexander Gillis, from Sunart, 1842–80. Died on Eigg.
Coll MacDonald, from Lochaber, on Canna 1850–1. Went to Knoydart.*
James J. Dawson, 1881–2.
Donald A. MacPherson, 1882.
Donald MacLellan, from South Uist, 1882–8.
Donald Walker, from South Uist, 1888–1903.
John MacNeill, from Barra, (later Monsignor Canon MacNeill, Morar) 1903–5.
John MacMillan, from Barra, 1905–8.
Frederick McClymont, 1908–14. Not a Gaelic speaker. Joined Benedictines after leaving the Small Isles.
Donald MacIntyre, from South Uist, 1914–19. Went to Craigston, Barra, and left with emigrants for Canada in 1925.
Patrick MacDonald, from South Uist, 1919–23.
Malcolm MacKinnon, from Barra, 1923–8.
Duncan Campbell, 1928–31.
William MacLellan, from Morar, 1931–4.
Joseph Campbell, from Barra, 1934–40.
Angus MacSween, from Barra, 1940–1.
John MacCormick, from South Uist, 1941–8.
Alexander MacKellaig, from Morar, 1946–8.
John MacLean (now Canon), 1948–52. Last diocesan priest on Eigg.

Since he left, the Small Isles were served from Bornish in South Uist until the direct steamer service linking Canna and Lochboisdale ended in the spring of 1964; since then usually (once a month) from

* See Odo Blundell, *Catholic Highlands of Scotland*, II. 75. There would have been no point in his continuing on Canna after the eviction of 1851.

Knoydart, occasionally from Arisaig; at Christmas and Easter before 1970 occasionally, and since then regularly served by the Benedictine Abbey at Fort Augustus.

APPENDIX VI CHURCH OF SCOTLAND MINISTERS

(a) While united with Sleat

Neil MacKinnon, c.1624–33 (see Chapter 7).
Angus MacQueen (Episcopalian), 166– to 1694 (deprived) but still present in 1709.

(b) Small Isles separate

Donald MacQueen, born about 1700, presented by the Presbytery 16 March 1727, ordained 19 May 1727; translated to North Uist in 1755. A believer in Second Sight. Died 28 March 1770.

Malcolm MacAskill, Rubha 'n Dunain, born 1723, minister 1757–1787 (died) 'Am Ministear Làidir'. His letter on second sight in *Miscellanea Scotica* iii. 160.

Donald MacLean, born 1752, presented by George III 5 June 1787. Wrote account of parish for *Old Statistical Account*.

Neil MacLean, presented by George Prince Regent 13 February 1811–7 March 1817.

William Fraser, born 1754, presented by George Prince Regent 13 September 1816, drowned 28 October 1817 between Arisaig and Eigg.

Donald MacLean, born 1793, ordained missionary Rum and Canna 16 September 1818, presented by George Prince Regent 17 November 1818, deposed for intemperance 21 November 1838, died 6 October 1839.

John Swanson, born Gravesend 10 May 1804, former grocer and schoolmaster, ordained missionary Fort William 1835, presented by Queen Victoria 26 March 1839. Joined Free Church in 1843, minister Free Church Small Isles 1843–7.

Henry Beatson, presented by Queen Victoria 1843, transferred to Barra 1847 (originally presented Stenscholl by William IV, 7 February 1837).

Peter Grant, born 1796, presented by Queen Victoria 12 October 1847, admitted 20 April 1848, died 4 June 1864.

John Sinclair, born 1825, presented by Queen Victoria 29 July 1864, admitted 1 November 1861, died 5 November 1908 after five years in Nova Scotia.

Alexander Fraser, 1909–11.
Angus MacDonald, born 1865, 1913–17.
George MacKenzie, 1920.
Hector Cameron, born 1893, Tiree-man, 1923–5, to S. Knapdale.
John Stewart, 1926–9.
William MacWhirter, MA, 1930–9.
Neil MacKay, 1940–5.

Since when the Small Isles have ceased to have a resident ordained minister, being now served from Mallaig.

APPENDIX VII POPULATION STATISTICS

Year	Source	Canna Males	Canna Females	Sanday Males	Sanday Females	Total	Inhabited Houses
1593	'Description of the Isles'					120	
1728	SPCK Minutes					236*	
1755	*Webster's Census of Scotland*					231	
1768	Revd M. MacAskill's count					233	
1794	*Old Statistical Account*					304	
1805	Clanranald Map						*c.*70
1815	Gaelic Schools Report					400	
1801	Census		No separate figures				
1811	Census		No separate figures				
1821	Census	206	230	Included		436	73
1831	Census	124	140	Included		264	not given
1841	Census	116	139	Included		255	44
1851	Census	125	113	Included		238	45
1861	Census	55	72	Included		127	29
1871	Census	26	22	29	29	106	25
1881	Census	30	18	27	35	110	23
1891	Census	22	18	31	31	102	21
1901	Census	21	21	20	24	86	21
1911	Census	15	14	20	21	70	20
1921	Census	15	14	21	16	66	16
1931	Census	22	18	9	11	60	14
1938	Count	7	10	12	9	38	11
1951	Census	8	3	13	9	33	12
1961	Census		No separate figures			24	
1971	Census		No separate figures			33	
1981	Count	4	7	2	5	18	7

* Not including children under five years of age.

Notes to Table

The earlier figures can only be approximations.

1593   Based on the statement that Canna could produce 20 fighting men. See p. 199.

1728   Letter of the Revd Donald MacQueen to the Committee of the SPCK, 5 September 1728. 16 Protestants, 220 Catholics.

1755   Scottish History Society, 1952, p. 34, footnote. 8 Protestants, 223 Catholics.

1805 The Clanranald map shows approximately 50 to 52 houses on Canna and 21 on Sanday; but some buildings shown could be small cattle sheds, on the other hand some could be double houses. Seven buildings shown SE of Creag Liath might well be the houses of small tenants shifted from Lag a' Bhaile on the Canna side to Sanday before 1805 to make kelp.

1821 The Gaelic Schools Report of 1823 gives the same figure (436) and says that all were Catholics except one family.

1841 There were 32 inhabited houses on Canna, and 12 on Sanday.

1851 There were 15 inhabited houses on Canna, and 30 on Sanday.

1861 There were 12 inhabited houses on Canna, and 17 on Sanday.

1901 Canna and Sanday had been ceded by Argyllshire to Inverness-shire in 1892, a fact still not realized by some Post Office sorters on the Scottish mainland.

1921 The Census this year was taken in June, when there were also 71 fishermen in Canna harbour.

1938 This is the writer's recollection of the numbers when he came to Canna in May of that year. There were only two young families, one of them of a shepherd from North Uist; half the population was then over forty-five years of age.

1941 There was no Census (Second World War).

1951 The figures for Canna and Sanday seem to have been reversed.

APPENDIX VIII THE NORSE HERITAGE OF CANNA

by Alf Sommerfelt (translated by Professor Angus McIntosh)

Professor Alf Sommerfelt, the famous Norwegian Celtic scholar, visited Canna in August 1943 when he was Minister of Education in the Norwegian Government-in-Exile in London, and published an article, *På Gamle Tomter i Suderøyene*, on the subject of the archaeology of Canna in the Norwegian Forces' journal *Norsk Tidend* the following month, on 4 September. A translation of that article was made by Professor Angus McIntosh, and a slightly shortened version of it is reproduced here with his kind permission.

A lecture tour to Scotland enabled me to make use of a standing invitation I had from a Scottish friend, Mr J. L. Campbell, Laird of the Isle of Canna, to visit him in the Hebrides. The journey took me via Dumbarton up through the Highlands past the north end of Loch Lomond, past Ben Nevis and on to Mallaig, through uplands covered with heather, through grass-covered glens, and down to the densely wooded hollows by the sea lochs. It is so like parts of Southern and Western Norway that one is moved by the likeness.

At Mallaig I was met by my friend's motor fishing boat and we set out on the old Viking route: to the north was the Sound of Sleat through which Haakon Haakonsson sailed with the whole of his great fleet in the summer of 1263 when he was driven back by the Scots at Largs on the south side of the Firth of Clyde. To the west were the islands of Eigg and Rum. Eigg looks like an 'egg' (Norse 'edge, knife-edge', etc.) and Norsemen must have found the name peculiarly fitting, but the resemblance is accidental for the word is Celtic or pre-Celtic. To the north-west could be seen the Cuillins of Skye. The old ruling family of MacLeod still lives in Dunvegan Castle on the west coast of Skye; according to tradition this dates back to the Norse era in the ninth century. The MacLeod line is descended from the Norseman Ljótr, a member of the royal family in the Isle of Man who got Skye as compensation when Norway relinquished its claim on Man and the Hebrides at the treaty of Perth in 1266. In the book about his tour with Johnson in 1773, Boswell relates that Lady MacLeod bemoaned having to live in so lonely and uncomfortable a place as Dunvegan Castle. They would have been pleased to know that after another one hundred and seventy years, the castle is the residence of the head of the Clan, and claims to be the oldest inhabited house in Scotland. The Cuillins loom out of the sea like mountain walls on the journey north, and the weather is like that of Northern Norway, with a brisk breeze from the north, and spray coming on to the exposed parts of the boat. There is no protecting belt of outer rocks here, and the Atlantic makes its way in among the islands.

We rounded the high desolate rocky island of Rum and came into calm water in the harbour of Canna which lies between Canna itself and the island of Sanday. Canna calls to mind islands in the south of Norway; a few nooks in the hills are cultivated and one finds woodland here too. The bird life too is reminiscent of home – birds with their young on the shore and puffins and gulls in the cliffs. The island is covered with grass in terraces with dark rock-cliffs between the terraces.

I was welcomed with a hospitality for which the Highlands are noted and have been ever since the memorable tour of Boswell and Johnson in 1773. In one of the corners of the hall of my friends' big modernized house the Norwegian flag is hanging beside the Scottish, British, and American flags. Mrs Campbell is American-born. In the well-stocked library there are not only English books about Scotland and Gaelic language and literature, but also Norwegian works. Campbell and his wife have travelled to Norway, among other things to study the Lofoten fisheries.

Here one suffers no material wants; the island is exempted from a number of administrative regulations about food production so one gets here as much butter, milk, cream, and eggs as one could wish together with Norwegian *rømme* ('old cream'). My friend bought Canna a number of years ago, and is trying to improve the estate. The situation in the Hebrides, as in the Highlands, is not easy. Canna had formerly between 200 and 300 inhabitants and now it has not more than 30 or 40. The island originally belonged to Clanranald, by origin a Norse family – Ranald is the Norse Ragnvald.

It has been said that the most living of all historical associations in the Hebrides are with the Norsemen and with the Forty-Five. Norway was called 'Lochlann' in Gaelic, which is probably – as Professor Marstrander has shown – a reshaping of the word 'Rogaland'. I at once got the impression that Norse history is not forgotten here; when the hotel keeper at Mallaig heard I was Norwegian, he said that almost all the names on the islands there are Norse and the skipper of the motor boat said that there was a Norse 'King's grave' on Canna, and if anyone digs it people believe that there will be a thunderstorm. I knew that in the Outer Isles there was a great number of Norse names – the language there has been studied by a young Norwegian philologist called Carl Borgstrøm. But it was a surprise to find that they were so preponderant also in the Inner Hebrides and on an

234 THE NORSE HERITAGE OF CANNA

island like Canna. Many of the names are clearly Norse, even to a layman. Others require a knowledge of the peculiar Gaelic sound-system and the curious Celtic grammatical system before they are clear. Coming to Canna is like coming to the west coast of Norway. South of the island lie Humbla (Norse Humla), Heidhsgeir (prob-ably Old Norse *Heiðsker* – 'the light rock'*), and An Steidh (Old Norse *Steði* – 'anvil', which is a common rock-name). 'An' is the Gaelic definite article, plural 'na', genitive plural 'nan'. A number of rocks lying in a row off the shore are called Na Garraidhean, which is a Gaelicizing of Old Norse *garðarnir* – 'fences'. Off the west of the island lies Sgeir nan Sgarbh, which is Old Norse *Skarvasker*. There are many clefts (ON *gjá* – 'cleft') running up into the hillside, called *geð* and pronounced 'geâ', and reefs (*baer*) in the sea are called *bódh*, pronounced 'bo'.

South of Canna and separated from it by a narrow channel which is dry at low tide lies Sanday (Old Norse *Sandey*). The channel itself bears the Old Norse name *vaðill*, 'ford-place', and in Gaelic this has become Fadhail. A headland a little to the west of the modern bridge over to Sanday is called Bruairnis (Old Norse *Brúarnes*). On the north-west of Canna there runs out into the sea a long and quite high point which is covered with grass and slopes back up into the hills, and is called Langanis (Old Norse *Langanes*). In the west of the island lies Garrisdale where there was a milking place for cows; this is probably Old Norse *garðastaðull* (or -*stöðull*) – 'milking place with a fence round'. Many other names could be given; it has been sup-posed that the name Canna itself is the Old Norse *kanna* ('can, tankard'), but this is doubtful for the Norse word would not account for the form in Gaelic. [See p. 10].

Small though Canna is (it is not more than six miles long and two broad), it is full of prehistoric remains. Some of them are mentioned in a report of the Royal Commission on the Ancient and Historical Monuments of Scotland, but the Commission cannot have made a very thorough investigation, for there are many to be found which are not mentioned in the Report. On Sanday there are the round cairns which cover graves from the Stone and Bronze Ages. In the middle of Canna there is a collection of so-called 'earth-houses' – subterranean houses with passages down into them resembling those into a cellar. The oldest of such 'earth houses' dates from the Bronze Age.

Canna has also relics of the oldest Irish Christian period. When Ireland was Christianized in the fifth century by St Patrick, Irish monks and nuns made their way in fragile craft, skin-covered boats

---

* Or *Hellsker*, 'Flat skerry', with *ll* now vocalized. Cf. Dean Monro, *Helsker na caillach*, in the Monach Islands; or *Helsker* 'dangerous skerry'. It is black.

(coracles), to lonely places where they built monasteries. They came all the way to Iceland where Norsemen came across them, and where Papey on the east coast is a reminder of them; the Icelanders called the Irish monks 'papar'. In the west of Scotland, the Irish monk St Columba founded the famous sanctuary of Iona, which time after time was plundered by our forefathers.

On the south shore of Canna there is a shelf in the hill called the Rubha Sgor nam Ban-naomha, 'the point of the scree of the holy women'. Here there are traces of stone houses which were probably once an Irish nunnery; here they must have been far away from the temptations of the world for it is not possible to put in from the sea except in good weather and nothing but a dangerous and precipitous path up the loose cliff-side leads on to the island there. In the old churchyard there is one of the peculiar Celtic crosses with relief-carving. On the top of a very steep rock north of the harbour there are the remains of an old eyrie-like castle called 'The Prison'. Tradition says that one of Canna's overlords was so jealous of his young wife that he kept her up there, where she died.

The skipper was right about there being Viking graves, not only on Canna but also on Sanday; they are mentioned in the archaeological report. Meanwhile nothing but formations of stones are left. On Canna they are to be found on Langanis, close to the sea. We came down from the hills by the grassy slope, and up on to the point. There was a blazing sun and sky and sea were extraordinarily blue. Thirty or forty miles out to the north-west the Outer Isles were floating in a thin haze. It was here that the Vikings were buried, facing the north-west, whence they had come: one of the graves lies right out on the edge of the sea where in bad weather sea spray would without a doubt reach it. One grave was long and narrow and must have contained a boat.

My friend told me that further to the south there were some mounds which I ought to look at. We clambered up again and then down on a broad grass slope which ran seawards and then fell quickly away with clefts and cracks under which the sea washes in and out. On this slope there was a whole cluster of Viking graves which, as far as one can judge, have never been disturbed. Only down at the edge is one which is open. The mounds are round but one is long and narrow and there must be a boat inside, though the effect of the earth has probably been such that it is unlikely that there are anything but nails left. These grave mounds are not mentioned in the archaeological report, and the same is true of some which Campbell showed me on the south-east shore. To the north, there are more than a dozen Bronze Age mounds which are not included in the Report either. Canna is entirely unmentioned in the survey which

Professor Shetilig has given of the reports of finds by Norwegian archaeologists in *Vikingeminner i Vest-Europa* (1933).

Langanis must have been an old haunt of the Vikings but those who are buried there probably lived in the middle of the island. Here there is nothing but grazing land now, but formerly there was cultivated land and right beside the peculiar earth houses lie the ruins of a house which closely resembles the remains of farm lay-outs in Lista and Laeren which Norwegian archaeologists have excavated in recent years. The Norsemen probably dwelt throughout the island, but on the east side tilling has caused many of the traces they left to disappear. Our forefathers must certainly have held sway throughout the Hebrides since they left so many place-names behind them. The pattern of building in the islands is also clearly Norse. In the Outer Hebrides and in Skye are still to be found some of the so-called black houses which Boswell* describes thus:

The cottages . . . are frequently built by having two stone walls at several feet distant filled up with earth, by which a thick and very warm wall is formed. The roof is generally bad . . . They are thatched sometimes with straw, sometimes with heath, sometimes with ferns. The thatch is fixed on by ropes of straw or heath; and to fix the ropes there is a stone tied in the end of each. These stones hang round the bottom of the roof, and make it look like a lady's head in papers.

These houses have earthen floors and are without chimneys. The peat fire is in the middle on the floor and the smoke goes up through a hole in the roof. At one end is the byre with an entrance through to the living room. The Danish architect Aage Roussel has shown that this type of house agrees with 1,500-year old Stone Age houses on Jaeren and in Jylland. There must have been a number of Gaelic communities existing among the Norse ones and after 1263 when the islands were ceded, the Gaelic inhabitants gradually assimilated the Norse. Now and then however they were extirpated in battle: Campbell noted down in Barra, one of the Outer Hebrides, a story about the son of a Norse woman who went under the name of Tvilens son (Gaelic Mac an Amharuis – Son of Doubt) because he did not know who his father was. People believed that it was MacNeil of Barra who was his father and the young man plagued him to acknowledge it. MacNeil grew tired of his importunings and said to Mac an Amharuis that he would recognize him if he would slay all the Norsemen. The Norsemen lived on a little island called Fuday (Norse *Utøy*). His mother decided that she would rather have a father for her son than save her own people, and she told her son that he should kill the Norsemen at night because they were weak and

* *Journal*, Viking Press edn., pp. 219–20.

listless then whereas during the day they were strong and powerful. Mac an Amharuis slew all the Norsemen. The story has obviously been influenced by a very old bit of Irish tradition which tells that the Ulstermen had a periodic condition of weakness, and it has been thought that this is a case of the curious custom which is known among the Basques and in various different parts of the world, of the father going to bed and being treated like a woman when, or just before, his wife is giving birth to a child. The tale may well be a memorial of the fact that a Norse community *was* massacred. Massacres of this sort are recorded in Scottish history over a long period of time.

It is not easy to decide how long the Norsemen in the Hebrides preserved their language, but it was probably for several hundred years after the cession of the land. The Orkneys and Shetlands became Scottish in 1468 but the language did not die in Shetland before the end of the eighteenth century. It seems to have survived equally long in Orkney because Campbell in the minutes of the SPCK report came across a letter from a Presbyterian minister in 1725 from Sandwick in Orkney, in which the minister bewails the fact that Presbyterianism makes very little progress because the inhabitants spoke 'the old broken Danish language'.

Prehistoric remains in Britain are not so thoroughly protected by law as in Norway, but Campbell well understands the importance of having the graves in Canna excavated by trained archaeologists and he will see to it that no-one else gets a chance. It is to be hoped that the graves will be investigated in a Norse–Scottish academic co-operation: both nations have an equally great interest in them. Co-operation of this kind has already been established in the philological sphere – the surviving Gaelic dialects were investigated under the direction of Professor Marstrander; the work was financed out of Norwegian funds and by the Scottish Lord Glentanar. That ought to be a prelude to intimate co-operation in matters of learning between Scotland and Norway after the war.

NOTE

See also *Norsk Tidsskrift for Sprogvidenskap*, XVI 231–4 (1952), where some of the Norse place-names of Canna are discussed in an article 'Norse-Gaelic Contacts' by Professor Alf Sommerfelt.

APPENDIX IX CANNA PLACE-NAMES

by J. L. Campbell

In any inhabited Hebridean island (and some, like Mingulay, no longer inhabited) every geographical feature, every nook and corner, has or until recently had, its own particular name. Inland most of these names are Gaelic, and usually easily intelligible, except when they depend originally on some lost allusion, or when they embody obsolete words; around the shores, and in the case of the larger hills, they are often Norse, sometimes explicable, at other times obscure. But all these names embody, to Gaelic speakers, memories and associations and sometimes anecdotes, which have a very important place in local traditional Gaelic memories. Indeed some knowledge of such things is inseparable from having real roots in island life.

It is particularly fortunate that a large number of Canna place-names has been preserved traditionally, and not alone from the point of view of correcting errors in Ordnance Survey maps. These errors arose not only from the pressure on the Survey to assign pronounce-able names to features on their maps, but from the unwillingness of the Survey to employ adequately qualified Gaelic scholars to correct their transcriptions and to avoid pseudo-learned restorations. We have examples of both cases on Canna, where the name of the rock between Canna and Heiskeir used to appear on OS maps in the garbled form 'Umaolo', and Heiskeir itself, an obvious Norse name, was transposed into the absurd Gaelic–Norse bastard 'Oigh-sgeir' 'Virgin-Skerry'. As will be seen, there are or were other OS names on Canna needing correction.

The preservation of Canna place-names, which were still well remembered in the 1930s and 1940s, has been due to several collectors. Foremost of these was the late Alexander Nicolson, for many years secretary of the Gaelic Society of Inverness, whose father was the first state schoolmaster on Canna (Sanday) after the 1872 Education Act, and who made a collection of over four hundred Canna and Sanday place-names during vacations spent on the island in the 1920s, written in pencil in a shorthand notebook which the present secretary of the Society, Mr Hugh Barron, kindly sent to the writer several years ago. Apart from this source, the writer and his wife separately took down many Canna place-names from the late Angus MacDonald, born on Canna in 1863, soon after coming here in 1938, and later recorded others on tape from his son the late

Hector MacDonald, and from Charles MacArthur, Duncan MacLeod, and Allan MacIsaac, all of the next generation. Finally, the chief authority on Canna place-names today is Mr Ian MacKinnon, farm manager, born in 1934 and brought up in the house of Angus MacDonald, who was his grandfather. All these collections have been collated, and with the help of Mr Ian MacKinnon, the situations of many little-known names in Mr Nicolson's collection have been determined.

Taking the names of the principal islands first, *Canaidh*, 'Canna' is of unknown origin. As the ancient fort at the west end of Canna is called *Dùn Chana*, the island may have been called after the person (or thing) for which the fort was called, adding Norse *ey*, 'island'. (For a discussion of this, see p. 10.) Sanday is the Norse term for an island with a sandy beach; there is a Sanday in Orkney and another in the Faeroes. But only the Gaelic equivalent is used in everyday Gaelic speech, *An t-Eilein* Gainmhich*. Humla, the bare little island between Canna and Heiskeir, is Norse for 'Hummer', refering to the surf that breaks on it, and Heiskeir probably means 'Flat Skerry'; it is only thirty-two feet high at the highest point.

If we start at the East end of Canna the most conspicuous feature is Coroghon Prison, built on the top of a broad stack. The name of Coroghon was also formerly given to the farm at the east end of the island and to the situation of the tenant's dwelling, and could be applied to Canna House. It is the Gaelic *Corra-dhùn*, 'odd (or 'peculiar') fort'. Originally this part of Coroghon farm was called *Corra-dhùn thall*, 'yonder (or 'nether') Coroghon' as compared with the tenant's house, now the Bothy near Canna House.

Nearby is the tidal island Hal(a)man, clearly Norse and possibly from *Hallholmr*, 'sloping islet'. This is separated from *Corra-dhùn* by a tidal channel called *Caol Haighleir*, meaning of the second word uncertain. *Caol* in Gaelic means 'narrow' or 'narrows', but the Norse *kíll*, 'narrow inlet, canal', may be involved here. (In passing, it may be said that the Old Icelandic dictionary is not necessarily enough to explain Norse place-names in the Hebrides; one would like to know much more about the terms used in the Faeroese language and its possible relationship to the Norse dialect spoken by the Viking settlers in the Hebrides.)

The point on which Canna pier is situated is called *Rubha Cairinis*, meaning uncertain. On the west side there is a rock, submerged at high spring tides, called *Leum an Dobhrain*, the Otter's Leap; I have seen an otter sitting on it. The tidal rock on the inside of Canna Pier is

---

* *Eilean* 'island' is a Norse borrowing, as is *sgeir*, 'skerry'. Colloquially the genitive *eilein* is used for the nominative *eilean*.

called *Sgeir an Fhang*, possibly from Norse *Fangasker*, 'Fishing Skerry'.

Inland from Coroghon Bay beside the Prison, the nearby piece of arable ground is called *Lag a' Bhaile*, 'the dell of the village'. The green slope above this and the neighbouring, unseparated ground *Liana mhór*, 'the big meadow', is called *Uchd nam Breac*, 'the hill-breast of the spots' (?). Possibly the 'spots' were primroses visible in early summer. *Breac* usually means 'trout' but there is no trout-stream there. One cannot ignore the possibility that this was formerly a Norse name ending in *-brekka*, 'slope', garbled into Gaelic.

Other fields: *Druim an Ùstraich*, north of the Presbyterian Church, 'the ridge of the (?)'. *Tioramanaich*, east of Canna House, 'the drier'. *An t-Iomaire Fada*, 'the long rigg', formerly cultivated ground above *Uchd nam Breac*; *Na h-Ealan*, long narrow field east of Tigh Ard, is from an obsolete Gaelic word *eala* or *iola* meaning 'terrace'. *Pàirc an Taigh Sheins*, 'Changehouse park' west of Canna House. West of the Square is *Bial na Fadhlach*, 'Edge of the Sea-ford' – *fadhlach* is the genitive of *fadhail* from Norse *vaðill*, 'sea-ford'. Above this is the large field called *Clàrach*, 'flat' (Gaelic); unfortunately the new Ordnance Survey map has planted the name *A' Chill* plumb in the middle of this field, which is totally wrong. (The mistake could have been avoided had proofs of the new map been submitted to any knowledgeable person.)

Around Keill or *Cill*, the melancholy site of the original religious foundation and main village on the island, place-names are plentiful. Going west from the Changehouse park the first feature is the long ridge known as *Druim Bù*, meaning of the second word uncertain. (Norse *bú*, 'livestock'?) At the north end of Druim Bù, west of Tighard plantation, is a grassy dell called *Cùil a' chàise*, 'Cheese Corner'. The next ridge, west of Druim Bù, is called *Cnoc Dubh nam Braonan*, 'the Black Mound of the Earth-nuts', though none have been found there in our time. The high mound near the Square is called *Cnoc nan Còrr*, 'The Mound of the Herons', while the small promontory near the Square is called *Rubha nan Còrr*, 'The Point of the Herons'.

West of the ridge called *Druim Bú* comes the field called *Calbhach*, pronounced *kala'ach*, now partly planted with trees, probably a Norse name connected with *kálfr*, 'calf'; compare the island name 'Calvay', The ridge between this and the present graveyard is called *Cnoc nam Ban* 'the knowe of the women', a name that had become nearly forgotten, but which was taken down by Margaret Fay Shaw from Angus MacDonald in 1939, and was later found in Alexander Nicolson's list. The site of St Columba's chapel, near the famous standing carved cross, was called *An Teampull*, 'the Temple' and the building itself was called *An Tigh Pobuill*, 'the House of the People'. The nearby standing stone on top of a mound with the small depression in it is called *Clach a' Pheanais*, 'the Punishment Stone'. A wrong-doer's thumb could have been wedged in the hole and the stone become the equivalent of the stocks. The name of the mound on which this stone stands is forgotten. The name of the mound near the western gate of this field is *Cnoc a' Bharain Duibh*, 'the Mound of the Black Baron'.

The fields at Keill are called *Earrann Mhór*, 'Big Piece', which is beside the plantation (1959) at *Guala nam Fàd*, 'the shoulder of the peats', and *Earrann a' Chlaidh*, 'the graveyard piece', the stony two acres beside the present graveyard. The small mound near the graveyard gate is called *Cnoc na Ceàrdaich*, 'the mound of the (fairy) smithy'. Plough irons used to be left there for the fairies to sharpen in olden times. The cleft in *Cnoc nam Ban* above the graveyard where the sticks for carrying coffins are kept was called *Uamh nam Marbh*, 'the cave of the dead'. North of *Cill* the green hill-slope is called *Uchd a' Bhaile*, 'the hill-breast of the village'. The stream which runs down this hillside is called *Abhainn Buaile Èarlaid*, 'the river of the cattlefold of Earlaid', whoever or whatever *Èarlaid* was. In the Hebrides even the smallest streams are called *Abhainn*, 'river'. This one was presumably diverted to provide water for Hector MacNeill's water-mill in the 1780s, and put underground later. The stream that comes down from the hill above *Guala nam Fàd* is called *Abhainn na Glasbhuaile* 'the river of the green cattle-fold' (*Uaine* is the ordinary Gaelic for 'green' but avoided as unlucky, green being associated with the fairies). Near *Guala nam Fàd*, 'the Shoulder of the Sods', is *Cnoc Shomhairle* (? *Chomhairle*) 'Samuel's' or perhaps 'Council' mound. Here there was a fairy mound where the fairies were disturbed by a man cutting turf, who let the rain into their dwelling, which they left in anger.

The low ridge separating the fields *Clàrach* and *Bial na Fadhlach* is called *Druim nan Seanag*. The meaning of *seanag* is uncertain, unless it is a metathesized form of *seangan*, 'ant'. 'Ant' however is *sneagan* on Canna. West of this at the place where the road to Tarbert diverges from the road to Sanday, is a corner now planted with trees, called *Lag nam Boitean*, 'the hollow of the sheaves'. Going towards Sanday, the mound beside Mrs MacLean's house is called *Cnoc an t-Salainn*, 'the salt mound', and the point of land beyond it is called *Bruairnis*, Norse Brúar-nes, 'bridge headland'. There is a Bruairnis on Barra.

Further west, the field below the sheep-fank is called *Liana nan caorach*, 'the sheep meadow', and the spot where the new house, built in 1971, stands is called *Caslum*. If the *-lum* of this word is the metathesized form of Norse *holmr*, 'islet', it may imply that this was a duelling place in Norse times, as duels were then first fought on little islets. Above the sheep-fank, built after 1851, the green valley now often used for camping is called *Lagan a' Ghrùmadail*, 'the hollow of Grùmadail', this obviously a Norse name containing *dalr*, 'dale, valley'. The stream and the good spring beside it, that runs through this valley, are called after it. Further west, the stream that falls in a waterfall beside the road is called *Abhainn Ghiùrain* (but heard by Mr Nicolson as *Geobharan* – see his p. 11). West of this stream in the hill above the road is a fairly large wet hollow called *Lagan na Sart*. If *sart* represents the Old Irish word meaning 'fleece', it is a remarkable survival.

Going along the shore on the way to Tarbert one passes a number of flat fertile grassy ledges, formerly cultivated, called in succession *Cùil a' Bhainne* 'the milk corner', *Losaid an t-Sagairt* 'the priests kneading-trough', *Losaid Mhór* 'the big kneading-trough', and *Losaid Eig*, 'the gapped (?) kneading-trough'. *Losaid*, plural *Loisdean*, 'kneading-trough', is used in Gaelic place-names to denote a fertile piece of land. Off *Losaid Eig* is a tidal island, climbable in only one place, called *Dùn nam Beirbh* (pronounced *beriv*, possibly connected with Norse *berg*, 'boulder, cliff'). Here a grass and peat fire once revealed the foundations of a small building and some pieces of pottery. It was doubtless an early place of refuge. The island off the end of the promontory here is called *Ha'aslum* (not *Hàslum* – the hiatus is distinct; clearly Norse). The dangerous rocks off this island were called *Na Fiaclan*, 'the Teeth'.

Beyond *Losaid Eig* on the way to Tarbert there is a long sea-chasm called *Geò na h-Ighne Duibhe*, 'the chasm of the black-haired girl', after a young woman who fell into it and drowned. The road then rises above a steep slope called *Croiseabrig*, a Norse name containing *-brekka*, slope, passing by the *Sgrìob Ruadh* or *Sgrìob Ruadh nan Each*, 'the red track of the horses' (*Ruadh* means rust coloured or auburn). Below this is *Cùil nam Marbh*, 'the corner of the dead'. We have thus reached Tarbert, *An Tairbeart*, the usual term for an isthmus in the Highlands. Here the old fields still retain their traditional names, though most of them are now unfenced. That in the valley between the stone dykes is called *An Strath*, 'the strath'; it was tile-drained by the former proprietor in 1942, and last cultivated in 1966. The ground north of this is called *Druim nam Port*, 'the ridge of the ports' (*Port* used in the Hebrides for any little sea entrance that could be used by a small boat). At the site of the present sheep-fank there used to be *Buaile nan Gobhar*, 'the fold of the goats'.

The old field-names at Tarbert were *Tobhta Tarra*, 'Homestead of Tarra', Norse *topt*; *Beanna Ruadh*, 'the russet hill'; *Na h-Athannan*, 'the Kilns', field where the piles of stones are, the site of the former village at Tarbert; *Leaba na Luatha*, 'Bed of Ashes'; *Lag an Tobhta Mhóir*, 'the hollow of the great homestead', the two acres above the Tarbert farm buildings; and *Iomair an t-Sneachda*, 'the snowy rigg', eight acres by the boundary dyke.

Inland west of Tarbert may be noted the names *Fang na fala*, 'the fank of blood', being the wet place into which cattle were driven to be bled in the old days of famine to provide food for humans in the springtime. Three names incorrectly entered on the Ordnance Survey map should be noted: *Cnoc Rùgail* should be *Cnoc Ghrùgail*, 'G.'s mound'; *Ceann Creag Àiridhe* should be *Ceann Creig Àird*, 'the end (or 'head') of the high crag'; and *Leòb an Fhionnaidh* should be *Leòb an Fhiantaich*, 'the piece of land of the Fingalian'.

The shore names on Canna are numerous and in many cases Norse. Often they contain the Norse term *skor* in the Faeroese sense of a steep slope where sheep can graze, between two cliffs.* Going round the shore clockwise (Gaelic *deiseal*) starting south of Tarbert, there is *Sgor an Duine*, 'the *Sgor* of the man' (but probably this is a corruption of the Norse name), then *Cràcasgor* 'the *Sgor* of the crows', Norse *krákaskor*; ravens nest there to this day. Next comes *O'osgor*, obviously Norse but meaning uncertain; *Sgor nam Ban Naomh*, 'Sgor of the Holy Women', the site of the ruins of the Columban nunnery situated above the *Rubha Reamhar*, 'the thick promontory', west of which is the *Geò Uaine*, 'Green chasm'. Then *Sgor an Fraoich*, 'the heather *sgor*', possibly a Gaelic translation of a Norse *Lyngaskor*. *Iolasgor*, where there is a colony of the Transparent Burnet moth, possibly a compound of Norse *ill-*, 'evil'. Next west is *Bré-sgor*, Norse *Breiðskor*, 'Broad *sgor*'; compare *Brevik* 'broad bay' in Barra, and *Broadford* 'broad fiord' (not 'ford') in Skye. South of *Brésgor* is the little island called *Steidh*, Norse *Steði*, 'anvil'; it looks like an anvil. To the west is *Boro'osgor*, Norse *Borðaskor*, 'table sgor', in which is *Uamh nan Gillean,* in Gaelic the 'cave of the lads', into which young men were lowered on ropes to hide in the times of the press-gang in the Napoleonic Wars.

Near this is *Dùn Chana*, 'the fort of Canna', an ancient place of refuge on a high rock, with some masonry. Nicolson writes this at different times as *Dun Chanute, Dun Channa*, and *Dun Channadh*. If a personal name is involved, i.e. 'C.'s Fort', the name of the island may be derived from this, with the addition of Norse *-ey* meaning island, *Canaidh, Cannay*, but see p. 10. The scenery here is very Faeroese.

* 'SKOR. Graesbevokset fremspringende parti i et stejlt bjaerg, hvor får og beder settes for at fedes'. Jakob Jakobsen, *Ordsamling*, Faerøsk Anthologi, II. 300. In Gaelic on Canna the word is pronounced with a single r and a short o.

We have now come to Garrisdale Point, at the far west end of the island. Off this point there is a large reef called *Am Bodha Mór*, 'the big reef', frequented by seals; the grey Atlantic seal breeds at the far west end of Canna. *Bodha* from Norse *boði*, a submerged rock. This part of Canna is generally called Garrisdale, Norse *Garðastöðull*, 'enclosed milking place', see p. 234. The flat green ground below the cliffs is called *Coine'egearraidh*, of which the first element, pronounced with clear hiatus, is uncertain, the second Norse *gerðr*, 'enclosure'; the hiatus seems against a derivation from *Konugerðr*, 'woman's enclosure'.

Going further east, one comes to *Càrasgor*, cliffs; the name might be connected with Norse *kárr*, 'curl' as the cliff here has a circular shape. The grassy terrace to the east is called *Cùil Chòlainn*, 'Còlann's Corner'; the *Cumha Chalain* of the Ordnance Survey map is wrong. The big bay north of Tarbert is called *Camus Thairbearnis*, according to George Henderson from Norse *Herbergines*, 'harbour headland bay'.* East of this land above the cliffs is called *Èarnagram*, derivation uncertain, and the long headland is called *Langanes*, pure Norse, 'long ness', wrongly written as *Langan-innis* on Ordnance Survey map. There is a double line of stones there suggesting a rifled grave, known as *Uamh Rìgh Lochlainn*, 'the grave of the King of Norway'. It has been suggested that this is actually the foundation of a sheiling, but on practical grounds this is hardly acceptable; the situation and the shape of the figure seem wrong for a sheiling. Any interference with it was believed to provoke a thunderstorm.

South of *Èarnagram* the big flat piece of peaty land with open drains is called *An Lòn*, 'the marsh', and the green mound where the earth houses are is *Cnoc buidh' a' Lòin*, 'the yellow mound of the marsh'. Preceding eastwards around the shore, one comes first to the cliff *Buidhesgor*, then the headland *Rubha Bhuidhesgor*, then *Sloc a' Ghallaich* (not *Ghallabhaich* as on Ordnance Survey), 'the pit of the Lowlander' (?). Nicolson has *Slochd a Ghalaidh* on p. 6, *Sloc a Ghaladh* on p. 7. From here until the stack known as *Iorcail*, 'Hercules', the cliffs, the highest on Canna, are called *Geugasgor*, Norse *Geiguskor*, 'Dangerous Cliff'. Beyond *Iorcail* there is *Làmasgor* (wrongly 'Laum Sgòr' on the OS map), Norse *Lambaskor*, 'cliff for lambs'; the grass is very rich here from the droppings of sea-birds. A natural arch here is called *A' Bhriogais*, 'the britches'. The next stack is called *An t-Each*, 'the horse', from its shape. Nicolson also records *An Leomhainn*, 'the Lion', for this.

Further East the last northern cliff is called *Tialasgor*, a name which is possibly a compound of Nors *hjalli*, a 'ledge'. We are now at

---

* *Norse Influence on Celtic Scotland*, p. 148.

Compass Hill, *Cnoc a' Chombaist*. A prominent upright bending boulder on the shore, which may be the stone into which St Columba's curse on reptiles turned the toad that swam over from Rum, is now called *Ord 'ic 'Uirich*, 'MacVurich's Hammer', for knocking limpets off the rocks. The steep mound above this shore nearby is called *Coir' 'earg* (apparently; Nicolson has *Cairfhearg, Coor Dhearg*, p. 6, *Corfharg*, p. 18; 'Red Corrie'(?) but it is not a corrie). The rocky point between this and *Corra-dhùn* (Coroghon) is called *Gàradh Aisginis*; Ordnance Survey *Garbh Àsgarnis* is wrong. The name contains Norse *garðr*, 'enclosure, wall' and *-nes*, 'headland', but can hardly be connected with *askr*, 'ash-tree', unless in the metaphorical sense of a 'small ship'. The steep slope between *Coir' 'earg* and Coroghon Prison is called *An Sgor Dhearg*, The 'Red Sgor', from the iron ore there.

We are now back in Canna Harbour with Sanday and the small tidal islands in the harbour to consider. The latter are called *Eilein a' Bhàird Ruaidh*, 'the island of the red-haired bard', and *Eilein 'ille Mhàrtain'*, 'the island of Martin's servant'. Outside the harbour is the large skerry called *Sgeir a' Phuirt*, 'the Port Skerry', which is the home of many seals. The submerged rock nearer the harbour, which only shows at very low spring tides, is called *Bodha nan Gall*, 'the reef of the Lowlanders'; presumably a Lowland ship or boat struck on it.

Starting on Sanday after crossing the footbridge from Canna, one enters a piece of green land above the sandy bay, which is called *An Tràigh Bhàn*; this part of the crofters' common grazing is called *Mialagan*, meaning uncertain. Nicolson writes *meadh lagan* and *midh lagan*. The stream which runs into the head of the bay, one of the very few streams on Sanday, is called *Abhainn Leiceadail*, obviously Norse – *Lekidalr*, 'leaking dale'? The small headland nearby is called *Rubha Leiceadail*. Above the shore a short way further on is *Cnoc an Tionail*, 'the mound of the gathering' or 'convening'. A collection of stones off the shore is called *Sgeir a' Bharp*, 'the skerry of the barp' or artificial place of refuge, made in a round shape; Norse *Hvarfasker*. The stones would have been taken for other buildings long ago.

The point of Sanday opposite Canna House is called *Rubha nam Feannag*, 'the point of the hoodie crows'. Further on the low black cliffs where black guillemots breed is called *Creag Màiri nighean Alasdair*, 'the crag of Mary the daughter of Alasdair'. Angus MacDonald had a story about a Clanranald drowning a woman of that name there in the old days by tying her hair to the seaweed at low tide. Further east the low cliffs are called *Tùrnasgor*, Norse, and then *Camus Stianabhaig*, Norse *Steinnavágr*, 'stony bay' (which it is). Further east one comes on a cave called *Uamh Ruadh*, the 'Red Cave'. The cliffs from there to *Ceann an Eilein*, 'the End of the Island', are called *Griomasaig* (Nicolson *Gremasaig*), Norse, the first part perhaps the personal name *Grímr*, compare the island named Grimesay between Benbecula and North Uist, 'Grímr's Island'.

At the south-east corner of Sanday are *Sgeir nan Crùbag* and *Geò Sgeir nan Crùbag*, 'the cleft or chasm of the skerry of edible crabs' (possibly a Gaelic translation of Norse *krabbasker*). Turning west, the stacks called *Dùn Beag* and *Dùn Mór* are prominent features with their puffins, and the gulls give their names to *Slocan nam Faoileag* and *Creag nam Faoileann*, 'the gully, the crag of seagulls', and *Creag nan Seagairean* 'the crag of the kittiwakes', where kittiwakes nest. Further east is the slope called *Eisebrig*, obviously containing the Norse word *-brekka*, slope, and perhaps *eisandi*, 'foaming'. Also compounded with *-brekka* are *Tallabrig*, Norse *Hallabrekka*, 'sloping hill', and *Gruinebrig*, Norse *Groenabrekka*, 'green slope', west of the bay called *Sùileabhaig*, Norse *Súlavágr*, 'Gannet Bay'. A short distance east of *Eisebrig* are large sea-caves called *Uamh Chriomain* and *Uamh Eisebrig*.

At the west end of Sanday below *Tallabrig* is *Geò a' Spùtain*, 'the spouting Cleft', and further north, *A' Chreag àrd*, 'the high crag', off which there are a number of rocks, called *Na Sgeirean Dubha*, 'the black skerries'. Further out are *Grob* (or *Gnob*) *nan Dallag*, 'the bare rock of the dogfish' – Norse *grúpa*, 'a peak', here used of a sea-mount, and *Na Gàraidhean* (see p. 234), *Mollachdag*, 'cursed little one', and *Am Bodha Liath*, 'the grey submerged rock', furthest out and very dangerous.

It remains to say something about the springs on Canna and Sanday, which were and are so important as sources of water for both humans and animals. They produce water of very good quality with no trace of peatiness. There was a St Columba's spring on Canna, *Tobar Chaluim Chille*, but its exact location is not remembered; and a *Tobar Mhoire*, St Mary's Well, near the sands at Tarbert. Other springs at Tarbert are *Tobar a' Chlachain Duibh*, 'the spring of the black clachan'; and *Tobar Lag a' Bholla*, 'the spring of the Hollow of the Boll'.

At the east end of Canna are *Tobar nan Ceann*, 'the spring of the heads', above the shore near *Coir 'earg*; *Tobar nan O'asdan*, meaning uncertain, near the cottage at *Lag nam Boitean*, 'the dell of sheaves'; *Tobar nan Giadh*, 'the spring of the geese', beside the road just west of Canna House; *Tobar a' Mhiosgain*, 'the spring of the meal measure', the source of the drinking water for the Square. The *miosgan* was a stone with a hollow in it used for measuring the first barley of the new crop in autumn for use in making the Michaelmas cakes called *struthan*. Near the field called *Earrann Mhór* at Keill there was a spring called *Tobar a' Bharain Duibh*, 'the spring of the black-haired baron', supposed to have had curative properties; it was blocked up with stones at the time of the Clearance.

Springs were particularly important on Sanday, after so many people were moved there in kelp-making times. Here are *Tobar Mhialagain*, below the house on the Steele croft; *Tobar na h-Aibhne*, 'the spring of the stream', behind Angus MacKinnon's croft; *An Tobar Mór*, 'the big spring' on Ronald MacIsaac's croft; *Tobar na Losaid*, 'the spring of the kneading trough' behind Ian MacKinnon's croft; *Tobar nan Uadhag*, beyond the Catholic church; the meaning of *Uadhag* is uncertain. The piece of ground is called *Na h-Uadhagan*.

These names are a representative portion of the place-names of Canna, but only a portion; there are many others. It is not possible to explain all of them, but still they give a rich picture of the topography and history of the island.

Canna Place-names Entered Wrongly on Ordnance Survey Maps

A'CHILL – name is wrongly placed in the modern map in the field called CLÀRACH. It should be moved east to field containing the Stone Cross.

ALMAN should be HALAMAN.

AN STÒL, rather AN T-EACH, 'The Horse'.

BOD AN STÒIL, rather IORCAIL, 'Hercules'.

CAMAS DANABHAIG should be CAMUS STIANABHAIG.

CEANN CREAG ÀIRIDHE should be CEANN CREIG ÀIRD (west of Tarbert).

CNOC BHRÒSTAN should be CNOC BHORO'OSDAN.

CNOC RUGAIL should be CNOC GHRÙGAIL.

CONAGEARRAIDH should be COINE'EGEARRAIDH.

COROGHAN should be CORRA-DHÙN ('odd or extraordinary fort').

CUMHA CHALAIN should be CÙIL CHÒLAINN.

DÙN TEADH at west end of Island should be DÙN TEÒ.

EALAIST should be placed above 450-foot contour.

GEÒDH where it occurs should be GEÒ (Norse GJÁ).

GEUG SGÒR should be GEUGASGOR (Norse, 'Dangerous cliff').

HÀSLUM should be HA'ASLUM. (OS transcriptions ignore hiatus in place-names, but it is important for the interpretation of Norse names.)

IOLA-SGÒR should be IOLASGOR.

LÀUM-SGÒR should be LÀMASGOR (Norse, 'lamb-cliff').

LEÒB AN FHIONNAIDH should be LEÒB AN FHIANTAICH (the strip of land of the Fiantach, the Fingalian).

NAHAGHEAN should be NA H-ÀTHANNAN ('The Kilns', at Tarbert).

OIGH-SGEIR should be HEISGEIR (or HEILLSGEIR).

RUDHA CARR-INNIS should be RUBHA CHAIRINIS or CHEARAINIS (the word is not a compound of Gaelic INNIS, but of Norse NES).

RUDHA LANGAN-INNIS should be RUBHA LANGANAIS. (*Rubha* is historically a better spelling than *Rudha*. *Langanais* is pure Norse, meaning Langanes, 'Long Ness or Headland'.)

SGÒR where it occurs should be SGOR, short vowel. (Used on Canna in the Faeroese sense of a steep slope on which sheep could graze, between two sheer cliffs.)

SLOC A' GHALLUBHAICH should be SLOC A' GHALLAICH, ('the pit of the foreigner').

TIAL-SGÒR should be TIALASGOR.

UMAOLO should be HUMLA or HUMALA.

NOTE

Professor W.B. Lockwood informs me that the meanings suggested for *Geugasgor*, p. 244, and for *Leiceadail*, p. 245, are unlikely.

APPENDIX X SOME LOCAL TRADITIONS

Anns na Laithean a Dh'fhalbh

Aonghus Eachainn a dh'inns; Dr Calum Mac 'ill' Eathain a sgrìobh; eadar-theangaichte le Iain L. Caimbeul.

Clann 'ic Nill an Canaidh

'S ann a nuas a Cinn-tìre a thàinig Clann 'ic Nill a bha seo. Bha tuathanachas aca 'sa Mhaoil, Maol Chinn-tìre, aig Gob na Maoile. 'Iain Ìleach' a chanadh iad ris a' chiad fhear dhiu.

Bha fear a mhuinntir an Eilein Sgitheanaich, bha pìos aige a' seo. 'S e Alasdair an Eilein a chanadh iad ris. [Alasdair Domhnallach.]

Bha fear eile a mhuinntir an Eilein Sgitheanaich, agus bha pìos aige a' seo. 'S e Fear a' Choire a chanadh iad ris. 'S e Teàrlach [Mac Fhionghuin] a bh'air.

Chuir Clann 'ic Nill uabhas dhaoine as an eilean. Cha chreid mi nach d'fhalbh trì fichead teaghlaichean as a' seo ri linn m'athair a bhith 'na dhuine òg. 'S e a' rud bu mhiosa dheth, cha n-fhaigheadh iad fuireach as a' rìoghachd seo fhéin. Bha iad air son iad a dhol fairis co dhiù. 'S ann a Chanada a chuireadh iad. Chuala mi gun deach iad air bòrd an Tobar Mhoire. Bha iad a' gealltainn dhaibh gum bitheadh iad gu math nuair a ruigeadh iad a null, ach 's ann a bha iad na bu mhiosa.

Chuala mi nach e an t-uachdaran, nach e bu choireach ris, uile gu léir, 'gan cur air falbh idir. Athair Mhic Nill mu dheireadh, thug e tuathanach a' seo, agus bha an t-àite an uair sin fo chruiteirean; agus chuir sin an truaighe air. Bha na cruiteirean uile air an taobh thall air aghaidh a' mhonaidh, agus iad 'ga àiteach cha mhór air fad. Dh'fheumadh an tuathanach a thàinig na daoine a shioftadh as, gu faigheadh esan an talamh. Bha an talamh ['n] sin 'ga àiteach air fad.

Thàinig a' chuid a bha thall a nall a' seo (gu Sandaidh), agus bha tuilleadh 's a' chòir ann an uair sin. Cha b'urrainn dhaibh a bhith beò ann. Chuir iad na daoine as an taobh thall uile. Fear Mac 'ill' Eathain* a thàinig a' seo 'na thuathanach, agus bha e treis mhór ann an Eige a rithist. Bha crodh dubh aig an tuathanach, agus rinn e feum mhór.

Bha mo sheanair fhéin agus cha robh facal sgoile 'na cheann, agus cha n-fhaca sibh duine na b'fheàrr na e air na thàinig riamh a ch-uile

---

* 'Mac Phàil' a thuirt Aonghus, ach 's e Mac 'ill' Eathain an fhine aige. Dh'fhaoidte gur h-e fear Pàl a bha 'na athair dha.

latha dha'n bhliadhna. Bha naidheachdan aig is òrain is sgialachdan.

Bha móran de dhaoine 'san àite an uair sin, agus cha robh aca ach bìdeagan beag fearainn ris an canadh iad 'luach péighinn'. Feumaidh nach robh unnta ach bìdeagan beaga.

Bha còrr is ciad duine air an eilean, nuair a bha mi fhìn òg. 'S ann thall mu'n a' Phrìosan★.a bha móran dha na daoine, 's ann a' sin a bha na taighean aca. 'S e 'n t-ainm a bh'air an àite far a' robh na taighean aca ann a' siod 'Lag a' Bhaile'.

Sin far am biodh iad ag ràdha a bhiodh iad a' faicinn bòcan uabhasach, thall an Lag a' Bhaile a' sin. Tha àite bog ann a' sin, agus bhiodh iad ag ràdha gur h-ann a' sin a bhiodh e a' fuireach. Bha aon sùil a's a' bhathais aige. Bhiodh iad ag innse dha'n chloinn mu 'Bhòcan Lag a' Bhaile'. Bhiodh iad ag ràdha riutha gum beireadh Bòcan Lag a' Bhaile orra, nam bitheadh iad a' dol a mach air an oidhche. Nuair a chluinneadh iad sin, chumadh e a' chlann bho na cladaichean. Bhiodh iad 'ga fhaicinn air an latha.

Nuair a bhiodh na daoine ag iasgach ann a' seo, bhiodh iad a' dol a bhuain cairst, air son na lìn a charstadh, sìos do'n chreig† ris an abair iad Géigeasgor.

Chuala mi iad a' bruidhinn gu robh boireannaich shìos ann, latha, agus bha iad a' buain cairst, agus thubhairt cuid gu robh gu leòr aca, ach dh'fhan té dhiu air deireadh. Chaidh i leis a' chreig mu'n dàinig i as. Cha d'fhuaireadh i gus an latha 'r-na-mhàireach. Chaidh bàta sìos. Fhuair iad an uair sin i.

'Sna creagan a bhios iad a' fhaighinn cairst. Tha e 'na chnapan móra. 'S ann 'sa bhun aige a tha feum. 'San talamh a tha e, am miosg nan creagan. Bhiodh iad 'ga bruich agus a' toirt aiste a' sùgh, agus 'ga chur air na lìn, leis an aon chairst a bhiodh iad a' carstadh nan seicheannan nuair a bhiodh iad a' deanamh bhrògan. Bhiodh a' sùgh aca ann an tuba mhór, agus bhiodh iad a' cur na leathrach ann. Nuair a thòisich bàtaichean air falbh 's air tighinn, thòisich iad air a' chairst Ghallda.

Bhiodh iad a' dèanamh nam brògan aca fhéin cuideachd. Chunnaic mise gu leòr a bhoireannaich agus bhiodh iad a' falbh cas-ruiste gu math tric.

Nuair a bha mise òg, bhiodh iad a' dèanamh feum de dh'ola nan ròn. Bha latha àraid aca a' rachadh iad 'gam marbhadh gu Haoisgeir. Bha an t-eilean sin làn dhiu. Bhiodh iad 'gam feannadh agus a' toirt dhiu na saille. Bhiodh cuid dhiu ùine mhór 'gan leaghadh cuideachd. Tha ola nan ròn uabhasach math do bheothaichean.

★ Corra-dhùn. Ach chuireadh a mach iad barrachd is lethchiad bhliadhna mu'n d'rugadh Aonghus Eachainn, chaidh an sioftadh chon an Eilein Ghaimmhich gu cealpa a dheanamh.

† 'sgeir' 's e thuirt Aonghus, ach 's e creag a th'ann.

Chunna mi feadhainn a bha 'ga bruich agus 'ga *refineadh* cho math is a b'urrainn dhaibh, agus iad fhéin 'ga h-òl cuideachd.

Mac Nìll, nuair a bha e a' seo, bhiodh e a' cur nan ròn aig bun nan craobhan ubhall 'sa ghàradh. Dhèanadh iad leasachadh uabhasach math. Cha robh iad a' dèanamh feum 'sa bith dhe'n fheòil aca. A' ròn bu mhutha a chunna mi riamh, bha e seachad air leath-tunna. Mharbhadh leis a' ghunna e. Cha robh agad ach buille a thoirt dha mu'n t-sròin, agus bha e marbh. Dhèanadh aon bhuille an gnothach.

The Old Days

Told by Angus MacDonald (b. 1863); recorded and transcribed by the late Dr Calum MacLean; translated by J. L. Campbell.

The MacNeills of Canna

It was from Kintyre that the MacNeills who were here came. They had a farm in the Mull of Kintyre, at the point of the Mull. 'John from Islay' the first of them was called.*

There was a Skyeman who had a piece of land here. They called him 'Alasdair of the Island'.† There was another Skyeman who had a piece of land here. They called him 'the Tacksman of Corrie'. His name was Charles.**

The MacNeills put a terrible number of people out of the island. I believe that sixty families left when my father was a young man. The worst of it was that they couldn't remain in this country. Anyway they wanted them to go over [seas]. They were sent to Canada. I heard that they embarked at Tobermory. They were promised that they would be well off when they had arrived over there, but in fact they were worse off.

I heard that it was not the laird who was altogether to be blamed for sending them away at all. The father of the last MacNeill brought a farmer here; the place at that time was under crofters; that annoyed him. The crofters were then all on the Canna side, on the hill face, which was nearly all cultivated by them. The farmer who came had to shift the people off it, so that he could get the land. The land was then all cultivated.

Those of the crofters who were on the Canna side came over to Sanday, where there were then too many people. They couldn't

* Presumably 'Iain Ìleach' was the father or grandfather of Hector MacNeill who got the lease of most of Canna in 1781.
† Alasdair MacDonald, who held the east part of Sanday, see lease of 18 June 1781.
** Charles MacKinnon of Coirechatachan. See Boswell's *Journal*, 1961 edition, p. 120.

survive there. They put all the people off the Canna side. It was a man called MacLean who came here to farm, later he was on Eigg for a long time.* The farmer had black cattle and did very well.

My own grandfather hadn't a word of schooling in his head, and you never saw a better man than he for any job that ever turned up any day of the year. He knew anecdotes and songs and stories.

There were many people on the place then, and they only had little pieces of land called 'pennylands'. They could only have been very little pieces.

There were then more than a hundred people on the island (Sanday), when I myself was young. It was over near the 'Prison' (at Coroghon) where many of the people were (originally), it was there they had their houses. The place where their houses were was called *Lag a' Bhaile*, 'the hollow of the township'.

That's where they used to say they saw a fearful bogey, over at Lag a' Bhaile there. There is a wet place there, and they used to say that the bogey was staying there. It had one eye in its forehead. They used to tell the children about the 'Bogey of Lag a' Bhaile'. They used to tell them that the Bogey would catch them, if they were going out at night. When the children heard that, it would keep them from the shores. They used to see it in daytime [too].

At the time when men here were at the fishing, they used to go to cut tormentil to tan the nets, along the cliff on the north side of the island called Geugasgor. I heard them saying that there was a woman up there one day when they were cutting tormentil. Some of them said they had enough tormentil, but one of the women stayed after the others. She fell down the cliff before she got out. She wasn't found until the next day. A boat went up there; then they got her.

It was on the cliffs they were getting tormentil. It grows in big lumps. It is the roots that are used, [they grow] in the soil amongst the cliffs. They used to boil the roots and take the juice out of them and put it on the nets, with the same tanning that they used when they were tanning the hides when they were making shoes. They had the juice in a big tub and used to put the leather in it. When boats started coming and going, they began to use Lowland tanning.

They used to make their shoes too. I saw plenty of women who were going barefoot often enough.

When I was young, they used to make use of seal oil. They had a special day on which they went to kill them on Heiskeir. That island was full of them. They used to skin them and take off the blubber.

* At Kildonan. His name is given as 'MacPhail' in Dr Calum MacLean's transcription, but this is certainly a slip. It is well known that he was John MacLean, see Chapter 17.

Some of it took a long time to melt, too. Seal oil is terribly good for cattle.

I saw people boiling it and refining it as well as they could, and drinking it too.

When MacNeill was here, he used to bury seals at the foot of apple trees in the garden. They made excellent fertilizer. They didn't make any use of the flesh at all. The biggest seal I ever saw weighed more than half a ton. He was killed with a gun. You only needed to give a seal a blow around its nose and it was dead. One blow was enough.

Canna in the 1870s

Memories recorded from Mr Angus MacLeod at Clydebank by J. L. Campbell on 15 December 1949, translated from the Gaelic.

I haven't got much to tell you but what Canna was like to begin with when I was first living there. There was a large number of people there, I am sure there was twenty-eight families in Canna when I was young. They were all working for the Laird. Working at the harvest. At the time of the sowing. They were getting very little pay for it. I was about eighteen years old at the time. We were only getting perhaps about 1 shilling a day. Perhaps we wouldn't even get that.

One night I said to my father when we were in the house that I was going to try to get away from Canna altogether. 'I don't know', said my father, 'how you are going to get away. You haven't got a penny.' 'Well,' I said, 'I have got to get away from here anyway.' 'Well,' said my father, 'I have not got a penny to give you.' There were fishermen on Canna then. My father went to see if they could give a loan of money and – did you know William Campbell? Well, it was he who gave 7 shillings to my father. The fare then to go to Glasgow on the steamboat was only 7 shillings. I reached Glasgow anyway. I did not know in the world what I should do, looking for work. I, and the brother of Annie MacKinnon (Annie who is in the Post Office on Canna), we reached Glasgow. I went with him, and it was along to Loch Striven that we went to work. What was the work that we did but putting up deer fences. We spent the whole winter working at that. When the summer came we went back to Glasgow and started to look for ships. Anyway, while we were in Glasgow we found a ship. We sailed from Glasgow. We spent two or three weeks with the ship then when we came back home, I went to the Isle of Bute, Rothesay, and I took a job with a farmer. That was the last work I did on the land.

Q. What stock did MacNeill have?

A. MacNeill of Canna had an enormous quantity of stock of cattle and sheep. I think he had about 2,000 sheep. The place was full of sheep and Highland cattle. They were out all through the year both summer and winter, and the calves at their feet. Herdsmen going with them all the time.

Q. Were there sheilings there?

A. [Question not understood.] Yes, they were taking the calves over there then. They were putting calves apart over on Sanday. The calves would be over on Sanday and the cows would be on the Canna side, and the herdsman was there all the time with them. There were eighteen or nineteen head of Ayrshire dairy cows as well as Highlanders. What he was making from them was cheese. He was selling the cheeses and sending them away, and selling the cattle beasts.

Q. Were they making cloth in those days?

A. My mother was making yarn with the spinning wheel. They were sending it to the weaver. When they had the cloth ready then they had the great night waulking it. Then they got hold of the tailor and it was £1 the tailor was getting for making a suit of clothes. I knew him well. We called him 'Allan the Tailor'. He belonged to Eigg. He was going from house to house in those days making suits of clothes. Suppose that you and one or two friends were at home, he would make suits for them all. You had to keep him as well as pay him his pound.

There were not any sheilings at all. There was a big number of Barra-men fishing out of Canna. You would see the harbour full of Barra boats in those days, at the time of the fishing. They were always coming over to Canna for the winter fishing. You do not see a single one of them nowadays.

There was always smuggling going on in those days. The brother of my grandfather, he used to smuggle. When the excise men used to come over after smugglers, to Canna by boat, there was a piper amongst the crew and when they landed on the island he used to start playing his pipes and the piper would go ashore and play the pipes all the way to Murdo's house and Murdo would hide everything. When the excise man called Campbell arrived at Murdo's house, Murdo would ask him whether he would like to have a drink. He would take him to the closet. He would take out a bottle and two or three tumblers. There was not an illicit still – they were getting the stuff over from Tobermory, Mull.

Q. What kind of man was MacNeill?

A. Oh, an odd fellow. If he took a spite against you, you might as well clear out. He had a big belly. He would watch the men working for him. He would sit apart from them keeping a watch on them to see if you did anything wrong, what you were doing. If you weren't working hard, you were cursed and were told to go home. I and the Barra chap called MacPhie, we were taking our food in the old house, where Tam Campbell was.* One night we went in there, the cook in the big house said that they had nothing for breakfast, they hadn't got a speck of meal. He came along and asked us to go and get a bag out of the kitchen of the old house where Tam used to stay. Well, I and the Barra lad went along. We lifted the sack of the 'Hieland Mary's', they called them, a big sack [probably a boll, 140 lbs.]; we lifted it on to the table. The Barra lad said to me, 'Are you thinking that we will be able to carry that up the garden?' 'If we can't,' I said, 'there is nothing to do but to leave it here.' I went up with the sack on my back from the old house through the big garden. There was a window at the big house opposite the kitchen door. He was in there. 'Oh, look you,' he says, 'see the children of the devil coming.' He was a terrible man.

Q. How did he lose his money?

A. The way he lost his money, it was when he was a young man and out the way of Edinburgh and in the Lowlands like that. They had a big night in Edinburgh, a big ball, and what did he do but take a notion to one of the ladies who were at the ball and they made a bargain, you know, the lady and himself, that he would lose the place, of Canna, and that she herself would have to pay as much to him if she didn't keep the bargain. The next day when the ball was over, and I am sure that the drink was going on there, the next day what happened but he met this lady and regretted his bargain. She had only been painted and polished up. Then they went to Law. It was MacNeill of Colonsay that won the case for him so that he had to pay her so much a year as long as she was alive, and the money he had was to be paid to her, and it was running out like that. Well, when MacNeill of Colonsay won the case, you know, that he would get the place and that he would have to pay her so much a year. Well, then he came home and stayed on the place.

He married a girl who belonged to Eigg.† A girl called MacLean and with the money he was spending on matters connected with the estate and everything like that, he ran through it. He was thousands of pounds in debt. The big house cost him an awful lot of money. He had four sons and a daughter. There was Donny, Johnny, Harry, and Peter. Harry is still alive [1949] or was until recently, over in

---

* The house below Canna House, where the MacNeills first lived. Now converted into stores and a bothy. Tam Campbell was a rabbit trapper and drainer from Alyth who worked on Canna.

† Isabella MacLean. Her father had the farm of Kildonan on Eigg after giving up Canna.

Manitoba. The daughter died young. He had to give up the place eventually.

I was there when Thom came to Canna. I was on Canna. Thom did not get so much as a knife and fork with the place when he bought Canna. It was Thom who brought in all the silver, bed-clothes, and everything. Thom had a skipper for his yacht – an Englishman. When he went up to the house – MacNeill had a housekeeper then – the Captain went up to the front door, and rang the bell. She came to the door and she took hold of the door and shut it in his face. He went back and told Thom what had happened. Thom went up to the house himself and ordered MacNeill out 'right off the reel'. MacNeill then went to Tobermory. He spent a while in Tobermory. Anyway he got hold of enough money for that. Then he went off to Manitoba. He was not missed much.

Q. Was he keeping many horses?

A. Yes he was. I have seen three pairs of horses working in one of the fields. In the Changehouse Park I have seen three pairs of horses working there at the time of planting potatoes and turnips. He had ten or twelve young horses out on the hill.

Q. Were you born at Tarbert [on Canna]?

A. No, I was born in Arisaig.

Q. What house were you living in on Canna?

A. You know where the 'house of the rams' is down at Tarbert? That was the house. And the shepherd was living up in the place where the shepherd's house is now. There were a lot of people on Canna at that time.

Q. Do you remember anyone being at Garrisdale?

A. No, but I remember the houses still standing there.

Q. Was it MacNeill that evicted the people?

A. No, it was not he who evicted them at all. I think it was the people who were in charge before him, the trustees, who evicted them, whoever they were. I have heard a great deal of talk about it.

Q. How many families went away then?

A. Well, I will tell you what families were there at that time. My grandfather was there; Calum the carpenter was there; Donald his brother was there; Murdo my uncle; the family of Donald, son of Calum; the blacksmith; Murdo of the shebeen who was smuggling; the family of Calum, son of Duncan; Big Hector, the grandfather of Aonghus Eachainn; Archie, the smith; Neil, son of Kenneth, son of Neil; John MacNeill, and my grandfather; and then the sisters of my grandfather – there were two of them; and Colla, he was there. I'm sure there were eighteen or nineteen families then. There was no school then . . . the schoolmistress whom the laird brought, she didn't stay long.

Q. Where was the Church then?

A. It was where the Post Office is. And there was a flour mill where the smithy is now.

Q. Who was the Priest then?

A. Old Mr Alasdair [Fr. Alexander Gillies]. Unless you were punctual to the minute going to confession, he would send you home.

Q. Did you ever hear of the 'press-gang'?

A. Yes, I have heard of the cave where two brothers hid down at the west end of the island in the face of the cliff when the press-gang came after them, the press-gang could not get hold of them. The chap who was going along with the Government, said to the soldier, 'You keep what belongs to you till you get what you haven't got.' They failed to get them. They were inside the cave. They were firing on them above the cliff.

Q. What year were you born?

A. 1862.

Sgeul mu Haoisgeir na Cuiseig

(Mac Talla, Leabhar III, Àireamh 43)

Bha triùir choimhnearsnach ann an ìochdar Mhuile aig an robh briuthas. Air dhaibh beagan uisge-beatha a dheanamh, dh'fhalbh iad leis 'nan triùir g'a reic do Eilean Thirithe. An déidh dhaibh an t-uisge-beatha a reic, thill iad air an ais; ach nuair a bha iad faisg air cladach Mhuile – oidhche na Nollaige Bige – shéid a' ghaoth 'nan aghaidh le cur ro-ghailbheach shneachda. Bha an oidhche dorcha, agus am fuachd do-ghiùlan, ionnas gun do bhàsaich dithis de na fir mun robh iad ach goirid an déidh fuadach a ghabhail.

Mhair an treas fear beò, agus stiùir e 'm bàta cho math 's a b'urrainn dha. Beagan an déidh miadhain oidhche chuala e gàirich-cladaich; rinn e air, agus nuair a thàinig e 'm faisge, ghlaodh fear bho thìr ri fear a' bhàta:

'Gabh mar seo!'

'Có thusa?'

'Mise Mac 'ille ruaidh.'

'Gabh mar seo' ars an darna guth.

'Có thusa?'

'Mise Mac 'ille dheirg.'

'Gabh mar seo' ars an treas guth.

'Có thusa?'

'Mise Mac 'ille bhàin.'

Fhreagair am fear a bha 'sa bhàta 'Gabhaidh mi a dh'ionnsaigh an àite 'san cuala mi a' chiad ghlaodh.'

Chaidh e air tìr, agus chunnaic e gur h-i sgeir-mhara a nis anns an robh e, le glé bheagan talmhana oirre. Rinn e toll leis a' bhiodaig, anns an robh e laighe gun bhiadh, gun deoch, ach aon chàrd de dh'im. Chaidh e 'n sin a shealltainn an robh duine no creutair air an sgeir ach a fhéin; thuig e nach robh. A thuilleadh air a seo, sheall e air na h-àiteachan bho'n cuala e na guthannan, agus chunnaic e gun robh e eucomasach dol air tìr ach a mhàin far an robh a' chiad ghlaodh.

Dh'fhan e air an sgeir bho oidhche Nollaige Bige gu Là'ill Phàdraig. Bha e teachd beò air bàirnich a' chladaich air am buain le sgithinn agus air an cur ris a' ghréin an uair a bhiodh i a' dearrsadh. Dh'itheadh e 'n sin iad le beagan dh'an ìm 'nan déidh. A h-uile h-oidhche chluinneadh e glaodhaich agus sgreadail mar gum biodh muinntir 'gam bàthadh; ruitheadh e sìos gus an cladach, 's an uair a ruigeadh e, cha robh creutair beò air thoiseach air. Lean e mar sin gus an d'fhàs e sgìth de bhith air a mhealladh.

Bha e air an sgeir gus an do thog bàt'-iasgaich e an déidh Féill Phàdraig, agus thugadh e do dh'Uibhist, far an robh e o thaigh gu taigh 'ga eiridinn leis a h-uile caoimhneas gu Bealltainn. Thàinig e air ais gu ruige Muile, agus an latha thàinig e, bha a bhean a' roupadh no a' reic a h-uile nì a bh'aice. Nochd am fear a bha air a shaoilsinn a bhith bàithte a fhéin, agus thill gach duine na nìthean a chaidh a cheannach a dh'ionnsaigh na mnatha.

Tha an sgeir air an robh e faisg air Eilean Chanaidh, agus is e a h-ainm 'Haoisgeir.'

A Story about 'Heiskeir of the Rushes'

There were three neighbours in the lower part of Mull [the Ross of Mull] who had a still. Once when they had made a little whisky the three of them went to Tiree with it to sell it.

After they had sold the whisky, they went back, but when they were close to the shore of Mull – it was New Year's Eve – the wind blew against them in a blizzard of snow. The night was dark, and the cold was insupportable, with the consequence that two of the men died before they had gone a short distance. The third man survived; he steered the boat as best he could. A little after midnight he heard the sound of surf on the shore; he made for it, and when he had come close, someone on shore shouted to him, 'Take this way!'

'Who are you?'

'I'm the son of the Auburn Fellow.'

'Take this way!' said a second voice.

'Who are you?'
'I'm the son of the Red Fellow.'
'Take this way!' said a third voice.
'Who are you?'
'I'm the son of the White Fellow.'
The man in the boat answered, 'I'll take the way to the place where I heard the first shout.'

He went on shore, and he saw that he was now on a skerry with very little soil on it. With his dirk he made a hole, in which he lay without food or drink, but for a gallon of butter. Then he went to see if there was anyone or any creature on the skerry beside himself; he perceived there wasn't. Besides this he looked at the places from which he had heard the voices, and he saw that it was only possible to land where he had heard the first voice.

He stayed on the skerry from New Year's Eve until St Patrick's Day [17 March]. He lived on limpets from the shore, which he detached with his knife and put in the sunlight when the sun was shining. Then he would eat them with a little of the butter after them. Every night he used to hear shouting and screaming as if people were being drowned; he used to run down to the shore and when he reached it, there wasn't a living creature before him. He kept on like that until he got tired of being deceived.

He was on the skerry until a fishing boat took him off after St Patrick's Day and took him to Uist, where he was from house to house being taken care of with every kindness until Beltane [1 May]. He returned to Mull; and the day he came back, his wife was auctioning or selling everything she had. When the supposedly drowned man appeared in person, everyone gave back the things they had bought, to the wife. The skerry on which he was is close to the Isle of Canna, and its name is 'Heiskeir'.

Ghaoth Thig a Canaidh

Fhuaras an t-oran seo anns an leabhar-notaidh a bha aig Domhnall C. Mac a' Phearsain, a bha cruinn'eachadh nan oran mu'n bhliadhna 1865. Chuir e a mach an *Duanaire* aige 'sa bhliadhna 1868, ach cha n-eil an t-oran seo r'a fhaighinn ann.

> Ghaoth thig a Canaidh,
>   Gum fairich mi blàth i;
> 'S tòil leam bhith coimhead
>   An rathad a thà thu;
> 'S goirid an ùine

Gu'n till mi g'ad ionnsaigh,
Gun d'fhalbh mo chluas-chiùil,
   Cha n-eil sunnd orm ri ceòl-gàire;
'S acain mo ghaoil dhomh,
   Cha n-ioghnadh mar thà mi,
Cumha na h-ògmhnaoi
   'S bòidhche 'san àite;
Cruth mar an sneachda,
A sùil mar an dearca
'S a gruaidhean air lasadh
   Air dhath mhucag àileag.

Nuair théid mi do'n leabaidh,
   Cha chadal 's cha tàmh dhomh,
'N amm éirigh 'sa mhaduinn
   Gur h-airtealach thà mi;
Théid mi 'nam dheannaibh
Gu Cnocan a' Bhaile,
Choimhead na mara,
   Fiach am faic mi am bàta.
Gun ghuidh mi Di-Luain
   A' ghaoth tuath mar a b'àill leam
A lìonadh a bréid
   Gun éirigh le bàirlinn,
Soirbheas gun dìobradh
Gun bhagradh le rìghneas,
Ach rogha gach sìde
   Gus an tìm sin am màireach.

Nam faighinn ort naidheachd
   Nach biodh tu 'nad shlàinte,
Gheobhainn na feara
   'S gum faradhainn àm bàta;
An seòladh no 'n iomradh
Cha rachamaid iomrall,
Eadar Rubh' Àird-na-Murchainn
   Gun ruigeamaid Àros;
Nuair théid thu 'nad dheise
   Gur deas am measg chàich thu,
'S math thig an gùn dhut
   As ùire bho'n t-snàthaid;
Caol ann an cumadh,
Am fasan a Lunnainn
Bho d' bhrògan gu d' mhullach
   'S leat urram na h-àilleachd.

Nam faiceadh tu 'n iùbhrach
Is siùil rithe an àirde,
Sgoltadh nan tonnan,
   'S 'gam pronnadh fo sàil;
Bu chianail an sealladh
Air bhaideala geala,
A h-aghaidh air Canaidh
   Mo Anna 'gam fhàgail . . . .

The Wind that Comes from Canna

This song was found in a rough notebook of D. C. MacPherson's, who was collecting Gaelic songs in the 1860s.

[1]

The wind that comes from Canna, I feel it warm; I like to be looking in your direction; short is the time until I'll be coming back to you; my ear for music has gone, I have no pleasure in the sound of laughter, I sigh for love, it is no wonder how I am, missing the most beautiful girl in the place. Her form is like the snow, her eye like the berry, and her cheeks are alight with the colour of the wild rose-hip.

[2]

When I go to bed, I cannot rest or sleep; at the time of rising in the morning, I am weary. I go in a hurry to the hillock of the village, to look at the sea, in case I can see the boat. On Monday I prayed for the north wind I wanted, to fill her sails, without raising billows, a mild steady breeze without threatening stiffness, but rather the choicest of weather until this time tomorrow.

[3]

If I were to get news that you were not well, I would get men and load the boat; sailing or rowing we would not go astray, between Ardnamurchan Point, until we reached Aros. When you put on your dress you are pretty amongst all others, well the gown becomes you, newest from the needle, slender in shape, in the fashion from London; from your shoes to your head-tip, you have the honour of beauty.

[4]

If you were to see the ship, with her sails raised aloft, cleaving the waves and pounding them under her keel, the sight of her white topsails would be a sad one, her bow towards Canna, my Anna departing . . . .

APPENDIX XI WILD ANIMALS AND FISH OF CANNA

Mammals, Reptiles, and Amphibians

Amphibians

Smooth Newt, *Triturus v. vulgaris.*
Palmate Newt, *T. h. helveticus.*

Reptiles

None as far as is known, though the presence of the Common Lizard, *Lacerta vivipara*, has been rumoured.

Land Mammals

Hedgehog, *Erinaceus europaeus* (introduced in 1939).
Pigmy Shrew, *Sorex minutus.*
House Mouse, *Mus m. musculus.* Uncommon.
Hebridean Mouse, *Apodemus hebridensis.*
Brown Rat, *Rattus norvegicus.*
Rabbit, *Oryctolagus cuniculus.*
Otter, *Lutra lutra.* Around the shores, e.g. in sea caves.
Feral Goats: there is a flock of about 20 on the cliffs of Geugasgor and Làmasgor.
Bats: one or two were seen flying around the trees of Canna House garden in 1945, but the species was uncertain.

Sea Mammals

SEALS

Harbour Seal, *Phoca vitulina.*
Grey Seal, *Halichoerus grypus.* Common, breeds at the west and south-west shores of the island.

WHALES AND DOLPHINS

Northern Bottlenose Whale, *Hyperoodon ampullatus.*
Common Porpoise, *Phocoena phocoena.*
Killer Whale, *Orcinus orca.*
Risso's Dolphin, *Grampus griseus.*

Common Dolphin, *Delphinus delphis*.
Bottlenose Dolphin, *Tursiops truncatus*.

These have been noticed. There are probably other species in the
Minch from time to time.

TURTLES

Turtles, probably Common Loggerheads, *Caretta caretta*, have been
taken by fishing boats in neighbouring waters occasionally. A small
dead specimen was found on the shore of Canna around 1939.

The Fishes of Canna

Long-spined Sea Scorpion, *Cottus bubalis*.
Grey Gurnard, *Trigla gurnardus*.
Mackerel, *Scomber scombrus*.
Spanish Mackerel, *Scomber colias*.
Tunny, *Thunnus thynnus* (once).
Horse Mackerel, *Cananx trachurus*.
John Dory, *Zeus faber*.
Lump-sucker, *Cylopterus lumpus*.
Grey Mullets, *Mugilidae*.
Ballan Wrasse, *Labrus maculatus* or *Labrus bergylta*.
Striped, Red, or Cuckoo Wrasse, *Labrus mixtrus*.
Cod, *Gadus morrhua*.
Haddock, *Gadus aeglefinus*.
Saithe, *Gadus virens*.
Whiting, *Gadus merlangus*.
Pollack, *Gadus pollachius*.
Ling, *Molva molva* or *vulgaris*.
Five-bearded Rockling, *Motella mustela*.
Greater Sand Eel, *Ammodytes lanceolatus*.
Lesser Sand Eel, *Ammodytes tobianus*.
Plaice, *Pleuronectes platessa*.
Lemon Sole, *Pleuronectes microephalus*.
Dab, *Pleuronectes limanda*.
Flounder, *Pleuronectes flesus*.
Sole, *Solea vulgaris*.
Turbot, *Rhombus miximus*.
Pipe-fish or Needle-fish, *Syngnathus acus*.
Herring, *Clupea harengus*.
Sprat, *Clupea sprattus*.
Eel, *Anguilla vulgaris*.

Conger, *Conger vulgaris*.
Blue Shark, *Carcharias glaucus*.
Basking Shark, *Selache maxima*.
Lesser Spotted Dogfish, *Scyllium canicula*.
Picked Dogfish, *Acanthias vulgaris*.
Skate, *Raja batis*.
Lamprey, *Petromyzon* or *Lampetra fluviatilis*.

APPENDIX XII BIRDS OF CANNA

by Robert L. Swann

The first recorded visit of an ornithologist to Canna was in 1881 by Harvie-Brown. He was followed by others, many of whom kept lists of the birds they had seen on their visits. In 1939 Carrick and Waterston wrote the first paper on the island's birds. Entitled 'The Birds of Canna', it appeared in the *Scottish Naturalist*, Jan.–Feb. 1939. It used the author's own records plus those of earlier visitors and also many records from the Thoms, the owners of Canna at the time, who took much interest in the island's bird life. In 1967 this paper was updated by Evans and Flowers, 'The Birds of the Small Isles', which appeared in *Scottish Birds*, Vol. 4, No. 6, and which used all available records till 1966.

In 1969 the island was visited by a group of students from Aberdeen University under the leadership of A. D. K. Ramsay. Their aim was to count the island's sea-birds as part of the Operation Seafarer project being organized by the Seabird Group in the aftermath of the Torrey Canyon disaster. This marked a turning-point in the island's ornithology. Prior to this, visits by ornithologists had been sporadic and by differing groups. Since 1969 the island has been visited annually in order to conduct long-term studies into the numbers, breeding biology, and movements of the island's sea-bird populations. During these visits (usually four a year in April, May, July, and August or September) detailed notes and counts have been kept of the island's bird life. This new list of Canna's birds uses the records from these visits along with observations from the islanders, in particular Dr and Mrs J. L. Campbell and Ian and Angus MacKinnon and their families. All records up till April 1982 have been used and the birds are listed in the revised Voous order. (1977, List of Recent Holarctic Bird Species.)

In all 157 species have been recorded on the island, an increase of 18 since the 139 recorded up to 1966. Of these 71 have bred, 56 of which have done so regularly over the past fifteen years. In the same period 10 or 11 new species have been added to the islands' breeding list. These are: Heron, Greylag Goose, Red Breasted Merganser, Collared Dove, Sparrow Hawk, Wood Pigeon, Mistle Thrush, Blue Tit, Siskin, Linnet, and probably Tree Creeper. During this period only one species has ceased to breed regularly, the Golden Eagle. It is of interest to note that 8 of the new breeders are woodland species.

A Blackbird's Song

Canna House garden, June 1949. Noted by J. L. Campbell.

Another Blackbird's Song

Canna House garden, June 1957. Noted by Francis Collinson.

The area of woodland on Canna has increased with the development and subsequent growth of the several small plantations, which has greatly benefited many species on the island. Apart from the woodland, there has been little apparent change in the island's land use in the past twenty years. Small changes like the decrease in the amount of actively worked croft land and the increased amount of drainage will have affected some species, details of which can be found in the species accounts which follow.

Red Throated Diver, *Gavia stellata*. Ones and twos are occasionally seen offshore in spring and late summer.

Black Throated Diver, *Gavia arctica*. Scarce visitor. One in June 1930 and one in June 1969.

Great Northern Diver, *Gavia immer*. A regular visitor offshore in small numbers chiefly between November and April.

Little Grebe, *Tachybaptus ruficollis*. Rare winter visitor with a few old records from the 1930s and one in 1956.

Fulmar, *Fulmarus glacialis*. First bred in 1930 on Sanday, and sites were occupied on the north side of Canna in 1936. There was then an increase to a peak of 669 occupied sites in 1977. Lately numbers have fluctuated around 600 sites, mainly on Geugasgor, Tialasgor, the Eisebrig area of Sanday with smaller numbers elsewhere.

Puffin, *Fratercula arctica*. Although this species has been noticed on the island since 1887, there have been few counts. At the moment there are two large colonies: Dùn Mór and Geugasgor. Numbers are decreasing at the former, due to erosion, but increasing at the latter. Other small colonies are found at An Stòl (An t-Each) around Iolasgor, and near the lighthouse and at Tallaibrig on Sanday. We estimate there to be between 500 and 1,000 pairs on the island. Birds arrive in April and leave in early August.

Manx Shearwater, *Puffinus puffinus*. About 1,500 pairs breed mainly along the grassy slopes on the north side of the Tarbert road, where numbers appear to have remained unchanged since the 1960s. Formerly other parts of the island like Compass Hill and the cliffs along the north side were reported to have breeding colonies. Nowadays the only other known colony on the island is at Bre Sgor where there are 50–100 pairs. Birds arrive in late February and depart by October. Ringing recoveries show that many winter off the east coast of South America.

Storm Petrel, *Hydrobates pelagicus*. There are unconfirmed reports of breeding having taken place in the 19th century. They regularly appear offshore during the summer months and although there are no recent reports of breeding it remains a possibility.

Leach's Petrel, *Oceanodroma leucorrhoa*. Only one record of a specimen taken by Gray prior to 1871.

Gannet, *Sula bassana*. Regularly seen offshore in good numbers from March till October.

Cormorant, *Phalacrocorax carbo*. Regular winter visitor in small numbers.

Shag, *Phalacrocorax aristotelis*. The colony on Canna is one of the largest in Scotland and was estimated to hold 15 per cent of all Scottish pairs in 1969. There are four large colonies: Geugasgor, Boro'osgor, Lamasgor, and Sgor am Fhraoich, plus many smaller groups. Numbers have fluctuated in recent years from a peak of 1,900 pairs in 1971 to only 200 in 1970. However, 800–900 pairs would be about the recent average number. Ringing recoveries show that most birds disperse from the island (with only 50–100 remaining to winter) throughout west Highland waters with 59 per cent of recoveries coming from the Outer Hebrides.

Heron, *Ardea cinerea*. Since the late 1960s one pair has bred regularly on a cliff site near Tarbert. In some years a second pair also breeds. There are regularly up to 15 non-breeders on the island.

Spoonbill, *Platalea leucorodia*. Two in November 1907.

Mute Swan, *Cygnus olor*. Very scarce winter visitor with no recent records. One in July 1958 is the only summer record.

Whooper Swan, *Cygnus cygnus*. Regular on passage when groups of up to 15 can be seen flying over the island and occasionally landing in the bay.

Pink Footed Goose, *Anser brachyrhynchus*. Occasionally seen on spring and autumn passage overflying the island. Singles have summered in the bay, usually with the feral goose flock.

White Fronted Goose, *Anser albifrons*. Seen on passage, when occasionally birds land, particularly during bad weather. Single birds occasionally remain on the island for several days, one as late as 23 May 1980.

Greylag Goose, *Anser anser*. Regular passage migrant especially in spring when birds often land due to bad weather. Birds summered in 1964 and in both 1980 and 1981 a single pair nested on Sanday. Occasionally seen in winter, e.g. 30 in January 1982.

Barnacle Goose, *Branta leucopsis*. Regular passage migrant over the island though small flocks often land. There are old winter records, e.g. 9 in January 1933. One bird was present as late as 23 May in 1981 and 2 were seen in August 1959.

Brent Goose, *Branta bernicla*. Six in May 1935 and one in October 1952.

Shelduck, *Tadorna tadorna*. In 1933 one pair bred. This had increased to 2 pairs in 1956, 4 pairs in 1963 and 1965, and up to 8 pairs in the early 1970s. In recent years only 4 or 5 pairs have bred and with a very low rate of success. Birds leave the island in late summer and return in December or January.

Wigeon, *Anas penelope*. One in January 1957.

Teal, *Anas crecca*. Between 5 and 10 birds winter on Sanday, mainly at the lochan. Single pairs summered in 1970 and 1973.

Mallard, *Anas platyrhynchos*. Resident. Since 1973 up to three pairs have bred most years. Small flocks totalling between 10 and 20 birds winter.

Pintail, *Anas acuta*. Four in April 1935 and in October 1938 are the only records.

Scaup, *Anthya marila*. One in February 1956.

Eider. *Somateria mollissima*. Common breeder all along the coast. Numbers appear to have dropped from about 100 pairs in 1969 to around 50 pairs in recent years. A flock of up to 60 moulting birds is regular in the bay in summer. Over 100 birds winter in flocks scattered round the island.

Long Tailed Duck, *Clangula hyemalis*. Two offshore, April 1970.

Common Scoter, *Melanitta nigra*. Seen offshore in March 1970.

Red Breasted Merganser, *Mergus serrator*. Up to 12 birds have been seen wintering in the bay. Since the mid-1960s birds have occasionally summered and in 1977 a pair bred. They have continued to do so since with two pairs breeding in 1981.

Goosander, *Mergus merganser*. One record of 4 in the bay on 1 November 1979.

White Tailed Eagle, *Haliaëtus albicilla*. The last known nesting attempt was in 1875 though birds were seen up to 1920. Since 1977 birds have been regularly seen on the island due to the reintroduction programme taking place on the neighbouring island of Rum.

Hen Harrier, *Circus cyaneus*. One November 1936 and one in the late 1960s which had been previously ringed as a young bird in Orkney.

Goshawk, *Accipiter gentilis*. One male 2–5 April 1977.

Sparrow Hawk, *Accipiter nisus*. Originally a scarce passage migrant. In the 1970s a pair bred on at least four occasions. Nowadays, even when breeding has not taken place, birds are regularly seen.

Buzzard, *Buteo buteo*. Four to six pairs bred in the 1930s. A crash in the rabbit population in the 1950s due to myxomatosis resulted in a reduction to only 3 or 4 breeding pairs. In the 1960s, the numbers rose to a peak of 11 pairs in 1971. In the mid 1970s a further major myxomatosis outbreak led to another crash so that in recent years only about 6 pairs have bred. Breeding success varies greatly with rabbit numbers but some birds have become adept at catching Shearwaters at night.

Golden Eagle, *Aquila chrysaetos*. The first pair was recorded on the island in 1935, though singles had been seen prior to that. In the 1950s and 1960s two pairs regularly bred, one around Geugasgor and the other at Iola Sgor. The last successful breeding took place in 1969 and although both pairs remained on the island up till 1976 no young were reared. This may well have been connected with a change of diet from rabbits to Fulmars. Since 1976 the only records have been of wandering immatures.

Kestrel, *Falco tinnunculus*. Several pairs were reported to have bred in the 19th century. Since the 1930s only one pair has bred or attempted to breed most years, with the exception of 1974 when two pairs bred.

Merlin, *Falco columbarius*. Regular passage migrant in spring. Occasional summer sightings probably are wanderers from Rum.

Peregrine, *Falco peregrinus*. Has nested since at least 1549. From the 1930s to the 1960s two pairs bred regularly. During the 1970s both pairs were normally present but breeding success was low with the young being reared on only three occasions. In 1981, however, both pairs again bred successfully.

Red Grouse, *Lagopus lagopus*. Last recorded in 1936.

Quail, *Coturnix coturnix*. One, 5–9 July 1976.

Pheasant, *Phasianus colchicus*. Introduced before 1914 but did not survive.

Water Rail, *Rallus aquaticus*. Rare winter visitor with only four known records.

Corncrake, *Crex crex*. During the 1930s 12 to 15 pairs were recorded but this had decreased to 5 calling birds by the late 1950s and 1960s. Recently there have been up to 15 calling birds. They arrive in late April or early May and are mostly found in the hay fields round the bay. They depart in September to overwinter in Central Africa as shown by an adult ringed on Canna and recovered in January 1978 in Congo Brazzaville.

Moorhen, *Gallinula chloropus*. Rare winter visitor. One summered in 1962 on Sanday lochan.

Coot, *Fulica atra*. Another rare winter visitor with only two known records.

Oystercatcher, *Haematopus ostralegus*. First recorded in 1889. Common in the 1930s, 30-plus pairs in 1963, and 72 pairs in 1969. Breeds all round the coast and numbers fluctuate between 50 and 80 pairs. Numbers drop in winter to about 40 birds, which are mostly seen in the bay. A young bird ringed on Canna in July 1972 was found dead at Arcachon, Gironde, France, in November 1975.

Ringed Plover, *Charadrius hiaticula*. Up to three pairs regularly breed. Small flocks can be seen in the bay in late summer consisting probably of both local and passage birds.

Golden Plover, *Pluvialis apricaria*. Bred until 1902 after which it was only seen in winter. One summered in 1963 and in 1976 a pair bred. Breeding was again proved in 1979 and suspected in other years. Small flocks are seen regularly on spring passage and birds occasionally winter, e.g. 12 in January 1982.

Lapwing, *Vanellus vanellus*. Resident. Three to five pairs bred in the 1930s. Breeding was not then recorded till the 1960s when two pairs bred. Nowadays 7 to 8 pairs breed; one group on Sanday and the others just west of Tarbert.

Knot, *Calidris canutus*. Occasionally seen in small numbers on passage, usually overflying the island.

Sanderling, *Calidris alba*. A few records of birds mainly on autumn passage.

Purple Sandpiper, *Calidris maritima*. Occasionally seen in winter in small numbers, also on spring passage, and two in July 1976.

Dunlin, *Calidris alpina*. Used to be a regular winter visitor. Nowadays it is mainly a passage migrant with small groups of up to 10 being seen in the bay.

Jack Snipe, *Lymnocryptes minimus*. This bird was a regular winter visitor with up to 5 being seen on the marsh on Sanday. There have been no records since 1973 when the marsh was drained.

Snipe, *Gallinago gallinago*. Resident and common breeder on Sanday and the moors of Canna. No accurate count has been made but possibly up to 40 pairs have bred. Recently there has been a decrease, mainly on Sanday, due to improved drainage schemes.

Woodcock, *Scolopax rusticola*. A regular winter visitor often in good numbers, e.g. 50-plus during the cold weather in January 1982.

Bar-Tailed Godwit, *Limosa lapponica*. Singles and small flocks of up to 3 have been recorded in the bay on passage.

Whimbrel, *Numenius phaeopus*. Regular spring migrant. Occasionally seen in late summer.

Curlew, *Numenius arquata*. There is a large flock of up to 80 birds on the island. They remain till mid-April and start to return in June. Their origin is unknown.

Redshank, *Tringa totanus*. Winter visitor in small numbers, usually about 10. On passage larger flocks of up to 30 have been recorded. Rarely, birds have been known to summer.

Greenshank, *Tringa nebularia*. Regular in ones and twos throughout the summer, with a few winter records, e.g. 2 in January 1982.

Common Sandpiper, *Tringa hypoleucos*. Summer visitor. Two pairs were reported in 1936 and 4 pairs in 1961 and 1963. Between 1969 and 1971 8–9 pairs bred and by 1977 12–15 pairs were breeding. Since then 11 or 12 pairs have bred, all in coastal sites. There is one record of a Spotted Sandpiper in autumn 1981.

Turnstone, *Arenaria interpres*. There are old winter records between 1935 and 1944. Most recent records have been of birds in small numbers on spring passage.

Pomarine Skua, *Stercorarius pomarinus*. One shot (? November 1890).

Arctic Skua, *Stercorarius parasiticus*. Singles occasionally seen offshore in summer.

Great Skua, *Stercorarius skua*. Commoner than Arctic with birds being seen offshore in early and late summer.

Franklin's Gull, *Larus pipixcan*. One adult in the bay from 5 to 11 July 1981 is only the second record of this American gull in Scotland.

Little Gull, *Larus minutus*. One shot, August 1912.

Black Headed Gull, *Larus ridibundus*. Up to 20 occur in the bay during winter, spring, and autumn, but summer records are scarce.

Common Gull, *Larus canus*. A few pairs nested in 1933 on Sanday. Four pairs were breeding in 1963. It is now a regular breeder in small numbers, averaging about 11 pairs, mainly along the Tarbert road. Small flocks are common in the bay in late summer and winter.

Lesser Black-Backed Gull, *Larus fuscus*. A few pairs bred in 1933 and 12 pairs were counted in 1963. From 1969 to 1978 numbers fluctuated around 60 pairs but there has since been a decrease to just under 40 pairs. This species is a summer visitor arriving in March or April and departing in August. Ringing recoveries show that Canna birds winter as far south as Morocco.

Herring Gull, *Larus argentatus*. In 1936 probably about 100 pairs nested. This had increased to 335-plus pairs in 1963 and to 1,449 pairs in 1969. Since then numbers have fluctuated around the 800 to 900 pairs mark. The main colonies are at Lamasgor, below Geugasgor, Buidhesgor, on Rudha Langanais, Coine'agaraidh, Boro'osgor, Rubha Sgor nam Ban-naomha, and on Sanday. Ringing recoveries show that all young and most adults disperse from the island in winter mainly to the populated areas of Central Scotland and Northern Ireland.

Iceland Gull, *Larus glaucoides*. One record of an immature which was present from 3 to 5 April 1982.

Glaucous Gull, *Larus hyperboreus*. One shot, winter 1890s, and one seen at the pier 4 March 1982.

Greater Black-Backed Gull, *Larus marinus*. Resident. Ten pairs nested in the 1930s, 17–18 paris in 1961 and 1963. From 1969 to 1981 numbers have remained stable at around 60 pairs. They are well scattered round the coast with small concentrations at An Steidh and Ha'aslum, both islets.

Kittiwake, *Rissa tridactyla*. A large colony was reported in the 1880s and 768 pairs were counted at two colonies in 1936. In the 1960s the Geugasgor colony held 400 nests and the Eisebrig colony on Sanday 120 nests. Both these colonies have continued to increase with 640 nests at Geugasgor and 341 on Sanday in 1981.

Ivory Gull, *Pagophila eburnea*. One shot, December 1922.

Sandwich Tern, *Sterna sandvicensis*. Singles are occasionally seen in summer.

Common Tern, *Sterna hirundo*. Two old records: June 1933 and July 1936.

Arctic Tern, *Sterna paradisaea*. Birds were present on Ha'aslum in the 1930s but were not proven to have bred. There are reports of breeding having taken place in the early 1950s on small islets in the bay. They are now regular in small numbers in the bay in summer, mainly feeding groups from the colony on Heiskeir.

Guillemot, *Uria aalge*. There are major colonies below Geugasgor and around Dun Mor on Sanday. This species has increased from about 1,200 pairs in 1974 to an estimated 2,000 pairs in 1981. This expansion has been coupled with the establishment of new colonies such as the small ones at Boro'osgor and Sgor an Fhraoich. Birds leave the colonies in late July and August and both young and adults disperse widely from Scandinavian to Spanish waters. Most adults do not return till March, though some do winter locally.

Razorbill, *Alca torda*. We estimated there were 400 breeding pairs in 1974 which had increased to around 700 pairs by 1981. The main colonies are below Geugasgor with smaller numbers on Sanday, and in the boulders amongst the Shags at Sgor an Fhraoich, Iola Sgor, Boro'osgor, and Lamasgor. Birds leave the colonies in

July and most winter in the Southern North Sea, English Channel, and Brittany area, though some birds do get as far as the Mediterranean.

Black Guillemot, *Cepphus grylle*. Said to be common in the 1880s but only 10 pairs in 1933, which had increased to 17-plus pairs in 1961. In 1974 36 individuals were counted which were thought to represent about 25 pairs. There has been a continued increase with 144 individuals being counted in 1981. The main sites are the north coast of Sanday, Sgor an Fhraoich, Carasgor, Buidhesgor, and Rudha Carr-innis. At the latter site there has been a noticeable decrease in recent years, possibly due to rat predation. In winter numbers drop.

Little Auk, *Plautus alle*. Three old records of birds found dead or dying prior to 1932, also two recent records in winters 1971 and 1973.

Rock Dove, *Columba livia*. Flocks of up to 20 are regularly seen. Nests in coastal caves.

Wood Pigeon, *Columba palumbus*. Originally this species was an unusual summer visitor with occasional autumn influxes, e.g. up to 200 in November 1935. In 1969 an old nest was found and since then birds have been resident in increasing numbers (up to about 10) and in 1980 a pair almost certainly bred.

Collared Dove, *Streptopelia decaocto*. Must have colonized Canna in the late 1960s. By the 1970s about 10 pairs were breeding and flocks of over 30 were common. In the last few years there has been a decrease with only 10–20 birds being seen.

Turtle Dove, *Streptopelia turtur*. A few records, mainly of single birds, between June and August.

Cuckoo, *Cuculus canorus*. Summer visitor in varying numbers. One or two calling birds is the norm but 4 were recorded in 1978 and 5 in 1936.

Barn Owl, *Tyto alba*. Four records between 1910 and 1962.

Snowy Owl, *Nyctea scandiaca*. One, November 1942.

Tawny Owl, *Strix aluco*. Last positive sighting was in July 1937.

Long-eared Owl, *Asio otus*. Single birds recorded in the winters of 1923, 1938, and the 1960s, usually at Tighard.

Short-eared Owl, *Asio flammeus*. One old winter record in December 1935. Three recent records in the last fifteen years, all in summer.

Swift, *Apus apus*. Unusual summer visitor overflying the island.

Skylark, *Alauda arvensis*. Resident and common breeder. Flocks of up to 200 are recorded in spring, mainly at Coroghon. Some winter and large hard-weather movements have been noted, e.g. 'hundreds' in January 1946.

Sand Martin, *Riparia riparia*. Rare visitor, usually on spring passage.

Swallow, *Hirundo rustica*. Up till the 1960s a single pair occasionally bred. Between 1969 and 1974 two or three pairs bred. Breeding then ceased till 1978 when a single pair bred and has continued to do so up to 1981.

House Martin, *Delichon urbica*. Regular spring migrant and occasional in autumn. A pair was seen in June 1977 and in July 1981 two spent several days round Canna House.

Tree Pipit, *Anthus trivialis*. One, 4 August 1964.

Meadow Pipit, *Anthus pratensis*. Common breeder. In spring large flocks of over 100 birds are common. Many of these are Icelandic migrants.

Rock Pipit, *Anthus spinoletta*. Resident and common breeder all around the low coasts with possibly up to 50 pairs.

Grey Wagtail, *Motacilla cinerea*. Now a regular spring visitor in small numbers. Occasionally seen in late summer, and in 1970 a single bird summered.

Pied Wagtail, *Motacilla alba*. One pair in the 1930s and 1–2 pairs in 1956 had increased to about 4 pairs in 1961 and 10–15 pairs by 1981. In spring and autumn up to 80 birds roost at Sanday Lochan. Most birds leave the island in winter. Two ringing recoveries suggest that they may winter in the English midlands with one being found in Wolverhampton and the other in Liverpool. White Wagtails are regular on spring passage mainly in late April.

Waxwing, *Bombycilla garrulus*. Recorded December 1946 and 1958.

Dipper, *Cinclus cinclus*. Rare winter visitor. One in January 1956 and one in February to March 1977 are the only recent records.

Wren, *Troglodytes troglodytes*. Resident and common breeder. Found in the woods and plantations and also along the coast. One pair is regularly found at the west end of Geugasgor.

Dunnock, *Prunella modularis*. Resident. Has increased from 4 pairs in the 1930s to between 10 and 15 pairs since the 1960s. This is mainly due to the planting and subsequent growth of the plantations.

Robin, *Erithacus rubecula*. Resident. This is another species which has benefited from the increase in the woodland areas. Only 1 or 2 pairs were recorded in the 1930s but now about 10 pairs breed.

Redstart, *Phoenicurus phoenicurus*. Two records: one 18 July 1969 and one 26 August 1970.

Whinchat, *Saxicola rubetra*. Summer visitor. Numbers fluctuate from year to year, e.g. 1 or 2 pairs 1930s, 1 pair 1961, 8 pairs 1963, 2 pairs 1975, 6 pairs 1978.

Stonechat, *Saxicola torquata*. Numbers also fluctuate with this species depending on the severity of the winter, e.g. 7 pairs 1962 down to 2 pairs 1963 and 10 pairs 1976 down to 1 pair 1978. They tend to recover quite quickly in the years following a bad winter.

Wheatear, *Oenanthe oenanthe*. Summer visitor and common breeder with between 50 and 100 pairs.

Ring Ouzel, *Turdus torquatus*. Rare summer visitor with no records since 1931.

Blackbird, *Turdus merula*. Resident. Has also increased owing to the development of the woodland areas. In 1933 there was one pair, in 1940 3 pairs, in the 1960s about 6 pairs, and now between 10 and 15 pairs. In winter there is an influx of birds probably of continental origin.

Fieldfare, *Turdus pilaris*. Occasionally winters but more often seen on spring and autumn passage in small numbers.

Song Thrush, *Turdus philomelos*. Resident. Between 5 and 10 pairs breed in the woodlands.

Redwing, *Turdus iliacus*. Regular spring and autumn passage migrant often in large flocks of several hundred. Measurements from the few caught on the island suggest they are mainly of the Icelandic race. Small numbers occasionally winter.

Mistle Thrush, *Turdus viscivorus*. One pair bred in 1972 and 1973. The only record since was one in March 1976.

Grasshopper Warbler, *Locustella naevia*. Two singing birds, June 1973.

Sedge Warbler, *Acrocephalus schoenbaenus*. Summer visitor with one to four pairs breeding, mainly on Sanday at the marsh and Lochan.

Whitethroat, *Sylvia communis*. Summer visitor. In the 1950s and 1960s up to 6 pairs bred. Nowadays only 1 to 3 pairs breed, mirroring the national decline which took place in this species in the late 1960s.

Blackcap, *Sylvia atricapilla*. No records prior to 1969. Now an occasional spring visitor.

Chiffchaff, *Phylloscopus collybita*. Regular spring visitor in ones and twos. Has occasionally summered, e.g. 1963, 1975, and 1981.

Willow Warbler, *Phylloscopus trochilus*. Summer visitor. Up to 6 pairs were recorded in the 1930s though they were scarcer in the 1960s. In the 1970s an average of 5 or 6 pairs were present with a maximum of 9 pairs in 1975.

Goldcrest, *Regulus regulus*. Resident. Single birds were recorded in 1930 and 1943. They first bred in 1956 and annually thereafter apart from a gap in 1962 and 1963 after the severe winter. Nowadays 2 to 4 pairs breed each year.

Spotted Flycatcher, *Muscicapa striata*. First recorded 1936 though the first breeding was not proved till 1961. Two pairs then bred in 1962. Breeding has since been sporadic with only 3 records in the last thirteen years.

Pied Flycatcher, *Ficedula hypoleuca*. One in August 1970.

Long Tailed Tit, *Aegithalos caudatus*. Two records: October 1935 when a flock of 8 was seen, and March 1949.

Coal Tit, *Parus ater*. Three in January 1946 and one in spring 1972 are the only records. Seen twice in January 1986.

Blue Tit, *Parus caeruleus*. Four records between 1928 and 1961, mainly in winter. Singles were then reported in spring 1970 and 1972, and in 1974 a pair bred successfully. A single pair has continued to breed round Canna House each year since.

Great Tit, *Parus major*. Seven records, all in winter between 1929 and 1979. Seen twice in November 1985.

Tree Creeper, *Certhia familiaris*. One in authumn 1957 and one in August 1964. Birds summered in 1975 and in 1976 a juvenile was caught and a second bird found dead, indicating that they probably bred.

Jackdaw, *Corvus monedula*. Present summer 1953 and 1961. It is mainly an unusual winter visitor with only 3 records, all in early spring, in the last thirteen years.

Rook, *Corvus frugilegus*. Occasionally recorded up till 1938. The only recent record is one which remained from February to April 1978 at Coroghon.

Hooded Crow, *Corvus corone*. Resident with up to 20 pairs nesting on crags round the island. Large non-breeding flocks used to be common, e.g. 100 in 1956, but these have declined to under 30 in the 1970s. Carrion Crows occasionally turn up though since 1969 there are only two records: one in winter 1976 and two, January to April 1982.

Raven, *Corvus corax*. Resident which has increased from 2 pairs in the 1930s to 3 pairs in 1961 to 5 or 6 pairs in recent years. In 1972, a year with much carrion, 9 pairs nested.

Starling, *Sturnus vulgaris*. Numerous up till the 1930s when large numbers bred and a roost of 300-plus was present round Canna House. Decreased during the 1940s and 1950s but in the 1960s several tens of pairs nested in the cliffs and buildings. There has been yet another decline and now only about ten pairs nest, all on the cliffs or crags. An autumn roost on Sanday Lochan holds 40–60 birds.

House Sparrow, *Passer domesticus*. Resident. None in the 1900s but common by the 1930s. It is now plentiful and many tens of pairs nest wherever there is human habitation and hens.

Tree Sparrow, *Passer montanus*. Resident. Under 3 pairs in 1933 then none till 1961. A pair bred in 1962 and they have continued to breed ever since, mainly around Canna House where there are now 5-plus pairs.

Chaffinch, *Fringilla coelebs*. Two to three pairs in the 1930s which increased to 10 pairs in the 1950s and to several tens of pairs in the 1960s. This increase is again due to the growth of the plantations. Flocks of over 100 are common around Coroghon and A'Chill in winter and spring.

Brambling, *Fringilla montifringilla*. One in March 1970.

Greenfinch, *Carduelis chloris*. First recorded in 1933 with odd birds thereafter until 1961 when a flock arrived in January and 6 pairs bred the following summer. A similar number have continued to do so ever since.

Goldfinch, *Carduelis carduelis*. Singles in December 1927, May 1934, June 1969, and June 1972.

Siskin, *Carduelis spinus*. A single pair probably bred in one of the plantations in 1969 and 1970. No subsequent records.

Linnet, *Acanthis cannabina*. One in June 1963, then bred 1964. Summered 1970 and 1972 to 1974 when it may have bred in the latter year. A single pair then bred in 1977 and 1978.

Twite, *Acanthis flavirostris*. Resident. Ten-plus pairs breed. Flocks of 60-plus build up round the bay in spring and autumn, with a maximum count of 120 in August 1977.

Redpoll, *Acanthis flammea*. Four records between 1936 and 1959 and a pair bred in 1940. Only two records since: June 1969 and May 1975.

Crossbill, *Loxia curvirostra*. Small flocks between June and August 1910, 1927, 1953, and 1958. None recently.

Bullfinch, *Pyrrhula pyrrhula*. A few spring records up to the 1940s. Since then only one record of 3 in August 1970.

Snow Bunting, *Plectrophenax nivalis*. One record: 20-plus, November 1935.

Yellow Hammer, *Emberiza citrinella*. During the 1940s one or two pairs bred. There were no records till 2 birds were seen in summer 1962. The only two recent records were singles in June 1970 and March 1972.

Reed Bunting, *Emberiza schoeniclus*. Originally an unusual winter visitor. In the 1960s a single pair was reported to be breeding. Nowadays 2 or 3 pairs breed most years on Sanday.

Red Headed Bunting, *Emberiza bruniceps*. Two records; though both are probably escapes, August 1970 and August 1976.

Corn Bunting, *Emberiza calandra*. Common breeder in the nineteenth century, but only one or two pairs remained by the 1930s with no records after 1949 till the early 1970s when singles were seen in spring 1971 and 1974 and a pair in 1973. No records since.

APPENDIX XIII BUTTERFLIES AND MOTHS OF CANNA

by J. L. Campbell

For reasons of space, only the more interesting species of noctuid and geometrid moths and microlepidoptera are given here. A full list of the macrolepidoptera of Canna can be found in Volume 82 of the *Entomologist's Record*, with some additions in subsequent volumes. For the microlepidoptera, see Dr M. W. Harper and Dr M. R. Young, 'Additions to the Microlepidopterous Fauna of the Isles of Canna and Sanday', *Entomologist's Record*, Vol. 93, pp. 150–3, where other references are given.

The arrangement and nomenclature correspond to that built up in my Hebridean collection, which was started in 1936, and is now the property of the National Trust for Scotland.

Butterflies

Resident

Green-Veined White (*Pieris napi*). (Double-brooded.)
Small Tortoiseshell (*Nymphalis urticae*).
Dark Green Fritillary (*Argynnis aglaia*).
Small Pearl-bordered Fritillary (*Brenthis selene*).
Grayling (*Satyrus semele*).
Speckled Wood (*Pararge aegeria*). (Greatly increased in recent years.)
Meadow Brown (*Maniola jurtina*).
Small Heath (*Caenonympha pamphilus*).
Green Hairstreak (*Callophrys rubi*).
Common Blue (*Polyommatus icarus*).

Resident Reinforced by Immigration

Large White (*Pieris brassicae*). (It seems that the local population is single-brooded.)

Regular Migrants

These come practically every summer, lay eggs here on their food-plants, and produce a generation that apparently flies south again, as the puffins do. At least that life habit makes sense – the idea that these summer broods simply wait to die off in the winter in Britain hardly favours their survival.

Painted Lady (*Cynthia cardui*).
Red Admiral (*Vanessa atalanta*).

Rare Migrant

Clouded Yellow (*Colias croceus*). Not certainly seen here since 1947.

A Common Wanderer

Small White (*Pieris rapae*). First noticed, in the garden, in 1978.

Suspected Wanderer

A few years ago I saw an unexpected large fritillary in the garden. When it settled on a flower I was able to see that the underside of the hind wings had silver stripes instead of silver spots. It might have been a Silver-washed Fritillary (*Argynnis paphia*), common in Ireland, but not yet certainly recorded from Scotland.

Extinct

Peacock (*Inachis io*). This was first observed in 1939; common in 1947, a great year for butterflies. It has not been seen here since 1961. I understand it has also disappeared from Rum and Eigg, although one was seen on Rum in August 1983. Seen again 1984.

Butterflies on Neighbouring Islands

The Large Heath (*Coenonympha tullia*) occurs on Rum; the Scots Argus (*Erebia aethiops*) on Skye, opposite Soay. Has anyone ever looked for the Mountain Ringlet (*E. epiphron*) in the Coolins?

Interesting Moths

A great many records are due to the mercury-vapour light trap started in 1951 and used fairly intensively until the great rise in the price of diesel oil that began in 1973. Apart from known migrants (marked here with an asterisk) quite a number of moths that have only turned up once or twice in the trap, especially woodland ones, must be considered wanderers.

Hawk-moths (Sphingidae)

Poplar Hawk (*Smerinthus populi*).
*Death's Head Hawkmoth (*Acherontia atropos*). Two in the house in 1956. The squeaking sound made by one was recorded and used in a broadcast nature programme.
*Convolvulus Hawk (*Herse convolvuli*). Singly in the trap a number of times, but not since 1969.
Elephant Hawkmoth (*Deilephila elpenor*). One in 1977 and one in 1982.
*Humming-bird Hawk (*Macroglossa stellatarum*). One in 1975 in trap. Seen in 1947.

Prominents (Notodontidae)

Sallow Kitten (*Cerura furcula*). Singly in trap, 1969 and 1974.
Puss Moth (*Dicranura vinula*).
Swallow Prominent (*Pheosia tremula*). Once, in 1955.
Lesser Swallow Prominent (P. dictaeoides). Four times, 1957, 1963, 1968, 1983.
Pebble Prominent (*Notodonta ziczac*).
Iron Prominent (*N. dromedarius*).
Coxcomb Prominent (*Lophopteryx camelina*).
Buff-tip (*Phalera bucephala*).

Thyatiridae

Peach Blossom (*Thyatira batis*).
Poplar Lutestring (*Palimpsestis or*).
Yellow Horned (*P. flavicornis*). Once only, 1965.

Eggars (Lasiocampidae)

Pale Oak Eggar (*Trichiura crataegi*). One in 1969.
Northern Eggar (*Lasiocampa quercus* var. *callunae*).
Fox Moth (*Macrothylacia rubi*).
Drinker (*Cosmotriche potatoria*). Rarely in trap, males only. No females or caterpillars found here so far.

Emperors (Saturnidae)

Emperor (*Saturnia pavonia*).

Nolidae

Least Black Arches (*Nola confusalis*).

Tiger Moths (Arctiidae)

White Ermine (*Spilosoma menthastri*).
Buff Ermine (*S. lubricipeda*).
Ruby Tiger (*Phragmatobia fuliginosa*).
Wood Tiger (*Parasemia plantaginis*).
Clouded Buff (*Diacrisia sanio*). Five males singly in trap 1954–64.
Garden Tiger (*Arctia caja*).
Cinnabar (*Hypocrita jacobaeae*). Introduced in 1949 to control ragwort, the colony lasted until 1956. A specimen which was taken in the house in June 1976 must have been a wanderer.

Footman Moths (Lithosiinae)

Dew Moth (*Endrosa irrorella*). An interesting inhabitant of rocky bouldered places on the south shore.
Common Footman (*Lithosia lurideola*). One found on Canna in 1957 by Dr Michael Harper.

Noctuids (Noctuidae)

One hundred and twenty species have been recorded. Only the most interesting can be given here.

Nut-tree Tussock (*Demas coryli*). One in 1961 and one in 1968, two in 1972.
Miller (*Acronycta leporina*). One in 1980, sitting on a house.
Light Knot-grass (*Acronycta menyanthidis*).
Sweet-gale Moth (*A. euphorbiae* var. *myricae*). One in 1952.
Coronet Moth (*Craniophora ligustri*). One in 1971.
Archer's Dart (*Agrotis vestigialis*). In 1956 and 1964.
Garden Dart (*A. nigricans*).
*Dark Sword-grass (*A. ypsilon*).
Portland Moth (*A. praecox*).
*Pearly Underwing (*A. saucia*).
Northern Rustic (*A. lucernea*).
Dotted Rustic (*A. simulans*). One only, indoors in 1956.
Double Dart (*Noctua augur*). Three only, two in 1968 and one in 1971.
Broad-bordered Yellow Underwing (*Triphaena fimbria*). One in 1955, three in 1968.
Green Arches (*Eurois prasina*).
*Great Brocade (*E. occulta*). One in 1960; two in 1964; one in 1966; one in 1973. All of the dark form.

Grey Arches (*Aplecta nebulosa*).
The Grey (*Dianthoecia caesia*). First taken, in the trap, in 1952, the first record from Scotland.
Hedge Rustic (*Tholera cespitis*).
Brindled Green (*Eumichtis protea*). One in 1955, one in 1966.
Minor Shoulder-Knot (*Bombycia viminalis*).
Straw Underwing (*Cerigo matura*). Two at sugar in 1945; one in trap in 1966.
Haworth's Rustic (*Celanea haworthii*). Thirteen records.
Light Arches (*Xylophasia lithoxylea*).
Deep-brown Dart (*Aporophyla lutulenta*).
Brindled Ochre (*Dasypolia templi*). .
Green-brindled Crescent (*Miselia oxycanthae*). One in 1974.
Merveille-du-Jour (*Agriopis aprilina*). One in 1968.
Angle-shades (*Phlogophora meticulosa*). Partial migrant?
Gothic (*Naenia typica*).
*Large Wainscot (*Calamia lutosa*). Four, 1960, 1962, 1967, and 1971.
*American Wainscot (*Leucania unipuncta*). 1964, 1966, 1973.
The Clay (*L. lithargyria*). One in 1969.
*Small Mottled Willow (*Laphygma exigua*). 1952, 1966 (ten).
Small Dotted Buff (*Petilampa arcuosa*). Two only, including one from Heiskeir light.
Brown Rustic (*Rusina tenebrosa*). Three, all males, 1955, 1964, 1965.
Pine Beauty (*Panolis flammea*). First caught in 1981.
Twin-spotted Quaker (*Taeniocampa munda*). One only, 1965.
Centre-barred Sallow (*Cirrhoedia xerampelina*). One in 1958 and one in 1966.
Flounced Chestnut (*Amathes helvola*). Two only, 1960, 1962.
Chestnut (*Orrhodia vaccinii*). One only.
Satellite (*Eupsilia satellitia*). One in 1956, one in 1960.
Small Purple-barred (*Prothymnia viridaria*). One in 1970.
Herald (*Scoliopteryx libatrix*). One in 1961.
Gold Spangle (*Plusia bractea*).
*Silver Y (*P. gamma*). Regular migrant.
Scarce Silver Y (*P. interrogationis*). One in 1966, one in 1971.
Dark Spectacle (*Abrostola triplasia*).
Pinion-streaked Snout (*Hypenodes costaestrigalis*). One in 1971.

Geometrids (Geometridae)

Ninety-six species have been recorded. The most interesting are recorded below.

Large Emerald (*Geometra papilionaria*). One in 1952 and one in 1956.

Riband Wave (*Acidalia aversata*). One in 1963, one in 1965.
Smoky Wave (*A. fumata*). One in 1945, one in 1974.
Manchester Treble Bar (*Carsia paludata*). One in 1956, one in 1963.
Barred Tooth-stripe (*Lobophora polycommata*). One in 1969.
Early Tooth-stripe (*L. carpinata*).
Yellow-Barred Brindle (*L. viretata*). One in 1971.
Small Phoenix (*Eustroma silaceata*). One in 1968, one in 1969.
Juniper Carpet (*Thera juniperata*). One in 1969.
Welsh Wave (*Venusia cambrica*). Two in 1965.
Grey Mountain Carpet (*Entephria caesiata*). One in 1956.
Yellow-ringed Carpet (*E. flavicintata*). Three in 1969.
Galium Carpet (*Xanthorhoe galiata*).
Argent and Sable (*Eutype hastata*). One in 1966.
Beautiful Carpet (*Mesoleuca albicillata*). Not seen since 1953. One 1985.
Rivulet (*Perizoma affinitata*).
Double-striped Pug (*Gymnoscelis pumilata*).
Oblique Carpet (*Coenocalpe vittata*). One in 1945, one in 1955, one in 1957.
Slender-striped Rufous (*Phibalapteryx lapidata*). One in 1956.
*The Gem (*Percnoptilota fluviata*). One in 1956.
Clouded Border (*Lomaspilis marginata*). One in 1969.
Barred Red (*Ellopia prosapiaria*). First taken in 1966.
Lunar Thorn (*Selenia lunaria*).
Bordered Beauty (*Epione apiciaria*). One in 1976.
Peacock Moth (*Semiothisa notata*). One in 1959, 1963, 1968, 1970.
Pale Brindled Beauty (*Phigalia pedaria*).
Belted Beauty (*Nyssia zonaria*). This species is well known on sandhills ('machair') in the Hebrides. Other species on Canna with wingless females besides this and the preceding are: the Scarce Umber (*Hybernia aurantiaria*), Dotted Border (*H. marginaria*), Mottled Umber (*H. defoliaria*), and the Winter Moth (*Cheimatobia brumata*).
Peppered Moth (*Pachys betularia*).
Mottled Beauty (*Boarmia repandata*). Var. *conversaria* occurs.
Dotted Carpet (*Cleora jubata*). One in 1971.
Scots Annulet (*Gnophus myrtillata*).
Bordered White (*Bupalus piniaria*). One in 1971.
Bordered Grey (*Selidosoma ericetaria*).
Grey Scalloped Bar (*Scodiona fagaria*). One in 1945, one in 1977.

Burnets (Zygaenidae)

Transparent Burnet (*Zygaena purpuralis*), spp. *Caledonensis*, Reiss. One colony on cliff near west end of Sanday, another on Iolasgor beyond Sgor nam Ban Naomh. Numbers fluctuate greatly; possibly emergence is postponed in bad summers. In some recent years the moth has also been seen on some of the cliffs between the latter colony and the Sgriob Ruadh on the road to Tarbert.

Six-spot Burnet (*Z. filipendulae*).

Swifts (Hepialidae)

Ghost Moth (*Hepialus humuli*).
Orange Swift (*H. sylvina*).
Map-winged Swift (*H. fusconebulosa*).

Microlepidoptera

The following interesting species have been noticed. There are many other species.

Bee Moth (*Aphomia sociella*).
Pine Knot-horn (*Dioryctria abietella*).
Brown China-mark (*Nymphula nympheata*).
*Rusty Dot (*Pyrausta martialis*).
Dingy Pearl (*P. fuscalis*).
Garden Pebble (*Mesographe forficalis*).
Mother-of-Pearl (*Sylepta ruralis*).
*Rush Veneer (*Nomophila noctulata*).
*Small Magpie (*Eurrhypara hortulata*).
Many-plume Moth (*Orneodes hexadactyla*).
Green Oak Tortrix (*Tortrix viridana*). Two in mercury-vapour light trap a good many years ago on the same night.

APPENDIX XIV
NATIVE TREES OF CANNA

There are few species, and individuals are scarce. No doubt this is due to cutting for firewood when the island was well populated; the introduction of rabbits and sheep would make things worse. The native species that survive are:

The Rowan, *Sorbus aucuparia*. There is one good specimen at Garrisdale, and another growing out of a cliff face above Tighard.

Hazel, *Corylus avellana*. This survived in the Abhainn Ghiùrain gulley, and reappeared in the Haligary gulley after the rabbits died out in 1955 from myxomatosis. Neither these nor introduced hazels ever seem to produce nuts.

Sallow, *Salix aurita*. This survived higher up in the Haligary gulley, where it is now protected, and also high up on the slope below the cliff at Iolasgor.

Creeping Willow, *S. repens*.

Aspen, *Populus tremula*. There is a good specimen at Garrisdale, near the Rowan there, and small individuals occur in some cliff situations inaccessible to sheep. There is also one near the Post Office.

Pollen analysis has shown that the Scots Pine, Alder, and Birch formerly existed on Canna. See Flenley and Pearson, *New Phtytologist*, Vol. 66.

More than forty different kinds of trees have been introduced, mostly since 1881. Those that seed themselves naturally here are the Sycamore, Wych Elm, Cherry, Hawthorn, Ash, and Elder. Introduced Birches have shown no signs of seeding. Of the others the most interesting are the Lime, Whitebeam, and Serbian Spruce (*Picea omorika*). Exotica, all of which are flourishing, are the Antarctic Beech, *Nothofagus antarctica*, and the Southern Beech, *N. procera*; these trees from wind-blown southern South America seem particularly suitable for introduction into the Hebrides. There are also flourishing single specimens of the Dawn Redwood, *Metasequoia glyptostroboides*, in the plantation east of Canna House, and of the Daisy Tree, *Olearia* sp., in Canna House garden.

APPENDIX XV   WILD FLOWERS OF CANNA
by Elizabeth Anderson

Based on the list recorded by Elizabeth Anderson; the order is that of MacGregor Skene's *A Flower Book for the Pocket.* *Introductions or escapes. †Confirmation desirable.

Meadow Rue, *Thalictrum flavum.*

Alpine Meadow Rue, *T. alpinum.*

Ivy-leaved Crowfoot, *Ranunculus hederaceus.*

Lesser Spearwort, *R. flammula.*

Celery-leaved Crowfoot, *R. sceleratus.*

Meadow Buttercup, *R. acris.*

Creeping Crowfoot, *R. repens.*

Lesser Celandine, *R. ficaria.*

Marsh Marigold, *Caltha palustris.*

Corn Poppy, *Papaver rhoeas.*

Fumitory, *Fumaria officinalis.*

Watercress, *Nasturtium officinale.*

Cuckoo Flower, *Cardamine pratensis.*

Hairy Bittercress, *C. hirsuta.*

Scurvygrass, *Cochlearia officinalis.*

Charlock, *Brassica sinapis.*

Shepherd's Purse, *Capsella bursa pastoris.*

Sea Rocket, *Cakile maritima.*

Sea Radish, *Raphanus maritimus.*

Marsh Violet, *Viola palustris.*

Wood Dog-violet, *V. riviniana.*

Heath Milkwort, *Polygala serpyllacea.*

Common Milkwort, *P. vulgaris.*

Sea Campion, *Silence maritima.*

Moss Campion, *S. acaulis.*

Red Campion, *Lychnis dioica.*

White Campion, *L. alba.*

Ragged Robin, *Lychnis flos-cuculi.*

Lesser Mouse-ear Chickweed, *Cerastium semidecandrum.*

Common Mouse-ear Chickweed, *C. viscosum.*

Greater Stitchwort, *Stellaria holostea.*

Lesser Stitchwort, *S. graminea.*

Bog Stitchwort, *S. uliginosa.*

Thyme-leaved Sandwort, *Arenaria serpyllifolia.*

Sea-purslane, *A. peploides.*

Common Pearlwort, *Sagina procumbens.*

Knotted Pearlwort, *S. nodosa.*

Corn Spurrey, *Spergula arvensis.*

Sea Spurrey, *Spergularia marginata.*

Blinks, *Montia fontana.*

*Square-stalked St John's Wort, *Hypericum quadrangulum.*

Creeping St John's Wort, *H. humifusum.*

Slender St John's Wort, *H. pulchrum.*

Purging Flax, *Linum catharticum.*

Dovesfoot Cranesbill, *Geranium molle.*

Jagged-leaved Cranesbill, *G. dissectum.*

Herb Robert, G. *robertianum*.
Stork's-bill, *Erodium cicutarium*.
Wood Sorrel, *Oxalis acetosella*.
*Gorse, *Ulex europaeus*.
*Broom, *Cytisus scoparius*.
*Spanish Broom, *Genista hispanica*.
Zigzag Clover, *Trifolium medium*.
Hares-foot Trefoil, *T. arvense*.
White Clover, *T. repens*.
*Alsike Clover, *T hybridum*.
Yellow Trefoil, *T dubium*.
Hop Trefoil, *T procumbens*.
Lady's Fingers, *Anthyllis vulneraria*.
Birds-foot Trefoil, *Lotus corniculatus*.
Marsh Birds-foot Trefoil, *L. uliginosus*.
Tufted Vetch, *Vicia cracca*.
Bush Vetch, *V. sepium*.
Meadow Vetchling, *Lathyrus pratensis*.
Bitter Vetch, *L. montanus*.
†Marsh Pea, *L. palustris*.
Meadow Sweet, *Spiraea ulmaria*.
Bramble, *Rubus fruticosus*.
*Raspberry, *R. idaeus*, spread into plantations.
*Loganberry, *R. loganobaccus*, an escape.
Wood Avens, *Geum urbanum*.
Tormentil, *Potentilla erecta*.
Creeping Cinquefoil, *P. reptans*.
Silver-weed, *P. anserina*.
Marsh Cinquefoil, *P paustris*.
Lady's Mantle, *Alchemilla vulgaris*.
Dog Rose, *Rosa canina*.
Burnet Rose, *Rosa spinosissima*.
Starry Saxifrage, *Saxifraga stellaris*.

Golden Saxifrage, *Chrysosplenium oppositifolium*.
Grass-of-Parnassus, *Parnassia palustris*.
Roseroot, *Sedum rosteum*.
English Stonecrop, *S. Anglicum*.
Biting Stonecrop, *S. acre*.
†Bog Stonecrop, *S. villosum*.
Round-leaved Sundew, *Dropsera rotundifolia*.
Mare's Tail, *Hippuris vulgaris*.
Water Starwort, *Callitriche aquatica*.
Rosebay Willowherb, *Epilobium angustifolium*.
Broad-leaved Willowherb, *E. montanum*.
†Square-stalked Willowherb, *E. tetragonum*.
Marsh Willowherb *E. palustre*.
Marsh Pennywort, *Hydrocotyle vulgaris*.
†Alexanders, *Smyrnium olusatrum*.
Bishopweed, *Aegopodium podagaria*.
Sweet Cicely, *Myrrhis odorata*.
Wild Chervil, *Chaerophyllum sylvestre*.
Fennel, *Foeniculum vulgare*.
Parsley Water Dropwort, *Oenanthe lachenalii*.
Fools Parsley, *Aethusa cynapium*.
Loveage, *Ligusticum scoticum*.
Angelica, *Angelica sylvestris*.
Cow Parsnip, *Heracleum sphondylium*.
Wild Carrot, *Daucus carota*.
Honeysuckle, *Lonicera pericylmenum*.
Northern Bedstraw, *Galium boreale*.

Lady's Bedstraw, *G. verum.*
†Hedge Bedstraw, *G. mollugo.*
Marsh Bedstraw, *G. palustre.*
Cleavers, *Galium aparine.*
Field Madder, *Sherardia arvensis.*
Valerian, *Valeriana officinalis.*
Devil's Bit, *Scabiosa succisa.*
Field Scabious, *S. arvensis.*
Hemp Agrimony, *Eupatorium cannabinum.*
Golden Rod, *Solidago virgaurea.*
Daisy, *Bellis perennis.*
Cat's-foot, *Antennaria dioica.*
Marsh Cudweed, *Gnaphalium uliginosum.*
Yarrow, *Achillea millefolium.*
Sneezewort, *A. ptarmica.*
Corn Marigold, *Chrysanthemum segetum.*
Ox-eye Daisy, *C. leucanthemum.*
Corn Camomile, *Anthemis arvensis.*
Scentless Mayweed, *Matricaria maritima.*
Rayless Mayweed, *M. discoidea.*
Tansy, *Tanacetum vulgare.*
Mugwort, *Artemisia vulgaris.*
Butterbur, *Petasites vulgaris.*
Groundsel, *Senecio vulgaris.*
Ragwort, *Senecio jacobaea.*
Lesser Burdock, *Arctium minus.*
Spear Thistle, *Carduus lanceolatus.*
Melancholy Thistle, *Carduus heterophyllus.*
Field Thistle, *C. arvensis.*
Marsh Thistle, *C. palustris.*
Knapweed, *Centaurea Nigra.*
*Chicory, *Cichorium intybus.*
Nipplewort, *Lapsana communis.*
Hawsbeard, *Crepis capillaris.*
Mouse-ear Hawkweed, *Hieracium pilosella.*

Cat's ear, *Hypochaeris radicata.*
Hawkbit, *Leontodon autumnalis.*
Dandelion, *Taraxacum officinale.*
Corn Sowthistle, *Sonchus arvensis.*
Common Sowthistle, *S. oleraceus.*
Water Lobelia, *Lobelia Dortmanna.*
Bearberry, *Aretostaphyllos uva-ursi.*
Ling, *Calluna vulgaris.*
Cross-leaved Heath, *Erica tetralix.*
Bell Heather, *E. cinetrea.*
Thrift, *Armeria maritima.*
Primrose, *Primula vulgaris.*
Yellow Loosestrife, *Lysimachia vulgaris.*
Yellow Pimpernel, *L. nemorum.*
Sea-milkwort, *Glaux maritima.*
Bog Pimpernel, *Anagallis tenella.*
Periwinkle, *Vinca minor.*
Centuary, *Erythraea centaurium.*
Field Gentian, *Gentianella campestris.*
Buckbean, *Menyanthes trifoliata.*
*Comfrey, *Symphytum officinale.*
Evergreen Alkanet, *Anchusa sempervirens.*
Bugloss, *Lycopsis arvensis.*
Sea-Lungwort, *Mertensia maritima.*
Forget-me-not, *Myosotis palustris*
Greater Bindweed, *Convolvulus sepium.*
Lesser Bindweed, *C. arvensis.*
Figwort, *Scrophularia nodosa.*
Foxglove, *Digitalis purpurea.*
Greater Field Speedwell, *Veronica persica.*
Thyme-leaved Speedwell, *V. serpyllifolia.*

Common Speedwell,
   V. officinalis.
Germander Speedwell,
   V. chamaedrys.
Marsh Speedwell, *V. scutellata.*
Brooklime, *V. beccabunga.*
Eyebright, *Euphrasia officinalis.*
Red Eyebright, *Bartsia odontites.*
Marsh Lousewort, *Pedicularis
   palustris.*
Heath Lousewort, *P. sylvatica.*
Yellow Rattle, *Rhinanthus crista-
   galli.*
Thyme Broomrape, *O. alba.*
Lesser Bladderwort, *Utricularia
   minor.*
Butterwort, *Pinguicula vulgaris.*
Water Mint, *Mentha aquatica.*
*Horse Mint, *M. longifolia.*
Corn Mint, *M. arvensis.*
*Pennyroyal, *M. pulegium.*
Wild Thyme, *Thymus serpyllum.*
*Clary, *Salvia verbenaca*; found
   once on Sanday by J. L. C.
Skullcap, *Scutellaria galericulata.*
Self-heal, *Prunella vulgaris.*
Wood Betony, *Stachys officinalis.*
Marsh Woundwort, *Stachys
   palustris.*
Hedge Woundwort, *S. sylvatica.*
Field Woundwort, *S. arvensis.*
Variegated Hemp-Nettle,
   Galeopsis speciosa.
Common Hemp-Nettle,
   G. tetrahit.
Gipsywort, *Lycopus europaeus.*
Red Dead-Nettle, *Lamium
   purpureum.*
White Dead-Nettle, *L. album.*
Wood Sage, *Teucrium scorodonia.*
Bugle, *Ajuga reptans.*
Buckshorn Plantain, *Plantago
   coronopus.*

Ribwort Plantain, *P. lanceolata.*
Great Plantain, *P major.*
†Hoary Plantain, *P. media.*
Shoreweed, *Litorella uniflora.*
White Goosefoot, *Chenopodium
   album.*
Orache, *Altriplex patula.*
Marsh Samphire, *Salicornia
   herbacea.*
Sea-blite, *Suaede maritima.*
Saltwort, *Salsolsa kali.*
Knotgrass, *Polygonum aviculare.*
Spotted Persicary, *P. persicaria.*
Amphibious Persicary,
   Polygonum amphibium.
†Alpine Persicary, *P. viviparum.*
Broad-leaved Dock, *Rumex
   obtusifolius.*
Curled Dock, *R. crispus.*
Sorrel, *R. acetosa.*
Sheep's Sorrel, *R. acetosella.*
Sun Spurge, *Euphorbia helio-
   scopia.*
Petty Spurge, *E. peplus.*
Dog Mercury, *Mercurialis
   perennis.*
Stinging Nettle, *Urtica dioica.*
*Bog Myrtle, *Myrica gale.*
   Introduced by J. L. C. from
   South Uist. Planted by loch
   on Sanday.
*White Water Lily, *Nymphaea
   alba.*
Common Horsetail, *Equisetum
   arvense.*
Marsh Orchis, *Orchis latifolia.*
Spotted Orchis, *O. fuchsiae.*
Heath Spotted Orchid,
   O. ericetorum.
Fragrant Orchis, *Habenaria
   conopsea.*
Greater Butterfly Orchid,
   Platanthera chlorantha.

Yellow Flag, *Iris pseudacorus*.
*Snowdrop, *Galanthus nivalis*.
*Daffodil, *Narcissus pseudo-
narcissus*.
*Crocus, *Crocus purpureus*.
Wild Garlic, *Allium ursinum*.
Vernal Squill, *Scilla verna*.
Bluebell, *Scilla nonscripta*.
Bog Asphodel, *Narthecium
ossifragum*.
Toad Rush, *Juncus bufonius*.
Heath Rush, *J. squarrosus*.
Common Rush, *J. communis*.
Jointed Rush, *J. articulatus*.
Common Duckweed, *Lemna
trisulca*.
Arrow Grass, *Triglochin palustre*.
Broad-leaved Pondweed,
Potamogeton natans.
Grasswrack, *Zostera mariana*.
*Bulrush, *Scripus lacustris*,
Planted by loch on Sanday.

Cotton Grass, *Eriophorum
angustifolium*.
Flea Sedge, *Carex pulicaris*.
Sand Sedge, *C. arenaria*.
Common Sedge, *C. goodenovii*.
Meadow Foxtail, *Alopecurus
pratensis*.
Yorkshire Fog, *Holcus lanatus*.
Reed, *Arundo phragmites*.
Purple Moor Grass, *Molinia
caerulea*.
Cock's Foot, *Dactylis glomerata*.
Sheep's Fescue, *Festuca ovina*.
Perennial Rye Grass, *Lolium
perenne*.
Mat-Grass, *Nardus stricta*.
Lady Fern, *Alnyrium felix-
femina*.
Common Polypody,
Polypodium vulgare.

APPENDIX XVI   GEOLOGY:
CLIFF SECTION, LANGANES, CANNA

by D. R. M. Pattison (University of Edinburgh)

This one small cliff section exposes very clearly a rather unusual feature of the geology of Canna. (See illustration, p. 239.)

Most of Canna consists of a succession of Tertiary basaltic lava flows, with some interbedded coarse conglomerate and agglomerate, which has been intruded by a number of dolerite sills that have cooled in sheets parallel to the flows. The interlayered basalt flows and dolerite sills have produced the island's terraced topography.

At Langanes (and also on the western cliffs of Sanday) a coal seam is present as a 1–4 cm-thick layer above a graded sedimentary sequence and below a lava sheet. The seam is visible at a distance as an irregular, roughly horizontal crack in the sea cliff.

At the base of the Section (see photograph), coarse conglomerate consisting of light-coloured lava pebbles and dark dolerite fragments is irregularly bedded with coarse volcanic sand. Above this is a thicker zone comprising a more uniformly bedded, medium–coarse volcanic sand. This is succeeded upwards by a still finer sand, at the top of which is a thin coal seam. The coal is variably shaley, but is pure enough to burn and glow like medium–grade bituminous coal.

Above the coal is the base of the basaltic lava flow. The bottom of the flow is a light-coloured, fine-grained, vesicular (containing gas bubbles) lava, which develops upwards into a darker, less vesicular zone in which polygonal basalt columns have begun to form. Above the top of the photograph, these columns become quite well formed.

The course, round pebble conglomerate at the base of the section suggests erosion and deposition in a marine environment of high wave and current energy, such as exists along the present Canna coast line, with its headlands and coarse-pebble beaches. The large (fist-sized) rounded lava cobbles must have been locally derived from earlier lava flows by wave erosion. The irregular lenses of variably sorted coarse-pebble sand and cobbles suggest sporadic, and frequently vigorous, current activity.

Following this initial stage of erosion and irregular deposition of coarse material, wave and current activity decreased (the sand becomes finer and more evenly bedded). This was probably due to the reduction of the cliffs and headlands that provided the source for the conglomerate, and a gradual rise in the sea level. The sand consists of small volcanic fragments, which become finer as the top of the section is reached.

The organic material that has ultimately produced the coal was probably a type of peat or hardy sea-grass that existed in quiet flats and marshes. Some very fine clayey material also accumulated in these areas, resulting in the impure, shaley coal.

At this point, igneous activity resumed, erupting basaltic lava that flowed over the area. The heat and weight of the lava reduced the organic material to a thin coaly layer. The weight of the overlying lava variably compressed the peat-topped sandy sediments, producing the irregularities in the thickness and orientation of the seam.

The overlying basaltic lava flow, at its base, is very fine-grained, massive, and full of gas bubbles. This is due to sudden cooling, (chilling) at the base of the lava flow as it encountered the cold surface, freezing the gas bubbles into the rock. Above this zone, the lava had longer to cool – it is less fine-grained, the density of gas bubbles has decreased, and the regular polygonal surfaces of basalt columns have begun to develop. Upwards, the columns become well formed, similar to those in the larger basalt flows on the island.

Repeated deposition of lava flows followed by marine erosion is very common on Canna. However, the presence of this coal-capped, graded sedimentary sequence, so beautifully exposed in the cliff at Langanes, suggests that Canna experienced a more prolonged period of igneous inactivity at sea-level conditions. Judging by the apparent absence of equivalent sequences between other flows on the island, this section is therefore notable.

Further information on the geology of Canna can be obtained in 'Memoirs of the Geological Survey of Scotland, Sheet 60 – The Geology of the Small Isles of Inverness-shire', A. F. Harker, 1908.

APPENDIX XVII THE VISITS OF EDWARD ELLICE OF INVERGARRY AND RICHARD DOYLE TO CANNA

After the typescript of this book was in the hands of the publishers, Mr I. F. MacIver of the National Library of Scotland kindly drew my attention to the fact that the papers of Edward Ellice (1810–80; MP for Huddersfield and later for Stirling Burghs) contained diaries with allusions to visits to Canna on his yacht *Ladye* in 1856, 1857, and 1859. On the last of these occasions his guest was Richard Doyle (1824–83) the well-known artist and caricaturist; Doyle left a journal of his trip, which is also in the Edward Ellice papers.

None of these yachting tours is mentioned in Sir Arthur Mitchell's *List of Travels and Tours in Scotland, 1296–1900*. Edward Ellice was an early photographer, but very few of his photographs are to be found in his papers; they include one of the entrance to Canna harbour, taken from a position above the present mansion; this shows buildings beside Coroghon barn that no longer exist. His diaries also include sketches of Canna harbour with directions on the best place for anchoring; this he indicates as in the centre when Rubha na Feannaig and the summit of Mialagan on Sanday could be seen in line. Ellice's diary for 19 October 1859 also included sketches of a 'Bothy on hillside', probably that on Guala nam Fàd, and a 'Stone house at head of harbour', which is obviously the Change-house and its barn. His sketch map of the harbour, made in his diary on 15 August 1856, shows two 'slated houses' west of this, probably the present smithy and RC chapel (formerly post office), but likely to have been made by Hector MacNeill in connection with his water-mill.

Ellice recorded on 18 October 1859 that he 'landed and photographed. Paid visit to Mrs MacNeil. Mr M'N absent at the market. Went to the highest top above the house.' There is nothing to suggest that Donald MacNeill had built, or even started to build, the new mansion, now called Canna House, by that date. The 1856 sketch map of the harbour shows the old MacNeill house clearly as the 'mansion'.

The 1859 cruise had reached Canna by sailing around the north of Skye, stopping at Stornoway, Loch Shiel, and Dunvegan. The last leg of the journey before reaching Canna was extremely rough, and Richard Doyle was miserably seasick. He went ashore on

18 October with great relief. He was particularly impressed by Coroghon stack with the ruins of the 'Prison', which he was later to paint two pictures which are now in the Victoria and Albert Museum (one of them is reproduced in this book). They are dated by him '1875'; he came in Viscount Sherbrooke's yacht to Canna on that occasion. He repeated an erroneous tradition that Lady Grange was incarcerated in the 'Prison' 'during the rebellion' (of 1745 – actually she was imprisoned first on Heiskeir off North Uist from 1732 to 1734 and on St Kilda from 1734 to 1741, having threatened to expose her husband as a Jacobite sympathizer. Doyle also repeated the exaggerated tradition that a Lord of the Isles had imprisoned his wife on Coroghon until she died (see chapter here on Domhnall Dubh of Clanranald).

These allusions occur in the previously unknown journal kept by Doyle of this 1859 yachting trip. He was also impressed by some basaltic columns, which he sketched; by seeing a lady in crinolines through his telescope; an eagle, many hooded crows and starlings, and cows. He described Canna as the most fertile of Hebridean islands, and said the population was only twenty or thirty persons, which was quite wrong. Ten pages torn from his journal suggest that they may have carried sketches of Canna scenes which he gave away; it is greatly to be hoped that some day these and the photographs taken by Edward Ellice of Invergarry will be discovered somewhere.

APPENDIX XVIII

THE CANNA EVICTIONS: 1849, NOT 1851

A few years ago the writer came into the possession of a very interesting collection of Canna papers, which for the most part deal with the period between 1848, when old Donald MacNeill, who had bought Canna from Clanranald in 1827 died, and 1854, when his natural son and heir young Donald, born in 1833, came of age; and then again with the period 1878 to 1882, when Donald MacNeill II, deep in debt, was trying to sell Canna, and eventually did so to Robert Thom, a Glasgow shipowner.

The papers dealing with the first period are of great interest because until Donald II came of age in 1854 the Estate lawyers Nisbet and Sproat in Tobermory, Isle of Mull, a small town which was then to Canna what Mallaig is today, were obliged to make annual reports on what was happening on Canna, to young Donald MacNeill's Curators in Edinburgh, Captain Archibald MacNeil of the Ninth Volunteer Battalion and Hector Archibald MacNeil WS. Though in these papers young Donald is always respectfully alluded to as the Proprietor, in fact Canna was actually being administered by two urban committees. As soon as Donald I died on 10 November 1848, the administrators must have found themselves in a difficult position; and in this situation the best thing to do seemed to be to accept the offer of John MacLean, a sheep farmer at Glenforslan in Moidart, of a rent of £300 a year for the farm of Keill – one of the important divisions of the island – on what was practically MacLean's own terms. There is about the tone of Messrs Nisbet and Sproat's reports and comments something which reminds one of the Gaelic proverb *Cha n-fhidir an sàthach an seang* meaning that the replete does not perceive the starving.

The statement on p.162 (*supra*) that the Clearance of Keill took place in 1851 is quite wrong; in fact it took place in June 1849 immediately after John MacLean had entered into a five-year lease of Keill, obviously timed to end the year that Donald MacNeill II would come of age. The rent was to be £300 a year, payable in equal amounts at Martinmas and Whitsuntide. Donald MacNeill 'with the consent of his Curators binding himself to remove when practicable the Tenants presently upon the farm of K[e]ill to that part of the Sandy Island not presently occupied by Tenants [there were three there already] and also to leave twelve acres of good arable ground on the said Main Island and sufficient quantity of Manure for turnips this incoming season.'

The grounds intended for crops are to be enclosed as soon as possible with stone dykes; fanks for sheep are to be made 'and such other enclosures for sheep as may be judged necessary for the use of the farm by one or two respectable persons to be mutually chosen, who understands the management of Cheviot sheep stock. John MacLean was to get the service of 20 days from each family of the small tenants of Sandy Island if required, he being bound to supply them with victuals during the time he employed them'. MacLean was to take over Donald MacNeill's livestock, mostly black cattle at valuation; on his outgoing the proprietor was to take them back on valuation, the difference being settled either way.

A very interesting clause is the statement that 'the said John MacLean hereby agrees to allow Mistress Mary MacKinnon, Mother of Mistress Captain Melville, and Mrs MacIsaac each a house and a cow's grass on the Main Island, and the use of a horse when required'. 'Mistress Captain Melville' was Jean MacNeill, the natural half-sister of Donald MacNeill, who married George Melville of Beechhill House, Campbeltown, in 1840, and was left £3000 under Donald I's will, which was eventually paid over eight years after Donald I's death. Presumably Donald I's other natural son Archibald, who was left £1000, was Jean's full brother; the papers reveal elsewhere that he had been drowned off the Isle of Man at the end of 1842 when in charge of a smack. Donald II's mother was presumably Mistress MacIsaac. The lease was subscribed by John MacLean and Donald MacNeill and his Curators Archibald MacNeil and Hector Archibald MacNeil, on 28 May 1849, and witnessed by Alex Campbell, Lachlan MacLean, John MacKenzie and J. A. Longmore of the firm of MacKenzie and Longmore WS. It marked the beginning of the misfortunes and the hardships of the 36 families which had occupied Keill from immemorable times. All thirty-six families were compelled to remove themselves to the windswept overgrazed island of Sanday on the south side of Canna Harbour. In the course of these documents they are frequently referred to as 'the Islanders'. Throughout these reports one can perceive a note of irritation that the devotion of the Canna people to their ancestral home is obstructing the plan of Donald MacNeill II's Curators in Edinburgh and their agents Nisbet and Sproat in Tobermory to solve their difficulties by making John MacLean king of the island for £300 a year and removing as many of its inhabitants as possible.

Names of the Tenants on Canna and Sanday in 1848

Keill

John MacIsaac	Angus MacInnes
Angus MacDougall	Allan Jamieson
John MacArthur	John MacLean
Hugh MacDonald	John MacKinnon
Neil MacInnes	Charles MacArthur
Murdoch MacLeod	Andrew Jamieson. £3 10 –
Widow MacKinnon	Alexander Jamieson. £3 10 –

All paid rent of £7 a year unless otherwise stated.

Tarbert

Charles McKennan
Donald MacKinnon
Murdoch MacLeod.

Each paying £7 a year.

Sanday Island

Angus MacArthur	Ronald (Donald) MacArthur
John McKennan	Malcom MacArthur
Angus MacKinnon	Alexr. MacArthur
Lachlan MacArthur	Lachlan MacKinnon
Rory MacDonald	

Each paying £3 a year.

Sandy lately in Proprietor's Possession £250

Total . . . .   £400★

Deductions

Cannot be deducted	Land Tax	£ 3 10 –
	County Rates	£18 13 8
	Minister's Stipend	£31 16 6
	Bishop's Teinds	£ 7 0 –
	Schoolmaster's Salary	£ 7 4 8

Assessment for Property Tax £396   9 2

★ All money statements are in pounds, shillings and pence, of course.

The Ground Officer's Report on conditions on Sanday after the Evictions

Canna 22 Nov. 1849

Having minutely gone over the Sandy Island of Canna which is now divided into four allotments

1. Division West end on which there are	12 settlers
2. Do. Middle Division on which there are	15
3. Do. South Division on which there are	9

Settlers 36

4. Do. A Common for their horses &c being the South end of the Island.

Remarks

I consider that the horses should be reduced to 12, that is, a horse between every 3 settlers gives this work of a horse two days in the week to each settler – by which arrangement each settler would be enabled to keep two cows from which they will be able to rear a calf and keep the same until it is 12 or 18 months old which should pay about their rent and give them a supply of milk – but if they are allowed to keep a horse each they can hardly keep a cow each, and which can pay them nothing nor do I think they can stand their ground two years.

I can't see how they can winter the stock now on the ground, except by hand feeding as I never saw such bare land this season of the year. Their great anxiety for keeping so many horses is the distance they have to carry peats. If they were to sell their extra horses and lay out £2 a year in buying coals they would be more comfortable themselves, and more enabled to do justice to their Landlord. For their own interest they should be forced into a proper arrangement.

Arrangement of Rents

No. 1. West Division 12 Settlers at £3 stg. each	£36
No. 2. Mid Division 15 do. at £3 stg. do	£45
No. 3 South Do. 9 do. at £3 stg. do	£27

£108

Say 12 horses at £1 10 – £18	
72 cows at £1 5 – £90	

This rent to be payable from Whit^y. last and such as have extra Stock to be charged in proportion to the benefit given to those who are deficient in Stock.

Dr. Sir,

The above are the only remarks that occur to me necessary just now – any questions that may occur to the Curators of Canna I shall be glad to answer to the best of my knowledge – I am Dear Sir

Your most ob^t. servant

(signed) H. McDougall

To Henry Nisbet Esq.

The following rental of Sanday for the year ending Whitsunday 1851 shows how things actually worked out. Only one tenant has been able to pay his rent, and only four are mentioned as being involved in fishing.

Tenant	Rent due	Rent paid	Remarks
1. Duncan MacArthur	£3		Has nothing – neither money nor stock. Young man.
2. John MacArthur	£3		One cow. Is anxious to leave the country. Has no family.
3. Alexander MacArthur*	£3		One cow. Will pay balance when fish sold.
4. Flora MacArthur	£3		Has no means, money, nor cattle. Very poor.
5. Donald MacArthur	£3		Cow and stirk. Balance when fish sold.
6. Alexander MacArthur sr.	£3		Has nothing, not even a cow or stirk. Very poor. Large family.
7. Alexander MacArthur jr.	£3		One cow, has no money.
8. Malcom MacArthur	£3		Has only one cow, and will give it or its price at Martinmas.
9. Donald MacArthur	£3		Poor and has nothing.
10. Donald Campbell, now John MacLeod	£1 10		Will pay when he sells his fish. MacLeod entered at Martinmas and half a year orig. charged.
11. Angus MacInnes	£3		Stirk.
12. Neil MacInnes	£3		Has nothing – very poor – young man with family – willing to leave home but can't for want of means.

* Some of the Canna MacArthurs eventually settled in the Codroy Valley in the SW end of Newfoundland, see Margaret Bennett, *The Last Stronghold. Scottish Gaelic Traditions of Newfoundland*, Canongate Pubishing Ltd, 1989.

Tenant	Rent due	Rent paid	Remarks
13. Allan Jamieson	£3		Two year old (stirk). Balance when stock sold.
14. Andrew Jamieson	£3		Proposes leaving the island. Has only one cow which he can't part with as it is in his support. Young family.
15. Alexr. Jamieson	£3		Promises payment from a legacy which he expects shortly from America.†
16. Murdoch MacLeod sr.	£3		Ground officer. Overseer of fishings. See remark about this in Report.
17. Murdoch MacLeod jr.	£3		Two year old heifer
18. Donald MacPhee, smith	£3		Allowed this year same as last year £2 for service as a blacksmith. Stirk for balance.
19. Lachlan Mackinnon	£3		Has nothing. Old man. Is bordering on pauperism.
20. No entry			
21. John MacKinnon	£3		One cow, large family, and very poor.
22. Archd. MacKinnon	£3		Has nothing. Was engaged at fishing in John MacKinnon's boat, but was unsuccessful.
23. Angus MacKinnon	£3		Stirk.
24. Chas. MacKinnon 2 crofts	£4 10		W(idow?) MacLean to pay £3 in October.
25. Allan MacKinnon	£3		Two year old.
26. Widow Hector MacKinnon	£3		Has nothing, and is as poor as the church.
27. Hugh & Archd. MacKinnon	£3		Has no money, cattle, or means. Very poor.
28. Dugald MacDougall	£3		Two year old and a stirk.
29. Widow MacKinnon or Peggy MacIsaac	£3		Pauper. Still give a heifer.
30. Archd. MacIsaac	£3		Stirk – very poor.
31. Hugh MacDonald	£3	£3	
32. John MacDonald	£3		Has only one cow and cannot give it up. Proposes leaving island but hasn't means to do so. Large family.
33. Angus MacDonald	£3		Three year old heifer.

† See *supra* p. 224, 'Many years ago a family of Jamiesons came from Canna. One of them, Lauchlin, settled at Piper's Glen, and married a MacIntyre'. This was in Cape Breton.

Tenant	Rent due	Rent paid	Remarks
34. Donald MacDonald	£3		Has nothing. V. poor. Is anxious with his brothers along with a sister to leave the island and go south. No means to do so.
35. Rory MacDonald	£3		Two year old.
36. Schoolmaster			No rent exigible.

Notes of Visit to Canna, June 1851
by Will Sproat

Rents

The tenant Mr MacLean stated that he expected to be in a position to settle immediately after the September Falkirk Tryst [the great annual cattle sale to which beasts from the Highlands and Islands used to be driven to be sold], as till then he would dispose of no Stock, and in consequence could not till then, make any arrangement. A state of the Debt owing by him will be prepared, and as he will pass homewards by Tobermory it will be presented to him for settlement.

A meeting of the whole tenants on Sanday Island was convened, and held at the house of Hugh MacDonald. All attended it, but I regret to say the Collection of Cash was worse than I could have anticipated – Hugh MacDonald being the only one who paid down in full. A rental is herewith furnished with remarks taken from the mouths of the parties at the time they were seen, and as they were called into the room one by one, they had not an opportunity of hearing each other's Statements. The present worth of the Cattle which I got is about £27, but as they were in such poor condition I would not risk shipping them until they improved, and was forced to leave them on the Island for a few weeks, after having seen them marked, and after taking delivery on behalf of the Curators. I would recommend that they be removed to better grazing so soon as it would be safe to make the change.

Reference is made to the remarks in the rental as to the conditions of the parties and if I might be allowed to judge from appearances I would say that in one or two instances the statements are true.

The Blacksmith was allowed last year £2 extra and as his services in that capacity this Year were as Valuable as last Year a similar allowance has been made to him.

A number of the Islanders voluntarily came forward and

Expressed their willingness and anxiety to leave the Island either for the South or for America. They asked me if I could provide them Assistance. They got no encouragement in that Respect tho' a promise was made, that their Statements would be made known to the Curators. The parties along with their families are Neil MacInnes, John MacDonald, and Andrew Jamieson. The two latter have large grown up families some of whom are already in the South at service, who I stated should be able to render their parents assistance and were bound to do so.

I am sorry to state that an idea has got into the minds of the people in consequence of Sir John MacNeil's letter to the Skye Boards that the Proprietor and his Curators are bound to support them* should they be needful, and that it is not necessary for them in order to get this, that they should look out for work or go off the Island in search of it. I told them distinctly that no such law existed, that the Curators would not hold themselves bound to do anything of the sort, and that as soon as the dykes and other works were completed, the aid at present extended would be withdrawn from all, except those whom the law would compel us to support as impotent paupers. I spoke seriously to them on the subject and pointed out the necessity of exerting themselves and by that exertion to make themselves independent of all aid. I am under the belief that a number of them will do this, but there are others of them so tied down with laziness and sloth, and in them I have no faith. There are a number (indeed the greatest number) of young men and women who might go to the South and earn fair wages and be able to remit sums of money in aid of their indigent parents. Rather than this however *they remain at home and assist to make their parents paupers*, and live on fare which is brought to them without labour. I pointed this out to them but the answer I received was 'we have no clothes nor have we money to carry us away'.

There are three Widows of the name of MacKinnon on the island as tenants; one of them gave me a small heifer and I got a two year old from another. The animals are ill wintered and of little valued. Two of these women have sons at the work, Each receiving a stone of meal per week, and they say this is the whole upon which they have to depend and that as there are four or five in each of their houses the quantity is much too small. I told them this was true but

---

* See J. P. Day's quotations from Sir John McNeill's *Report to the Board of Supervision*, 1851, and the idea that he had about their having a right to aid from the Destitution Funds, in his *Public Administration in the Highlands and Islands*, p. 103. Some proprietors gave generous help to their small tenants, but they were far wealthier men than Donald MacNeill II of Canna.

that it was plenty for the one at work and the Widow and that the Younger branches of the family who were grown to womanhood should provide for themselves. The Boys at work are healthy but ill clad. If a pair of shoes each, could be sent them I think it would be a great charity, as it is difficult to work among sharp stones with bare feet and Cuming to whom I mentioned their names speaks favourably of them. The women wanted me to give them some assistance as paupers but I refused. They have the appearance of poverty. I instructed Cuming* without letting them know it, that he was not to allow them to starve for want – but beyond this he was not to go.

Murdoch MacLeod who acts as sort of Ground Officer and superintends the fishings† has paid no rent. He must be made some allowance for his services but I could not fix anything until the Curators were consulted. He Expects his Croft free but is willing to abide by anything that we may allow. I think for the first Year 30/– or £2 sufficient. He is a steady man and will be able I think to take charge after Cuming's services can be dispensed with. . . .

The Quay is still uncompleted. I daresay a week of 10 or 12 Men would make it all right and as it is nearly useless in its present condition I desired Cuming after the dykes were finished to put it in proper order.

The Islanders are all anxious backed by Mr MacLean to work the whole week and be paid for it 2 stones of meal. The matter was allowed to remain in abeyance till I went out, but on hearing their statements I refused to alter existing arrangements, the more especially as Cuming stated that he could take as much work out of 20 as double that number. The relay system is still therefore in Existence in terms of the minute to that effect entered into when Mr McNeil was here.

The meal was nearly out – when I left, there was in store only two loads which I am sure is out before this. A fresh supply must be sent out immediately which will cost considerably more than the last, as the article has risen in the market. I think if Indian Meal is cheaper one might supply it in equal portion with the oatmeal. I mention this merely on the grounds of economy and throw it out only as a hint.

---

* Cuming was the contractor from Tobermory who was building the dykes. He and John MacLean did not get on.

† Henry Nisbet reporting to Hector Archibald MacNeil on 12 April 1851 said there were four boats with five hands each fishing out of Sanday each boat at the time taking on an average 60 ling a day.

Fishings

A statement of the sums due by the various fishermen is made up and sent herewith. The three first mentioned in that account will pay in full, but I fear we will sustain loss from the last two. The cause of this as far as I could learn was that the crews were attacked and suffered much from smallpox.* I took or rather caused Murdoch MacLeod to take possession of their fish and to retain it with all they might still take, until he heard as to its disposal. The fish taken by the first three boats is still in their possession as they would be able to dispose of it better than we could and at less Expense. I have confidence in them that they will pay.

There are some lines and hooks sent to Canna still undisposed of, and a quantity of nails sent to repair their Boats have not been used.

The fishing at Canna will soon cease and those Engaged are anxious that permission should he got for them to land on the adjacent Island of Rum for the purpose of camping† on their operations during the winter months. They say that the fishing at Rum during the Winter is good, while at Canna there is none to be got. They say that the Proprietor the Marquis of Salisbury thro' his Manager hitherto has refused them permission to land and if it were possible that this could be got I think the application should be made. I don't know the regulations of the Board of fisheries on this head, but I daresay the Secretary would give the requisite information.

General

(Under this heading Mr Sproat goes on to discuss a visit to Eigg, where the Minister and the Schoolmaster are anxious to get their roofs repaired, which would be at the cost of the proprietors on the Small Isles, including Canna. He concludes the account of this visit by saying that 'Mr MacKenzie the Manager at Rum was from home and I could [not] see him.')

Mr Sproat continues: The Islanders, Mr MacLean stated, had refused to work for him the 20 days mentioned in his lease. When I had them together I got a consent from all and so settled the matter. To make the transaction have the appearance of certainty I caused each man to sign a paper to this effect and I hope to hear no more complaints on this head.

Mr MacLean has sent a letter in reference to some land which he

---

* According to another account, eleven men had come down with smallpox.

† This would mean camping in sheilings by the shore; the remains of these may still exist.

wishes to take in at Keill, a copy of which is enclosed. While there Mr MacLean pointed out the spot and on examination I found that about a dozen acres might be got in, of as good crop land as on the Island. I could give no encouragement to the application and more especially as the subject had already been brought before the Curators and refused. The other points in Mr MacLean's letter explain themselves and do not require to be commented on by me.

There will be about a dozen gates required for the Enclosures which are being made at Canna and Mr MacLean says these must be supplied at the Expense of the Estate. They will soon be needed and the cheapest plan would be to send out some Scotch larch and get them made on the spot. There is a Joiner on the Island who would do the work for 2/– or 2/6 Each. The Blacksmith would make the Iron work on being supplied with material without any Extra charge. The Timber would not cost much. It is a matter for consideration which whether or not the Curators consider themselves bound to make these, but I would only remark so far as I am able to judge that an Enclosure without a gate is no Enclosure at all. NB I am glad to have it in my power to say that the Priest* left the Island for the Mainland while I was there. I expect that he is left for good and all and at this I am not sorry.

I have thus far endeavoured to make a true report of all that came under my notice and to make it as full and Explicit as possible, that so the Curators may be able in Edinburgh to understand the matters going on on the Island as fully as if they were there themselves. The Report is a simple relation without Comments – but I cannot close without saying a word as to the future prospects of the Islanders and I regret to say that the conclusion at which I have arrived is far from favourable. They cling in all their poverty with a tenacity to the Island which is truly surprising – Many of them in consequence of their condition have lost heart, have become almost apathetic, and wish to depend entirely of the charity of the Proprietor.† Their live stocks have now betwixt death and otherways been reduced each to one cow and a horse and a few of them have not even that same. The Crop at present in the lands will be consumed by many of them long before the Winter has run, and how they are to survive or get

* Rev. Fr. Coll MacDonald, a native of Lochaber, born 1812, ordained in Rome in 1850. Canna must have been his first appointment, and no doubt he had made himself unpopular with Messrs Sproat and Nisbet by speaking up for the victims of the 1849 evictions. In June 1851 he was transferred to Knoydart, where he was fated to witness even worse evictions.

† Hardly surprising in view of the Highland tradition that it was the duty of a laird to help his tenants and employees in hard times, and that Donald MacNeill II's mother herself belonged to the island people. Like many urban people today, Mr Sproat has no idea of *noblesse oblige*.

through the next Spring and Summer is a matter beyond my powers of conception.

That their condition from year to year will grow daily worse is evident from the falling off in their appearance and circumstances since I last visited the Island and that they will become still more destitute and helpless is a fact, on which no one need have a doubt. The only permanent cure for the Evil which I can see is Emigration and I trust that Sir John McNeill may recommend to Government to come forward on a liberal Scale in aid of the Highlands and that Canna will come in for its share of the benefits.

All which is humbly reported
Will Sproat for
Mr Nisbet
Tobermory 27 June 1851

Inventory and Valuation of the Stock of Black Cattle, Horses, Sheep . . . Belonging to the Deceased Donald McNeil Esq of Canna taken at Canna on the 28th day of February and 2nd and 3rd days of March 1849 by John Campbell Auctioneer and Appraiser residing in Tobermory Mull.

30 Cows valued at £6	£180
40 do. do. at £4 15 –	£190
15 do. do at £3 10 –	£ 52 10
16 three year old heifers at £4 10 –	£ 72
37 two year old do. stots at £4	£148
30 do. do. do. at £3 10	£105
50 Quey and stot stirks at £2	£100
1 Ayrshire Cow	£ 6
2 do. at £3 10	£ 7
1 Bull	£ 10
2 do. at £8	£ 16
1 do. at £4	£ 4
1 Bull stirk	£ 2 10
2 Old Mares at £3 10	£ 7
7 Horses at £4	£ 28
1 Entire Horse	£ 8
92 Ewes at 18/–	£ 82 16
27 3 year old Wedders at 21/–	£ 28 7
12 2 year old Wedders at 15/–	£ 9
77 Wedder Hoggs at 12/–	£ 72 12
44 Ewe Hoggs at 12/–	
22 2 year old Ewes	£ 16 10
3 Aged Tups at £2	£ 6

50 Bolls Bear or Barley at £15	£	37 10
48 do. Oats at 10/–	£	24
500 stones Hay	£	12 10

Giving totals of 226 head of cattle and 227 sheep and ten horses in 1848.

List of Stock on Canna
stated by Mr Mac Neill
6 Dec. 1880

1002 Cheviot Ewes
 287 Cheviot Ewe Hoggs
 278 Cheviot Wether Hoggs
 115 Cheviot Dinmonts
  82 Cross Wether Hoggs
  88 Cross Ewe Hoggs
 194 Two year old Blackfaced Wethers
  74 Blackfaced Ewes
  28 Highland Cows
   5 Three year old Highland Heifers
   8 Two year old Do. Do.
   5 Quey stirks
   6 Cross stirks
   1 Two year old Stot
   3 Highland Bulls
  21 Highland Calves
  14 Ayrshire Cows
   2 Ayrshire Quey Stirks
   2 Galloway Queys
  12 Cross Calves
   5 Work Mares
   1 Entire Horse 8 years old
   1 do. do. 2 years old
   1 Filly 2 years old
   1 Colt 2 years old
   3 Fillies one year old
   1 Colt 1 year old
   1 Foal
   6 Pony Mares
   3 Fillies
   2 Colts

Dinmonts – wethers between one and two years old
Queys – young heifers; stots – young oxen

The 1848 and 1880 figures are not directly comparable, as Donald MacNeill II had more land at his disposal than his father did in 1848. Also the 1880 figures may have been increased if Donald II was keeping back sheep to sell at valuation with the Estate. The Cheviots were possibly South Country Cheviots, whereas those now on Canna are North Country ones, a larger type. It is interesting to compare the numbers handed over by the writer at the time of his outgoing in May 1983 after having been owner–occupier of Canna from 1938 to 1981 and farming tenant of the National Trust for Scotland from May 28 1981 to May 28 1983:

483 Cheviot Ewes	466 Blackface Ewes
189 do. Ewe hoggs	146 do. Ewe hoggs
379 do. lambs	384 do. lambs
5 do. wethers	114 do. shearling rams
8 shearling rams	12 do. 2, 3, 4 shear rams
13 do. 2, 3 shear	4 do. aged rams
4 do. aged rams	
1081 Cheviot sheep	1026 Blackfaces

Total number of sheep, 2107.

Crossing Cattle	*Highland Pedigree Herd*
1 AA Bull	1 Black Highland bull
24 Cows	21 Cows
16 Heifers	25 Heifers
19 Calves	13 Calves
60 head	60 head

The total, 2107 sheep and 120 head of cattle, compares very well with the 2115 sheep, 107 head of cattle, and 23 horses and ponies possessed by Donald MacNeill II in 1880. The present herd of Highland Cattle was founded by Mrs Campbell of Canna in 1946. There are no horses on Canna now.

By 1880, by when Donald MacNeill II was in deep financial trouble, owing a consolidated debt of £15,000 to the Scottish Amicable Association and £7612 19 7 on private accounts, and Canna was up for sale, the number of tenants on Sanday had fallen to twelve, all paying £4 a year. Their names were:

Angus MacInnes	Donald MacIsaac
Charles MacKinnon	Donald MacLeod
Murdoch MacLeod	Angus MacKinnon

Malcolm MacArthur	Arch^d. MacKinnon
Angus MacDonald	Arch^d. MacLeod
John MacKinnon	Widow MacArthur

Angus MacDonald was presumably the Angus MacDonald known in Gaelic as 'Aonghus Eachainn', Angus son of Hector, born in 1863 the last person born of Canna parents on both sides, who married a lady from a well-known Barra family and lived to become the last Canna tradition-bearer, dying in 1947. He taught Iain MacKinnon, the late Canna farm manager who died in 1992, the Canna place-names and the stories attached to them. The 1880 list adds:

Valuation by County Valuator of the lands unlet in Mr MacNeill's possession	£500
Mansion House and offices	£ 60
Lands let	£ 48
	£608

Public burdens:

Property tax (last year)	£23	8	5
Road Assessment	£ 9	10	—
Land Tax	£ 3	13	—
Synod Dues	£ 6	18	10
Minister's Stipend	£32	—	—
Schoolmaster's salary	£ 6	16	—
Poor Rates	£15	—	—
	£97	7	10
Deducted	£23	8	5
	£73	19	5

Tenants on Sanday in May 1938

From West to East.
1. Neil Steele, widower, from South Uist. Left a fishing boat to help at the harvest around 1908, and stayed on Canna for the rest of his life. Two crofts.

Paid £13 8 –

2. Donald MacKinnon, married to Jessie MacDonald, sister of Hector. Father of Iain MacKinnon, late farm

manager who died in 1992, Angus, Hector, Charles
and Effie.*   Paid   £ 7 2 –
3. Hector MacDonald, son of former grieve Angus
MacDonald, the Canna shenachie; married to Chris-
sie, sister of Donald MacKinnon; no children. Iain
MacKinnon was brought up in this household and
learnt a lot from his uncle and his grandfather. Two
crofts.   Paid   £10 10 –
4. Charles MacArthur, lobster fisherman. His house-
keeper and her son young Angus MacDonald came
from South Uist. He and Charles MacArthur and
Donald MacKinnon crewed a lobster boat.   Paid   £ 5 4 –
5. Ranald MacIsaac, brother of Allan. One croft. Paid   £ 6 5 –
6. Duncan MacLeod. Lived in Square, employed as
cattleman. Married Morag MacIsaac, sister of Ranald
and Allan, in 1939 after prolonged engagement, then
worked on Eigg and Muck. Returned to live in Canna
after retiring. His brothers-in-law worked his croft.
                                                        Paid   £ 6 10 –
7. Allan MacIsaac.Double croft near R. C. chapel,
given to him by A. G. Thom in respect of his 1914–18
war service, in which he earned a commission. Allan,
Ranald and his sister Penny lived in the old MacIsaac
house; no children.   Paid   £ 9 9 –
Allan MacIsaac kept a horse, which had the grazing of
Creag Liath assigned by the Land Court.   Paid   8 –
                                            TOTAL   £58 17 0

Notes

At the time of the writer's entry, the souming of each croft was 2
cattle beasts and 2 followers, while the proprietor had the right to
winter 100 ewe hoggs all over Sanday. So far as the crofts, which
then had to be unfenced, were concerned, the writer renounced this
right in 1942, after which they were fenced and the tenants could
keep what stock they liked within their fenced arable ground, but
the souming still applied to the crofters' common.

1. Neil Steele was the official Wreck Receiver. His wife had been
from Barra; I never heard him speak English. His daughters
Morag and Mary Flora kept house for him and his two sons,

* Angus and Hector are now in New Zealand, Charles is in Fort William, Effie is
deceased. Only croft then with children. Iain married Norah Boyle from Donegal,
two sons and four daughters.

Hugh and Sandy who worked a lobster boat; Sandy Steele was a good joiner.

2. Donald MacKinnon was a Relief Lighthousekeeper. He was also a good joiner. He died in 1949; in 1951 his family came over to live at the Square.

3. Hector MacDonald received the Royal Highland Society's Long Service Medal after 48 years working on Canna farm in 1964. He retired from managing Canna farm in 1972, when his nephew Iain MacKinnon succeeded him. He had been manager since 1951. Hector was the piermaster.

4. Charles MacArthur died in 1947; his housekeeper's son Angus MacDonald lost his life on a minesweeper in the 1939–45 war.

5. Ranald and Allan MacIsaac worked a part-time lobster boat. For a number of years Allan MacIsaac acted as postmaster. The MacIsaacs claimed some relationship or connection with the MacDonalds of Clanranald. Their elder brother Malcolm lived on Colonsay and used to visit Canna in his yacht, a converted lifeboat; another brother was the Rev⁴. Samuel MacIsaac, formerly parish priest of Craigstone on Barra, latterly at Carstairs.

Persons on Canna, not holding land

John MacLeod, horseman, brother of Duncan, a first class agricultural worker; retired 1947; died 23/4/1962, age 89.* Lived at the Square along with his brother Duncan the cattleman and his sister Annie; John and his sister later moved to the 'Skipper's House' on Sanday. Tractors were not used on Canna until after his retirement. These MacLeods were said to have some connection with the chiefly house of Dunvegan. Annie MacLeod was dairymaid.

Donald MacLeod, retired horseman, gardener for Canna House and Tighard, lived with his sister Kate in the cottage at Guala nam Fàd. He is mentioned by Angus MacLellan in the book *The Furrow Behind Me* pp. 165–71; Angus knew him when they both worked on a farm near Dalmally.

Annie MacKinnon, postmistress when the P.O. was in the building now used as the Canna R.C. St Columba's chapel, which it originally was; retired in 1949; among her successors were Michael MacLean and Allan MacIsaac.

Mary Anne MacLean, a sister of Hector MacDonald, returned to Canna after working in Glasgow; was given a croft of two acres on the Canna side of the Sanday bridge, let with Doirlinn House,

---

* John MacLeod's Gaelic patronymic was Iain 'ill' Easbuig, perhaps son of Archibald MacLeod, p. 304.

which she improved with a DOAS grant to use as a guest-house. Later for some unexplained reason the National Trust removed its dormer windows. She died in 1987 at Fort William. Mother of Michael MacLean, for a while postmaster of Canna, who died in February 1964.

More Notes on the MacNeills

The Canna Papers contain a copy of the Will of Elizabeth MacNeill, widow of Donald MacNeill of Bealachnahully in Kilkivan Parish in Kintyre, written in 1775; she names her sons as Colin MacNeill, Merchant in Campbeltown, Hector MacNeill, senior merchant there, Malcolm MacNeill and Stephen MacNeill, both deceased, late shipmasters in London, and Archibald MacNeill shipmaster in Campbeltown, her youngest son. Unfortunately Elizabeth Mac-Neill does not give her maiden surname as one would expect; but Colin and Elizabeth are favourite Campbell names, and there is a good chance that she herself was a Campbell. It is also likely that her son Hector was the Hector MacNeill who got a lease of Canna from Clanranald in 1781. Hector is a favourite MacNeill name.

It is possible that the Gaelic poem (below) the writer took down from Allan and Penny MacIsaac on Sanday was made to Elizabeth's husband.

The Designer of Canna House

The late R. V. G. Thom wrote to me, in a letter dated 11 April 1980, that Canna House was designed by 'MacNeill's sister' who was an architect by profession. This must have been Jean MacNeill, who married George Melville around 1840.

The late Henry Nisbet MacNeill

Known as Harry MacNeill, became a successful lawyer in Manitoba. There is a cutting of his obituary amongst the Canna Papers, but most unfortunately it is not dated.

Song to MacNeill of Canna, taken down by J. L. Campbell from
Allan and Penny MacIsaac, Sanday, Canna, about 30 years ago
(1986). There are obviously verses missing.

Oran Do Mhac Neill Chanaidh

Ailean agus Penny Mac Iosaig
a ghabh e

O gur bòidheach an cnocan air an suidheadh Cloinn Nìll,
B'e siod na fir ghasda bhiodh 'g òl air an fhìon
Treis ag iomairt air cairtean gun mhionnan gun strìth,
Nuair thigeadh sibh dhachaigh 's ann libh a liginn mo sgìos.

O gur éibhinn, gur éibhinn, gura h-éibhinn gach slògh,
O gur éibhinn na sléibhtean far an éireadh an ceò,
Gur bòidheach an Losaid 's Baile Ghrogain 'na còir
'S gur h-éibhinn Ceann Locha far 'm bi mo sheachd rùn-sa ag òl.

Thusa Domhnall 'nat ònar, bha sùil bhòidheach 'nad cheann,
Gu math thig dhut an triubhas tighinn bho shiubhal nam beann,
Cha n-eil òigbhean 'sa ghleannan nach eil fhortan an geall
Agus cuachag na coille fo leann dubh as do dhéidh.

'S truagh nach robh mi mar shionnach air a' chnocan ad shuas
Agus tusa mar eala air an lochan ad shìos,
Gu rachainn 'nad choinneamh 's gu meallainn thu leam
Òigear ùr a' chùil chlannaich, 's ann ort tha mi 'n geall.

Translation

Pretty is the knoll on which Clan MacNeill used to sit; they were
the fine fellows who used to drink wine – a while playing cards without oaths or strife; when you'd come home, 'tis with you I'd relax.

O happy, o happy, happy each band; happy the hillsides where
the mist used to rise; pretty is Lossit and Balligrogan nearby, happy
Campbeltown where my dearest love drinks.

You, Donald, by yourself, had a fine eye in your head; the trews
become you well, coming from walking the hills; there is not a
young woman in the glen to whom his fortune is not pledged; the
cuckoo of the wood is melancholy after (i.e. missing) you.
('Cuckoo of the wood' probably a kenning for a young woman).

'Tis sad that I am not, like a fox, up on yonder knoll with you like
a swan on yon lochan below; I'd go to meet you and beguile you,
young man with curly hair, 'tis with you I'm in love.

GLOSSARY

arrestment, a seizure or attachment of property or money by legal authority (Scots Law).

baillie, bailie, a steward of an estate.

bailliery, stewardship.

Bairn's Rights, the rights of the children to one-third of the father's estate under Scots law.

bere, beare, four-rowed barley, formerly much grown in the Hebrides.

blench, a quit-rent, a very small nominal rent.

Caisteal Tioram, 'Dry Castle', the old castle residence in Moidart of the chiefs of Clanranald.

calliver, caliver, 52, a light kind of harquebus, fired without a rest (O.E.D).

caschrom, 163, the old Highland foot plough.

changehouse, an inn, Gaelic *Taigh Seins* (so called because coach horses used to be changed at such places).

caschrom, 163, the old Highland foot plough.

Colum Cille, the Gaelic appellation for St Columba.

deeply sworn, 211, solemnly sworn.

depone, to testify (Scots Law).

factory, 'had their lands in factory', i.e. held them as agents for a feudal superior.

feu, a possession (land) held by a vassal from a feudal superior in return for payment of a certain rent, services, etc.

feu-duty, see below.

feu-farm, the annual rent or duty paid to a superior by a vassal for the tenure of lands (Scots Law). In the case of Canna, between 1627 and 1690, the duty paid by the Earls of Argyll as vassals of the Bishops of the Isles, and in turn the rent paid by the MacDonalds of Morar and later the MacDonalds of Clanranald as vassals of the Earls and Marquesses of Argyll.

forfeiture, the loss of an estate in favour of a feudal superior in consequence of some crime or offence (such as rebellion) or failure to fulfil some engagement.

gressum, lump sum paid by an incoming tenant of a farm on entry.

I, Icolumkill, Hi, Iona.

infeft, given formal occupation of heritable property under the feudal system (Scots Law).

intromitt, to take to do with someone else's property, usually illegally (Scots Law).

Justice Air, a court of justice (Scots Law).

melioration, milleration, compensation for an improvement made on his farm by a tenant.

Merk, two-thirds of a (Scots) pound, thirteen shillings and four pence.

merkland, a unit of land assessment, land which originally (a very long time ago) had the annual value of a merk (two-thirds of a pound).

penny-land, originally land that paid a penny tax in Norse times. The area varied according to the quality.

sasine, the act of giving possessions of feudal property (land). (Scots Law.)

skaithless, unharmed.

sorn, to exact the service of hospitality of free quarters required of vassals by superiors for themselves or their men (Scots Law).

spoolyee, 51, plunder.

superior, a person who has, or whose successor has, granted an estate of heritable property (land, buildings) to another (called his **vassal**) in return for the annual payment of certain rent and the performance of certain services. The ultimate Superior under this system was the King, or in the case of Church land before the Reformation, the Church.

tack, the tenure of a farm, the period of tenure (Scots Law).

tacksman, in the Highlands a person holding a farm on lease; in the seventeenth and eighteenth centuries often a relative of the clan chief. Tacksmen in turn would have subtenants, who mostly paid rent in kind and by services.

teinds, tithes paid to the Established Church (Scots Law).

vassal, see **superior**.

wadset, to sell land with a conditional right of redemption, *e.g.* on repayment of a debt (Scots Law).

A MODERN BIBLIOGRAPHY

Books and documents about the Scottish islands, including those that refer to them incidentally, are extremely numerous, and it would be quite impracticable to give a full list of them here. The notes to each chapter contain bibliographical references to the sources consulted. There is a full list of books and MSS connected with visits to and tours in Scotland down to 1900 in Sir Arthur Mitchell's *List of Travels and Tours in Scotland 1296 to 1900* (Edinburgh, 1902), which should be of interest to readers. References to Canna in modern literature, scientific and popular, so far as discovered, are listed below.

(A) SCIENTIFIC

Alcock, Leslie. 'The Supposed Viking Burials on the Islands of Canna and Sanday, Small Isles.' *From the Stone Age to the 'Forty-Five*, Edinburgh, 1983.

Berry, R. J., Evans, I. M., and Sennitt, B. F. C. 'The Relationships and Ecology of *Apodemus sylvaticus* (the Longtailed Fieldmouse) from the Small Isles of the Inner Hebrides, Scotland.' *Journal of Zoology*, Vol. 152 (1967), pp. 333–46.

Boyd, John Morton and Bowes D. R. (ed.). *Natural Environment of the Inner Hebrides*. (Foreword, Introduction, and thirty-four articles by various authors). Royal Society of Edinburgh, 1983 (Volume 83 of the Society's *Proceedings*). 648 pp.

Bertram, D. S. (General Editor). 'The Natural History of Canna and Sanday, Inner Hebrides. A Report upon the Glasgow University Canna Expeditions of 1936 and 1937.' *Proc. Royal Phys. Society* XXIII. 1–72 (illustrated).

Bradley, J. D. 'Microlepidoptera from the Islands of Canna and Sanday, Inner Hebrides.' *Entomologist*, Vol. 91, pp. 9–14.

Canna Expedition, The, 1961. Report of the Repton, Ardingly and Merchant Taylors, Crosby, Expedition.

Campbell, J. L. 'The Macrolepidoptera of the Isle of Canna.' *Scottish Naturalist*, Vol. 66 (1954), pp. 101–21.

—— 'Macrolepidoptera Cannae, Butterflies and Moths of Canna.' *Entomologist's Record*, 1970.

Carrick, B., and Waterston, George. 'The Birds of Canna'. *Scottish Naturalist*, 1939, pp. 5–22.

Davidson, Maurice. 'Canna Bedived'. *Scottish Diver*, Nov.–Dec. 1982, pp. 122–6.

Dempster, George. 'An Account of the Magnetic Mountain of Canna.' *Archaeologia Scotica I*, 1792.

Evans, P. R., and Flower, W. U. 'The Birds of the Small Isles.' *Scottish Birds*, Vol. IV (1967), pp. 404–45 (illustrated).

Flenley, J. R., and Pearson, M. C. 'Pollen Analysis of a Peat from the Island of Canna (Inner Hebrides).' *New Phytologist*, Vol. 66 (1967), pp. 299–306.

Harper, M. W., and Young, M. R. 'Additions to the Microlepidopterous Fauna, of the Isles of Canna and Sanday, Inner Hebrides'. *Entomologist's Record*, 93, 150–3.

Lethbridge, Thomas, C. 'Exploration of a Cairn on Canna.' *Proc. Soc. Antiquaries of Scotland* LIX, 1925.

Napier, Ramsay. 'Some Birds Notes from Canna.' *Glasgow and West of Scotland Bird Bulletin*, Vol. IV (1955), p. 3.

Report of the Joint Schools Expedition made by members of Merchant Taylors Crosby and Monkton Combe School, Bath, to the Island of Canna, Aug.–Sept. 1948.

Royal Commission on the Ancient and Historical Monuments of Scotland, *The Outer Hebrides, Skye and the Small Isles*, 1928.

Royal Society of Antiquaries. *Scottish Archaeological Tour* (in conjunction with the Cambrian Archaeological Association). Dublin, 1899 (Canna, pp. 64–7).

Sommerfelt, Professor Alf. 'Norse Words on and round the Island [of] Canna.' *Lochlann*, Vol. XVI (1952), pp. 231–4.

Swann, R. L., and Ramsay, A. D. K. Canna Report, 1979–80 (ornithological).

Wormell, Peter. 'Lepidoptera in the Inner Hebrides.' *Proceedings of the Royal Society of Edinburgh*, 83B, 531–46, 1983.

(B) POPULAR

Anonymous, 'An Isle of Enchantment'. *The People's Friend*, 29 Mar. 1975.

—— 'A Tour to the Hebrides and Highlands of Scotland'. *The Imperial Magazine*, London, 1819 (an account of what must be the earliest yachting trip to the Hebrides). See Sir Arthur Mitchell's *List of Travels and Tours in Scotland*, where a MS account of the same trip by John Scott of Hawkshill, since lost, is described, pp. 199–200. Sir Arthur Mitchell was not aware that an account of the trip by another party member had been published in the *Imperial Magazine*. It is preceded by an engraving by Thomas Dixon from a drawing by John Bird of Coroghon Prison and Halaman, made for the *Imperial Magazine*.

Barnett, Dr T. Ratcliffe. 'The Isle of Canna; Its Ancient Lore'. *Scotsman*, before 1939.

Campbell, J. L. 'A Home on Canna.' *Scots Magazine*, Feb. 1953, pp. 383–93 (illustrated).

—— 'As I See It.' *Scots Magazine*, Apr. 1965.

—— 'Danger in the Minch.' *Scots Magazine*, Sept. 1959 (illustrated). On the presence of Killer Whales in the seas around Canna.

—— 'Farming in the Hebrides.' *Scottish Farmer* (Special Album), 1942, p. 43.

—— *Statements on Behalf of the Island of Canna*. Stornoway, 1963.

Clark, E. M. 'Calling at Canna.' *Scotland's Magazine*, May 1961, pp. 12–15 (illustrated).

Collingwood, W. G. 'Some Antiquities of Canna.' *The Antiquary*, Oct. 1906, pp. 372–7 (illustrated).

Cooper, Derick. 'Islands for Sale.' *illustrated London News*, Apr. 1975. (Not that Canna was for sale!)

Cowan, Bailey. 'Skye Way.' *Yachting Monthly*, Apr. 1964, pp. 192–5.

Currie, Peter G. 'The Isle of Canna'. *Scotland's Take Note!* June 1952, pp. 20–3 (illustrated).

Doria, Rosemary F. 'A Magnetic Island.' *The Lady*, 1 May 1969, pp. 804–5 (illustrated).

Giertych, Jedrzei. 'Na Katolickich Hebrydach.' *Zycie*, Nr. 17, 1952. (Written after a visit to Canna.)

Harker, Alfred. 'Canna and Sanday' in *The West Highlands and the Hebrides: a Geologist's Guide for Amateurs*, 1941, pp. 73–75.

MacKay, James A. *Islands Postal History No. 4, Skye and the Small Isles*. Dumfries, 1978.

MacLeish, Kenneth, and Uzzell, R. Stephen. 'Isles of the Western Sea.' *National Geographic Magazine*, Vol. 146, No. 5 (Nov. 1974). The Canna photographs are by Thomas Nebbia.

MacQuarrie, Alan. *Iona through the Ages*. The Society of West Highland and Island Historical Research, 1883.

Mitchell, Isabel M. 'I often think of Canna.' *Scots Magazine*, Jan. 1970, pp. 368–76 (illustrated).

Rae, George. Holiday Rambles by Land and Sea, 1899. Vol. II, p. 59. (Describes a yachting visit early in Robert Thom's ownership.)

Redfern, Roger A. 'Lighting Up the Western Isles.' *The Lady*, 10 Apr. 1980 (about Heiskeir).

Robertson, R. N. 'Weeds, Tweeds, Rockets and Rackets.' *Gourock Magazine*, No. 17 (last number issued).

Ross, Sir Archibald, KCMG. 'McNeills of Canna.' *The Scottish Genealogist*, Vol. 30, No. 4, Dec. 1983, pp. 126–33.

paper of the Norwegian Forces then in Britain; written after a visit
to Canna).

Svensson, Roland. 'Host på Hebriderna.' (Autumn in the Hebrides.)
Vi, 16 Nov. 1951 (Stockholm; illustrated by sketches, the first of
which is of Canna pier and harbour).

Villiers, Alan, and Sisson, Robert F. 'Scotland from her Lovely
Lochs and Seas.' *National Geographic Magazine*, Vol. 119, No. 4
(Apr. 1961; the photograph on p. 518 is of the cliffs of Canna, not
of Rum).

Weir, Tom. 'Campbell of Canna.' *Scots Magazine*, July 1971.
(Describes the broadening of Canna Pier.)

—— 'Canna and Rhum Revisited.' *County Life*, 10 Aug. 1972.

—— 'Mail. Steamer to the Small Isles.' *Post Office Magazine*, Nov.
1952.

There are a number of references to Canna in some of the books of
Seton Gordon, Gavin Maxwell, and T. Lethbridge, and in the
poetry of Kathleen Raine.

Pictures painted on the island by Reynolds Stone and by Winifred
Nicholson have been exhibited in London, and those painted by
Ronald Svensson have been exhibited in Stockholm.

Index

In order to avoid overloading the Index, material occurring in the bibliographical notes at the end of each chapter is not included. In the case of Appendixes II, V, VI, VIII, IX, XI to XVI, only items occurring elsewhere in the book are noted in the Index. In the case of Appendix IV, only persons actually born on Canna are included.

MacCormick, *see* MacCarmic and
  M'Ormet
MacCulloch, John, mineralogist, 116
Mac Cumhaill, Fionn, hero in traditional
  ballads, 114
MacDermots, of Connacht, 53
MacDonalds, so called from Domhnall,
  grandson of Somerled, 13, 21, 22. *See*
  Lords or Kings of the Isles
MacDonalds of Ardnamurchan (patronymic
  'Mac Iain', often anglicized 'Johnston'),
  22, 33, 37
MacDonald of Benbecula, Ranald
  (Raghnall mac Ailein 'ic Iain), 60, 61,
  205
—, of Boisdale, Alexander (Alasdair Mór
  nam Mart), 82, 126, 128, 140, 170*n*,
  210, 215, 215*n*; Hector MacNeill,
  tenant of Canna his son-in-law, 122,
  134; his acquisitions, 206; and the
  Forty-Five, 206; his marriages and
  progeny, 206–7; and the Catholic
  religion, 207
—, Collin (Colin), brother-in-law of
  Hector MacNeill, tenant of Canna,
  122; his residence at Kilbride in South
  Uist, 132; his daughter Jean married
  John MacDonald XIX of Clanranald,
  127; as guardian of this John
  MacDonald approved lease of Canna to
  Hector MacNeill, 217; his acquisition
  of Ulva, 122*n*; his marriages and estates,
  207
MacDonalds of Clanranald (patronymic
  'Mac 'ic Ailein'), 1, 27, 37, 39–40, 58,
  122, 311; origin of clan appellation,
  24; relations with the MacLeods
  of Dunvegan, 39. *See* Appendix II;
  Clanranald; Lords of the Isles
MacDonald of Clanranald, Allan, IV, 32,
  204
—, Allan, XIV, son of Domhnall Dubh,
  killed at Sheriffmuir, 90, 108, 109, 111,
  205, 210
—, Anna, dau. of Iain Muideartach XII
  of Clanranald (married Ranald II of
  Benbecula), 64 and *n*
—, Catriana, dau. of Iain Muideartach XII
  of Clanranald (married Gill' Eóghanain
  MacNeil of Barra), 64 and *n*
—, Donald, XI, 44, 45, 51, 205
—, Donald, XIII, Domhnall Dubh na

Cuthaige, the 'Young Clanranald'
  of the Montrose wars, 64, 70, 74–7;
  'excommunicated' by the Covenanters,
  71, 73; his marriage to Janet of Sleat,
  72; his charges against his MacLeod
  wife, 82; gets charter of Canna in 1672
  and 1684, 208; his death on Canna,
  83–4; 206
—, Donald, XVI, succeeded 1725, 97, 205
—, Flora, widow of Ranald XVIII of
  Clanranald, mother and guardian of
  John XIX, 217
—, John, XII, 'Iain Muideartach', Captain
  of Clanranald at the time of the
  Montrose wars; his marriage to Mór
  (Marion) MacLeod, 51, 66, 69; Synod
  of Argyll demands that he surrender
  priest, 71; excommunicated by the
  Synod, 72, 73
—, John, XIX, and the British Fisheries
  Society's interest in Canna, 122, 126,
  127; under age at time of lease of
  Canna in 1781, 132–3, 205–6, 216–17
—, Margaret, widow of Donald XVI, 210
—, Mór (Marion), sister of Donald XIII,
  64*n*
—, Ranald, XV, son of Domhnall Dubh,
  97
—, Ranald, XVII, 'Old Clanranald' of the
  Forty-Five, 94–5, 206, 209
—, Ranald, XVIII, 'Young Clanranald' of
  the Forty-Five, 95, 205, 206, 215
—, Reginald George, XX; purchased
  superiority of Canna from the D. of
  Argyll, 24, 136; his marriages, 149; his
  sales of the Clanranald estates, including
  Canna, 150
—, Ronald, brother of Allan XIV, 211
MacDonald of Dalilea, Revd Alexander,
  father of Alexander MacDonald the
  Gaelic poet, q.v., 97–8
—, Lt. Angus, 100
—, Lt. Angus, tenant of Kenachreggan in
  1798, 140
MacDonald of Dunnyveg, Angus, 44, 45,
  57; his sister Margaret, 61
MacDonald of Glenaladale, Alexander, 99,
  100 and *n*
—, Angus, 99
MacDonalds of Glencoe, 22, 36; massacre
  of, 88
MacDonald or MacDonnell of